# FREEDOM AND LIMITS

# AMERICAN PHILOSOPHY

*Douglas R. Anderson and Jude Jones, series editors*

# FREEDOM AND LIMITS

JOHN LACHS

*Edited by Patrick Shade*

FORDHAM UNIVERSITY PRESS   NEW YORK   2014

Fordham University Press has no responsibility for the persistence or accuracy of URLs for external or third-party Internet websites referred to in this publication and does not guarantee that any content on such websites is, or will remain, accurate or appropriate.

Fordham University Press also publishes its books in a variety of electronic formats. Some content that appears in print may not be available in electronic books.

Library of Congress Cataloging-in-Publication Data

Lachs, John.
  Freedom and limits / John Lachs ; edited by Patrick Shade. — First edition.
      pages cm. — (American philosophy)
  Includes bibliographical references and index.
  ISBN 978-0-8232-5674-7 (cloth : alk. paper) — ISBN 978-0-8232-5675-4 (pbk. : alk. paper)
  1. Philosophy.   2. Life.   I. Shade, Patrick, 1965–, editor of compilation. II. Title.
    BD31.L28 2014
    128—dc23

                                                                    2013036333

Printed in the United States of America

16  15  14    5  4  3  2  1

First edition

# Contents

# Abbreviations

CI     *A Community of Individuals* (New York: Routledge, 2003)

GS     *George Santayana* (Boston: Twayne, 1988)

ILL    *In Love with Life* (Nashville: Vanderbilt University Press, 1998)

IM     *Intermediate Man* (Indianapolis: Hackett, 1981. Paperback edition: 1983. Second printing: 1985. Published as *Modern Man and Responsibility* by Harvester in Great Britain)

MP    *Mind and Philosophers* (Nashville: Vanderbilt University Press, 1987)

OS     *On Santayana* (Belmont, CA: Wadsworth, 2006)

RPL   *The Relevance of Philosophy to Life* (Nashville: Vanderbilt University Press, 1995)

SP     *Stoic Pragmatism* (Bloomington: Indiana University Press, 2012)

TR     *Thinking in the Ruins: Wittgenstein and Santayana* (With Michael Hodges; Nashville: Vanderbilt University Press, 2000)

# Acknowledgments

Pat Shade labored long and hard to bring this project to fruition. I am deeply grateful for his perseverance and devotion. Special thanks go to Shirley, my beloved wife, for her passionate commitment to this project. Kenneth Faber kindly compiled and scanned most of the articles composing this volume.

The following works appear in this volume with the kind permission of the original copyright holders:

"The Personal Value and Social Usefulness of Philosophy," in *The Philosophical I: Personal Reflections on Life in Philosophy*, ed. George Yancy (Lanham, MD: Rowman & Littlefield, 2002), 231–248.

"The Impotent Mind," first published in *The Review of Metaphysics* 17, no. 2 (December 1963): 187–199.

"Santayana's Philosophy of Mind," *The Monist* 48 (1964): 419–440.

"Fichte's Idealism," *American Philosophical Quarterly* 9 (1972): 311–318.

"Peirce, Santayana and the Large Facts," *Transactions of the C. S. Peirce Society* 16 (1980): 3–13. Reprinted with permission from Indiana University Press.

"The Transcendence of Materialism and Idealism in American Thought," in *Doctrine and Experience: Essays in American Philosophy*, ed. Vincent G. Potter (New York: Fordham University Press, 1988), 190–204.

"Primitive Naturalism," in *The Future of Naturalism*, ed. John R. Shook & Paul Kurtz (Amherst, NY: Humanity Books, 2009), 65–74.

"Two Views of Happiness in Mill," *The Mill News Letter* 9 (1973): 16–20.

"Questions of Life and Death," reprinted from *The Wall Street Journal* © March 31, 1976. Dow Jones & Company. All rights reserved.

"On Selling Organs," *Annals of Internal Medicine, Forum on Medicine* 2 (1979): 746–747.

"A Community of Psyches: Santayana on Society," *Rice University Studies* 66 (1980): 75–85.

"The Cost of Community," in John Lachs, *Intermediate Man* (Indianapolis: Hackett, 1981), 9–21.

"Public Benefit, Private Cost," in *Ethical Principles and Practice*, ed. John Howie (Carbondale: Southern Illinois University Press, 1987), 65–89.

"Leaving Others Alone," *The Journal of Speculative Philosophy* 18, no. 4 (2004): 261–272.

"Relativism and Its Benefits," *Soundings* 56 (1973): 312–322.

"The Element of Choice in Criteria of Death," in *Death: Beyond Whole-Brain Criteria*, ed. M. Zaner (Dordrecht: Kluwer Academic Publishers, 1988), 233–251. Reprinted with kind permission from Springer Science+Business Media B.V.

"Human Natures," *Proceedings and Addresses of the American Philosophical Association* 63 (1990): 29–39.

"Persons and Different Kinds of Persons," *The Journal of Speculative Philosophy* 8, no. 3 (1994): 155–163.

"Grand Dreams of Perfect People," *Cambridge Quarterly of Healthcare Ethics* 9, no. 3 (July 2000): 323–329. Reprinted with the permission of Cambridge University Press.

"Philosophical Pluralism," published originally as "The Future of Philosophy," *Proceedings and Addresses of the American Philosophical Association* 78, no. 2 (2004): 5–14.

"To Have and to Be," *The Personalist* 43 (1964): 5–14.

"Drugs: The Fallacy of Avoidable Consequences," *Peabody Journal of Education* 51 (1973): 53–56. Reprinted by permission of Taylor & Francis (http://www.tandfonline.com ).

"Loving Life," in John Lachs, *In Love with Life* (Nashville: Vanderbilt University Press, 1998), 1–17.

"Aristotle and Dewey on the Rat Race," in *Philosophy and the Reconstruction of Culture: Pragmatic Essays After Dewey*, ed. John J. Stuhr (Albany: SUNY Press, 1993), 97–109.

"Improving Life," in *In Dewey's Wake*, ed. William J. Gavin (Albany: SUNY Press, 2003), 199–211.

"Stoic Pragmatism," *Journal of Speculative Philosophy* 19, no. 2 (2005): 95–106.

"Pragmatism and Death," in John Lachs, *Stoic Pragmatism* (Bloomington: Indiana University Press, 2012), 53–61. This material appears courtesy of Indiana University Press.

"The Relevance of Philosophy to Life," in *Frontiers in American Philosophy*, ed. Robert W. Burch and Herman J. Saatkamp Jr. (College Station: Texas A&M University Press, 1992), 58–65.

"Both Better Off and Better: Moral Progress Amid Continuing Carnage," *The Journal of Speculative Philosophy* 15, no. 3, (2001): 173–183.

"Education in the Twenty-First Century," in *A Pedagogy of Becoming*, ed. Jon Mills (Amsterdam: Rodopi, 2002), 219–228.

"Learning about Possibility," in *Education for a Democratic Society*, ed. John Ryder and Gurt-Rudiger Wegmarshaus (Amsterdam: Rodopi, 2007), 177–183.

"Moral Holidays," in John Lachs, *Stoic Pragmatism* (Bloomington: Indiana University Press, 2012), 95–107. This material appears courtesy of Indiana University Press.

"Good Enough," *The Journal of Speculative Philosophy* 23, no. 1 (2009): 1–7.

"Physician Assisted Suicide," in *Contemporary Debates in Bioethics*, ed. Robert Arp and Arthur Caplan (Hoboken, NJ: John Wiley and Sons, Inc., 2014).

# FREEDOM AND LIMITS

# INTRODUCTION

Patrick Shade

Since publishing his first article, "Consciousness and Weiss' Mind," in 1959, John Lachs has worked with determination and distinction to advance the philosophical discussion not only within the discipline but also in the public arena. He has published consistently and widely in both professional and public venues for over fifty years. In addition to more than 160 articles, Lachs has written ten books, with three additional volumes now in preparation. He has also collaborated with other thinkers throughout his career, translating Fichte's *Wissenschaftslehre* with Peter Heath; coediting and writing a book and two articles with his wife, Shirley; and writing a variety of papers as well as *Thinking in the Ruins* with his Vanderbilt colleague Michael Hodges. This cooperative spirit has aided in the realization of his signature commitment to ensuring that practitioners and the public see the relevance of philosophy to life. Unsurprisingly, Lachs's work has earned the respect and critical reaction of colleagues and laypersons alike. It is a testament to his stature and influence that others' responses have been published alongside his articles on values (for example, by Erazim Kohák), the status of contemporary philosophy

(Charles Scott), and our material and moral progress (Cynthia Willet, Dennis Schmidt, Andrew Light, and Nikita Pokrovsky). Significantly, Lachs is a beloved and celebrated teacher, having received six teaching awards and having taught many reputable thinkers in American philosophy.

Lachs has created a corpus that is diverse in its topics, resources, and audience. Two books and more than twenty-five articles address Santayana's thought. Lachs began his career defending and critiquing Santayana's epiphenomenalism and ethics; the effects of this early work remain notable throughout the long course of his career. Lachs has also been a thoughtful expositor and critic of Peirce, James, Dewey, and Royce, making him a prominent commentator on the American tradition.[1] He is equally at home discussing Hume, Kant, Fichte, Hegel, and Schopenhauer. Taking seriously the endeavor to infuse public discourse with the fruits of philosophical reflection, Lachs has made numerous public addresses and written on contemporary problems concerning social interaction, violence, education, and bioethics. One book, *In Love with Life*, was written with the public as its primary audience; while this approach reduced the number of citations offered, it did not sacrifice sophistication of insight or complexity of ideas. One of Lachs's animating impulses is to ensure that we consider a wide array of perspectives and take seriously overlooked ideas or unpopular positions. This orientation accounts in part for his careful engagement with epiphenomenalism as well as his sober and critical consideration of euthanasia and physician assisted suicide. Lachs approaches none of these as mere academic issues, but rather considers their vitality as well as their consequences and likely limits.

In the midst of this prodigious output on a rich diversity of topics, recurrent and interwoven themes give his work coherence and depth. This volume's title offers one distillation of these themes. *Freedom and Limits* underscores the complex tension that arises in Lachs's thinking, for while he celebrates human individuality, intelligence, and creativity, he is nevertheless mindful of the real conditions that curb our endeavors. Meaningful and enriching living are not thereby sacrificed but rather contextualized. As a result, Lachs celebrates moments of immediacy even as he recognizes the comforts and costs associated with material and moral advance.

Each of the five parts of this volume highlights a dominant theme in Lachs's philosophy, and each is organized chronologically to map the development of specific arguments and ideas across the years.[2] Two significant features become apparent when surveying Lachs's work. The first is that although he frequently reflects on a number of different topics at the same time, roughly each decade of his career is characterized by a dominant concern. For instance, his 1960s articles tend to address topics in the philosophy of mind, while his work in the 1970s develops his views of mediation, individual agency, and liberty. Second, Lachs rarely abandons a good idea, frequently returning to it as his work in other areas prompts new insights. This is especially true of his treatment of the notion of activity, an idea that runs from his early critiques of epiphenomenalism to his later espousal of stoic pragmatism.

One who reads Lachs's individual journal articles separately may fail to see the patterns emerge, especially given the wealth of articles from which to choose, and it is my hope that this volume foregrounds the core themes in their vibrant development. Moreover, we gain new appreciation for the full import of Lachs's positions when we contextualize them. For instance, while most of his positions on bioethics invite controversy, each is rooted in and develops his other key ideas. Mediation proves a significant factor in the arguments of "Questions of Life and Death" and "On Selling Organs," while Lachs's articulation of choice-inclusive facts is central to "The Element of Choice in Criteria of Death." Hence, although it is reasonable to consider as a whole his various articles on bioethics, such an approach obscures their role in the development of his thinking and weakens their connection with other arguments from the relevant time period. The advantages of adopting a developmental structure are thus twofold. First, it enables us to see how Lachs's ideas mature so that we appreciate more fully their complexity and organic unity. Second, it reinforces the context within which articles arise and thereby minimizes misinterpretations that arise from considering ideas and arguments in abstraction from their living origin.

Any attempt to do justice to a thinker like Lachs in a single representative volume inevitably omits or downplays significant themes in his work. For instance, while Santayana figures prominently in our selections, Lachs devotes considerable attention to Santayana's treatment of spirituality. That view is not absent from the articles here, but it functions far less prominently in them than the related theme of immediacy that arises in Lachs's later discussions. To compensate for this general problem of omission, I discuss relevant further readings pertinent to each part at the end of the volume.

In the remainder of this introduction, I trace the main lines of development in Lachs's thinking. A thinker who insists that we attend to the relevance of philosophy to life would be woefully inconsistent if he failed to reflect on its role in his own life. That is precisely what Lachs does in the prologue, "The Personal Value and Social Usefulness of Philosophy," an article in which he reviews his own development and summarizes his achievements. Lachs speaks perfectly well for himself, introducing the trope of philosophy's personal value and social usefulness, so I will only add two points. The article heralds from 2001, and Lachs's ideas have of course continued to grow over the past decade. This is most apparent in his presentation of stoic pragmatism, an orientation that aptly captures much of his perspective. Additionally, Lachs has recently developed an argument against perfection. Though implicit in his early work, the new articles articulate more fully and deliberately the problems with aspiring for perfection and its corresponding notion of infinite obligations.

Lachs's early works mark the beginning of an abiding interest in metaphysical issues. All of the arguments in Part I concern important figures in the history of philosophy. Their significance to Lachs is captured in the final point of "Santayana's Philosophy of Mind" when he urges that we "use the past the way we use food, for the sustenance of life." This attitude characterizes the approach he takes to the philosophical tradition throughout his career. His chief interest in metaphysical issues concerns their impact on how we understand and ultimately promote human flourishing, and so his early focus is understandably on the mind-body relation and the status of the self. Lachs critically explores epiphenomenalism, or the impotence hypothesis as he sometimes calls it, in our first selection, "The Impotent Mind" (1963). He groups objections to the hypothesis into three main categories and argues that they all assume a dubious connection between consciousness (whether it be of volition, pain, or logical inference) and efficacy. The article has a modest goal—to demonstrate the inconclusiveness of prominent objections

to epiphenomenalism—but it shows Lachs hard at work "chopping logic," as he later describes it. His defense of epiphenomenalism comes in "Santayana's Philosophy of Mind" (1964). Lachs highlights Santayana's use of the Aristotelian distinction between process and activity to argue that mental life is an impotent byproduct of the body. Processes involve movement from potentiality to actuality and so are temporally differentiated. Activity by contrast is complete and self-contained, lacking heterogeneous parts or any essential temporal reference. Consciousness (or spirit, to use Santayana's terminology) is the actualization of physiological processes, possessing the perfections of pure activity. Being fully actualized, it lacks the power to bring anything into existence. Lachs argues that this position preserves our experience of the duality of mind and body while also leaving the world open to scientific investigation, unimpaired by mental or nonphysical forces. He is not wholly convinced by Santayana's argument, however, objecting that the fixed nature of the system inclines Santayana to dismiss rather than investigate the unknown and mysterious. This marks Lachs's first critical departure from Santayana.

Lachs does not restrict his attention to a single thinker or school of thought, as we see in later articles that move beyond Santayana. He deliberately challenges his own approach and assumptions about the mind and self by turning to thinkers such as Fichte, a move that he believes rendered his philosophical approach more dialectical. In discussing Fichte's view that the self posits itself (and posits itself as positing) in "Fichte's Idealism" (1972), Lachs again draws attention to the relevance of activity. He notes that positing is a nontemporal act whose model is the Aristotelian concept of activity. Relating Santayana and Peirce in "Peirce, Santayana and the Large Facts" (1980) brings out the significance of individuals in Lachs's thinking. He notes seven important similarities these two thinkers share, but he finds their respective views of the individual (isolated or social) and of reality (independent or communal) to be the source of their more apparent differences.

The benefits of these explorations in the philosophies of Fichte and Peirce (as well as Kant and Dewey) manifest themselves in later articles in which Lachs distinguishes his view more fully from Santayana's. In "Transcendence of Materialism and Idealism in American Thought" (1988), Lachs argues that what is distinctive about American philosophy is its

transcendence of the materialism-idealism option and with it a host of related dichotomies (subject-object, mind-matter, process-product). Criticizing Santayana's insistence on the impotent mind, and with it his emphasis on the realm of essence, Lachs distances himself from his earlier embrace of epiphenomenalism, but argues that Santayana's view of animal faith, with its emphasis on human action, offers vital insights for a philosophy of life. He builds on these insights in the later article, "Primitive Naturalism" (2009), defending the view that the world in which we live and act is one continuous with our bodies and their agency. Lachs derives this position from Santayana, but while sharing Santayana's commitment to animal faith, he has at this point largely set aside Santayana's ontology.

While issues in the philosophy of mind dominated his writings in the 1960s, problems in ethics and social philosophy assume greater prominence in the 1970s, as is apparent in Part II. Perhaps Lachs's chief development is his theory of mediation, which addresses alienation in a novel manner. Lachs argues that mediation is not the special consequence of a particular social arrangement but of social organization per se. It carries the obvious boon of enabling us to engage in the more efficient concerted efforts that typify human civilization, yet it also harbors often hidden costs. Indeed, Lachs here sounds what becomes a recurrent theme: social life is unavoidably complex, with costs and benefits always attending one another.

His early reflections continue to draw on Santayana and Aristotle, though Mill plays an increasingly important role. In "Two Views of Happiness in Mill" (1973), Lachs appeals to Aristotle's treatment of eudaimonia to distinguish two views of happiness in Mill's *Utilitarianism*. In addition to the "official" view that happiness is pleasure, Lachs argues that Mill also understands happiness in reference to the life pattern of a person. Recognizing this second view renders more intelligible Mill's support of liberty, for without liberty, Lachs argues, an individual cannot develop the voluntary self-expressive life patterns (of thought and action) needed to be "happy" in the larger sense. Lachs expands on the role of life patterns and liberty in two bioethics articles from the same period, "Questions of Life and Death" (1976) and "On Selling Organs" (1979). Calling attention to the costs arising from new technology that

helps extend life almost indefinitely, Lachs urges that we consider the seasons of life when determining how to spend social resources. He argues that "extraordinary medical and surgical intervention at social cost should be available only to those who are not in their terminal season." Technological advances concerning organ transplant also generate new issues, and Lachs believes liberty is significant in addressing them. Arguing that the poor have a right to make use of their bodies in securing wealth, Lachs contends that the government has no right to interfere with the sale of skills and bodies, so long as this activity does not harm others.

The success of these arguments rests on a defense of the primacy of the individual, a case Lachs offers in "A Community of Psyches: Santayana on Society" (1980). Lachs argues that the individual is the only moral substance (not atoms, not the state), for it alone is the seat of consciousness and desire required for action. Communities and organizations may "act" but only through the actions of their individual members. Individuals are ultimate in the social world, and the hallmark of a good society is tolerance of different individuals with their different goods. This view of society bears the mark of Santayana, though Lachs is critical of the sketchy nature of Santayana's moral and political philosophy. He offers his theory of mediation as a more detailed analysis and explanation of social life.

Lachs develops this theory in a series of articles that culminate in *Intermediate Man* (1981). The opening chapter, "The Cost of Community," defends the central point that, since social relations and structures are predicated on the notion of one individual performing a task on behalf of another, mediation lies at the heart of every society. Mediation's chief benefit is making possible complex communal behavior, but its costs include readiness to manipulate others, a growing sense of passivity and impotence, and an increase in the psychic distance between humans and their acts. The later analysis in "Public Benefit, Private Cost" (1987) explains costs and benefits in reference to the notion of a unified act, since mediation necessarily breaks up the unity of an act. In simple single-agent acts, the act is a continuous process of initiation (defined by intention), performance, and enjoyment (or suffering). This tripartite unity provides a context for understanding liberty and responsibility, since

liberty is the unity of intention and act, while responsibility concerns the act and its consequences. The dismemberment of an act created by mediation generates problems for both. Mediation on a large scale results in each individual performing an act-fragment in ignorance of the act's other parts. Removal from decisions that initiate acts leads to impotence and passivity on the part of actors, thereby curtailing liberty. Distance from the consequences of our actions breeds indifference and irresponsibility. Lachs proposes reimmediation as a means of overcoming these costs. His proposals—including the educative efforts of leaders—are modest but require continuous effort in a world in which mediation is ubiquitous.

Given his attention to liberty and the costs of mediation, it is no surprise that Lachs attends to the benefits of keeping a positive distance from others. Mediation unifies many actors in the same web of act-fragments, often crushing individuality as a result. Self-affirmation may be an understandable response to the claustrophobia of mediated life, but projecting the ego and its values over the world—beyond the scope of one's true agency—is nevertheless deleterious. In "Leaving Others Alone" (2004), Lachs argues that we do better when we learn to leave others alone, especially those with natures and hence goods different from our own. This means leaving them enough "operational space" to exercise their choices and enjoy their goods. Leaving others alone does not amount to indifference, since its flip side is helping them when they need it and when doing so is consistent with the integrity of their (not our own) needs. Since individuals have different natures and so different satisfactions, Lachs advocates a positive pluralism that both tolerates and encourages diversity, generating a society more conducive to human flourishing.

In addition to mediation, one of Lachs's key innovations is the identification of what he calls "choice-inclusive facts," an idea he develops in the 1980s and 1990s. This idea undermines the fact-value dichotomy by acknowledging that facts come in a variety of kinds, some of which include a significant element of choice. In Lachs's early discussions of values, he explicitly defends a form of relativism. In "Relativism and Its Benefits" (1973), he argues that belief in the uniformity of human nature underlies dogmatism about absolute values. Lachs rejects this view since

he finds that the natures of individuals vary. Values are relative not to individuals' thoughts and feelings but to their natures. This form of relativism does not lead to anarchy, however, since natures are similar and compatible enough to make social organizations possible, even if their overlaps do not constitute or consist in a uniform essence. Relativism has the chief advantage of promoting human liberty so that individuals can pursue their unique forms of perfection, allowing as Lachs says a hundred flowers to bloom.

When he later considers matters of death and human nature, Lachs draws on this pluralism but adds to it an appreciation of the variable ways in which we categorize events and entities. In distinction from objective facts, whose existence is independent of human activity, and conventional facts whose existence depends wholly on our thoughts and actions, Lachs describes choice-inclusive facts as an intermediate or hybrid kind of fact that arises when "human choice and action build on preexisting things or conditions to create a novel object." In "The Element of Choice in Criteria of Death" (1988), Lachs employs this notion to helps us understand death. He contends that those who defer to scientists to articulate the criteria of death treat it as a merely factual affair, overlooking the fact that death's significance is in part its social consequences. By contrast, Lachs argues that "locating death along the continuum of organic decline involves a social choice"; indeed, death is best understood as a "biologically based social status." When thinking about criteria for determining what is "dead," we thus need to consider relevant social factors, such as the way technologies affect decisions about the costs and benefits of keeping alive those in organic decline. In keeping with his pluralism, Lachs endorses an individually centered, multiple-criterion approach that allows for a *good* death.

Choice-inclusive facts are also useful in better understanding human nature. The designation of an entity as a "human" or "person" depends, as Lachs argues in the twin articles "Human Natures" (1990) and "Persons and Different Kinds of Persons" (1994),[3] on facts but also on choices about how best to carve and organize the continuum of living beings. At the heart of the argument are two elements of choice involved in choice-inclusive facts. One is the emphasis we give to some features at the expense of others in creating classifications, while the other arises when we determine the degree of similarity necessary for an individual's admission to a specific class. Acknowledging the many differences humans exhibit, Lachs proposes that we recognize distinct human natures, each distinguished on the basis of the desires, activities, and satisfactions of individuals.[4] Diverse desire-act-satisfaction triads account for the valuational differences that structure different kinds of lives. Lachs's position aims to take the sting out of the dubious appeal to the "natural" as a means of dismissing or censoring what is different, rendering us more tolerant and appreciative of human variation. It further requires us, as he argues in "Grand Dreams of Perfect People" (2000), to recognize that designating states as "normal" rather than "diseased" is a choice-inclusive act. No simple appeal to the human genome, then, can defend the grand dreams of the proponents of eugenics. This argument foreshadows Lachs's antiperfectionism (developed in the final part of the volume). Acknowledging the limits of being finite gives us reason to reject perfection as an appropriate demand or goal. Such an acknowledgement leaves us better prepared to focus our attention on the concrete details of actual individuals. Lachs's commitments to individuality, liberty, pluralism, and antiperfectionism thus interweave into a cohesive whole.

Lachs also applies these commitments to the profession of philosophy, as is apparent in "Philosophical Pluralism" (2004). Animated by attention to diverse desires and ways of viewing the world, Lachs recommends that philosophy departments be as pluralistic as they can be. An appreciation for the variety of philosophical schools of thought, made manifest through the study of its history, provides one ground for pluralism. Another is the fact that, as Lachs says, "no field of study shares the ambition, scope and consequent uncertainty of philosophy. Making room for widely divergent approaches is, therefore, even more important in philosophy than in other contested disciplines." Pluralism, then, can and should play a role in keeping philosophy vital and relevant.

As we have seen, Lachs has an abiding interest in issues that shed light on questions concerning meaningful living. His treatment of these questions results, as is apparent from the selections in Part IV, in a celebration of the fulfillment and joy of the activities in which we energetic beings engage, coupled with the sober assessment of our limitations. Given its dominance to his thinking, we unsurprisingly find significant discussions of meaningful living throughout his career. In two early articles, "To Have and To Be" (1964) and "Drugs: The Fallacy of Avoidable Consequences" (1973), Lachs explores concrete problems in contemporary society concerning possession, progress, and indiscriminate experimentation.[5] Behind these lies a preoccupation with the future—both its promise and its openness—that blinds us to the joys of the present and draws our attention from the very real consequences of our actions. Lachs proposes careful consideration of the assumptions of these problems (giving them colorful titles such as "the Consumer's Fallacy about the Ends of Human Life," "the Fallacy of Separation" of means and ends, and "The Fallacy of Avoidable Consequences") and offers the more promising prescription of an active life directed by self-knowledge.

In addition to the critique of specific contemporary social problems, such as the above, Lachs believes that understanding and pursuing meaningful living requires consideration of the big picture and so of the dominant dynamics of life. "Loving Life," the first chapter of *In Love with Life* (1998), addresses this broader horizon. The notion of activity plays a central role here and is linked to Lachs's view of humans as energetic beings, seeking and finding satisfaction in the release of their energies. The chapter's central message is that we should love life as long as there is something worth loving. There is, Lachs argues, plenty that is worth loving, from the joys of childhood to the pleasures of the body (the organ of our activities) and the comforts afforded by technology. That we love rather than merely like life is evident by the delight we take in its activities; we throw ourselves into life with boundless enthusiasm, never getting enough of it. Retaining his sensitivity to the correlativity of costs and benefits, Lachs nevertheless cautions against wanting life at any price, for the price is sometimes simply too high.

Attention to costs informs the trio of articles critiquing Dewey's treatment of the means-end relation. Dewey's position challenges the activity-process distinction that has dominated the history of philosophy and Lachs's own thinking. In "Aristotle and Dewey on the Rat Race" (1993), Lachs examines Dewey's notion of means-end integrated actions by embracing his denotative method and so seeking its empirical warrant. Though love and play offer concrete examples of means-end integrated actions, Lachs concludes that these are limited and not representative of the range of human experiences. Though Dewey hoped that technology could aid us in making life more artful, Lachs's perspective is more guarded. Drawing on his theory of mediation, he stresses that techno-logical mediation severs rather than integrates means and ends. Social advances, even when aimed at enhancing freedom and enabling us to enjoy more of our actions, are similarly limited. "Improving Life" (2003) continues this analysis, focusing on three distinct ways in which we can understand the unity underlying means-end integrated action. In the first, every means is an end and every end a means; in the second, means are constituents of ends (as flour is to bread); and in the third, ends are fulfillments of means (so there is a unity of purpose and outcome). Lachs argues that the first is limited to a few activities (e.g., play, sports, or con-versations) with little promise of extension, and he finds the latter two problematic, especially given the fragmentation mediation generates.

Lachs resolves his ambivalence toward Dewey in "Stoic Pragmatism" (2005) by granting that pragmatists see half of the human puzzle, while Stoics see the other half. Pragmatists celebrate what we can accomplish by exercising intelligent freedom, while Stoics reminds us of the limiting conditions that precede and follow our accomplishments. Arguing that the two are not incompatible and need one another's insights, Lachs es-pouses a stoic pragmatism that generates a wiser pragmatism—one that knows how and when to stop pressing onward—and a more active Sto-icism that does not retreat into itself. Stoic pragmatism accords with the import Lachs gives, most notably in his discussions of bioethics, to the seasons of life. Norms appropriate to the young need and often should not apply to the elderly, and vice versa. Lachs thus keeps our attention on specifics, on concrete problems, even as he underscores the value of hav-ing a broader, more cosmic view on human life. This is one way in which he reconciles loving life even while recognizing its costs. As a result, Lachs's philosophy offers us tools for recognizing as well as thinking about and acting amid the inevitable complexities of the good life.

An example of the fruit of stoic pragmatism is apparent in "Pragma-tism and Death" (2012). Responding to objections that pragmatism is in-adequate in helping us face death, Lachs emphasizes the unique satisfactions that come with the different stages of the life cycle (enthusiasm in youth, achievement in adulthood, peace in old age). Those who believe we can and should defeat death—a belief attributed to pragmatism (erroneously, if the pragmatist is a stoic)—are insufficiently attentive to consequences and to the values made possible by our unavoidable finitude. Lachs advises that "if life is satisfactory, we should avoid death for as long as we can." Death is not a matter of indifference to the pragmatist, but neither is it an absolute foe to one who recognizes achievement in the context of limits.

Lachs's recent work explicitly addresses our obligations and our capacity for advancement, although there are suggestions concerning these issues in earlier works. In the articles that constitute Part V, Lachs focuses on education on the one hand and on concepts such as moral holidays and what is good enough on the other, each of which are significant if humans are finite beings with multiple natures and goods. A recurrent thread that links these topics is integration; Lachs argues for the unification of theory and practice, of the material and the moral, and of the technology represented by the Internet with the human contribution unique to education. He interprets our obligations in relation to the sources of human advance, remaining sensitive to their limitations in the process. In "The Relevance of Philosophy to Life" (1992), Lachs offers five reasons philosophers have a general obligation to make philosophy relevant to life, thereby unifying theory with practice—albeit *in practice*. The conviction that to believe something is to have a tendency to act on it, for instance, obligates us to embody our commitments. We should also be attentive to be conditions of material and moral advance, as Lachs argues in "Both Better Off and Better: Moral Progress Amid Continuing Carnage" (2001). He identifies three areas of improvement—our understanding of the human body, the development of technology, and the spread of democratic values and practices—that have increased the range of our choices and so our opportunities for intelligent control of events. Telecommunication and pervasive commerce have provided a "mechanized imagination" that has increased our contact with diverse others, rendering us more knowledgeable about and sympathetic to their needs. Material prosperity has increased the magnitude, the reach, and the possible institutional support for widespread benevolence.

One might wonder, however, whether technological advances radically alter or diminish the value of traditional practices, such as education.

Computers, for instance, put increasing amounts of information at our fingertips. Together with his wife, Shirley, Lachs argues in "Education in the Twenty-First Century" (2002) that schools cannot be replaced by computers, for they provide unique intergenerational connections that define the broader context in which learning and growth occur. The individualized investment teachers have in students and that students have in one another generate immediate and ongoing interactions that cannot be enacted by or on computers. The Internet can, however, help shift the educational focus from collecting information to investigating hypotheses and enhancing critical judgment and appreciation. Such a shift would allow for greater integration of the theoretical and practical components of the learning experience; Lachs argues that "better coordination of practical life on campus with the abstract materials of the classroom offers a splendid opportunity for improving education and providing a more attractive alternative to the Internet." Moreover, teachers—but not computers—can teach students to challenge the status quo and explore alternate possibilities. In "Learning about Possibility" (2007), Lachs recognizes the limiting reality that, even with the protections of tenure, few foster an awareness of alternate possibilities for fear of upsetting the status quo. He nevertheless calls on educators to teach the young how to think and act on possibilities. Such a call is rooted not only in the need to integrate theory and practice but also in recognition of the optionality of our ways of framing the world. Educators who attempt to cultivate critical thinking skills without promoting critical reflection of the actual prove to be hypocritical. That our material prosperity has made available to us even more resources for thinking differently only strengthens the obligation to teach possibilities.

While our advances both embolden us and underscore our duties to the young, Lachs is nevertheless sensitive to the limits we must acknowledge in forming and pursuing our obligations. In "Moral Holidays" (2009), he examines these limits in the context of Royce and James. Though both thinkers are wary of permitting moral holidays (the former forbidding them and the latter recommending against them), Lachs argues that downtime is both needed by finite creatures like us and justifiable, given our plural natures and diverse goods. Rather than supposing our obligations are infinite, we should acknowledge our limits, for this enables us to set clear achievable objectives and to hope for some degree of completion. Consequently, we can justifiably take a moral holiday when it is needed and circumstances permit, though determining when each of these conditions is met requires careful judgment.

Lachs completes the previous argument in "Good Enough" (2009) by carefully distinguishing between what is "perfect" and what is "good enough." The former may promise the security of a permanent good or the stability of an absolute standard, but in addition to the fact that these promises are abstractions relative to our actual experience, Lachs notes that celebrating the perfect leads to the misery of endless seeking and striving. This leaves us incapable of any satisfaction, destroying human relationships in the process. Lachs distinguishes what is good enough, whose mark is experienced satisfaction, from the compromise implicit in the idea of that with which we can "make do." What is good enough has an integrity of its own that indicates that it does not need to be better; it is satisfactory on its own terms. We may deem it unsatisfactory, but that is relative to another experience or situation. Consequently, embracing the good enough does not warrant indifference or settling for less than what is possible, though it does enable us to enjoy satisfactions and counteract the impossible drive to have and do everything.

The final selection in the volume offers an apt epilogue to the work of a thinker who attends to the personal value and social usefulness of philosophical reflection. "Physician Assisted Suicide" (2011) is both life-affirming and respectful of our limitations. Written in response to his mother's recent death at the age of 103, the article offers an analysis of a meaningful death in relation to our current social practices. It is a poignant synthesis of human emotion and reflection, of respect for human dignity and autonomy as well as the seasons of life. As such, it provides an apt conclusion to this volume.

Lachs's work is notable for both its form and its content. Richly productive, Lachs engages diverse audiences both critically and cooperatively. He explores and draws on the resources distinct philosophical traditions offer, advancing the philosophical conversation with his own contributions. His writing mixes careful argumentation and poetic expressions, and it can be both sobering and inspiring. In attending to the vital mission of infusing philosophical reflection into public life, Lachs has fashioned unique tools—from his theory of mediation to his notion of choice-inclusive facts—designed to render reality more comprehensible, thinking more practical, and acting more fulfilling. The result is that he provides us a perspective of human life and activity that is energetic and diverse, appreciative of immediacies as well as attentive to consequences, receptive to benefits but mindful of accompanying costs, celebratory of individuality yet committed to social values, and in love with life's multifarious stages while still aware of its finite constraints.

# PROLOGUE

*The Personal Value and Social Usefulness of Philosophy*

I was born on July 17, 1934, in Budapest, Hungary. There was little in my family background to suggest a future in philosophy: my father was a lumberman, and my mother, though a cultured woman, occupied herself primarily with taking care of our home. No one on either side of my family had gone to college.

Enduring daily bombings in the Second World War, the long Soviet siege of Budapest, and the subsequent Russian occupation provided ample opportunities for the development of latent reflective tendencies: nothing jolts one into thinking about life as effectively as the sight of gratuitous violence and sudden death. I started thinking about the evanescence of life and the uncontrollability of fortune even though I was only ten, and tried my hand at rendering my ideas, and my distress, in poetic form.

The "nationalization" of my father's small business by the communist government and my family's consequent passing without passports through two patrolled borders to flee Hungary created additional invitations to reflect. Immigration to Canada, and later to the United States, gave me a great deal of material for thought about language, differences among cultures, and the relations of individuals to their communities. I spent a year in a Canadian high school and then entered McGill University.

It was easy for philosophy to find me. My experiences predisposed me to be interested in momentous issues: I wanted to know about God, the meaning of life, and the right comportment toward death. I found working with ideas irresistibly attractive and wished to develop resources for effective reflection on human nature. At McGill, the only question I needed to ask was which of the many departments that vied for the attention of students dealt with the topics I wanted to investigate. Upon being told that it was philosophy, I signed up as a major.

McGill University offered me a thorough, historical introduction to philosophy. Although the faculty lacked high-profile published authors, it included a wealth of good scholars. Cecil Currie taught me Kant and exquisite attention to texts. Alastair McKinnon, whose love of Kierkegaard was contagious, engaged in a losing struggle to meet the department's absurd requirement that he teach logic. Raymond Klibansky, the scope of whose knowledge was legendary, but whose thought was severely handicapped by excessive learning, set the highest standards for dealing with works in foreign languages and for mastery of the history of thought.

For a while at McGill, I thought I was called to the ministry. Reading Hume's *Dialogues* had a devastating effect on this career option: I could not imagine serving a God whose existence I was unable to demonstrate. It took me many years to realize that rational proofs do not need to play a significant role in one's religious life. I came to this conclusion partly as a result of listening to Paul Tillich in New Haven and discussing religion with John Burbidge, a fellow student, who later distinguished himself as a commentator on Hegel.

As philosophers must, I now reserve the right to interpret and to embrace the mysteries of Christianity in my own way. My recent writings attempt to articulate ways in which a commitment to transcendence can be combined with cold-eyed naturalism. My interest is in seeing religion as a celebration of life, rather than as a consolation for its losses and our finitude.

The thought of George Santayana found me through the agency of T. G. Henderson, chair of the McGill department, who had written on Santayana with Whitehead, and decided to teach *Scepticism and Animal Faith* in a senior seminar. I struggled for months to find the decisive weakness of the book, believing that in some fashion that kept eluding me, Santayana was clearly cheating.

I fought the book so hard that it became a part of my life. Both my master's thesis and my doctoral dissertation were focused on Santayana's philosophy of mind and, for perhaps ten years, I may have been the only living epiphenomenalist in the world. The articles I published in the 1960s on this odd but permanently tempting theory did not attract much attention. When philosophers feel compelled to adopt the view, they seem to want to think through its ramifications each time anew, all on their own.

By tradition, McGill sent its philosophy graduates to Oxford; Charles Taylor, Storrs McCall, and Andre Gombay, among other good philosophers, followed this path. For me, going to Yale seemed more natural. In those years, Yale stood out as the one program that took metaphysics, the philosophy of religion and the history of philosophy seriously. Paul Weiss boasted that Cornell's Max Black was sending his students to New Haven to point their fingers at him in amazement as he spoke of potentiality and God. Brand Blanshard was an unabashed rationalist, John Smith discussed Royce and the infinite, and both Northrop and Margenau championed international, humane, and generous philosophical ideas.

The department had been built by Charles Hendel, who was by the time I got there in rapid decline, and it impressed me and many others as exactly the kind of diversified community that could nurture many different kinds of souls. Yale students organized the University of Texas department on the pluralistic model in the early 1960s; Vanderbilt began to flourish as a Yale outpost, upholding the legitimacy of multiple philosophical methods, a little later.

Although John E. Smith was a shining presence at Yale, I took no courses with him, opting instead to learn analytic philosophy from Arthur Pap and Wilfrid Sellars, metaphysics from Paul Weiss and judiciousness from Brand Blanshard. This work reinforced my native tendency to pluralism: the wide variety of philosophical styles and projects that flourished in the Yale department of the late 1950s convinced me that there is no royal road to philosophical insight. As if to demonstrate this belief, I chose Brand Blanshard and Wilfrid Sellars as codirectors of my dissertation.

The two of them could not have been further from each other in style and substance. They divided between them the conflicting features of a good thesis advisor: Blanshard was all encouragement and appreciation, Sellars all critical bite. I learned more from Sellars about technical philosophy, but much more from Blanshard about the virtues of loving-kindness. I discovered in graduate school that I was not easily led: I listened eagerly to whatever opinions were offered but retained the right to separate them into the potentially sound and the worthless or implausible.

I read Dewey in those years and found him terminally boring. I was expecting philosophy to reveal the hidden structure of reality, but all I found in Dewey was a description of our well-known everyday situation. It took me twenty years to realize that probably there are no arcane facts, and even if there were, philosophy would be ill equipped to unearth them. Reading Dewey again helped me understand this.

A pounding sense of reality convinced me that language and conceptual discourse constitute a relatively superficial play on the surface of events. I have a profound appreciation of the power of language, but I cannot live in a world of chattering the way Groucho Marx and some contemporary philosophers appear able to do. I view preoccupation with language, including the famous "linguistic turn," as the folly of academics whose lives are consumed by conversation, glib repartee, and argument. I am too close to the silent people, to the nonverbal non-intellectuals who constitute the bulk of humankind, not to know the places where the stream of words dries up in the sands of feeling or the mountains of action.

The same sense of a vast nonhuman environment makes it impossible for me to accord special metaphysical prerogatives to thought, minds, or persons. Of course, all the information that reaches us about the world is conditioned by our cognitive apparatus. But this equipment consists of earthbound organs, not transcendental faculties. Accordingly, it must be placed in the context of its biological role of sustaining our bodies and enabling us to find our way in the world.

Santayana taught me that the ultimate issue in philosophy and in everyday life is the health of one's soul. Unfortunately, he never experienced the joy of living in a supportive community, and hence did not offer an account of the intricate links between the personal and the social. I learned to think these relationships by reading Royce and Dewey, but full experiential understanding had to wait until I came to feel that my home was at Vanderbilt and in Nashville.

I was fortunate to begin my teaching at William & Mary. Eight years of attending to undergraduates made it impossible for me to forget that the ultimate purpose of teaching philosophy is to reach a broader audience. Mentoring graduate students who will carry on the task of reflection is a special joy, but in the end even that needs justification in terms of the good it will do future undergraduates and the community at large. Philosophy, unlike molecular biology, cannot be expected to uncover hidden facts. Even if it did, however, this arcane knowledge would demand application and practical results.

By the time I moved from William & Mary to Vanderbilt, I was ready to teach at the graduate level. I got lucky again: I found excellent students who worked hard and needed primarily guidance and encouragement to get on with their projects. Being by nature self-willed, I have great respect for the autonomy of others, which made it easy for me to support generations of graduate students in the pursuit of their ends. My tendency is to let them write on what they wish and derive instruction from how I suggest that they trim their luxuriant growths. The wide variety of their inquiries has broadened my interests and has in the aggregate taught me much more than I was able to teach any one of them.

At Vanderbilt, I started teaching American philosophy. This led me to read Dewey again. The second time around, I thought he was scintillating and in many particulars clearly right. I expanded my reading and reflection beyond Dewey to Peirce, James, Royce, and Mead, and more recently to Alain Locke, the personalists, Jane Addams, and a host of lesser-known or neglected thinkers. On certain topics, I now agree with the pragmatists, though on others I continue to be at a great distance from them.

I agree, for example, that thought is not an end in itself and that knowledge presupposes purposes. They are also on the right track in refusing to deal with decontextualized problems and in rejecting the separation of values from facts. But I cannot make myself believe that social construction goes all the way down; somewhere, there must be a residuum of things or facts on which the edifice of our thought is built.

This conviction is embodied in the distinctions I draw between objective, choice-inclusive, and conventional facts. We enjoy significant leeway in creating order by classification out of the welter of reality that surrounds us. Every item in our experience is saturated with features and relations; the plausibility of our conceptual schemes varies with the similarities and the differences among objects that we decide to stress. This means that there is an interplay between things and our choices in the creation of many of the facts we ordinarily, though mistakenly, consider objective elements of the world. Such choice-inclusive facts include those on which we base our social life, our psychological discernments, and our biology.

The interplay is possible only if there are elements of the world independent of our choices. We find these elements in the limits nature sets to our classifications and in the momentous difference between existence and non-existence. We can characterize human beings, for example, as persons, as animals and as gravitating bodies, but not as solar systems or two-volume dictionaries. Moreover, in whatever conceptual garb we dress beloved others, their death betokens our impotence; no construction or reconstruction of facts can lead them back to life.

Objective or independent facts provide, therefore, the ground on which or the material out of which we build the edifice of human knowledge. This conception allows for the post-Kantian claim that much of the world bears a human stamp, and yet retains the sanity of supposing that there are externally imposed limits to human creativity. It acknowledges a reconstructive element in much knowing and considerable flexibility in our schemes of classification, without abandoning the idea of an independent reality that is at least somewhat determinate. It pays equal heed to Dewey's claim of the social construction of reality and Santayana's sense that we are surrounded by a deep and ancient world.

This approach to the role intelligent agents play in structuring the world has rich implications for our view of human nature. It enables us to distinguish a variety of natures all of which are legitimately human, and can thereby serve as the philosophical underpinning of an ethics of toleration. Moreover, it deprives the word "natural" of its moral wallop, providing ample illustrations that widely divergent values and behaviors can be natural and, in their contexts, understandable.

The account of human natures that grows out of my theory of choice-inclusive facts is modestly original. I continue to work out its details and implications, and hope eventually to show its power in a single volume. I have already explored its bearing on issues in psychology, bioethics, and morality, but much more needs to be done to see it in full context and to assess both its social and its explanatory value.

The theory of choice-inclusive facts constitutes a good example of the sort of philosophical idea I value. I am interested in theories that have a close connection to concerns arising in the course of daily life. Ideas of great abstraction or generality hold little fascination for me; though I think philosophical reflection is intrinsically delightful—it certainly constitutes one of the great pleasures of my life—its ultimate value is closely tied to the contribution it can make to the improvement of the human condition.

Another example of such a theory is my account of mediation, designed to explain the sources of manipulativeness, irresponsibility, and individual powerlessness in industrial societies. A complex condition besets people in the crowded modern world. In spite of the rhetoric of respect for individuals, they feel insignificant and disregarded. Working in large institutions, they view themselves as passive and not in control of their lives. The sense that they fail to author their own deeds makes them reluctant to take responsibility for them. The more tightly integrated their social world becomes, the more they experience their existence as fragmented and lacking in meaning.

The syndrome is well known; social philosophers have identified it at least two hundred years ago. But they have not done well in explaining it and in prescribing remedies. They have called it "alienation" and supposed that it results from some social malformation or other. Their descriptions of the condition contained hidden value judgments and their prescriptions for eliminating it were meant to move us in the direction of their favorite utopias.

My theory of mediation explains the syndrome without reference to any social malfunction. The values it relies on, moreover, are not mine, but belong to the people who live the fragmentation. Improvement must be measured, accordingly, by their reduced frustration and enhanced ability to view their actions as their own.

I believe that alienation is simply the price we pay for corporate existence, the cost of our comfort. Passivity, manipulativeness, and irresponsibility flow naturally from operating in vast mediated chains. In such institutions, the natural unity of actions is shattered: planning, doing, and enjoying/suffering the consequences no longer reside in single individuals, but are distributed among different people. The condition is not fully curable, but we can improve things by taking steps to counterbalance the fragmentation. Openness within institutional chains, reducing the psychic distance between planners, doers, and sufferers, and giving a full hearing to all interested parties, among other strategies, help individuals understand their situations and accept them as appropriate.

Mediation theory has enabled me to see alienation phenomena with a clarity and to understand them with a simplicity that I have not found in more metaphysical and more tendentious accounts. Whenever I present these ideas to nonprofessionals, they need little effort to recognize their condition and apprehend its causes. Their responses bolster my confidence that the theory is on the right track.

A conviction underlying my views on several subjects is that solutions to problems tend not to be permanent or complete. Moreover, all improvements carry their own costs, which can readily grow into new problems needing solutions. If there are any permanent elements in the human condition, the inability to secure costless benefits is certainly one of them. Religious people call this "fallenness" or "original sin," which seems so pervasive that ironically, as I tried to show in a recent essay, it interferes even with formulating a viable notion of heaven and thus of a particularly desirable afterlife.

Believing in what hopes promise has, in any case, never much appealed to me. I think, on the contrary, that the dignity due our intelligence requires seeing the world and our prospects in it with unclouded eyes. Religion gets undue support from our desire to escape the pain of loss and the dread of death. Although they do not bring out the best in religion, I have no quarrel with such consolations. But philosophers should not need them. They ought to have the courage to look into the abyss alone and to face sudden tragedy and inevitable decline with equanimity born of joy or at least of understanding. I am prepared to be surprised to learn that we have a supernatural destiny, just as I am prepared to be surprised at seeing my neighbor win the lottery. But I do not consider buying tickets an investment.

Philosophers need courage also to leave the security and comfort of the university and address nonacademic people on issues of personal significance and public policy. As a profession in this country, we have reached a level of irrelevance that renders commercial presses reluctant to publish our work. The in-groupish abstraction of philosophy books makes them the butt of jokes. Yet the public is hungry for thoughtful commentaries on the affairs of life and for guidance on how to deal with its problems. The response to *In Love with Life* showed me the magnitude of the need people experience for philosophical reflections on what they do and what befalls them. Meeting this need is a project of the greatest importance for philosophers. I continue to contribute to the effort as a writer and to promote it through the Centennial Committee of the American Philosophical Association, which I currently chair.

The Centennial Committee was created to celebrate the hundredth anniversary of the founding of the American Philosophical Association by calling attention to the personal value and social usefulness of philosophy. The Centennial Committee's intention is to create an audience for philosophy and to encourage philosophers to address that audience. Both tasks are difficult, the first, because academics have little public relations experience, the second, because many colleagues lack the interest, the language, or the temperament to speak about matters beyond their technical specialties. Nevertheless, slow progress is possible, and I am in the process of collecting money for an endowment so that this work can continue. I am unable to think of anything more important for the future of academic philosophy in this country than for it to become less academic.

Having had more than my share of bad instructors, I sought a job in education as a way to earn a living while I continued my philosophical reflections. I never suspected that I would develop a passion for teaching. Yet, conveying to others the benefits I receive from philosophy has become a burning desire and a consuming activity in my life. I do it in a way that seems to some a form of witnessing, showing the immediate pertinence of philosophical ideas to my life.

Immense satisfaction attends my good fortune in having had the opportunity to make a contribution to the lives of thousands of undergraduates. I view this multitude of people as extended family: I keep in touch with as many of them as I can and cheer them on in the pursuit of their purposes. I hope philosophy has made a significant difference in their lives. I have also been fortunate in having launched more than sixty young philosophers on their careers. My relation to them is one of lifelong concern and support: helping them with their problems and careers is of vital importance to me. I think of these activities not as the result of optional commitments on my part, but as the continuing expressions of my philosophical beliefs.

People whose minds are energetic and who are interested in their fields find it easy to teach well. Bored instructors are boring and the self-absorbed fail to place themselves in the shoes of their students to see how what they say is received. Thinking before one's students' eyes—which means, among other things, teaching without notes—demonstrates what one expects them to do. Keeping in mind the interconnectedness of things and especially the relations of what one teaches to the ordinary concerns of students renders instruction vivid and, when things go well, even memorable.

By no means least, good teaching requires deep respect for students. The activity is hallowed because it enables one human being to contribute to the creation of another. Its chance of success is enhanced by embedding it in wider human relations; truly good teachers tend to offer caring companionship as the context of instruction. Perhaps all learning is imitation; if so, there is added reason for teachers to offer themselves as living examples to their students. Knowledge that makes little difference to the instructor's life is, in any case, rightly suspicious, and it may deserve to be disregarded by students.

The professionalization of the disciplines within the university has made teaching an activity to be minimized or, ideally, avoided. Although some colleges still prize good teaching and universities make a show of appreciating it, rewards in both employing institutions and in the profession closely track publication records. Tenure, promotion, increases in salary, reductions of teaching load, grants, fellowships, positions in professional organizations, and offers of employment depend in significant measure on research productivity. As a result, the primary loyalty of educators is no longer to the local institution and its students, but to the broader profession and peers who can write recommendations.

Philosophers play this game no less than do historians and literary scholars, generating vast quantities of publications of dubious quality. The price of this Niagara of printed words must be calculated in wasted trees, neglected students, and loss of devotion to the culture and values of the local university. The pluralists who revolted against the leadership of the American Philosophical Association in the late 1970s had professionalization as one of their grievances. Rhetorically, the revolt pitted analytic philosophers against Continentalists and pragmatists. But the causes of the conflict were deeper and more numerous than disagreement about philosophical method and style.

The APA was run by a self-perpetuating circle of people largely from elite East Coast graduate schools. They thought distinction gained through publications was evidence of ability to run the affairs of the Association. They viewed teaching institutions as useful primarily for placing graduate students and allowed them neither representation nor influence in the inner councils of the APA. Eastern Division elections occurred in the business meeting of the annual convention, effectively disenfranchising those who were not on the program and could thus not have their way paid to distant cities. The revolt was at least as much a reaction against the professionalized exclusiveness of the APA as an attack on the dominance of analytic philosophy.

Santayana is surely right that one's philosophy must be honest in the double sense that one must act on what one believes and that one must not believe what one cannot enact. The demand to act on my principles made me join the pluralist revolt and explains my continuing efforts to open up the APA when I was elected to various offices in the organization. My decisions to remain at Vanderbilt also express my commitment to my students and to the university that has become my home. I have an intense loyalty to people near to me, which shows itself in my readiness to go to great lengths to promote their good. This attitude defines my relation to friends, students, and family.

I also believe that, although some things matter intensely, many of the things that upset people are of little significance. This conviction has enabled me to live without condemning much and without the desire to run other people's lives. The connected respect for autonomy has been the source of great happiness for me: I attribute my deeply satisfying relations to my children to mutual acceptance built on caring and on love. Love and respect have also served as the foundation of the extraordinary relation my wife and I enjoy, sharing all the tasks and pleasures of life, and reflecting and writing together on the problems of education.

In graduate school, we are taught to write with footnotes, evoking authority for all questionable claims. Philosophers, like other human beings, find it consoling to run with the crowd and embrace few views that are out of favor. Knowing the fickleness of public opinion, I could never make myself believe that the number of people holding a position has anything to do with its truth. Accordingly, I have learned to write without footnotes and, when it seemed appropriate, I have embraced wildly unpopular, though not intrinsically outrageous, ideas.

I was for a while committed to epiphenomenalism, and I am one of few people insisting that philosophy imposes special demands on its practitioners. I have not many companions in trying to do metaphysics as a nominalist, and am in a tiny minority in speaking bluntly on behalf of euthanasia. My recent work on moral progress places me at odds with the vast majority of my colleagues, who find it difficult to affirm the superiority of Western values. I have not hesitated to publicize my view that a particular university administration was corrupt and called for the resignation of its leader. I view plain speaking about matters of significance not as a privilege of the educated but as the obligation of people who enjoy the benefits of tenure and professorship.

Pain and eventual loss appear to me inevitable elements of the human condition. Suffering and disappointment can be reduced by intelligent effort, but they cannot be erased. At the point where we run out of ameliorative strategies, graceful acceptance of whatever fate may throw our way makes for inner peace and better life. Such stoic equanimity has hardened me against disaster from an early age. I am careful, however, not to employ it too soon or as an alternative to energetic assault upon the world, rather than as a final stance after every effort has failed.

The consideration that in the end we die has disturbed my enjoyment of life just as little as the fate of the food I eat interferes with the delight of a good meal. Focusing on the destination makes us forget the pleasures of the road. Should the eventual extinction of the sun send cold shivers down our backs? Surely not; such issues simply do not matter. Untold generations will have basked in the light before the dark descends. Their joy redeems eventual disaster, or at least proves it irrelevant. Sometimes it is best to avert our gaze, for viewing matters in context liberates the mind, but seeing them in their ultimate outcome can paralyze it.

This is one of the many lessons of finitude we tend to forget. Descartes's view that the will is infinite needs to be supplemented by the observation that the mind finds it just as tempting to expand its scope beyond reasonable limits. If it is wise to look a week ahead, we suppose, it must be better to think of what may happen in a year or a decade. Reflecting on what is possible over an unlimited period generates foolish theories, baseless hopes, and unending worry. A part of the reason why animals live better than some humans is their freedom from ultimate concerns; they act as if they knew that finite creatures are not designed to deal with totality.

Up to a point, life gets better in proportion to our ability to get absorbed in the immediate. Failure rehearses memories, caution advises planning; future and past squeeze us from two sides until life becomes the hurried conversion of one into the other. Even universities have become beehives that leave little time for leisured reflection or the life-giving moments in which one can simply *be*. Few things are more difficult for our burdened and busy generation than focus and absorption. These are the gifts of immediacy, which is not some unconceptualized given, but simply the present in whose movement we can feel at home. Momentary forgetfulness can liberate us from the future and the past, and reveal the exhilarating beauty of whatever comes our way. This is transcendence— probably the only sort available to animals.

I am grateful for living at a time when I can contribute to the recovery of American philosophy, a great and greatly neglected national treasure. The founding of the Society for the Advancement of American Philosophy, in which I gladly participated, serves as clear evidence that just a few determined and persevering individuals can have a lasting effect on the future of a profession. We need to continue expanding the canon by adding to it thinkers whose work is excellent but who have, for one reason or another, been neglected over the years. I work on this, as I work on bringing philosophy into contact with a broader public, with the conviction that the energy and vision of a small band of people can make all the difference we need.

The activist element in American philosophy seems to fit well with my temperament. I value the sort of robust engagement with the world that evokes personal activity and aims at social improvement. Scholarly imprisonment in universities strikes me as intellectually narrowing and emotionally impoverishing. It tends to make professors timid and compliant souls. I am interested in ordinary people and their problems because I see myself as no different from them; I simply cannot take claims about aristocracy of any sort very seriously.

As a consequence, I love philosophy for the perspectives it offers on human difficulties and the tools it provides for their resolution. Thinking about what I see around me is one of the great pleasures of my life; acting on what I believe combines the satisfaction of being a whole person with the exhilaration of an experiment. Academics who live only in the mind sadden me; their truncated existence denies them the robust delights and the sound common sense of those who engage the world on multiple levels. A sense of practical reality is a badly needed balance to excessive cerebration.

Philosophy needs balance no less than do philosophers. Even if it could attain the precision of some of the natural sciences, philosophy would need the literary imagination to complete its task. Its product is not disinterested knowledge but a relationship that changes lives. To establish that relation, we need to communicate both discursive ideas and visions. The manner of the communication can be as important as its substance; people respond to what is well thought and well said. The magnificence of philosophical ideas and the excellence of their expression are, therefore, integrally connected to their effectiveness. My ideal has always been to write philosophy with the beauty and inventiveness of Mozart's music, though I would also like for my ideas to be true in some sense on which philosophers will never agree. The momentousness of this ideal is measured best by seeing how far I fall short of it.

In the end, I do not want to be absorbed in the technical details of the problems of philosophy. My passion is to deploy philosophy to deal with the important issues that face us as individuals, as a nation, and as members of the human race. There is a large public waiting anxiously for what philosophy can offer—for careful thinking, clear vision, and the intelligent examination of our values. That is where the future of philosophy lies, that is where American philosophy has always pointed us, and that is where I will continue to be.

# PART ONE

# MIND AND REALITY

# ONE

# THE IMPOTENT MIND

My task in this chapter is to show that epiphenomenalism cannot be disposed of in a "conclusive fashion."[1] Epiphenomenalism is a theory that consists of two universal propositions: one about the origin of mental events and another about their causal efficacy. They are (1) every mental event has as its total cause one or a set of physical processes; and (2) no mental event is a total or a partial cause of any physical process. I leave the question of the precise distinction between the mental and the physical for another time. For our present purposes, it will suffice to say that by "physical process" I mean such events as the explosions of supernovas, the ionization of gases, and the firing of neurons, and by "mental event" I mean such occurrences as the thought of feasting ghosts, the remembrance of things past, and the lust for life. I presume that all of us are acquainted with some such events. The nature of the causal connection between physical processes and mental events is an issue I have explored in another place.[2] My only concern here will be with the validity of the claim that epiphenomenalism (or, as I shall also call it, the "impotence hypothesis") is a "thoughtless and incoherent theory."[3]

To show that this contention is unfounded, I will examine six of the most popular arguments against the impotence hypothesis. Each of these arguments has been considered conclusive against epiphenomenalism by one distinguished philosopher or another. My strategy will be to separate the arguments into three major groups; I will then state each as clearly as I can, and attempt to assess their force impartially.

*I*

Professor Taylor contends that epiphenomenalism is "incompetent to take account of the obvious facts of mental life."[4] The claim is that our everyday experience acquaints us with numerous instances of the mind's action on the body, as well as of the body's action on the mind. I will term this set of objections "The Counterintuitive Arguments," since their essence is the insistence that careful attention to the plain facts of experience is sufficient to prove the epiphenomenalist wrong.

There are three forms of the Counterintuitive Argument, each stressing the efficacy of a different type of conscious experience. The first is the argument from volition; the second is based on a consideration of some special forms of thought or purely cognitive experience; and the third takes as its point of departure certain acknowledged features of the emotive life.

The Counterintuitive Argument from Volition runs as follows. Volition is a consciousness of effort that often stands in a peculiarly intimate connection with subsequent physical (or mental) events. There is a high degree of correlation between conscious efforts directed at performing certain actions and the actual execution of these actions. The relationship is especially intimate in that not only are volition and action constantly conjoined, but the former is precisely the attempt to bring the latter into existence. Further, an essential part of any volition is envisagement of its effect. It appears, therefore, that merely by reflecting on the nature of volition we can recognize that it is a cause, and that when we will something we have an actual experience of a causal process. All of this is borne out by the fact that we ordinarily believe that certain bodily movements occur at certain times *because* certain conscious events had occurred at immediately antecedent times, that is, that mental events are causal factors in bringing about at least some bodily states.

Now, I do not think anyone would have the audacity to deny that we do believe in the causal efficacy of volition. However, the possession of this belief proves nothing. The issue turns on what reasons we can give to support it. It seems that there are three distinct but interconnected reasons. First, in volition we seem to have firsthand experience of creative process; we seem actually to be observing the smooth passage involved in the conversion of a thought into reality. Second, it seems patent that the relation of volition to willed bodily event is intimate in the extreme since the volition forecasts the event and is "active" in the sense that it appears poised to bring it about. Finally, we have the overwhelming spectacle of effectuated will, the apparent harmony of will and nature. Our belief that the bond of volition with the willed bodily (or mental) state is authentic and indissoluble is enhanced not only by our appreciation of the intimate connection of the two and by the alleged experience of process, but also by the steady success of volition at fulfilling its promise.

If the claim that in volition we are immediately aware of causative process could be substantiated, the fate of epiphenomenalism would be sealed. However, there is nothing to be said for this dictum, and the remaining two considerations do not suffice to establish the truth of the belief in the efficacy of volitional consciousness. We are no more aware of causal process in volition than we are in observing the transmission of a shove down a line of freight cars. When I decide to wriggle my nose, what I experience is the conscious effort to do just that with the appropriate kinesthetic (and possibly visual) sensations immediately following. The experience, as Hume pointed out long ago, is that of one event succeeding another, not that of the *production* of the later event by the earlier. If *per impossibile* we could actually observe the creative process, we would not be in the dark as to how it comes about that sometimes our will is done; as it is, with the method of birth concealed we are left to delight in the occasional achievement.

But if we do not have immediate experience of the alleged creativity of consciousness, it is of no avail to insist on the intimate connection of volition and achievement, on the tendency of will to predict the future and the fact that it appears to be an "active" experience. The epiphenomenalist has a ready explanation. Volition gives the appearance of being a causal factor, because it is the mental counterpart of a process in the physical organism that is a causal factor. Instead of being the necessary and sufficient condition of a certain action, consciousness of effort to bring it about is a concomitant of the necessary and sufficient condition; instead of being the cause of the physical effect, it is the coeffect of the physical cause, the mental "transcript" of a physiological state. It is the physical processes of the body that cause the occurrence and determine the content of conscious events. The harmony of volition and achievement will, then, no longer seem mysterious once we recall that the processes that give rise to a consciousness of effort are the same that initiate fulfillment of its promise.

One might urge that if epiphenomenalism were true all states of consciousness would be "passive" accompaniments of physiological processes. This would eliminate the distinction between active and passive forms of awareness, yet volition clearly appears to be an "active" experience. But this argument also has a fatal flaw. Accounting for the possibility of the distinction does not present any difficulty for the epiphenomenalist, for if there are passive (receptive) and active (out-directed) states of the organism, then it is no secret why we have "passive" and "active" experiences. Now the organism is evidently passive with respect to external stimulation and active when outgoing process is centrally induced. It may, therefore, well be that the appearance of activity on the conscious level is due to the occurrence of movement and action within the animal. Volition throws lame sparks testifying that electric current is busily at work.

The epiphenomenalist's defense derives its strength from two quarters. First, it is clear that the premises of this form of the Counterintuitive Argument do not suffice to prove its conclusion. Second, facts that serve as the basis of this argument can as well be accounted for on the hypothesis of the impotence of consciousness. If epiphenomenalism were true, it would be reasonable to expect the kind of confusion about the efficacy of thought which is perhaps implicit in our everyday beliefs and which has been raised to the status of dogma by philosophers. The unsophisticated man easily confuses the conspicuous attendant of the cause with the cause; when the mainspring is hidden, what is really a part of the complex effect may itself be construed as the causal source. We still tend to believe that flashes of lightning cause thunder (instead of being its coeffects, since both the thunder and the lightning are brought about by the same electrical disturbance) and the early history of medicine is replete with cases where one of a set of symptoms is singled out as the unitary "cause" of the disease. The epiphenomenalist may well argue that the explanation of the miracle of effectuated will, the persistent harmony of will and nature, is not to be sought in some mind that mysteriously imposes its designs on the recalcitrant stuff of the world, but in a living animal that, struggling in the universal flux, for a brief moment overcomes the reniency of its surroundings and produces in the process an inner sense of its effort and passing dominance. Volition is a form of consciousness indicative of the fact that physical changes directed at the execution of some action are occurring or have just occurred.

Let me devote brief attention to the two remaining forms of the Counterintuitive Argument. The claim that cognitive experiences are physically efficacious is based on the following type of consideration. It is well known that the thought of ripe plums makes the mouth water, and recognition of a speeding car may be under suitable conditions a mental fact with radical issue in the realm of action. Now, the critic may urge, since experiences of this type are common, and the intimate connection between mental event and physical outcome is admitted on all sides, the epiphenomenalist's claim that the mind is causally lame carries no conviction.

This argument is open to the same objections as the previous one. The "intimate" connection of mental event and physical outcome does not imply direct causal relatedness: we may even make a fair case for the view that the antecedent probability of such a direct causal tie is not appreciably greater than that of the rival hypothesis that their tie is indirect, running through a common physical source. The fact that thought is followed by appropriate physical change is by no means unambiguous evidence for the view that it was a causal factor in bringing about that change. To argue as though it were may well be to commit the fallacy of *post hoc, ergo propter hoc*. At any rate, the claim that recognition as a mental fact has physical consequences is at best a hypothesis, and the fact that the common man tends to embrace it does not help in the least to show that it is a conclusively established one.

Exactly the same considerations apply to the Counterintuitive Argument from Emotion. The fact that fear is correlated with a wild pounding of the heart or rasping dry throat, or that anger tends to make a man breathe fast and even to cloud the eyes, is no evidence against epiphenomenalism. The sole fact that the Counterintuitive Arguments suffice to establish beyond all reasonable doubt is that epiphenomenalism is counterintuitive. However, I do not see why any exponent of the doctrine should consider this in the least alarming. The Copernican system of the universe is wildly counterintuitive, as are Freudian theories of subconscious motivation and any number of other respectable hypotheses. It is, of course, necessary to remind ourselves that it is no virtue for a theory to lack the recommendation of being in accord with the everyday intuitions of mankind. There have to be good reasons for preferring such counterintuitive hypotheses to their less counterintuitive rivals. But it is not my present purpose to consider the reasons *for* epiphenomenalism; I am concerned only with evaluating some of the arguments against it. And my conclusion is that none of the Counterintuitive Arguments comes even remotely near to refuting the impotence hypothesis. Moreover, the facts adduced against epiphenomenalism in these arguments can be readily and adequately explained on the hypothesis that epiphenomenalism is true. Finally, I must remark that the impotence hypothesis is by no means *completely* counterintuitive, for while it appears to run counter to a number of our common beliefs and experiences, certain other common experiences tend directly to confirm it.

## II

The unifying character of the next group of arguments I will consider is that each of them is based on a feature of "the natural history of consciousness."[5] I will give them the name "Arguments from the Distribution of the Intensity of Consciousness," a phrase that combines the vice of being cumbersome with the virtue of descriptive accuracy. The deployment of awareness is such, it is argued, as would be reasonable to expect if it were efficacious. It seems to be present whenever intelligent actions are performed, and absent whenever activity is restricted to an in variable, automatic level. Moreover, it is most intense when the need for intelligence is greatest, and sinks to a minimum when truncated forms of discernment suffice for the performance of the action. I will present two subsidiary forms of this argument. Although I intend to judge each on its own merits, I will make a general comment at once. It appears that any force this type of argument may have is derived from its successful application of the Method of Concomitant Variation. The claim is that the intensity of consciousness varies concurrently with some such feature as the complexity or the urgency of the action to be performed. Now my remark is that even on the most charitable interpretation, even if— and this is by no means beyond doubt—a clear case can be made for such concomitance, the argument cannot prove the causal efficacy of consciousness. Mill's Fifth Canon of Induction states quite explicitly that a phenomenon that varies whenever another phenomenon does "is either a cause or an effect of [the latter] . . . *or is connected with it through some fact of causation.*"[6] Mill goes on to point out with great acuteness that concomitant variation of two phenomena is no proof of the causal efficacy of either, since the same concomitance would be observed if they were "two different effects of a common cause."

The first form of the Argument from the Distribution of the Intensity of Consciousness is perhaps its most common one. We notice that we have to pay no attention at all to automatic actions such as the beating of the heart, and little if any to habit-actuated ones. However, consciousness is agonizingly intense in situations where indecision is great or the complexity of some task excessive. A person caught in some inimical state will think furiously to find a way out, or will, at least, be acutely aware of the danger to which he is exposed. Since conscious consideration appears necessary for the resolution of the worst predicaments and the consummation of exacting performances, the causal efficacy of at least some mental events cannot be reasonably denied.

Now even if there were such an invariable concomitance of intense consciousness with complex problem solving, it would, as I have suggested before, not prove the mind's efficacy. But not even this invariable concomitance can be established. For some of the most complex, non-habitual performances are executed without the least thought. Trying to prevent falling on the back of my head once I have slipped on an icy hill involves a series of actions of staggering speed and complexity. But even if I had an hour to reflect, I could not think out what to do and how. If it be objected that this example prejudices the issue, for what is involved here is a set of automatic body adjustments, it may be well to remind the critic that it is by no means a unique case. Solutions of complex mathematical or philosophical problems "pop" into our heads, sometimes without effort. And sometimes the intensity of attention directed at solving a problem is directly proportional to the resultant frustration: the only way the required result can be reached is by diverting attention from the issue or by "sleeping on it." The correlation of intense consciousness with high-grade problem solving is too spotty to serve as the premise of any compelling argument.

The general form of the epiphenomenalist answer to counterarguments should be clear by now. Confronted with an apparent instance of effective consciousness, the characteristic move is to disjoin efficacy and awareness, assigning the former to the physical organism while the latter, in its varied modes, is left as the distinguishing mark of the mental. The significance of this procedure is that it reminds us that the efficacy of consciousness is not "given": it is not an indubitable fact of experience but a theory we frame to account for observed conjunctions. The weaker the evidence in favor of this theory, the more epiphenomenalism remains unrefuted. Incidentally, of course, this method of rejoinder also calls attention to the fact that epiphenomenalism is itself but a hypothesis. This is an issue about which a great deal should be said; nothing, however, in this essay. Let me just remark, before I go on to the second form of the Argument from the Distribution of the Intensity of Consciousness, that while its refutation or confirmation is by no means independent of the findings of physical science, epiphenomenalism itself is not a scientific hypothesis.

An examination of our everyday beliefs would probably turn up considerable public support for the view that pain functions as a biological deterrent to action. I will not touch an electric wire because of the excessively disagreeable sensation of shock, and one may even check one's tendency to be a glutton, if only the memory of the previous night's dyspepsia is vivid enough. As is clear in the case of such experiences as toothaches, the more intense the pain, the more it functions as a signal to the organism to take remedial action. It is of the greatest moment for the welfare of the animal that pains be associated with function-impeding and plea-

sures with life-enhancing processes. An animal that would find suffoca-
tion irresistibly pleasurable and the consumption of food the source of
excruciating and perdurable pains, would not grow up to father broods
of young. Hence, it is clear that pain is biologically important and causally effective, the argument contends. But it is also a form of consciousness. Certain conscious events thus seem indispensable links in at least
some causal chains that result in overt bodily acts.

There is nothing to be said for this argument. Since pains are grounded
in the body or in the action of some external object on the body, the
claim that our acts of evasion and aversion, or our positive attempts at
suppressing the source of irritation are due even partly to the efficacy of
the feeling of distress, is pure hypothesis. Being on a plane with the noxious object or the injured organ, it is more likely that the physiological
counterpart of the consciously undergone pain occasions the avoidance
response, than that this purely physical response is due to a feeling of
helpless suffering. The Argument from Pain lacks even the apparent
plausibility of the Argument from Volition, for suffering is the most passive, most infuriatingly impotent of experiences. If suffering were efficacious in mending the rent fabric of organs, it would be criminal to
administer pain-relievers; as it is, the natural tendency of the sick man is
to sleep, that is, to "switch off" the mind altogether, and let the body
make whatever repairs it can. To reply here that the paradigm case of the
efficacy of pain is to be looked for in the influence it exerts over intelligent choice, not in the circumstances surrounding its questionable role
once bodily injury is sustained, is of no avail. The reason is obvious. For
the wisdom gathered from past pains to affect our choice, it must in the
first place be remembered. But there is little reason to suspect that consciousness of pain is a necessary condition of the formation of a trace
that will occasion our finding certain things or actions objectionable,
and there is even less reason to suppose that the avoidance response is
due to remembered pain rather than the activated trace. The same kind
of argument applies to the supposed role of pain in bringing about avoidance habits. It may well be that if pain accompanies the joint occurrence
of a kind of stimulus with a kind of behavior, the probability increases
that the behavior will not occur the next time the stimulus occurs. But

far from demonstrating the efficacy of pain, this shows only that under the circumstances either the pain or (what is more likely) its physiological counterpart was causally involved.

## III

I will now consider Pratt's interesting Argument from the Impossibility of Reasoning. The argument goes as follows. Reasoning in some sense involves the awareness of logical relations. Thus, it is permissible to affirm certain propositions as conclusions if certain other propositions have been affirmed as premises, and this only because the two sets of propositions stand in certain intimate logical connections. Awareness of some such logical connection is an indispensable co-cause of the mental act of affirming a proposition as conclusion on the basis of one or more propositions that serve as premises. If awareness of logical relations did not play a causal role in inference, no conclusion we reach could ever claim to be based on logic. Then if we happened to think logically, it would be merely "because the brain molecules shake down, so to speak, in a lucky fashion."[7] And the inevitable outcome of such an absurd view of inference would seem to be that even the best arguments its exponents can marshal to demonstrate its truth do not entitle them nor anyone else to believe it. For belief in a theory is the outcome of physiological changes in the brain, and never of the awareness of good arguments for it. Thus if epiphenomenalism were true, logical inference would be impossible. And if logical inference is impossible, then we cannot really know that epiphenomenalism is true, in the sense of "know" in which it implies the ability to give reasons upon demand.

I will restate the basic claim of this argument somewhat more precisely. By the statement that a person $P$ inferred the proposition $C$ from the propositions $A$ and $B$, we mean at least (1) that the occurrence of $C$ as a thought in $P$'s mind was due to a total cause of which $P$'s thought of A and $P$'s thought of $B$ were parts, and (2) that another cause-factor leading to the occurrence of $C$ in $P$'s mind was $P$'s belief that $A$ and $B$ jointly imply $C$. It is obvious that no claim is made to the effect that the original entertainment of $A$ and $B$ together with the awareness that $A$ and $B$ jointly imply $C$ represent the total cause of the assertion of $C$. No proposition or set of propositions entails only one proposition; hence, implication is not sufficient to determine the direction of inference. However, even a proof that mental events are indispensable parts of complex causes would be enough to evidence the bankruptcy of the impotence hypothesis.

But the argument cannot even establish this. If consciousness of logical relations were a necessary condition of inference, we would not be justified in believing any of the results of electronic brains such as UNIVAC, the RCA 501, or for that matter, the Kalin Burkhart Logical Truth Calculator. For surely these machines do not work by the apprehension of logical relations, although they do seem to manage quite well when it comes to tracing implications. Now if to do logic is to engage in a transformation game in accordance with rules, this is not a whit surprising. For the rules specify with complete determinateness the logically permissible moves in any situation, and it is simple enough to construct a mechanical model for this. The "passage" from proposition to proposition could be represented by actual motion; lack of a circuit, or a switch in the "off" position might serve to express in a material medium the absence of the logical relation of implication.

In order to work out the details, one has only to look at the blueprint of some recent logic machine. To say that a machine programmed to solve problems of the Lower Functional Calculus is working in accordance with logic merely because "the molecules shake down in a lucky fashion" is either to insist, quite correctly of course, that if the machine had broken down it would not have performed properly, or to remind us that we are here dealing with "molecules," that is, physical entities. So we are, but the fact that the brain is, among other things, a high-efficiency cybernetic calculator does not in any way imply that its operation in accordance with the physically coded rules of logical inference is a matter of "luck." If the brain is primed to function according to a system of rules isomorphic with the laws of logic, nothing could be more reasonable than that we should time and again have the conscious experience (brain-produced) of inferential passage from thought to thought. Thus the causal source of the "inference" of $C$ from $A$ and $B$ need have as its constituent neither $P$'s thought of $A$ and his thought of $B$, nor his conscious belief that $A$ and $B$ jointly entail $C$. If this is one of those comparatively rare occasions when the inference is fully explicit, the two thoughts and the belief will indeed occur, but both their occurrence and the passage from them to the conclusion *C* will be due to the steady whirr of the calculator below. Obviously, the soundest test that a machine works in accordance with the logical rules of inference is its ability to come up with the right answer consistently, just as the ultimate proof that a certain machine can play chess is to be looked for in its adroitness at out maneuvering opponent after opponent. Now, if after just having lost his game to the machine a player were to insist that the rules of chess "had nothing to do" with the moves of his opponent for it can only act in accordance with the way its "molecules shake down," we would at once know the source of his distress. And perhaps we know it in the current case, as well. For it is not easy to cede unique possession of a skill that we think attests our supremacy.

The upshot of my argument is this. None of the six objections I have considered comes anywhere near to refuting epiphenomenalism. Other objections, which I did not think essential to include, are equally inconclusive. There is good reason to believe that "epiphenomenalism . . . is a thoughtless and incoherent theory" is a claim both thoughtless and incoherent. This, of course, does not mean that the impotence hypothesis has been or may be proved true. It only means that it is not a theory that may be discarded or disregarded in quite as cavalier a fashion as too many philosophers have too often done. The detailed assessment of the evidence for epiphenomenalism is a task still to be accomplished. The probable truth of the impotence hypothesis cannot be established without such detailed investigation of the arguments for as well as against it; an investigation that has to be carried out in the context of equally thorough examinations of rival mind-body theories.

TWO

# SANTAYANA'S PHILOSOPHY OF MIND

The history of philosophy resembles a convention of deaf-mutes. Each participant attempts to communicate the secrets of his private imagination through a swirl of silent gestures. Intent on disclosing his own insight, each is confined in his own world: He has no ear for the language of others and often little knowledge of how to make them understand his. The carnival of controversy that ensues is grotesque in the eyes of the outsider but tragic for the thoughtful participant. For in the history of philosophy, many more messages are sent than are received, and the ones that are received come to us mutilated, infected by our own perspective and interests. In our own way, each of us distorts or discards the central judgments of almost everyone else. The dead sign language of the printed word is inadequate to span a century. Philosophers signal like wild semaphores that lost their common code.

If the philosopher who attempts precision and rigor is often misunderstood, the fate of the thinker who writes as though he were a poet is still worse. A picturesque style rich in metaphor invites misapprehension not only of its content and detail but also of the author's general intention.

The result of such misunderstanding and of the frustration attendant upon the attempt to explicate poetry in prose is disdain and eventually the total neglect of the thinker's work. The supposition is soon advanced that the author did not mean to write serious, systematic philosophy or, at least, that his thought is not a significant aspect of his work. In precisely this fashion, George Santayana has long been celebrated as a consummate stylist, a poet, and a literary psychologist, while the view that his philosophy does not warrant serious study has been gaining ever wider acceptance.

It has become fashionable to pay cursory homage to Santayana's "courageous naturalism" and, at most, to follow this by the expression of regret about the vague and almost mystical things he said about the realm of spirit. But, the official view runs, such mysticism, incoherence, and ambiguity should not surprise us for Santayana was, after all, a poet, and it would be rash to look to him for philosophical enlightenment or to judge him by the rigorous standards of rationality. I contend that this "official" view of Santayana's philosophical achievement is radically mistaken. If my purpose were to present a general refutation of it, I would begin by arguing that style and content cannot be dissociated, and that Santayana's picturesque mode of expression is not an accidental feature of his work. In his view, neither literary psychology nor philosophy is a source of clear and adequate knowledge, and it would be vain pedantry to affect precision of language where such is inappropriate. An imaginative style that evokes in us the intuition of particularly rich and comprehensive essences is singularly appropriate for Santayana, who believes that existence is ultimately unintelligible, knowledge is always symbolic, and one of the tasks of philosophy is to articulate "the large facts."

I will, however, not take this occasion to present a general rebuttal of this most influential of the current appraisals of Santayana. Instead, I hope that the destructive task of showing the inadequacy of this appraisal will be accomplished in the course of the constructive enterprise of developing a central segment of Santayana's philosophical thought. The segment of his system that I wish to explore is what may be called "the philosophy of mind," viz., his views on such subjects as the nature of mental acts, the nature of the immediate objects of consciousness, and in this paper especially, the relationship of mental acts to the animal organism.

In essence, I propose to do three things. First of all, I propose to point out some of the fundamental concepts of Santayana's philosophy of mind, along with the technical terms that fix these concepts in the public language. Second, I intend to exhibit the structure of Santayana's thought, the strong skeleton of a system that may be discerned once the bedizenments of style, all embellishment and vagary are cut away. This will be the major task of my essay. In order to accomplish it I will attempt to clarify his language, systematize his statements, and throw some light on his scattered arguments. Whenever necessary, I will introduce distinctions or make explicit the ones Santayana drew. In some discussions I will be reduced to conjecturing what he would or might say. In all such cases I will try to stay within the largely unstated intent of his thought. Finally, by a critical examination of some of its concepts and theories, I hope to demonstrate that Santayana's philosophy of mind has a unity of purpose and structure that is a considerable source of strength. Even though I will not hesitate to level serious criticisms against it, I hope to show that the easy dismissal of this aspect of Santayana's mature thought is as unjustifiable as it may be injurious to future progress in the philosophy of mind.

## I

By careful and elaborate ontological analysis, Santayana distinguishes four "realms" or irreducibly different kinds of being. First in the order of being, there are an infinite number of essences: This infinity of the forms of definiteness Santayana calls "the realm of essence." Essences are universals, and as such they do not exist. By existence Santayana means location in a space-time network with the consequent possibility of causal action. Essences do not exist because neither spatial nor temporal properties may be predicated of them. They are timelessly and hence changelessly self-identical forms of every degree of determination. Such timeless, changeless universals, Santayana maintains, are necessary conditions of the possibility of time and change and action, and therefore of the world as it exists.

In the order of generation, matter has primacy, even though its operation presupposes the availability of a plenum of essences. Matter is the principle by virtue of which essences are instantiated; it is the incalculable force that confers existence on the forms. In a fundamental sense, matter has no characteristics or nature. As the principle of selective instantiation it is merely the undifferentiated and inarticulate other of essence. No essence can yield an adequate description of its inner dynamism, and it does not derive its inexhaustible creative power from participation in some form. Matter is a primordial existential flux; it is an indescribable and unintelligible surd.

The world of substance, of physical objects acting and reacting in space, can be analyzed into the two components of matter and essence. The blind thrust of matter embodies, "existentializes" set after set of essence. And we must be careful not to put narrow limits on the conception of essence: Santayana claims that even events have essences. The essence or form of an event as distinct from its occurrence he calls a "trope." Substance may, then, be described as a set of instantiated tropes or, in plainer language, a large number of physical events. The realm of truth is the total inventory of essences instantiated by matter. It consists of the possibly infinite set of universals that have been, are being, and will be exemplified in the history of the world. In Santayana's view, then, truth is fully objective: it does not presuppose the existence of a knowing subject or mind. On the contrary, truth as an objective standard is a necessary condition of the possibility of true opinions. Judgments are true if and only if they faithfully reproduce a portion of the descriptive properties of the world-process.

The fourth irreducibly different realm of being Santayana distinguishes is that of spirit. By "spirit" he means nothing more mysterious than consciousness. However, the notion of consciousness, I am afraid, is mysterious enough for some philosophers. For this reason, I will presuppose in my discussion as little as I can, perhaps no more than their and my human experience. Human experience consists of a series of conscious acts, and consciousness is the total inner difference between being asleep and awake.[1] This difference itself is never the sole object of consciousness, but in retrospect it can be discerned with sufficient clarity. In conscious events we must draw a distinction between the objects of consciousness and our consciousness of these objects. The consciousness or consciou*sing* of the object is a pure act of apprehension. As such, it exists only in being enacted, and can never be its own object or the object of another conscious act. It is because the act of consciousness is never, and can never be, among the objects of our experience that so many philosophers tend to deny its existence. But its presence, though not all of its properties, is undeniable even on a Humean theory of mind: it is a necessary condition of experience and the correlate of every object of awareness.

Spirit in a man, then, consists of a series of conscious acts, each with its own manifold of objects. Santayana calls these conscious acts "intuitions." The objects of consciousness are always changeless and impotent essences. Since no conscious act can exist without some objects, and since any essence implicates through the internal relation of difference an infinity of other essences, the entire realm of essence is a necessary condition of the possibility of intuition and hence of spirit. In another and even more fundamental way, intuitions presuppose the existence of both matter and essence. Although consciousness is first in the order of knowledge, it is a late arrival in the causal order of nature. Its emergence presupposes the instantiation by matter of a set of enormously complex essences. This system of tropes, the hereditary movements and physical organization of an animal, Santayana calls "the psyche." The psyche is the mythological unity of the sum total of significant tropes embodied in the life history of an animal. Since it is wound up to aim at self-development and self-maintenance, the psyche has diverse groups of functions that conjointly define its nature. Being present in the seed, its first function is embryological and vegetative. Biologically, it is a self-regulating and self-repairing mechanism. In the search for food and shelter, it is the source of locomotion. Surrounding itself with a web of organs, its psychological function is to grow perceptive and intelligent in its responses. Socially, it is the agent in all interaction and the cause of all behavior. Morally, it underlies all choice, impulse, and interest, and is the natural ground of the distinction between good and evil. Its physiological and endocrinological function is to maintain the internal health and equilibrium of the organism. Finally, one of its neurological functions is to give rise to consciousness.

Spirit is thus totally dependent for its existence on the system of embodied tropes that constitutes the psyche. "Spirit, or the intuitions in which it is realized . . . (requires) the existence of nature to create it,"[2] Santayana says. And again, "The life of the psyche, which rises to . . . intuition, determines all the characters of the essence evoked."[3] In the light of this generatively secondary or derived character of intuitions, it is important to remark that even though spirit is causally reducible to the psyche and exerts no causal influence over anything, it nonetheless constitutes an ontologically irreducible and ultimate mode of being. At a later stage I will discuss Santayana's reasons for maintaining the irreducibility of consciousness to neurological process, of spirit to psyche. At this point, however, I must content myself with an unembellished statement of what Santayana holds.

## II

The significance of Santayana's distinction between psyche and spirit is best brought out by directing attention to the properties and functions of each. The psyche as a set of embodied tropes is a relatively stable vortex in the universal flux. Each psyche is a system of vital events: each system of this sort is a material organism. To say that something is material is to assert at least that it is publicly observable, that it is in a field of action continuous with the human body, and that under favorable conditions its behavior may be predicted and even controlled. To say that something is in a field of action is to say at least that it has a specific locus in physical space and a specific locus in physical time, that the behavior of its spatiotemporal neighbors may bring about changes in it, and that its changes may modify the behavior of its neighbors. A psyche, then, is an observable, spatiotemporally located system of operations that stands in close and constant interaction with its environment. No psyche is a substance: Only the physical universe as a whole is a substance in the sense of being an enduring and independent existent. Psyches are modes of substance, limited centers of dynamic equilibrium that the flux of existence temporarily sustains.[4]

By contrast with its material organ, spirit is immaterial and imperceptible. It is "the actual light of consciousness,"[5] "the light of discrimination,"[6] or "intelligence in act."[7] The essence of spirit or mind is cognitive awareness. Let me warn at once against two possible misunderstandings.

First of all, by "spirit" Santayana does not mean a single individual being or some cosmic Consciousness. Instead, he uses the word to refer to a category or type of being, the class of occurrences of which every particular thought, feeling, and sensation is a member. Second, the fact that he speaks of "minds" should not mislead us into supposing that he thinks of minds as substantial, independently existing things. Nothing could be farther from Santayana's intention than to admit the existence of enduring mind-substances or mental continuants. Consciousness exists only in the individual acts Santayana calls "intuitions." A mind, therefore, is simply a set of intimately connected intuitions. The intimate connection between the intuitions that constitute a single mind is at least of two sorts. First, all of them share the same psyche as their source of origin. Second, the essence disclosed in any intuition of the set is qualitatively similar to, or in some sense continuous with, the objects of intuitions that precede and succeed it. Since both the occurrence of intuitions and their specific objects are dependent on the psyche, it is clear that the continuity of our experience is due to the continuity through change of the animal organism, and the unity and identity of the mind is but a reflection of the unity and identity of the psyche.

Intuitions are intentional acts directed upon objects. The objects of intuitions are nonexistent essences of varying complexity. At this point, a problem arises. If all intuition is of essence but knowledge is always of some state or process of substance, how is knowledge possible? If nothing that is presented to the mind exists, how can we discern the phases of existence? If the immediate is, without exception, a changeless and eternally self-identical universal, how can we perceive the growth and the corruption that gnaw at the heart of each particular? Let me begin an answer to this problem by expanding the act-object terminology, which has been adequate for our purposes until now.

Santayana needs a threefold distinction here. He cannot be satisfied with distinguishing the act of consciousness from its immediate object. He must also draw a sharp line of separation between this immediate or "immanent" object of consciousness and its transcendent object in the knowledge-situation. The framework of distinctions Santayana has in mind parallels rather closely Meinong's act-content-object scheme. Intuition is the act of consciousing, changeless essences constitute its content or immanent object, and the enduring substance of the physical universe functions as its most frequent, though by no means only, transcendent object. It is important to insist that by speaking of intuited essences as the "content" of experience I do not mean to imply that for Santayana experiences form total and inseparable wholes of which such essences are parts or in which they are in some way contained. On the contrary, Santayana is a realist in the extreme sense of maintaining that both the immediate and the mediate objects of consciousness, both essence and substance, are logically as well as causally independent of mental acts.

Under what conditions will an intuited essence constitute knowledge of material substance? Intensely aware of the overwhelming difficulties of any copy-dualism, Santayana claims that knowledge presupposes neither the qualitative identity nor even the resemblance of what is "in the mind," and what physically exists. There are no reasons to suppose and there are excellent reasons to doubt that the simple, dramatic pictures of the eye trace faithfully the movements of the flux. If the animal organs and occasions of knowledge are taken into account, the probability of such a reproduction of the world in sense is at once seen to be infinitesimal. Literal possession of the object or of a replica of the object, however, is not a necessary condition of knowledge. The relation between the immanent and the transcendent object of consciousness is symbolic: The data of sense function as symbols of the presence and processes of physical objects. Santayana has never made a sustained attempt to explain the nature of symbols or to formulate the rules of symbolism. I suspect that in the claim that essences appearing in intuition are symbols of the modifications of matter, the word "symbol" is used in a quite nontechnical sense. It is used primarily to call attention to (a) the fact that the intuited essence and the properties of the encountered physical object are not numerically identical, and (b) the fact that the animal whose psyche gives rise to a series of conscious acts does not accept the essences intuited at face value, but habitually deputizes them to stand for and report the movement of ambient forces. As a test of the adequacy of such symbolism we do not need to compare the given with what is physically real and hence irrevocably beyond the reach of mind. The ultimate criterion of successful symbolization is appropriate action.

Knowledge, then, is always symbolic in character. Intuited essences serve as the vehicles of symbolism: The movements of substance, the phases of the world-process, are symbolized. I will not concern myself with special problems that arise in this connection, but I cannot avoid dealing with at least one issue of general significance. Intuition in its pure form is enjoyment of self-identical essence. How is it possible for an essence, intuited in its meaningless aesthetic immediacy, to acquire meaning and become a symbol of something other than itself? What is the factor or force that transforms the contemplation of essence into knowledge of substance?

In its current form, the question is misleading. It can readily be interpreted as implying that there is some mysterious psychic force that harnesses, at a certain point in our development, innocent intuition to the practical life. This interpretation of Santayana's point is incorrect for two reasons. First of all, common human experience does not consist of a string of pure intuitions. Probably even the earliest conscious experiences of the child are symbol-cognitive: For the adult, at any rate, the uncommitted contemplation of essence is an infrequent and difficult achievement. Second, since most of our experiences are substance-directed and hence involve symbolic cognition of facts or things beyond the experience, it would be clearly inappropriate to speak of the intuition of essences and of the factor that makes it possible for the essences to function as symbols as if they were in some sense separable. The factor that is present in all experiences that are symbol-cognitive and in no experiences that are not, Santayana calls "intent." Now even though intuition can exist independently of intent, as it does in moments of aesthetic enjoyment, on occasions of symbolic cognition the two exist inextricably interwoven. When our consciousness is symbolic, intent and intuition are at best distinguishable elements in the experience: it would, however, be a mistake to speculate about the way in which intent transforms essences into symbols. Strictly speaking, such a transformation does not occur. A pure intuition exists while it lasts; it can never be transformed into an act of knowledge. Similarly, moments of symbolic cognition cannot be stripped of their referential element and transformed into pure essence-directed acts. Like Athena out of Zeus's head, each moment of consciousness springs into existence full-grown out of the psyche's substance.

What then, it might be asked, is the nature of intent? It is the expression on a mental plane of the outdirected concerns of the psyche. Intent is the counterpart in consciousness of animal fear and the psyche's natural urge to live. The hidden agencies of the environment must be feared and fought: Animal life is eternal preparation for the impending blow. This preoccupation of the psyche with the distant, the absent, and the latent is reflected in the mind in our tendency to take the qualities of the given as revelatory of what is not presented. Intent thus is an agent of animal faith: it is external reference, unthinking belief in the not-given. Such tacit reference to what is not presented or what is yet to come is an essential condition of all perception, memory, and science. In the case of perception, intent takes the form, first of all, of the supposition that the essence presented stands for a physical object, and second of the belief that this object far outstrips in complexity the essence that is its symbol. In the former instance, intent deputizes an essence to stand for an existent, in the latter case one or a small group of properties is taken as the symbol of a larger set. In general, intent is the animal urge to use what is present and presented for the representation of the absent: by its means essence may become the symbol of existence, and the changeless may be made to yield knowledge of change.

In view of the central significance of the concept of intent in his account of the conscious life, one could reasonably expect Santayana to be detailed and specific in his explication of it. Unfortunately, however, such expectations are disappointed. Santayana leaves the matter on a level of high generality with almost all the technical details missing. Here Santayana might argue that since the major task of philosophy is the evocation of particularly comprehensive essences, once such an essence has been elicited little more can or should be done. This argument sounds hollow, and I suspect it had little to do with Santayana's scanty attention to the theory of intent and symbolism. A far more obvious explanation is at hand. Santayana was simply not interested in issues relating to the nature of intent. Even though he showed intense interest in certain special fields of symbolic activity such as religion and art, he had never managed to develop any great concern with the general problem of how symbolic cognition is possible.

The reason why Santayana has so little to say about intent is that its study does not further his central interests in the nature of spirit and of the spiritual life. The study of intent gives practically no direct insight into the nature of spirit. Even though intent can only exist in conscious experiences, it is not for that reason indigenous to consciousness. Spirit in its purest form is pure intuition. Pure intuition is free of all symbolic reference and all belief in the absent. Intuition with intent is a form of spirit, but it is not spiritual. Intent strips intuition of its spirituality by subjecting it to the principle of practical interest, the prejudices of its psyche, the grotesque limitations of a single perspective. If a mind could ever be fully spiritual, it would have no special interests, no predilections, and no preferences. If a life of detached contemplation could ever be sustained, it would consist of the impartial readiness to conceive without the urge to posit or possess. "All essences are grist for the mill of intuition": Spirit, as the principle of universal sympathy, would never be motivated on its own account to go beyond what is immediately presented.

As spirit is purified, it approaches the ideal of what it would be if it were left alone: pure contemplation of essence or *Wesenschau*. In a strict sense, of course, if spirit were left alone it would not even exist. The psyche, after all, is the sole and adequate source of consciousness, and it is this humble origin of spirit in the heat of organic adjustments that makes prolonged spiritual living an unattainable ideal. If it were free of external influence, intuition would be fully and solely essence-directed. Intent represents alien interests, the interests of the struggling body, in the realm of mind. It diverts the attention of spirit from essence to substance, and impels it to follow the fortunes of its organ. Santayana's interest in intent is slight because it is only the study of intent-free intuition that yields an insight into the nature of spirit. Once the nature of spirit is clearly conceived, the ideal of the spiritual life becomes inescapable. The central concern of Santayana's philosophy is with life, not theory, and specifically with the uniquely human, or divine, life of disinterested aesthetic enjoyment. In this subordination of theory to practice, Santayana is in the best tradition of the Ancients. As a consequence, the standard by which his work is to be judged cannot be the single one of theoretical adequacy. Like any philosophy that has at its heart a conception of the good life, it has to be judged at least partly by the satisfactoriness of the life it advocates.

## III

Santayana uses a general argument to show that mind and matter, knowledge and object known cannot be identical. The physical world is a spatiotemporal process. Change, coming into being and passing away, pervades the innermost recesses of every material thing. Change is substitution of event for event and quality for quality in relatively permanent surroundings. In the material world this substitution is total in the sense that the termini of change cannot coexist: whenever there is a change from any state $S_1$ to another state $S_2$, there is a time at which $S_1$ is actual and $S_2$ is not yet, and a later time at which $S_2$ is actual but $S_1$ exists no longer.

If the mind mirrored this total physical substitution of state for state, knowledge of change would not be possible. Change can only be known by "arresting" its temporal passage. Since it is a relation, it cannot be conceived unless its terms, separate and successive in physical time, can coexist in the conscious mind. The state that is no longer must be remembered, and the state that is not yet must be anticipated: only by such time-spanning, synthetizing actions of the mind is knowledge of temporal process made possible. Change and knowledge of change differ, then, in a fundamental way. Apprehension of the changing is synthetic and hence exempt from alteration and passage; change, on the other hand, involves successive substitution that is possible only in physical time. But the temporal and the nontemporal cannot belong to the same ontological realm, Santayana maintains. The act of intuition is not an event located in physical time, nor do the essences intuited in any way undergo substitutive passage. Each act of consciousness occupies what Santayana calls "the transcendental position appropriate to viewing";[8] each is "withdrawn from the sphere of the categories which it employs."[9]

This argument appears to me to be an exceptionally strong one. It is a reason sufficient by itself to justify the initial distinction between mental act and physical event, quite irrespective of what our ultimate theory of the mind-body relation will be. Santayana contends that no theory of the relation of consciousness to the physical world can disregard the difference between the temporality of change and the time-spanning vision or time-independence of the cognitive act. The pair of concepts that seems most succinctly to express Santayana's view of the contrasting nature of physical existence and mind is that of agent and spectator. Agency in a space-time field is the very essence of substance, and spirit consists of nothing but cognitive acts. Since all causation and generation belong in the sphere of action, it is here that we must look for the origin of consciousness. Since all cognition belongs in the realm of spirit, it is to spirit that we must look to discover the organ of consciousness and the laws or circumstances of its emergence.

No reasonable philosophy can ignore the fact that cognitive awareness arises on the occasions of physical existence. Santayana contends that consciousness emerges as a by-product of the activities of the psyche. This appears to be a difficult view to uphold. What specific sense can be attached to the claim that the spirit depends for its existence on the psyche? Since all generation is material, the psyche-dependence of spirit must be total: each moment of consciousness must be individually produced by some process in the physical organism, and no cognitive act can sustain itself in existence, change anything, or beget its own successor. The correlation of neural events with conscious acts, no matter how complete, would never suffice to establish such generative dependence. By the claim that *a* generates *b* we mean more than that *a*'s and *b*'s are highly correlated, although it is by no means clear what more. In any case, it is evident that if by causation Santayana meant nothing more than constant conjunction or regular sequence, he could not consistently maintain that all generation is physical. Consciousness precedes physical changes no less regularly than psychic process ushers in mental acts.

It is clear, then, that no science, not even the ideally complete unified science of physical nature whose possibility Santayana foresaw, can adequately support a theory of the unilateral generative dependence of consciousness on the material organism. There appear to be at least two reasons why Santayana's epiphenomenalism is not a scientific hypothesis. The first is that in speaking of the generation of spirit by psyche Santayana means to convey more than that there is a functional relation between the two: he wishes to maintain that in addition to the discoverable correlation between mental acts and physical events there is also an imperceptible though real derivation of the former from the latter. All such generation occurs "in the dark" of the realm of matter. As such, generative process is, in principle, unthinkable. Since only forms or essences may be intuited and they are the termini of change, the actual process of alteration, the process that renders essences existent, the process of the embodiment of forms is closed to inspection by the mind. Such generative process permeates the psyche and surrounds it. The body encounters it at every turn even though the mind finds its existence conjectural and can at best adumbrate it by the use of symbols. Generation is matter itself, and matter is the unintelligible other of essence. The unintelligible cannot be an object of scientific inquiry.

The second reason why epiphenomenalism is not a scientific hypothesis is that it is a theory about the relationship of two types of occurrences only one of which falls properly within the field of scientific investigation. Conscious acts are private in a way no physical object or particle is: their imperceptibility is not on a logical par with the imperceptibility of electrons. There is something logically odd even about the correlations between physical events and mental acts, for a direct correlation can only be established in the single case of the investigator's own experiences. For the rest, we must be satisfied with the indirect and tenuous method of attempting to correlate physical events with experiences through the verbal, introspective reports of others. Santayana's theory of the mind-body relation, then, cannot look to science for confirmation because one of the terms of the relation cannot be investigated by the scientific method, while the relation itself cannot be understood by the mind.

I will not hold it against Santayana's mind-body theory that it is not a scientific hypothesis: no mind-body theory is. However, I do wish to call attention to the difficulty Santayana has to face in his attempt to give an account of the relationship of consciousness to the physical organism. What appears to be needed first and foremost is a theory of causation. Santayana rejects the entailment view,[10] and his epiphenomenalism makes it impossible for him to hold either the activity theory or the regular sequence view.[11] He is left with the conviction that constant conjunctions are signs of causal connections, but that the generative act itself is beyond the pale of mind. When late in life he noted the fact that on the issue of the emergence of consciousness he has "not seen much new light,"[12] he should have felt no surprise or regret. There is nothing new to be discovered here for the simple reason that there is nothing to be known about the causal process that gives rise to intuitions. The most we can hope for is a more adequate knowledge of the physical occasions and the physiological antecedents of the emergence of consciousness. But no matter how much we may eventually learn about the psychic tropes that are the necessary and sufficient conditions of consciousness, we will never be able to understand the dark process by which something new, a mental act, is brought into the world.

It is tempting to terminate Santayana's credit at this point and file for theoretical bankruptcy. There is good reason to be dissatisfied with Santayana if this is all he has to offer. I tend to think he is quite correct in his contention that reality outstrips the human mind or that existence is a surd. But this single contention does not constitute a philosophy. In fact, if it is not to be construed as an outright denial of the possibility of philosophy, all avenues of rational inquiry must be explored until exhausted. If the principle of the ultimate unintelligibility of existence is not to beget wild mockery of reason, we must avoid seeking its protection at every turn.

I now wish to argue that Santayana in fact does not have direct and immediate resort to the unintelligibility of generation in his attempt to explain the relation of spirit to psyche. He conceives the mind-body relation in terms of concepts that, while they are inadequate to render a complete account of the generation of consciousness, at least confer upon it a degree of intelligibility by connecting it to the coherent system of concepts and theories that constitutes his ontology. The key to my argument is Santayana's distinction between what belongs in the realm of spirit and what is properly spiritual. Every type of consciousness belongs in the realm of spirit, but only intuition free of intent or animal faith is truly spiritual. Feeling, belief, and memory are forms of consciousness, but they do not possess the spirituality of pure intuition. Unbiased and uncommitted contemplation, aesthetic enjoyment of the immediate reveals most clearly the inner, spiritual nature of spirit. Spirituality is freedom from the concerns of animal life, release from the anxious selectivity of the psyche, liberation from the practical intelligence that is incessantly at work adapting means to ends. It is precisely this temporal separation of means and ends that is the most pervasive feature of the physical world. By contrast, for spirit in its purity each mental act is its own end: each is whole and complete in itself and a means to nothing beyond itself.

The difference between the physical and the mental is best expressed in terms of the contrast between the Aristotelian concepts of process and activity. A process (*kinesis*) is an event or series of events with internal reference to time. By this I mean that each process is temporally diversified: each consists of heterogeneous segments or parts, and cannot be considered complete until its last part has occurred or its end product has been brought into existence. No part of a process can meaningfully stand alone, for a process is only complete when completed, it is "whole" only in the whole time required for its occurrence. But since processes are changes or motions, there is an important sense in which they are never whole at all. For although they are "whole" in the whole stretch of time necessary for their existence, that stretch of time never exists as a whole. Being temporally variegated, processes are condemned to move from birth to death, from beginning to end, essentially incomplete.

An activity (*energeia*), by contrast, is a being or occurrence with no essential or internal temporal reference. Activities contain no heterogeneous or separable parts. They are complete and self-contained at each moment of their occurrence: their actualization is not accomplished piecemeal and by parts. Although an activity may be said to last a shorter or longer period of time, such time is not an intrinsic measure of it: the profound irrelevance of time to act is clear if we recall that activity is whole not only in the whole stretch of duration through which it exists but whole also in every measurable part of that duration. Activity, in brief, is act without motion (*energeia akinesias*), or an occurrence that is not a change.

The relation of spirit to the world of nature generally is that of activity to process. Borrowing further from Aristotle, Santayana describes the system of operations that is the psyche as the first actuality of a natural body possessing the power to live.[13] Consciousness, accordingly, is the second entelechy of the living body, or the psyche in act.[14] The relation of a particular spirit to its organ, then, is that of the second entelechy to the first or, in what is perhaps a less precise but more direct way of putting the matter, that of the actual to the potential. The ideal of spirit is pure actuality: Santayana models the spiritual life on the divinely active but unproductive existence of Aristotle's Prime Mover. Such divine perfection will, of course, be powerless in the sense of being unable to create change. Impotence is the price of perfection. For if existence is the movement from potentiality to act,[15] pure actuality once reached cannot give rise to any more existence. When the laborious process of physical life is transmuted into synthetic vision, existence achieves its aim and apex in actuality. In actuality, motion ceases and existence comes to rest. The actual light of consciousness is a terminus of life: Beyond this act of final consummation, existence has nowhere to go.

## IV

In the last few pages I have presented what I take to be Santayana's constructive account of the mind-body relation. On the whole, I have refrained from raising objections: I have reserved until now the task of critical assessment. The first difficulty that appears to be involved in Santayana's view is that the Aristotelian concepts he adopts have acquired their distinctive significance in a framework of teleological explanation. Concepts cannot readily be torn from the context that is their natural habitat. Aristotle is very plain in stating that potentiality exists for the sake of the actual and that the soul is the formal and final cause of the body. But Santayana, as an epiphenomenalist, cannot and does not leave room for formal or final causes, even though he wishes to retain the notion of the mind as the form or actuality of the body. Now what explanatory force do the concepts of potentiality and actuality possess if they are divested of all connotations of purposiveness and hence of value? Is purposiveness not tacitly assumed even in Santayana's own attempt to account for the impotence of mind by the claim that once existence achieves the actuality that is consciousness, it has nowhere to go, or that the end of a causal chain can only be something that is an end-in-itself (note the ambiguity of "end")?

This objection is readily answered by recalling Santayana's distinction between scientific and literary psychology. The science of the psyche consists of the description and explanation of the behavior of animals. Psychology can only be scientific if it aspires to be a part of biology: its aim is a system of theories that would be ideally adequate to explain the vital operations of animals in space. Since consciousness does not consist of publicly observable events in space and time, it cannot be an object of scientific inquiry. In clear contrast, then, to the behavioristic or physiological science of the psyche, the art of literary psychology is the imaginative exploration of the feelings and intentions on other minds. The literary psychologist divines the existence of thoughts and purposes in nature: the hallmark of his art is that it yields a reading of the flux of nature in terms appropriate only to spirit. The result of literary psychology is myth.

Now myth, properly understood, is adequate to convey a moral about regions of fact that are opaque to the intellect. It is, in reality, the only means at the disposal of the mind for gaining knowledge of what is recondite. If it is taken literally, however, it presents a grotesque and untenable view of the world. Teleology is a myth of the literary psychologist: it is the interpretation of nature in spiritual terms, the projection of desires and aspirations into the flux. Reading the fortuitous concourse of events from its own perspective, spirit might easily see a moral direction to history and believe that its own existence has from the first been the goal of evolutionary change. Such myths should be taken seriously but not literally. They should be made to yield whatever insight they can, but we ought to be wary of accepting them as accurate descriptions of reality.

Santayana's defense on this point consists, then, of the claim that the relation of consciousness to the body belongs in the sphere of literary psychology. Here the mystery of the generation of spirit by matter is transformed into the myth of the attraction of matter for the ideal and its potentiality to make it actual. It must be remembered that this is no more than a myth, and therefore less than knowledge, and even this myth has to be discounted and stripped of its teleology to bring it to fighting weight. But, it may now be objected, does the claim that psyche and spirit are related as first and second entelechy, or as the potential is related to the actual, in any way help us attach clear meaning to the "generation" of intuitions or specificity to the psyche-dependence of spirit? Is the concept of potentiality of any theoretical significance, or is it merely the ponderous expression of our conviction that things manage to bring into existence what we think they do?

This objection is well founded. A statement *ex post facto* that X had in itself the power to generate Y is not an explanation of the occurrence of Y. The claim that consciousness is the operation of a psychic power conveys no information about methods of action or modes of generation. But what kind of information are we looking for? What sort of "explanation" of the generative process would satisfy us? Santayana urges, rightly I think, that there are no ultimate explanations,[16] and that sooner or later we must face the facts and make our peace with the insane and inexplicable emphasis that arbitrarily raises some possible states of affairs to the status of existence. It is certainly true that we can only think of generation as "a transformation of one thing into another, involving two natural moments, and leaving the bond between them obscure."[17] If this is the best the human mind can do, it would be thoroughly unreasonable to ask for more. I, for one, do not find it difficult to conceive that the human mind may identify the unintelligible without understanding it, and that it lives by framing spontaneous myths to assimilate each recalcitrant fact into its structure.

Santayana's positive contribution to a better understanding of the mind-body problem was his recognition that epiphenomenalism is incompatible with any of the significant views of causation. While he was by no means the first philosopher to abandon the category of causation in the attempt to explicate the precise connection between consciousness and the animal organism, his introduction of the potentiality-actuality framework in its place was both adroit and auspicious. Not only was his epiphenomenalism made self-consistent in this way, but the concepts of process and activity also made it possible for his view of the mind-body relation to be incorporated in a coherent and comprehensive system of theories that derives its strength from, among others, a cogent ontology and a persuasive view of the nature of the good life.

The strength of epiphenomenalism is that it preserves the experienced duality of consciousness and physical fact, while it leaves the material world exempt from interference by nonphysical agencies and therefore open to total scientific scrutiny. The epiphenomenalist takes full account of the obvious facts of the physical dependence of consciousness, as well as the no less obvious fact that consciousness as we know it is a product of evolutionary, biological advance. There is no theoretical reason why any physical action or change could not be explained in terms of previous physical actions and changes, or why science could not develop a system of concepts and theories ideally adequate to account for the behavior and distribution of all physical things. Santayana's philosophy of mind has the advantage of allowing for this autonomy of science in the physical realm, while it retains as categoreally different the private and intentional mind. I also consider it a strength of Santayana's position that it avoids the pitfalls of the view, now in vogue, that phenomenalistic language and physicalistic language differ only in connotation but agree in referent, and that introspection and the observation of brains are but two ways of examining the same thing. Epiphenomenalism has its difficulties, and it will certainly not appear plausible to the man who has not seen himself forced out of other, initially more promising positions by overpowering objections, but these difficulties are relatively slight when compared with the problems of the monistic identity view.

The weakness of Santayana's philosophy of mind is the weakness of any system. No system is an open-ended set of theories that leaves room for investigation or research. There is nothing tentative about a system: it is not a dynamic tool or stimulus to inquiry, for it is nothing if it does not claim to give a full and authoritative account of all the facts. A system is a clear and total crystal; it may be beautiful but it is dead. Since it has to account for everything, it tends to establish an orthodoxy or a status quo and become a harassment to much-needed research. To bring but one example, Santayana's concept of intuition cuts across the distinction between thought and sensation. The system tends to sanctify the concept, and the significant differences between sensing and thinking are suppressed. The result is that the little known and rather complex similarities and divergences of sense and thought are no longer deemed worthy of serious investigation. The issue is considered as resolved once and for all. The instances could be multiplied, even though in such systematic dogmatism Santayana is by no means the worst offender.

I will not use his dogmatism, clearly an unavoidable attendant of every philosophical system, as a general argument against Santayana's philosophy of mind. For the weakness of systems is at once also their strength: Like castles and manor houses, they are recognizable landmarks for the mind. A hundred or five hundred years after the architect has died, we may still study the structure of the walls and spend an evening in his living castle. What is of import is not that we divine with accuracy the builder's every thought. His work belongs to the public treasury of mankind, to be used by each as his wits will allow. In this way, history sometimes converts the voiceless monuments into starting-points for another age. New thinkers will begin where Santayana left off. They will transcend or reject him; they may distort his thought or not even know that they are in his debt. All of this, I am certain, matters not the least; all of them will have profited from Santayana's work, and it is such facts that justify the man, not our eulogies.

Philosophy, like the human mind itself, lives only in being continually refashioned and recreated. The question of ultimate historical accuracy is irrelevant to the progress of philosophical thought. What matters is the continued integrity of the inquiring mind. What matters is that we should use the past the way we use food, for the sustenance of life. If in the last analysis our intuition will disclose essences that differ from those that constitute his philosophy, Santayana would have no regret. Man is not a disembodied searcher after truth: each must mirror the world in his own way. Every man must seek to make his thought the adequate expression of his personality: this is the sum and substance of philosophy. In this enterprise of self-fulfillment, Santayana would be the first to wish us luck.

# THREE

# FICHTE'S IDEALISM

Fichte is usually classified as an idealist, yet the precise nature of his idealism is rarely examined. Idealism is frequently taken as the view that only minds and their states are real. The temper of our times is such that this theory appears to need no refutation. The suggestion that the Ohio Turnpike is nothing but a state of your mind or mine, or even of some supermind, no less than the Leibnizian idea that it consists of an infinite collection of harmonized souls, seem to us to be manifestly absurd and to warrant serious examination only of the persons who are so deluded as to suppose them true.

It would be wrong, of course, to classify Fichte as an idealist in any such popular or easy sense. He does maintain that there is a watershed question for all of philosophy: the answer to this determines the total complexion of one's philosophical thought. The question is whether objects exist independently of the self. There are only two possible answers to this question, and of the two only one is right. The dogmatist, incorrectly, asserts the absolute and independent existence of the world of objects. The idealist, by contrast, maintains that no object can exist independently of some self.

Fichte does not think that the world of objects, what we normally call the physical world, is in any sense the creature of some finite individual self, group of selves, or the infinite individual we call "God." Such might be the view of "dogmatic" or absolute idealism, which, by Fichte's own profession, is in sharp contrast with what he calls his "critical idealism." According to the critical idealist, both finite individual selves and the correlative world of physical objects are the resultants of a single, unconditioned self. Much of the interest of Fichte's metaphysics derives from his fundamental claim that the undifferentiated primordial being that is the source of all is actually a self. The plausibility of his idealism hinges entirely on his ability to substantiate this claim.

The central concept in Fichte's thought, then, is that of the self. What does he conceive to be the nature of selfhood? Without a reasonable account of this, his idealism is certain to remain vacuous. In attempting to determine his position on this and a variety of other issues I shall be relying primarily on the 1794 version of the *Wissenschaftslehre*, the first complete English translation of which was published last year.[1]

The most convenient and most obvious starting point in developing Fichte's thoughts on the self may well be his famous aphorism, "*Was für sich nicht ist ist kein ich*"—what is not conscious of itself is no self.[2] Self-consciousness is a necessary condition of selfhood: nothing that lacks the ability to reflect on itself can qualify as a self. Fichte affirms in a variety of places and in a variety of ways his conviction that self-consciousness presupposes consciousness of objects. This view may well be open to argument, but it is not my present purpose to dispute it. I shall merely note that a self must be or at least must have the ability to be conscious of both objects and itself. But even this is not enough for full-fledged selfhood: the intellectual, attenuated property of consciousness can never be enough to constitute the essence of a real being.

What, then, are the conditions both necessary and sufficient for a given existent's being a self? Are they to be consciousness and creativity? Or cognition along with a certain organization or structure of the elements of the being? Or the presentational and reflective activity of consciousness in conjunction with the purposiveness of all the activities of the being and the purposiveness of their union? Characteristically, Fichte has given ample thought to the problem, and equally characteristically, he infuriates his readers by not disclosing his answer in any systematic or straightforward manner.

The magnitude of the reader's frustration may be evident from the fact that perhaps the best place for relevant hints on the nature of the self is in the chronically obscure Part III ("Foundation of the Knowledge of the Practical") of the *Wissenschaftslehre* of 1794. There Fichte discusses the activities of the absolute self in their purity; the activities and features that pertain to this primordial ego must be reflected, to a greater or lesser degree, in all finite individuals. The absolute self, Fichte maintains, has two divergent but interdependent fundamental drives. The two drives give rise to two divergent lines of activity; and since it is impossible to distinguish agent from activity on this level, the self is properly said to be constituted of these two sets of nontemporal acts.

The first activity of the self is its striving to fill out infinity. The practical drive urges the self on to infinite self-expansion, to an affirmation of itself and its own law without limit. The second activity is that of reflection or self-consciousness. The theoretical drive urges the self on to know itself as a unitary, self-expansive being. Using Fichte's physical model we could conceive the practical activity of the self as a line stretching outward from a center to infinity. By contrast, theoretical activity may be conceived as a line reverting back to the center; but throughout it is important to remember that the center is not to be thought of as any substantial or substantive being. The two activities are interdependent: reflection presupposes the outgoing activity that it restricts and turns back upon the self, while the effusive activity of self-assertion relies on the other to define its direction and to present it with the obstacles it must overcome.

These two closely interrelated activities define the nature of the self. Anything that is both self-assertive and reflective must be a self; nothing that lacks these characters can qualify as one. Reflectiveness is nothing but what I have previously referred to as self-consciousness and identified as a necessary condition of selfhood. If we combine it with expansive or assertive activity, we have the necessary and sufficient conditions of selfhood as Fichte conceives it. And this, incidentally, also gives us the clue to why Fichte thinks that, at least primordially, self-consciousness and the consciousness of objects are necessarily connected. The explanation is simple if we bear in mind that he thinks of reflection as an activity that restricts the infinite outgoing act of the self and drives it back upon itself. Since both activities are primordial, neither can overwhelm the other: no sooner is the assertive activity restricted than it renews itself, and the ensuing oscillation (*Schweben*), in a manner of speaking outside the self, yet totally dependent on it, is what Fichte calls the imagination. It is in this field of imagination that the presentations of which the empirical world consists are generated. The unavoidable conflict of the primordial activities manifests itself to the self in the form of the feeling of frustration and inability. These, in turn, are the source of the feeling of necessity or constraint that accompanies, in our experience, the presentation of external objects. In this way, the self's consciousness of itself is inseparable from the consciousness of external objects: the very activity of reflection is the cause, or at least a part of the cause, of the generation of objects.

What we have laboriously disentangled from the obscure parts of Fichte's work can also be found stated by him with the greatest clarity. Unfortunately, however, even the clearest and most elegant Latin is lost on the man who never learned the language. The meaning of some of Fichte's plainest statements becomes evident only after one has gone through some of his obscurest deductions: their clarity after one has understood them is often no less annoying than their vagueness had been before the light dawned. In a variety of places, Fichte reminds us that the self is what it does, that it consists of nothing beyond its activities in their dialectical relation. If we add to this his oft-repeated statement that the self posits itself and posits itself as positing, we have in an embryonic form everything that we have said so far. For positing is nothing but the self-assertive activity of the self; and to posit the self as positing is to think it, to reflect on it, to know it as engaged in characteristic activity. The very essence of the self, therefore, is summed up by saying that it is something that both posits and knows that it does.

But have we helped clarify by introducing the concept of positing? Not if we can give no better account of the mysterious activity it stands for than the few commentators who have written on Fichte in English.

Possibly the problem is one of translation: no English word captures the richness of the German original. The German word *"setzen"* is ordinarily translated as "to set," "to place," or "to establish." Its root significance is creative activity, an activity that can show itself in various modalities. It may be the simple physical act of placing an object in some location, the biological activity of bringing children into the world (*Kinder in die welt zu setzen*), or the exceptionally complex sociopolitical action of raising some person to the throne (*auf den Thron setzen*). What we have in each case is practical activity that is productive or creative; it is always purposive and often voluntary.

The activity *"setzen"* denotes, however, is not only practical. The word may be used to express agreement and opposition (*sich auf etwas, wider etwas setzen*), as well as the propositional attitudes of supposing and affirming. Its connection with the intellectual and the intelligible is further confirmed by the overtone we find of it in the German word for law, *"Gesetz."* The richness of *"setzen"* is due precisely to this amphibious character: it is equally at home in the realms of theory and practice. Fichte takes advantage of the ambiguity: he uses the word to denote an activity that is both cognitive and creative and represents the unity of reason and will, the theoretical and the practical.

The word "positing" is therefore at once revealed as inadequate to expressing what is conveyed by the word *"setzen."* "Affirmation" and "assertion" come close to capturing the volitional element in the activity Fichte refers to, and "self-affirmation" is certainly a central part of what he means when he says that the self *"setzt"* itself. But both the creativity and the cognitive action implied or suggested by "setzen" are lost in the word "affirmation," and we can safely say that there is no word in ordinary or, for that matter, in extraordinary English that comes any closer. What Fichte designates by this difficult word, then, is a fundamental cognitive-conative activity. It is a purposive and productive act, an act whose creativity is the source of all that is real. If we keep this in mind, it comes as no surprise that Fichte thinks the organ of positing is reason itself. Reason in its primordial unity is thus conceived as the infinite and intelligent source of all, totally absorbed in its creative, all-encompassing act. For lack of a better substitute, I shall continue to use the word "posit" to stand for Fichte's *"setzen."* But it is important to remember that I shall refer by this word to the cognitive-conative activity whose nature I have briefly indicated.

Positing is a nontemporal act. Its model no doubt is the Aristotelian concept of activity or "*energeia*" in which process and product, agent, act, and deed indistinguishably coincide. This concept of activity appears in Spinoza, whom Fichte frequently praises as the greatest and most consistent of dogmatists, as the infinite potency-in-act that is his all-creative Substance. Viewed dynamically, from the standpoint of the act, Substance or God is *Natura naturans*, an indeterminately infinite creative agency. Viewed statically, from the point of view of the deed, Substance or God is *Natura naturata*, an infinitely determinate, eternal modal order. Since productive act and completed deed are indistinguishable in the primordial, infinite potency-in-act and since no temporal lag separates activity from its end, creative energy and created world are inseparably one.[3]

I do not wish to minimize the difference between Fichte and Spinoza. But I also do not wish to overlook or underplay instructive similarities. Positing, as the absolute ego's primordial activity, is clearly analogous to what in Spinoza I have called potency-in-act. And the relation of Spinoza's God as creative act to God as created modal order has a clear analogue in the relation, in Fichte, of the absolute ego to the empirical world of subjects and objects. The progression from indeterminate infinity to infinite determinateness is present in both systems: it is by this gradual determination that, in both, finite fragmented beings are generated. And there is agreement that the progressive self-determination of the absolute is a necessary consequence of its nature. The two thinkers are in consonance even on the fundamental neo-Platonic dictum that determination is negation: the self-determination of the absolute, by its application to itself of ever more specific predicates, is at once a self-negation and self-limitation.

We may view Fichte's interesting theory of thetic judgments in the light of its relation to the emanation scheme that is one of his neglected, or at least little understood, versions of the generation of everything finite from the infinite ego. A thetic judgment, according to him, is one that consists of the affirmation of the existence of a subject without any reference to a predicate. The prime example he gives is the judgment "I am." Now it is clear that the being of the absolute self would have to be affirmed in a thetic judgment, and the peculiarity of such a judgment is that it leaves the concept of its subject unrelated to any other concept, and thus totally indeterminate. This is the infinite indeterminacy of the absolute ego; yet no sooner is the indeterminacy ascribed to the self than it becomes inapplicable. Even as general a predicate as indeterminateness limits and determines; the very indeterminateness of the primordial self constitutes the first step toward its inevitable total determination. The finite world of empirical selves and physical objects naturally flows from the necessary self-determination of the absolute ego, and in Part II ("Foundation of Theoretical Knowledge") of the *Wissenschaftslehre* of 1794 Fichte displays considerable ingenuity in tracing this dialectical development.

An obvious dissimilarity between Fichte and Spinoza, of course, is due to the historical fact of the presence of Kant between them. Spinoza strove to deduce the eternal modal order from the activity of his primordial substance. By contrast, Fichte no longer wishes to deduce an infinity of beings, but only the structures and categories of experience. I will not stop to explore this interesting point; it is peripheral to my main purpose here. I have set out to examine the nature and to determine the tenability of Fichte's critical idealism, and I have now managed to reach a stage where his terms have been, I hope, adequately clarified, and where we can set him a fundamental and, I think, disastrously destructive question.

Fichte spends considerable effort in deducing the categories, conceived as principles of unity in experience, from the self-postulation of the absolute self. It should be evident, therefore, that the primordial self itself is subcategoreal or precategoreal. We cannot say of it, for example, that it is a substance, even though we must think of it as, in a sense, nontemporally enduring. No predicate that is applicable in the world of experience is applicable to it univocally; in its primordial being, which may be affirmed in a thetic judgment, no predicate is applicable to it at all. I shall not discuss here Fichte's apparent violation of this principle in conceiving of the absolute self as the cause of the world of objects. Spinoza at least realized a part of the limitation on what we may predicate of the primordial being and conceived his infinite potency-in-act as neither mental nor physical, although in a sense the source of both. The question fundamental for Fichte's idealism that thus arises is the following: What conceivable reason can we offer for thinking of the primordial agency-activity as a self? If there is good reason for thinking of it that way, it may be difficult to escape Fichte's critical idealism; if there is none, his central views will surely appear as unwarranted dogmas.

To say, as Fichte does repeatedly, that the absolute ego is not in any sense an individual person does not eliminate the question. On the contrary, it only raises the additional problem of how anything could be a self without displaying at least some of the determinate tendencies, attitudes, and intentions that are the hallmarks of individual personality.

I think I can detect in Fichte three major lines of argument for his idealistic conclusion. Nowhere does he develop these arguments in detail. Their outlines, however, are clear enough and he hints at them in a variety of places. I shall consider them in turn.

The first argument starts from the premise that the task of philosophy is to give an account of the origin and nature of experience. Fichte appears to be of the opinion that this can be attempted in only two ways. In the first attempt, we proceed from the side of the object or unthinking thing, in the second from the side of the subject or self. Accordingly, as he insists in the First Introduction to the *Wissenschaftslehre*, there are only two possible philosophical positions: dogmatism, which attempts to deduce experience from a world of independently existing things or things-in-themselves, and idealism, which attempts to display experience as the result of the operation of an active self.[4] The two theories are contradictory: at most, one of them can be true and at least one of them must be. Fichte makes no secret of the fact that he thinks we can never account for lived experience by reference to things or objects alone. In some places, he goes so far as to assert that a dogmatism that attempts such an account is demonstrably false. If only two attempts at explanation are possible, the two are contradictory, and one of them is demonstrably inadequate, the other must clearly be correct. For this reason, idealism is the only tenable philosophy and the primordial existent must be a self.

This argument appears to me to have no merit. First of all, even if we grant that one of the tasks of philosophy is the relatively vague one of explaining the nature and origin of experience, we have reason to doubt the remarkable claim that this can be done in two ways only: either by sole reference to things and their laws or by reducing all to selves and their operations. This is surely a gross simplification and excludes by edict far more philosophical views than it permits. It is this oversimplified picture that leads Fichte to the mistaken thought that idealism and dogmatism are true contradictories and that hence by disproving the latter we can incontrovertibly establish the former. The contradictory of the proposition that in explaining the source and structure of experience we need no reference to anything beyond things and the laws that govern their behavior is the proposition that such reference is necessary, and not the proposition that we need reference to selves only. Even if we were to stay within Fichte's unreasonable thing–self dichotomy, the most that the refutation of dogmatism could show is that some concepts or laws other than those relating exclusively to things are necessary to give an adequate account of human experience. This would leave the door wide open to a variety of dualisms, among them the highly critical and attenuated sort held by Kant, who viewed experience as a unity of elements derived from self and thing.[5]

Let me wipe the slate clean, however, and permit the entire matter to be decided by an adequate refutation of dogmatism. On Fichte's own interpretation such a demonstration of the inadequacy of dogmatism would be tantamount to a proof of his idealism, and even on a less charitable rendering it would tend to increase substantially the probable truth of his position. Unfortunately, however, one looks in vain through Fichte's works for the demonstration. It is, in fact, not even seriously attempted, much less accomplished. And in a bold about-face in the work in which he claims the demonstrable falsity of dogmatism, Fichte asserts that ultimate philosophical positions are susceptible neither of proof nor of disproof: the view we adopt, without evidence and as a starting-point, is a function of personal interest, commitment, and disposition.[6] I shall come back to this point later and now proceed to Fichte's second argument.

Here his reasoning amounts to perhaps no more than a version of the previous argument stated in the material mode. Whatever else there may be in the world, it is generally agreed that there are at least some selves.

Now Fichte thinks it evident that no self can ever come from an unfeeling, unthinking not-self. If all is to have a simple, unitary source and the only conceivable source of an ego is another one, it clearly follows that the primordial reality must be a self. We can view Fichte's attempt to deduce finite objects and subjects from an absolute self as giving added point and poignancy to this argument. Since nothing that lacks self-consciousness and self-affirmation can be the ground of a self, nothing that is bereft of these features of selfhood can serve as an ultimate principle. His deduction aims at establishing that an ego, by contrast, is able to generate both selves and things, and thus amply qualifies as the ultimate source of all.

I cannot make myself believe that this argument has anything to recommend it. First and foremost, I am entirely at a loss as to why anyone should think it evident that a self cannot have its source in the not-self. I do not propose to argue here that it can or does, even though the entire weight of evolutionary thought supports this hypothesis. I shall content myself with the comment that if no good reasons are presented for accepting it, Fichte's putatively self-evident premise is simply an arbitrary dogma. The issue of whether or not things can function as the source of selves is at the very heart of the problem of idealism: the bold claim that they cannot serves only to start the controversy, not to resolve it.

Fichte was no less vocal in avowing belief in the view that things cannot give rise to selves than he was silent about his reasons. Although it is idle to speculate on what these might have been, it is appropriate to make two brief remarks. The first is that his reasons could not have been of the sort that supported Berkeley's conviction that objects cannot generate spirits. For Berkeley thought of causation as the exclusive property of minds; for him, physical objects were impotent. By contrast, Fichte in no way restricts causal activity to selves: following Kant he thinks of causation and of reciprocity as universally applicable. My second and more positive comment is that what might be behind Fichte's conviction that the not-self can generate no self is simply the time-honored causal maxim that decrees the impossibility of the like coming from the unlike. The putative emergence of mind, consciousness, or selfhood from the thoughtless and inanimate is surely a paradigm of the generation of the like from the unlike. To some it may also seem to demonstrate the absurdity of any such generation. In reality, however, there is nothing absurd about it, and if Fichte's argument is to be grounded in this maxim of causation, we are perfectly justified in asking for the grounds for it. The blow of the hammer does not resemble the pain it causes, nor the brain of Shakespeare a page of manuscript. The vast majority of the causal sequences we know involve the creation of like by unlike; what are we to do with a maxim that decrees all this impossible?

Let me, however, forget all that has been said; let us suppose that Fichte has proved, as he has not, that the source of every self is itself or another. Would this be adequate to show that the ultimate existent must be an ego? Clearly not. This by itself leaves the door wide open, once again, to dualism: it is perfectly compatible with the view that there are two ultimate existents, say, a transcendental ego and a transcendental object. Fichte thus needs an additional principle, viz., the one that maintains that all is to have a single source. Yet why should we accept this principle? Surely not because unity is boldly asserted to be a demand of reason. This may well be the demand of reason in a tight little mind perpetually at work imposing discipline on his children or the world, but it is surely no demand of universal reason. And even if it were, would it not be a begging of the question, an unwarranted assumption of the idealist principle that reason shapes the world—the very principle under examination—if we were to say that its demands are invariably met?

I now come to Fichte's third argument. This is never explicitly stated by him, but it appears to me to be behind what he says in a number of passages. We start with the assertion that the primordial being must engage in creative activity. Such an activity, since it is essentially self-assertive and expansive, resembles far more closely the activity of a self than that of some thing or not-self; self-assertiveness is in fact, as we noted, one of the marks of the ego. If the argument were correct, it would not of course prove that the ultimate source of all is actually a self. It would show, however, that such an unconditioned being must resemble selves far more closely than it resembles unconscious or inactive things—and this may conceivably be all that Fichte needs to establish his idealism.

This argument hinges on a fundamental unjustified assumption, namely that the activities of the self are the paradigm of creative activity. Fichte clearly wants to stop short of the extreme position of asserting that only selves can engage in causally creative endeavor; since he does, he has to justify his taking the dialectical self-expansive/self-limiting activity of the self as the model of all creative agency. Why should we say that the primordial creative act is more like the self-expansiveness of a self than like the self-expansiveness of a gas or of a healthy tree? We search in vain for Fichte's answer to this question. It is clear that reference to the self's voluntary or intelligent self-assertiveness is of no avail: the absolute ego's expansiveness is unavoidable and the self-expansion of a tree is law-governed and purposive. Similarly, there is little merit in the approach that professes to see in each tree's growth a pale replica of the ego's actions. These activities are different, and either one can be considered a pale or imperfect version of the other, depending on what features we select for emphasis. Fichte loads the dice by using the word "*setzen*" for the primordial activity: this suggests, without being evidence for, the view that the activity properly belongs in the sphere of the self. But what reason have we to suppose that the activity is self-like or self-connected and that "*setzen*" is not merely a misleading or question-begging name for it? As best I can see, none at all.

I must conclude, therefore, that Fichte's arguments for the view that the primordial being is a self fall altogether short of establishing their conclusion. As we have seen, each suffers from a variety of faults, but most blatantly the first fails because it presupposes an unprovided demonstration, the second because it must rely on an unacceptable maxim of causation, and the third because it begs the question by a prejudiced selection of the paradigm of activity. Does this leave Fichte entirely without defense? I do not think so. It would be open to him to use a version of his third argument, if not to attempt to show that the ultimate being is a self, then at least to justify supposing it to be that for the sake of increasing our knowledge. This regulative version of the argument is well known in the history of idealism, and the likely reason why Fichte made no reference to it is that he thought it both valid beyond all reasonable doubt and inextricably intertwined with the entire enterprise of Kantian and post-Kantian transcendental philosophy. The usual argument is that since we know the self and its structures and activities best of all, we must use them as our model for understanding everything else. Fichte, however, might subscribe to a somewhat stronger version. His acceptance of Kant's theory that all intelligible structure is due to mental activity might lead him to the view that all we ever know is the self, its structures and activities and therefore have in fact no choice but to use them as our models.

Now I can find nothing wrong with using the self as our model in the attempt to see how far it will take us and what important or unsuspected insights it might provide. One can have one's opinions about the ultimate value of this model, but when all is said and done there is no substitute for the actual full-scale attempt to push the idealist program as far as it will go. Surely this is all the justification Fichte needs for having attempted a deduction of the finite world of subjects and objects from a primordial self. It is an interesting and important fact that such a deduction is possible, and his having managed to complete it is a tribute to his dialectical skill. But the possibility of the deduction is one thing, its truth or bearing on the real world another. It is well worth keeping in mind that the way we choose between two deductions, say those of Spinoza and Fichte, is normally not by finding logical or dialectical slips in the one and none or fewer in the other. Philosophers notoriously have more logical than good sense, and though an idealist deduction proceeding on the basis of the regulative principle under discussion is clearly possible, it may well be severely at odds with reality.

So much for the weaker version of the regulative principle. The stronger version, according to which our only models for understanding the world are the cognitive, conative, and affective activities of the self appears, by contrast, excessive and question-begging. It assumes, without good reason, that all forms, structures, and activities are mental. By according such preeminence to the self and thinking of it as the source of all order, if not of all reality, were we not tacitly affirming idealism? And if such tacit affirmation is disavowed, what reason could conceivably be proposed for saying that the activity of gravitation or the orderliness in the growth of poison ivy reveal somehow the marks of intellect?

Let me conclude with some remarks on a characteristic, though typically exaggerated, claim of Fichte's. Acceptance of ultimate philosophical positions is a matter of personal inclination or interest, he maintains. Now, his argument continues, the highest and most exalted interest of every ego is that of self-affirmation or the free exercise of the intelligent creative powers of the self. This activity of self-creation and self-development is the source of all morality and goodness. But an activity of this sort presupposes a free and independent ego. The highest interest of man, the very possibility of morality demands, therefore, the primacy of the ego and its total primordial independence of determination by objects. This makes idealism, and with it belief in the primacy of the self, a demand of morality, Fichte concludes. But he refuses to stop even here and indicates that whoever does not acknowledge and exercise his freedom does not truly or for long possess it. And not to possess freedom is not to be a self, but a mere thing. For this reason, failure to subscribe to idealism is not merely a theoretical error: it is a practical act that disqualifies one from membership in the kingdom of ends. The dogmatist is not a person who is simply wrong; he is simply not a person.

It is difficult to think that this argument is anything but nonsense. It is a peculiar sort of morality indeed that sees the greatest requirement imposed on every man as self-assertion or the exercise of his native powers. But this peculiarity is nothing when compared to the singular claim that practical life determines or should determine one's beliefs about what is, and that a single wrong opinion can strip us of selfhood and turn us into things.

The ultimate problem here, however, is the easy confusion between the absolute ego and the finite selves of individuals. Fichte devotes considerable attention to the deduction of the world of objects, but almost none at all to the deduction of finite subjects. To establish his idealism, he would have to prove that the unconditioned being is a self. Showing, as he attempts to, that the demand of morality is to think of individual selves as unconditioned and free does not in the least contribute to proving this. Good sense impels us to believe in the existence of a variety of finite selves; but if there are more than one of them, none can serve as the primordial unity from which all flows. If, however, all individual selves are to share a single transcendental ego, the analogy, central to Fichte's entire enterprise, between our finite selves and this primordial ego inevitably collapses. And even if this near disaster could be averted, what account should we give of the relation, so peculiar on this view, of transcendental to individual self? To this question, though not to this alone, Fichte provides no answer.

## Bibliography

Fichte's works are readily available in German. His son, I. H. Fichte, brought out an edition of his collected works in 1845–1846 (*Sämmtliche Werke.* 8 vols. Berlin, Veit). This has now been supplanted by the *variorum* Gesamtausgabe of the Bayerischen Akademie der Wissenschaften (*Werke.* Stuttgart-Bad Cannstatt: F. Fromann, 1964–). There is a readily available reprint of *Grundlage der Gesamten Wissenschaftslehre* (1794) by F. Meiner Verlag, 1961. No English edition of the collected works exists. A substantial number of Fichte's epistemological and metaphysical writings remain, in fact, untranslated. An incomplete and inaccurate rendering of the *Grundlage* appeared in 1889 (*The Science of Knowledge.* Translated by A. E. Kroeger. London, Trübner). A new, complete translation (J. G. Fichte, *Science of Knowledge,* edited and translated by Peter Heath and John Lachs. New York: Appleton-Century-Crofts, 1970) incorporates also the First and Second Introductions to the *Wissenschaftslehre.*

There is a substantial body of scholarly and critical literature on Fichte in German. The following list is a selection from those most interesting or most relevant to the thesis of this article.

Friedrich Dannenberg, *Der Begriff und die Bedeutung der Erfahrung in der Fichteschen Philosophie.* Weida i. Th.: Thomas and Hubert, 1910.

Julius Drechsler, *Fichtes Lehre vom Bild.* Stuttgart: Kohlhammer, 1955.

Kuno Fischer, *Geschichte der neuern Philosophic* Heidelberg: C. Winter, 1897–1904. Vol. 6.

Dieter Henrich, *Fichtes ursprüngliche Einsicht.* Frankfurt a.M.: Klostermann, 1967.

Willy Kabitz, *Studien zur Entwicklungsgeschichte der Fichteschen Wissenschaftslehre aus der Kantischen Philosophie.* Darmstadt: Wissenschaftliche Buchgesellschaft, 1968.

Dietrich H. Kerler, *Die Philosophie des Absoluten in der Fichteschen Wissenschaftslehre* Ansbach: G. Brügel, 1917.

Richard Kroner, *Von Kant bis Hegel.* Tübingen: Mohr, 1961.

Johann H. Loewe, *Die Philosophie Fichtes: Nach dem Gesammtergebnisse ihrer Entwickelung und in ihrem Verhältnisse zur Kant und Spinoza.* Stuttgart: W. Nitzschke. 1862.

Fritz Medicus, *J. G. Fichte: Dreizehn Vorlesungen.* Berlin: Reuther & Reichard, 1905.

Baldwin, Noll, *Kants und Fichtes Frage nach dem Ding.* Frankfurt a.M.: Klostermann, 1936.

In English there is very little critical literature on Fichte's metaphysics that is worth reading. The following four books may be consulted, though without any great hope of enlightenment:

Robert Adamson, *Fichte*. Edinburgh and London: W. Blackwood, 1881.

Charles C. Everett, *Fichte's Science of Knowledge: A Critical Study*. Chicago: Griggs Philosophical Classics, 1892.

Ellen B. Talbot, *The Fundamental Principle of Fichte's Philosophy*. New York: Macmillan, 1906.

Anna B. Thompson, *The Unity of Fichte's Doctrine of Knowledge*. Boston: Grinn & Co., 1895.

Among histories of philosophy in English, by far the most adequate account of Fichte is in F. H. in Coppleston, *A History of Philosophy* (Garden City: Doubleday, 1965. Vol. 7, Part I). The article in P. Edwards's *Encyclopedia of Philosophy* is virtually useless. The most recent and most interesting English treatment of the *Wissenschaftslehre* of 1794 is an unpublished doctoral dissertation (Walter E. Wright, *Self and Absolute in the Philosophy of Fichte,* Vanderbilt University, 1971).

I shall mention only two recent works in French:

Xavier Leon, *Fichte et son temps*. 2 vols. Paris: Armand Colin, 1954.

A. Philonenko, *La liberté humaine dans la philosophie de Fichte*. Paris: Vrin, 1966. (A very thoughtful work.)

On the whole, however, one who is interested in Fichte's systematic philosophy will do best by proceeding to the texts directly. A remarkable scholar of the stature of Kuno Fischer can help to put Fichte in the proper historical perspective. But, alas, in dealing with the text one seeks in vain the aid of even one commentary as careful and sustained as exist in droves on the work of other major thinkers.

# FOUR

# PEIRCE, SANTAYANA, AND THE LARGE FACTS

Some earnest scholar will someday produce a study of the remarkable similarities between the thought of Santayana and of Peirce.[1] This is rich lode to mine. Imagine demonstrating that two major philosophers, frequently supposed as distant from one another as Ryle from relevance, share assumptions, theories, and approaches! The topic does not lend itself to an easy dissertation: any adequate treatment would require mastery of the material and the keen skill of dissecting to find matching parts. Perhaps some analytic philosopher who had tired of "could have done otherwise" and turned to the subtleties of the ontological argument will now move past God and reach Peirce and Santayana. The training and temperament of such a person would enable him to do an excellent job: Scholarship is scholarship, whether you deal with the dead or the nonexistent.

I will not undertake the full task of showing that in spite of obvious differences, Santayana and Peirce are astoundingly similar. I should like simply to assume that they are, as if the work of careful and piecemeal comparison were already complete. But I find that I cannot. For the task of showing that Peirce and Santayana hail from the same family has not even begun. If I fail to make that claim at least plausible first, it will not be surprising that on the things that matter our two philosophers do not see eye to eye.

Let me therefore give a few pointers that might help to pick out similarities of pattern. I shall focus briefly on *seven* issues. There are many more, of course, that a full treatment would disclose. But these should be enough to make the claim of family resemblance thoroughly plausible. The only other comment I must make is that similarity is a complex relation that always involves difference. So we should never be surprised if my love, revealingly like a red, red rose, nevertheless needs no water and has no thorns. Even the finest picture of Dolly Parton leaves something to be desired or, shall I say, fails the original in a number of respects. So let us think of similarities as embedded in a context of differences and making those differences more important and more interesting.

1. Both Peirce and Santayana are realists. They maintain that the object of perception exists independently of the perceptual relation into which it may on occasion enter. They are deeply committed to the idea that the world is real in an irreducible way, that it is not the figment of some mind. Though each in his own way has a deep respect for the work of mind, neither thinks that the intellect through its cognitive act creates reality.

2. Both Peirce and Santayana are naturalists. It is not altogether easy to express what this means: the idea of naturalism is as elusive as it is important. They agree that the world, with whatever magnitude of order it displays, is a single system that articulates itself in space and time. This system is governed by its own laws, which diligent inquiry may disclose. Man is in some fashion continuous with the natural world and may find his fulfillment within it.

3. We find in both Santayana and Peirce a remarkable and central stress on action. One could put this aggressively and maintain that both of them are pragmatists. But this label is not very useful because it is not sufficiently specific. The similarity I have in mind is better conveyed by focusing on the intimate and intricate relation Peirce thinks obtains between ideas and actions. Beliefs, for Peirce, are not primarily propositions entertained in consciousness. The element of awareness is clearly second-

ary; beliefs are constituted of habits of action. This line of reflection is nearly identical with Santayana's classical rejection of subjectivism in the early part of *Scepticism and Animal Faith* and the subsequent development of an entire philosophy based on animal action. For Santayana's point concerning animal belief is precisely that it is not an entertained essence or proposition but a habit of action as we work to pursue or avoid objects in our environment. This habit may rise to consciousness. But what is then immediately present to us has a deeper source and reality in the life of action; and what confirms it is not propositional evidence but unhindered, successful operation. This philosophy of animal faith is the central reason for calling Santayana an American philosopher. It overshadows his Platonism, his commitment to spirituality, his arcane, Scholastic terminology. And it is, at once, a point of fundamental kinship with Peirce.

4. If one wanted to explore Santayana's indebtedness to Peirce, one would have to start with the theory of signs. I am not aware of any direct evidence that Santayana read Peirce. We know that he read Dewey and Husserl and Heidegger; there are copies of their works with extensive marginalia in Santayana's hand. No one has identified any copies of *The Monist* or *Popular Science Monthly* similarly marked up. Yet Santayana was well aware of Peirce's work. He followed the journals. He attended some of Peirce's lectures. He was in continued and intimate philosophical contact with James and others who corresponded with or were influenced by Peirce. Most importantly perhaps, the similarity of his ideas on the function of symbols in cognition to those of Peirce is too great to be coincidental if we take into account the surrounding context of indirect contacts.

But whether Santayana owes something to Peirce or not, the similarity of their ideas on sign cognition is remarkable. Both maintain that the very heart of intelligence consists in signification and that the mind's relation to its object is always mediated. Moreover, they share the insight that *symbolic* knowledge is no handicap; on the contrary, identity, resemblance, and inclusion yield no knowledge at all without the triadic relation that signification involves. The impact of this recognition is vast and tends to color one's entire epistemology. The fact that Santayana left the notion of symbolization half-developed and moved it in a literary direction, while Peirce converted it into a romantic metaphysics in no way diminishes the substantial identity of their starting points.

5. Both Peirce and Santayana are committed to the independent reality of universals. To be sure, the world of universals is carved up in different ways by the two philosophers. Santayana sees no essential distinction between qualities and general ideas, while Peirce is committed to distinguishing them as firsts and thirds, respectively. But this difference pales by comparison with the importance of agreeing that there are universals, that they are embodied in nature and that their reality is in no way hostage to the whims of mind.

6. Both Peirce and Santayana reject the legitimacy of a universal skeptical reduction. Though Peirce does this by a theory of the nature and function of doubt, while Santayana follows the skeptical enterprise to the point where it reduces itself to senseless irrelevance, they join in recognizing wholesale skepticism as an intellectual game unrelated to the business of serious inquiry. Universal skepticism proposes a standard, a rationalistic standard, which all knowledge worthy of the name must meet. The rejection of the skeptical enterprise is at once the rejection of this criterion of absolute certainty. The removal of this standard, however, amounts to the elimination of the possibility of what we nowadays call foundationalism. For foundationalism requires that all knowledge rest on a bedrock of certainty: on intuitions or sensations or basic propositions by reference to which all other statements may be judged probable or true. Santayana and Peirce are unequivocal in stating their impatience with this view. The "myth of the given" is not exactly a recent discovery, nor was it Popper or some friend of his who first developed the notion that everything can be questioned in turn but not everything at once.

7. Last but not least, there are persuasive similarities between Peirce's and Santayana's fundamental categories. Once again, I am not inclined to deny that the resemblances provide a context for interesting differences: nothing is served by the futile attempt to show that everyone has the same ideas. But a close study reveals that what Peirce calls firstness is almost precisely what Santayana dubs spirit: the stress on self-contained feeling makes the connection unmistakable. Secondness is what Santayana and Peirce both call matter, the realm of force and brute interaction.

Thirdness may be thought to present problems because it cuts across objective law and subjective thought, realms that Santayana takes special pains to distinguish. But in fact Santayana's realm of truth comes very near to capturing what Peirce had in mind. Truth encompasses both matter and mind, for it consists of all those orderly tropes that gain actualization in any medium. And by "trope" Santayana means the complex essence of a process, a notion closely akin to Peirce's general idea or law.

In focusing on these seven points of similarity, I do not wish to imply that there are no others. Quite to the contrary. My purpose was only to render the claim of Santayana's similarity to Peirce plausible. The seven points should have accomplished this. If they did, I am free to go on to my main topic.

I find it remarkable that two philosophers who agree on so many important philosophical matters and on so many details should nevertheless hold such radically divergent views on the large facts. By "the large facts" (Santayana's phrase), I mean what he also calls "the moral truths" about the world. They are constituted by the alignment of circumstances of significance in the conduct of life. "The chief issue," Santayana staunchly maintains, "[is] the relation of man and his spirit to the universe."[2] The large facts are the ones truly important because of their bearing on this relation. They govern the role and prospects of the individual and the race. They determine the costs of happiness, the limits of existence, the forms of failure. They provide the necessary conditions of life and of the possibility of the good life.

Philosophers rarely analyze these facts. Some consider them too cosmic to permit close examination. For the rest, they are situated near the outcome of philosophies as those final, unchallenged realities to which proper thought enables us to assume the correct attitude. What we think of these large or ultimate facts of life, therefore, is too frequently a function of temperament and prior commitments. Even though Socrates said that the purpose of philosophy is to prepare us for death, we often find that our attitude to death prepares our philosophy. I do not suggest, of course, that one's philosophy is but the mindless expression of one's sentiments. Least of all is this true of two such self-conscious and methodologically sophisticated philosophers as Peirce and Santayana. Yet one must be struck by the similarity of their technical philosophical premises and the divergence of their human conclusions, the consequences they draw for the large facts. Suffice it to say that we understand too little of the interplay of rational considerations with individual temperament and circumstances in the generation of philosophical views. Is it not astounding that an age as deeply devoted to metaphilosophical, methodological, and evidential questions as ours should have kept itself ignorant on this issue?

Peirce worked under difficult circumstances and was largely unappreciated while alive. Yet his philosophy exudes a cosmic optimism about the prospects of man in nature, even about the very structure, the growing rationality of nature itself. Santayana, on the other hand, was a successful professor, the darling of Cambridge society for a while. Yet in one of his notebooks he penned, "I have been called many names: sceptic, relativist, materialist, epiphenomenalist. But no one has ever called me an optimist." He made no secret of the fact that he thought the human spirit was an alien visitor in the tearing world, yet he held out no hope of another place from which we hail and to which we repair.

Peirce's optimism is not a dispensable afterthought of his system. Some might suppose that his discussion of creative love or agapasm is an unneeded and best forgotten indiscretion. But in fact his entire philosophy *is* permeated with the cheerfulness of nineteenth century evolutionary thought. This is reflected even in the way in which the categories are related to one another. Although firstness, secondness, and thirdness are in one sense independent, separate, and irreducible conceptions, yet they are hierarchically arranged in the direction of enrichment and order. Peirce indicates this with extraordinary eloquence in one place where he temporalizes the interrelations of the categories. In describing the sort of metaphysics his ideas adumbrate he writes,

> ... in the beginning—infinitely remote—there was a chaos of unpersonalized feeling, which being without connection or regularity would properly be without existence. This feeling, sporting here and there in pure arbitrariness, would have started the germ of a generalizing tendency. Its other sportings would be evanescent, but this would have a growing virtue. Thus, the tendency to habit would be started; and from this, with the other principles of evolution, all the regularities of the universe would be evolved. At any time, however,

an element of pure chance survives and will remain until the world becomes an absolutely perfect, rational, and symmetrical system, in which mind is at last crystallized in the infinitely distant future.[3]

I chose to quote this passage at length because it displays, better perhaps than any other, the two great sources of optimism whose confluence shaped Peirce's philosophy. One is the empirically based theory of evolution, which promised to render the self-improvement of nature a matter of scientific fact. The disorder of spontaneous variation is harnessed—in a fashion that would make Royce proud—to provide enriching multiplicity for higher unities. The second source is romantic German metaphysics, which sees the actualization of mind as the ultimate motive force of all reality. Peirce knew this perfectly well, for he said, "my philosophy resuscitates Hegel."[4] It is just that he should not have neglected to add that his insistence on the infinity that must pass before the self-perfection of the world is complete also resuscitates that most bittersweet of German romantics, Fichte.

Peirce thus thinks that we live in a universe that is upward bound. It is purposive to its core and naturally tends to impose order on its multiplicity. The order is referred to variously as law and mind, habit and general idea. Man belongs in the highest reaches of this self-perfecting cosmos. For man is a sign,[5] and signs are thirds. Our beliefs and behaviors are habits. All of life is but a train of thought and all thought, in fact all mental action can in the end be reduced to the formula or law of valid reasoning.[6] Persons themselves are but general ideas[7] in no essential way different from the universals that structure the apparently nonhuman parts of the world.

There is, then, a cozy identity between man and the intelligible structure of the world. The identity is not only that of kind, however. For the principle of continuity makes the genuine isolation of any individual item impossible. We thus find ourselves fading into our neighbors on all sides; we are continuous with the cosmic stream of thought. Peirce expresses this idea in a variety of ways. In one place he says that being "welded into the universal continuum" is "what true reasoning consists in."[8] In another passage nearby he speaks of duty completing our "personality by melting it into the neighboring parts of the universal cosmos."[9] The unity of man and nature is rendered complete when we learn that "physical events are but degraded or undeveloped forms of psychical events."[10] We are in this way not only at one with the world but also represent its highest, most perfect form of manifestation.

I need to add only one more factor to complete this sketch of Peirce's optimism. Just as each individual belongs in the bosom of nature, so he is inseparable from the community. The development of truth and reality and the development of the community of investigators proceed isomorphically. Peirce says: "Every species of reality . . . is essentially a social, a public affair"[11] and the very "conception of reality . . . involves the notion of a COMMUNITY, without definite limits, and capable of a definite increase of knowledge."[12] The community to which we belong has no definite spatial limits and it stretches infinitely into the future. "Now you and I—what are we?" he asks. "Mere cells of the social organism," he answers without the least hesitation.[13] We can be and be fulfilled only as integrated members of the cosmopolitan, nay the cosmic, community of inquiring minds. But since we naturally belong there, we have reason to be of good cheer. The community of investigators is as secure as order in nature, as emerging reality itself. The fate of the individual is of no significance so long as the scientific community marches on.

It is interesting to compare this glowing description of the glory of rational man with Santayana's more sober assessment of the realities. It is best to begin by calling attention to Santayana's much-neglected positivistic tendencies. His firm commitment to ontology and to scholastic language tends to obscure the fact that Santayana is a firm advocate of the fact-value distinction and a vigorous opponent of speculative metaphysics. The latter is amply demonstrated in the depth of his disdain for German idealism. Much of the moralizing metaphysics of that tradition comes under what Santayana calls "dreaming in words." The fact-value distinction, on the other hand, occasioned him to look particularly closely at the moral or perfection claims frequently made on behalf of the theory of evolution. He quickly decided that no description of natural developments is by itself adequate to support value-judgments concerning what emerges. That more complex unities emerge in the course of natural evolution may well be a fact; that order is more perfect than chance or that complex unity is better than diffused flashes of protoplasmic feeling are judgments expressing the less-than-cosmic preferences of animals.

Neither one of the great nineteenth century sources of optimism is thus available to Santayana. He starts his philosophy, therefore, the way his admired Lucretius did, building on his observation of "the stars, the seasons, the swarm of animals, the spectacle of birth and death, of cities and wars."[14] There is little outside the sphere of human, or at most animate life to suggest purposiveness. Values are irreducibly relative; comparative judgments presuppose a private imagination with all the private value commitments that that involves. There is no reason to suppose that social organisms exist in any sense resembling the very real existence of individuals. Individuals enjoy, in Santayana's view, a reality that is—if not physically then at least morally—ultimate. States and societies derive their legitimacy from the way in which they express and satisfy the needs and values of individuals.

The philosophical paradigm here is the single animal making its way in a treacherous environment. The source of life, value, preference is the psyche, the tenuous material organization of the animal body. The life of the psyche itself is finite and precarious. Nature, indifferent to our good, permits us to flourish for a day and then with equal indifference cuts us down. The universe is too vast for us to count for much; since everything passes, even those to whom we mattered are soon gone. To be sure, man's spirit can transcend this flux and contemplate the eternity of essence for the nonce. Yet spirit or consciousness itself is but a momentary achievement of its material organ. Like the mayfly it, too, disappears and there is nothing to show for it but the cold, impersonal stretches of the realm of truth, which is a complete record of everything that was.

Of course, I do not want to say that in Santayana's view we can never rise above the mindless necessity of nature. On the contrary, a life of reason, a temporary reversal of the forces of death and decay is often possible. But there is nothing in the very structure of nature that especially promotes it, just as there is nothing in iron ore that especially invites or promotes the manufacture of cars. A clever animal or group may avail itself of existing opportunities; when the vessel runs dry, the good life, the bad life, all life simply ceases. Order holds sway contingently. And all the evidence points to the fact that soon this order will be replaced by another, perhaps without continuity and almost certainly without advance.

Santayana is no pessimist in the sense of thinking that everything is in vain. It is only the dispassionate mind viewing the world under the form of eternity, as "the chronicles of ancient wars," that *sees* the futility of everything. The heat of life is rarely affected. But the wise man's perspective on it all is framed in sadness. This surely is in sharp contrast to Peirce who maintains that the wise man or the scientific investigator is precisely the individual who understands how logic and ethics hang together, how signification and reality constitute a seamless, structured web.

When I reflect on the immensity of the difference between Peirce and Santayana in these all-important matters, I find it hard to resist the thought that technical philosophical agreements do not matter much. I am then tempted to view philosophical theses as but support for what the heart desires. They certainly do not determine what we think of matters of great importance, or else Peirce and Santayana would be in far closer agreement on the large facts. But temptations are there to be resisted. Attractive as it may be, it is surely simplistic to see philosophies as but rationalizations of private hopes and feelings. So I am impelled to look for philosophical reasons for the divergences. And I think I can find two.

There are two sets of divergent generative images from which Peirce's and Santayana's differences flow. The first set relates to the individual. I hinted at this before and now want to make it fully explicit. Santayana has no sympathy with the Cartesian view that the individual or the mind is an independently existing substance. As to existence, both body and mind are conditioned, finite, tenuous beings. The body is a mode of material substance. The mind *is* a fruit of physical organs; its content is culturally determined. But morally the individual psyche is a substance indeed; it is a self-contained arbiter of values. Santayana is committed to an isolationist individualism: there is an absolute gulf between persons and within each of us privacy is absolute. This view of essential loneliness is what Peirce rejects by means of his principle of continuity. Moral and personal privacy become matters of choice not of fundamental principle the moment we view the individual as constituted by others, as continually touching everything around it. Santayana thinks we are inescapably unto ourselves; Peirce retorts that we belong in and to the community.

The second set of formative images involves the community. Santayana is unequivocal in his realism about the world: he thinks that physical reality exists in absolute independence from knowers and their knowledge. The world is fully determinate, the job of knowledge is to recapture in mind as many embodied essences as may be possible or necessary. To be sure, Santayana runs into problems here. The idea that to know is to capture the truth commits Santayana to the ideal of literal knowledge, to something resembling the old and discredited correspondence view. Yet he also insists that probably knowledge is never literal, nor does it need to be. And if knowledge is symbolic, then to some extent at least we create a reality for ourselves, a world articulated in our language, expressed in our native medium.

But Santayana disregards this implication of his notion that knowledge *is* symbolic. For he is deeply convinced that reality and knowledge are separate affairs and no private image of the world can add anything to its structure or determinacy. Peirce, by contrast, is firmly committed to the notion that reality is always a social affair. The progressive self-determination of the world cannot occur without the stream of signification of which knowledge consists. In fact, Peirce's famous description of truth as that which the community of scientific investigators will in the end accept must not be taken merely as a statement extolling epistemic method. For the object of these future true opinions will be the real and the development of true opinions and of reality largely coincide. The real emerges as we get to know it and achieves full determinacy only as our beliefs come at last to rest in absolute truth. For Peirce, then, the social epistemic and the ultimate ontological mature together. We thus find the world, partly at least, a social product and ourselves the divine co-makers of reality.

These two sets of generative images should make it clear that the difference between Peirce and Santayana concerning the large facts is of vastly more than historical interest. For the first, the contrast between isolationist individualism and absorption of the self in the social fabric, is a continuing problem of paramount importance in our society. And the second, the clash between the physical science view of an independent reality and the historicist idea of social world-creation, is but a cosmologizing version of the battle of individualism. Renewed interest in Marx and attention to such recent philosophers as Habermas have now once again placed this issue at the center of intellectual controversy.

This is obviously not the occasion to adjudicate these matters. I want to make only one closing comment. It is immensely tempting to join Peirce and adopt his optimistic vision. The sense of belonging to a community of rational inquirers is exhilarating. The notions that we are integral parts of a self-improving nature and that our individuality is of no account because the community will accomplish everything we may have left undone provide infinite comfort. The thought of being partners in world creation is ennobling to the point of exaltation.

Yet I cannot help noting that most of those whose optimistic comments I read are now dead. I cannot think that that is a matter of indifference. It is, of course, nothing to them; but then that is the very point. They are gone irremediably, as we will be. And there is genuine loss in that, not only to those about to go but cosmically. Individuality is a genuine value and it is simply false that values are preserved. Whatever happens to the world and to our community, our own prospects are dim. So for you and me at least, cosmic optimism yields little consolation and will always sound hollow. And that is a fact unchanged by the consideration that in the short run we may be drunk with life and have a marvelous time.

# FIVE

# THE TRANSCENDENCE OF MATERIALISM AND IDEALISM IN AMERICAN THOUGHT

What is unique about American philosophy? Is there anything beyond the nationality of the authors that justifies us in grouping a broad range of philosophical books as works of "American philosophy"? We shy away from talking about Afghanistani philosophy, Armenian philosophy, and even Spanish philosophy. Many would argue that, similarly, it is appropriate to talk of philosophy in America or philosophy done by Americans, but not of philosophy that is in any important way American in character.

Yet we do not hesitate to speak of German philosophy, and when we do our minds are not empty. We understand in some general but important way what would be "Germanic" in philosophy, just as we understand what is usually meant by Catholic philosophy or medieval philosophy or even Platonic thought. It would be clearly Platonic, for instance, to look for *the essence* of Catholic philosophy or of American thought. And whatever American thought may be, it is clearly not Platonic. So let me begin with the reassurance that I am not interested in finding the one generic feature all American philosophy has that is not shared by anything else. The search for such essences is the work of tight, tidy minds that welcome conceptual games and invite frustration by reality.

The special character of American philosophy is, like all real things, a messy and difficult affair. There is a complex set of features, many of which are shared by a goodly number of the works in American thought. The features are there to differing extents in different philosophers. Some may be altogether absent in one or another, yet that does not take away from the American character of the work any more than the failure to have a four-chambered heart destroys the mammalian character of an animal. For no *one* feature is unique to American thought; none is a necessary and sufficient condition of its Americanness. It is the configuration of the characteristics, the total shape of the philosophy that makes it usefully classifiable as American. This is what I suspect Santayana meant when he spoke of the smell of philosophies.

I wish to focus on one member of the complex set of characteristics that defines American philosophy. It is, I think, one of the more interesting ones. Rightly understood, it shows the continuity of American and Continental thought, while it distinguishes the two by the intriguing, if not radical, twist in American thought on Continental themes. It would be rash to say that this difference in continuity has been altogether overlooked. Yet it has not received the critical attention it deserves.

Perhaps the best way to focus on the feature I have in mind is by reference to a standard though ill-defined distinction in much of modern philosophy. From Lucretius or before, philosophers have proudly declared themselves to belong to one or the other of two broad groupings. Some claimed to be materialists, while others announced their allegiance to idealism. These views were frequently conceived to be not only mutually exclusive but also conjointly exhaustive. All philosophical theories were to be classified *either* as materialistic *or* as idealistic, on an "if you are not with us, you are against us" mentality. Admittedly, conceptually there is little to be said for such an exclusive disjunction, yet intermediate dualisms have tended, on the whole, to be unstable and to revert quickly to one or the other of the fundamental monistic positions.

I take materialism to be the view according to which the ultimate ingredients of reality are spatiotemporal units that exist independently of mind, ideas, or will. The specific details of the conception of matter are relatively unimportant: whether we think that the ultimate units are indivisible atoms or charges of energy or minute vortices is irrelevant so long as we all agree that they are to be found in a single, continuous space, arrange themselves in a single, continuous time, and operate as a total system governed by autonomous laws.

I take idealism to be the view according to which the ultimate constituents of existence are ideas or minds or expressions of will or fragments of consciousness or moments of sentience. It is not that idealists deny the existence of a space-time world with all its apparently independent and apparently insensate furniture. But they are convinced a closer examination of this world shows the surprising result that what seems lifeless in fact quivers with sensitivity or, at least, that the spatial world is an eternally dependent product of creative minds.

It is evidently impossible to catch all the conceptual subtleties that have been developed in 2,500 years of defending the two positions. There are foolishly strong versions of materialism, such as that of Lucretius, who maintains that only atoms exist and then finds himself having to admit the reality of the empty space in which they move. And there are utterly implausible versions of idealism, such as that of Leibniz, according to whom each finite physical shape hides an infinite set of dull, minuscule minds. There are also methodologically cagey, weaker versions of each view. Thus, some materialists maintain simply that the ultimate ingredients of the world are more like the unconscious, purely spatial parts of our bodies than anything else. By contrast, sophisticated and careful idealists asseverate that the ultimate units of existence are more like our experienced sensings, cognizings, or desirings than anything else. I do not hesitate to lump all these views together because, however bold or however cautious, they all profess to give us information about the ultimate nature of reality, they all claim that it is of one sort and not another, and they all agree that, at least on the surface of it, the human body paradigmatically belongs in one sphere and the human mind in another.

The important thing about both materialism and idealism is that, however phrased or modulated, they are efforts on the part of theoretical reason to understand the world. Their very rivalry presupposes their agreement on the starting point, on the task and on the method of philosophy: Both claim that a purely cognitive grasp of the world is possible and necessary.

The moment we put the matter in this way, we are reminded of Kant's revolution in philosophy. The point of that radical reversal is not so much what it is frequently conceived to be—viz., the assignment of a central role to human cognitive faculties in the creation of reality—as the ultimate shift away from the primacy of theoretical reason. I suspect that Kant himself did not fully grasp the revolutionary significance of placing human creative activity at the center of reality. This, at least, is suggested by his disavowal of Fichte's philosophy, in which many of the radical consequences of Kant's departure are boldly displayed.

The primacy of practical reason, of *action* in the end, permits the development of a novel metaphysics, which undercuts the distinctions and categories of much earlier thought. It is remarkable that it took generations to draw the full implications of an activity-centered metaphysics. Fichte himself, even though he bravely declared that "in the beginning was the deed," failed to see that that insight, if adequately developed, would render obsolete the previous metaphysical distinction between materialism and idealism. It was this failure that made it possible for him to declare himself a "critical idealist" and to maintain that each philosopher belonged to one or the other of these warring camps.[1] He attempted to deduce all of reality from a primordial activity. But he failed to see that such a predeterminate burst of energy can be neither physical nor mental and that therefore his attempt to distinguish his own view from the similarly conceived but presumably materialistic theory of Spinoza was altogether without hope and merit.

The movement from the metaphysics of ultimate ingredients to a metaphysics of activity was essentially completed in the work of Fichte. Yet, amazingly enough, the self-understanding of the new philosophy was altogether inadequate, making the full development of its consequences impossible. Fichte still drew a sharp distinction between idealism and the conviction of the people he called "dogmatists." Idealists, he thought, attempted to explain human experience from the starting point of a self-like, free activity. Dogmatists, by contrast, undertook the same task by reference to independently existing, inanimate things. There were then, as there are today, philosophers of both kinds. But what Fichte overlooked was the way in which insistence on the primacy of the act destroyed the contrast between the two views and made room for the development of a new sort of philosophy.

The metaphysics of activity was present also in Hegel and in Marx, and it is their agreement on the primacy of creative act that makes the usual contrast drawn between them as idealist and materialist, respectively, so difficult to understand. This contrast is frequently conceived in the philosophically feeble-minded fashion popularized by Engels. "Those who asserted the primacy of spirit to nature and, therefore, in the last instance, assume world creation in some form or another . . . comprised the camp of idealism," he says. "The others, who regarded nature as primary, belong to the various schools of materialism."[2] Engels specifically focuses on Hegel in this context and characterizes the contrast between him and Marx, who supposedly "stood him on his head," as the simple one that the former believed thought creates nature while the latter denied this.

Engels' idea is, of course, a simplistic misreading of both Hegel and Marx. In fact, the fundamental metaphysical contrast between them is vastly more subtle and not at all easily drawn. If Lukács is right that the primary category of Marxism is that of totality, perhaps there is no such difference at all. Nevertheless, some maintain that there is one centered in a disagreement as to the *sort* of activity supposed primary. For Marx believed, and Hegel presumably denied, that the economically productive activities of the human race enjoy a special primacy in human life and that only by studying them can we understand the course of history. This view helpfully focuses on the fact that Marx was not interested in the ultimate constituents of the universe; his efforts were concentrated on understanding the human world, viz., the world that human activity creates. Yet why should insistence on the primacy of economic relations render him a "materialist"? It is futile to argue for this by reference to the fact that economic activities always involve the physical interaction of man and his environment. There is indeed an element of crude physicality in growing food and in eating, but Marx believed that in the end thinking was no less physical than mastication. And he also thought that social and legal relations which are, in this rudimentary sense, not physical were no less real and causally efficacious than the production and distribution of goods.

If there is a contrast between Marx and Hegel, it must be conceived as a function of divergent views of the nature of man. The primacy of "material" production in Marx can be justified only by a special theory of primary human needs that focus human energies on their satisfaction. Yet even this contrast tends to fade, if we take seriously the hints in the young Marx that the source of our world is the species-being, species-powers, or species-activity of the race. For these relatively undeveloped ideas of Marx take us back to the metaphysics of activity in its purest form. An indeterminate, all-creative, and primordial activity is then seen to beget a determinate, multifaceted world. The generation occurs with a necessity based on the freedom of the initial act; the act and its infinitely varied products stand in the relation of dialectical identity. Viewed in this light, the differences in detail and emphasis between Marx and Hegel do not disappear. But there emerges an overwhelming similarity in their patterns of thought, and we can see how both of them transcend the materialist-idealist dichotomy.

I have given but the barest sketch of the tradition of activity-metaphysics from which a fundamental trait of American philosophy hails. The primacy of action is at once the primacy of will and is paralleled in ontological theory by the primacy of the concept of activity. One way to put the matter is by saying that, for such a metaphysics, substance itself is an ultimate outcome of activity. This does not mean that activity is analyzed into substantial constituents or substance into portions of activity. The entire idea of analysis into elements is rejected, to be supplanted by a study of the dynamics by which creative activity fashions a real world. Engels's notion of creation by thought or matter is also transcended; the starting point of reality is taken to be an activity that is neutral with respect to such later or special determinations as materiality and mentality.

In William James and even in Josiah Royce there is a fundamental insistence on creative activity that derives directly from this metaphysical heritage. The view is of course preeminently clear in John Dewey. His entire philosophy presupposes the centrality of human purposive activity in the reconstruction of the world. Primary experience itself is a primordial activity in which subject and object, matter and mind, agent, action and deed, individual and society are not distinguished. His emphasis on human desires and purposes as undergirding our life is but his version of the thesis of the primacy of will. "Man," he says, "is the tool of tools," suggesting that we are essentially creatures of interactive transformation. And we are creatures of it in two important senses: first, in that we are beings who engage in such continued activity, and, second, in that we ourselves are products of our own activity and the activity of others. This fundamental activity-emphasis in Dewey is, in effect, the hallmark of his thought. Admittedly, he shies away from high metaphysics. Yet the philosophical task he sets himself is clearly metaphysical: he attempts to develop a general characterization of human experience in terms primarily of the purposes we have and the activities in which we engage.

Dewey was perhaps the first philosopher who understood that such a metaphysics of activity undercuts the distinction between materialists and idealists. Not all in the American tradition of philosophizing have reached this level of self-understanding. Some have altogether misread their alignment. A prime example of such a philosopher is George Santayana, who, contrary to popular opinion, fits squarely in the American tradition. He thought that he was in fact a materialist, "perhaps the only one living." What could have occasioned as shrewd a thinker as Santayana to misunderstand his own philosophy? This is a difficult matter to explain, and it may be instructive for my greater purpose to explore it in detail. If I can show that materialism is transcended even in Santayana, I will have gone a long way toward demonstrating my thesis.

Santayana draws a sharp contrast from the first between consciousness or spirit, consisting of what he calls intuitions, and the material world. Intuition, he thinks, is cognitive and synthetic. It is a unitary act focused upon a more or less complex object. He views unity as somehow central to consciousness: each intuition is unified as act and presents a unitary vista. By contrast, the material realm is necessarily granular; it is spread out through space and diversified in time. The reasons why Santayana feels compelled to draw this sharp distinction between body and mind are not of any significance to us here. We must begin with the fact that such a contrast looms large in his thought.

The moment the distinction is introduced, Santayana faces the task of giving an account of the two realms. His description of consciousness is specific, sensitive, and successful. Part of the reason for this success is the fact that instead of the futile task of describing the nature or constituents of mind, he focuses on the description of spirit's activities. He gives an eloquent account of the work of mind in art and religion, in social customs and in natural science. Even the later accounts of consciousness, such as those in *The Realm of Spirit* and in *The Idea of Christ in the Gospels*, focus on the work of mind in purified experience and in symbolic structures, with bold disregard for his self-confessed view of the impotence of consciousness.

The shift from the analysis of mind to description of its activities and products is natural for Santayana. Even on his own account, there is nothing in the act of intuition, which is the foundational and the only unqualifiedly mental thing, to describe. It is but an activity in Aristotle's sense, an evanescent union of doing and deed. By nature it is, in G. E. Moore's famous phrase, diaphanous: as with light or a pane of window glass, when we look at it, we see only what it reveals. To describe it to any extent, therefore, is to describe its objects or products, the vistas of imaged reality it reveals. We understand mind, then, only by developing a phenomenology of the world it lights up or creates.

By contrast with his confidence in the sphere of spirit, Santayana approaches his account of matter with caution and diffidence. He is quick to limit the task of the natural philosopher to identifying ontological realms. The nature of matter is something for scientists to determine, he insists again and again. Yet he himself knows that this easy disclaimer is simply not enough. If philosophers are to distinguish matter from other sorts of beings, they must have some specific notion of what it is. Perhaps they can afford to remain ignorant of the subtler laws of its behavior, but they cannot leave matter as a mere cipher or as the referent of a purely designative name.

With characteristic stubbornness, Santayana's first tendency is, not to develop a theory of the nature of matter, but to try to explain why we can know nothing of it. According to this account, matter is the formless other of essence. It is simply that which is responsible for the introduction of external relations, for existence, for the instantiation of any essence. This faceless force, frequently declared by Santayana to be a surd, can have no form. Any essence of it would still be only an unexemplified form intrinsically; even *that* form would have to be instantiated by something beyond itself, by some formless, natureless power. In one place, Santayana compares matter as it picks essences for instantiation with the shapeless wind that whips sand into a howling vortex.

Yet this account will obviously not do for at least two reasons. First of all, it is unintelligible how the formless or the natureless can be thought. Yet Santayana is clearly thinking it. The affair is best put in terms of a dilemma. If matter is natureless, it cannot be thought. And if it cannot be thought, it can be no part of a philosophy. If, however, matter can be thought, it is not without form after all. And if so, it is neither radically distinct from essence nor unknowable.

The second reason why this account fails to satisfy is that it makes a mockery of Santayana's own account of his materialism. He does not claim to be a materialist in the simpleminded Lucretian sense of maintaining the sole reality or sole existence of matter. He gladly admits the *existence* of both matter and mind and the *reality* of no less than four factors, namely, matter, mind, essence, and truth. At a dramatic juncture in *The Realm of Matter*, he announces that his materialism amounts merely to the claim that material reality alone has creative or generative power. Yet the force of this assertion is destroyed the moment we add to it the confession that this single source of generative power is, in the end, unknowable. There are philosophers who maintain that God is the ultimate or immediate source of all causation while they piously add that inquiries into God's nature reveal only contradictions, for He outstrips the power of our minds. How are we to distinguish such a view from Santayana's "materialism"? Admittedly, to call such ultimate unintelligible power "God" or "Providence" is unjustified and is but the expression of the hope or optimism of these philosophers. But is it any less unjustified to call the faceless power "uncaring matter"? This may well be no more than the expression of Santayana's pessimism about our place in nature and our ultimate prospects in the world. If we follow out the implications of this move, the difference between materialism and theism becomes but a difference in our attitude toward the unintelligible source of our being. What we then have is not ontological views, but expressions of our unjustified faith.

There are few philosophical problems about which Santayana is as ambivalent as he is about the nature of matter. He appears to have struggled with the problem over a span of sixty years, even though most of his changes of thought and reversals are hidden by a confident facade. He gives the appearance of having but one view about matter; in reality, however, a careful reading of the texts suggests three or four divergent and incompatible approaches. Santayana clearly sensed that leaving matter as an unintelligible, unthinkable surd is simply inadequate. The sense that he must do better and say more is surely what underlies the systematic confusion that exists in *The Realm of Matter* and elsewhere between the notions of matter and of substance.

There is a perfectly obvious distinction between these two concepts in Santayana's thought, a distinction echoing in some important ways Aristotle's original ideas on the subject. Substance consists of both matter and form: for Santayana, it is an ontological hybrid constituted of a "parcel" of creative energy and some essence harnessed to give it specificity. Essences do not exist on their own, and even matter is only a necessary condition of the possibility of existence. The two combined form individual substances or enduring existents. In a more extended sense, Santayana allows that there is but one substance and that is the sum total of the universe. The form of this substance is the staggeringly complex one that is displayed little by little in the total history of the world.

Given Santayana's contrast between intuition and the external world, it is easy to see why he can comfortably slide from matter to substance without even noticing the shift. For the world of substance is what we normally call the physical world. It has a reality that appears independent of our will and serves as the medium in which we live and in which our fortunes are made. If anything is "material," tables and dogs and fried liver with onions are, so if we want to study "matter," it is these things we must analyze. Yet these substances or modes of material substance are not "matter" in the technical, ontological sense in which Santayana uses the term. Matter stands related to them not very differently from the way in which Spinoza's *natura naturans* is related to elements of his *natura naturata*: Such physical things are the products of the creative activity of an indeterminate, infinitely fertile force. If we think of matter, therefore, as indeterminately infinite activity, we can think of the entirety of the world-substance as the infinitely determinate product of this act. Santayana himself approximates this language at the end of *The Realm of Spirit*, where he calls matter the self-actualizing indefinite potentiality of all things and says that in existence the "infinity of essence is determined to a particular complex . . . of forms."[3]

It is interesting to note that this shift from the attempt to describe simple, unitary, faceless matter to giving an account of its works parallels Santayana's move, noted earlier, from describing the act of intuition to giving a phenomenology of the works of spirit. This change is perfectly evident by the second chapter of *The Realm of Matter*. There Santayana sets himself the task of explicating the indispensable properties of substance. He proceeds under the assumption that he is detailing the generic features of the physical world, as these may appear to an animal engaged in the pursuit of its own purposes. Viewed in this light, it turns out that substance is diversified in space and time; its units, though unevenly distributed, compose a single field. The field is continuous with our bodies; it is, in fact, nothing but the dynamic domain in which we act and are affected, in which we move, seek, and respond. This idea is expressed by Santayana again and again throughout the volume, but nowhere as eloquently as when he says that substance is universal food. He means by this that the real world is a sphere of perpetual interaction that both presupposes and takes the primary form of the continued incorporation of agents into one another.

"There is no occasion for positing any substance save as an agent in the field of action,"[4] Santayana declares. Substance itself is but the dynamic continuum in which we live. The primary reality, therefore, is not a thing or a set of things, nor even a process or set of processes with some ontologically definite nature. It is, instead, the actions in which we and others engage. Whatever things there may be acquire significance and reality for us only as agents whose actions might affect us. The field itself is not a container in which transactions occur; to call it a single arena is but a summary way of describing the continuity that exists between all the beings that act and react.

Santayana is quite explicit in maintaining that there is nothing to be known about the real world beyond what our doings and sufferings reveal. What sense does it make to call this dynamic world "material"? Analysis of it reveals nothing but change, action, motion, energy. This is a world in which desires and purposes ride supreme, in which our psyches live only by the selective rejection or incorporation of alien beings and alien goods. The primary categories here must be purpose and action, not matter and mind. That everything belongs in a single sphere of interaction is no justification for calling that sphere material or mental. That action occurs in space and time is once again inadequate to show its materiality. On the contrary, Santayana himself insists that space and time are but properties of action or categories derivative from the primary one of activity.

I suspect that what happened at this stage in Santayana's philosophy is that the notion of the causally active has been collapsed with or has taken the place of the concept of the material. And as if to adduce evidence for this identification, Santayana again and again reminds us that the mental, the immaterial, is at once also the causally impotent. Epiphenomenalism thus becomes an analytic consequence of this new version of his "materialist" view.

I think we have come far enough to show that, in spite of his own protestations, even Santayana transcended the materialism/idealism dichotomy. For we have seen how he moved by insensible degrees from what he declared to be an outright materialism to a view in which the notions of action and interaction hold primacy. The entire philosophy of animal faith is in reality a shift away from the traditional mind-matter conceptual framework to an activity-metaphysics whose consequences Santayana worked out only in part and whose presence in his thought he never fully recognized. He reached only the stage of suspecting the collapse or coincidence of materialism and idealism. In the eloquent last chapter of *The Realm of Matter,* he argues that in accepting all the evidence and all the distinctions presented in our daily life of action, idealists have in effect shown themselves to be but materialists in disguise. The real world in which we live, he correctly remarks, is seen no differently by the one group of philosophers than by the other; the only difference between them is that of terminology. Berkeley, for instance, simply renamed the ultimate source of brute contingency "God," and the same elaborate project of renaming may be discerned in other idealists.

In his famous review of *The Realm of Matter,* John Herman Randall retaliated against this charge of the latent materialism of idealists by accusing Santayana, the materialist, of latent idealism. This mad exchange of labels in fact reveals a deeper truth than the parties to the conflict supposed. The insight that certain materialists can be viewed as idealists and certain idealists as materialists is at once the first step toward grasping that both sides have transcended the matter-mind dichotomy and are operating with categories that are neutral with respect to it. Santayana has clearly reached this stage, even though for reasons that might have been at least partly sentimental, he clung to the label "materialist."

I leave unexplored for the moment the radical impact this reading of Santayana has on the rest of his philosophy. One thing is clear. Had Santayana himself taken his philosophy of animal faith and the primacy of action seriously, he would have laid less emphasis on essence and would have altogether eliminated his view of the impotence of mind. The discovery of essence is the only positive outcome of the skeptical phase of *Scepticism and Animal Faith.* This phase leads to the rejection of the rationalist criterion of knowledge, of subjectivism, and of the whole skeptical enterprise. It is altogether surprising that in rejecting the method of seeking certainty by reversion into the mind, Santayana did not at once also reject whatever meager results the method yields. The introduction of animal faith is a new beginning: it might have been appropriate for Santayana to make a clean sweep of it and to develop the philosophy of animal activity without a doctrine of essence encumbering it. The pure intuition of essence itself is postulated only because the skeptical reduction left Santayana with unembodied forms; if the ontology of essence were removed, mind would no longer be the impotent observer of nature Santayana supposed it to be.

I also leave unexplored the outlines of a metaphysics of activity. Part of the reason for this is that there is no single, compelling metaphysics of this sort. There is a variety of ways in which the basic ideas have been developed; some of these constitute the gems of American philosophy. The differences among the various versions of activity-metaphysics are instructive and important, but they presuppose similarities of starting point and of certain developmental patterns. This is not the time to study any of them in detail; it should be sufficient to call attention to the presence of a primary activity-orientation in much of American thought.

The stress on activity is clearly there in Santayana. This shows, in contradiction to the usual appraisal of him as a Platonic or Scholastic metaphysician, that he is much closer to American pragmatism than is normally believed. Pragmatism itself is an interesting American development of activity themes that pervade post-Kantian German metaphysics. The notions that social activity is world-creative and that human nature itself is a human product had been widely present in philosophy since Kant. But it was in pragmatist thought that the mad metaphysical excesses of this idea were first eliminated. One might say that in much of American philosophy human world-creative activity was naturalized: the focus here fell not so much on some ontologically primordial, indeterminate creative act as on the continuing, piecemeal, animal, and cultural creativity of the species. And the object of the activity was at last conceived not as an alien and hateful medium to be subjugated or overcome, but as a tractable world continuous with our life and energy.

The notion of this fundamental activity undercuts the subject-object, process-product, mind-matter, individual-society, will-intellect distinctions. Such discriminations may have their point and usefulness. But they are derivative and partial, and they command no ontological prerogatives. For much if not all American thought, philosophy begins and ends with the examination of daily human practice. This is perfectly evident in Dewey, but elements of it may be found in all major American thinkers. I have tried to show that these ideas are there in more than trace form in Santayana, who is supposed to be paradigmatically a non-American non-pragmatist. I maintain boldly, without proof here, that they are there also in Chauncey Wright, in Peirce, in James and in Royce, not even to mention Mead and Perry and C. I. Lewis. The presence of these ideas or ideas like them is one of the great enduring traits of American thought.

An adequate philosophy of human values and of daily life seems systematically to elude us. Many among us have altogether surrendered the task of speaking to the human estate and feel fulfilled if we can clarify a stray, insignificant thought. Others continue to voice worn fallacies, as if we could lay siege to the truth and by repeating falsehoods make it capitulate. Many proceed in the old ways, trying to subjectivize the world or objectivize human nature, pretending to see little replicas of their minds all over nature or patches of inanimate nature in themselves. All these false starts and frustrations can be avoided by taking social activity in nature as our starting point. The development of a philosophy upon such a foundation is not without its pitfalls. But it offers our best chance for understanding human nature and human society.

In the American philosophical tradition we have ready at hand the starting point, many of the tools, and the proper aim of a full philosophy of life. A creative rediscovery of this tradition, along with its further development, would meet our intellectual needs. An adequate philosophy of life in turn would serve not only to enhance our understanding but also to guide our practice. To take human activity as our starting point, therefore, is in the end to render that activity more intelligent, more fulfilling, and more humane.

# SIX

# PRIMITIVE NATURALISM

Experience, even of a primitive sort, even the experience of primitive, untutored people, reveals a world continuous with our bodies. The hunted beast is vulnerable to our weapons; when it turns in anger, however, we are the ones endangered. The symmetry of causal influence, known to all as mutual endangerment, serves as the foundation and curse of animal life; we seek food and are food, in turn. This is the primitive naturalism of ordinary people who know, unreflectively, that they live in the same world as is populated by everybody and everything.

This world may have surprising regions, accessible only through special openings, such as the mouths of caves, or as a result of special events, such as death. Mysterious holes in the sides of mountains can open our eyes to a magical world of crystals and rivers, which is soon understood to be a part, a very special part, of the ordinary world. Similarly, death may reveal to us a fabled province of happy people given to singing the praises of God, or else a dark realm marked by screams of pain. These regions are also parts of the ordinary world, even though they can be reached only on condition that we die, just as Columbus could visit the West Indies only on condition that he leave Spain behind.

Primitive naturalism, which is the inarticulate conviction of all, is amply confirmed by our actions. We live in a single spatiotemporal world that is largely regular in its habits and hence somewhat predictable in its behavior. Beings that may seem supernatural—elves, spirits, guardian angels, and leprechauns—are all parts of this world; if they exist at all, they exist here and now or somewhere else at some other point in time, always ready to engage in mischief or protective action. Even if mental events are different from what takes place in the brain, they belong in this world and obey its laws. They exist at a time and for a while; they exercise influence over such portions of the world as the human body; and, since Locke is right that when we travel we do not leave our minds behind, they are clearly associated with certain regions of space.

Is there anything that does not belong in the natural world? God does if He listens to prayers, rewards the righteous, and punishes the wicked. So also do ghosts, poltergeists, and the Virgin Mary, who ascended to heaven and lives there with her son. Possibilities expand this world immeasurably, though they are not existing powers. Numbers pertain to the world as applicable abstractions, as do hypotheses and relevant errors. Ordinary people have few ontological problems; they know where to turn to deal with entities of virtually any sort.

Such a naturalism is undermined by those who wish to raise one part or another of this crowded world to prominence. They may want to call special attention to God and His angels, control mystical powers, or stress the prerogatives of mind. In doing so, they think they establish grand dualisms or display the ontological priority of one world-region over all the rest. In reality, however, they overlook the fact that in making the supposedly independent regions relevant to ours, they strip them of prerogatives and render them continuous with the mundane. So long as any being has a purchase on space and time and stands with what exists in them in causal relations, it cannot escape being a part of the single world in which we all live.

Philosophers who associate naturalism with the universe as described by science tend to forget about this more primitive, pervasive, and inclusive version of the view. Naturalism is not the position that there is a single world populated by entities that are the proper objects of science, but the unuttered conviction that the world is one and all its parts have access to all the others. The job of science is to determine the constituent regions of the world and to learn the nature of their populations. The Russian cosmonaut who returned from space informing us that there is no God, for he had been "up there" and saw only darkness, was not altogether foolish. He was right that if there is a God, we should be able to find Him, or at least feel His influence. But he may well have looked in the wrong place or failed to perform the proper rituals to invoke the presence of God.

Primitive naturalism makes all issues of existence empirical questions and provides reassurance that a being whose presence and influence cannot be ascertained need not be counted among the existing. The connection of the sciences to this view is primarily through their efficacy in resolving empirical problems. They can trace the source of hidden influences and more often than not provide definitive answers to the question of what exists and what does not. If deviation from the expected path of Neptune suggests a previously unknown object, astronomers can calculate the location of that body and identify it on their telescopes. Other specialists with the relevant expertise can determine whether there are quarks and muons, reproduction across species, and gold deposits under the sea. The evidence for the existence of ghosts and telepathy and for the efficacy of faith healing and prayer must be examined by the best available methods, which typically are—but may not always be—scientific ones.

The conditions for obtaining empirical evidence may, of course, be deadly. Anthropologists have been cooked and eaten by their subjects, and the astronomer who tries to determine the temperature of the sun by carrying a thermometer to it is vaporized long before arrival. Similarly, some areas of the world may exist behind trapdoors, permitting the investigator to enter but never to return. Black holes may function in this way, along with death as a condition of studying the afterlife. Once we realize this, we may be satisfied with never trying to enter, or else employ these limitations as spurs to inventiveness. The important fact is that what we want to explore lies open to our efforts even if we must be cautious and clever in how we investigate it; however difficult and dangerous it may be to get to some parts of the world, they can in principle be reached.

What we think of as mystical powers and miraculous events are no less natural than the most mundane forces and happenings. Lack of imagination and the desire for security make us believe that the sequences of the world are always regular and hold no surprises. In fact, the opposite of this is the case; even the most common of ordinary things, the weather, can be astonishing. Extraordinary forces and events surround us, due not to the intrusion of supernatural beings but to the natural operation of the restless world. If shamans know how to cure diseases by words and dance, and if the cures are not accidental, then they must have found a shortcut to the relevant mechanisms of nature. If some people know how to raise the dead by calling on them to rise, the sensible response is to learn the right words so we may be able to do it as well and to believe that some verbal rituals are more effective than resuscitation by pumping the chest or administering chemicals. And it is no miracle if only some people can do it and the rest of us can never learn: no one else can write music the way Mozart did, and only one person could paint like Mondrian.

Much has been made of the ineluctable privacy of minds and feelings. And indeed, my cousin who tends to bore me to tears has no idea of what I think of him. But the impenetrability is not intrinsic, or else I could dispense with making sure that my drooping eyelids and painful urge to yawn do not betray my secret. If the world is continuous with my body and envelops it, thoughts and feelings must find their places in the orders of space and time. Some think that naturalism is an inadequate view because feelings of anger and sensations of red cannot be discovered in specific areas of the brain. But the expectation that everything must be like mailboxes and Christmas trees, located in unique places with sharp spatial boundaries, is groundless. Radio waves spread everywhere and lack definitive borders; actions such as calling a friend in New Jersey are not located in a single place; and summer heat can suffuse an entire continent.

Philosophy suffers from an impoverished selection of examples; sometimes it operates with a single model and is quick to create dualisms when not everything fits that mould. But there is no need to invent arcane substances and a private world. When I get excited at a football game, I know exactly where my feelings are; they were admitted to the stadium with me and on my ticket. Worries about the existence of other minds and about our ability to communicate with them appear to be the specialty of loners too much in love with themselves to notice the movements of the world. The rest of us know how to get in touch with other people to monitor their feelings, to learn their thoughts and to annoy them. I could not drive home if I were unable to gauge the intentions of others on the road, and I would never kiss anyone if I thought they lacked feeling or experienced it as a stabbing pain. Success in our physical and social operations provides ample support for the one-world thesis of primitive naturalism.

The primitive naturalism I have described is the tacit belief and operational guide of everyone. We think, and when we act, we suppose that the world is a single place, all of whose inhabitants are, potentially at least, within our causal reach. Philosophically sophisticated versions of naturalism are derivatives of this mindset and of such experiential enactments. Is there anything that could disconfirm our silent belief that the world is a continuous field? Only repeated frustration of our plans due to the failure of actions to be efficacious could convince us that reality is, in structure at least, not an even playing field, and this conviction would dawn on us slowly.

If, for example, one day we manage to cross the Potomac on Memorial Bridge but the next, inexplicably and irremediably, we cannot, our faith in the one-world hypothesis may suffer damage. Imagine that the bridge is there, we can walk, no one is holding us back, and yet, as in a dream, we make no headway in getting to the other side. A few days later, we get across without trouble, but then the nightmare scenario repeats itself. We would of course invent a hundred naturalistic explanations for our failure and propose an equal number of remedies. But what if none of the explanations accounted for the irregularity and none of the remedies accomplished what we want? We would come over time to view ourselves as caged beasts, feeling our power yet witnessing our impotence. Since we can imagine many such disconfirming instances, primitive naturalism is not a view to whose truth we are committed no matter what. It lives or dies, as we do, by the success of our actions.

A point worth stressing is that primitive naturalists believe, first and foremost, in the efficacy of action in a field of agency continuous with our bodies and only derivatively in the regularity of the world. So what would concern them about Memorial Bridge–type experiences is not that they subvert the accustomed sequences of nature and even less that what goes on is difficult or impossible to understand. The problem as they see it is that we cannot do what we intend, that even well-executed actions bear no fruit. The idea that the order of nature has changed serves only as an explanation of this failure, and the desire to grasp why and how it has done so is part of the attempt to reestablish our power. Primitive naturalists are not theoreticians. They do not believe in the primacy of action in theory but by enacting it. Their interest in understanding and in the regularity of nature is practical to the core: they want to be able to achieve concrete results.

The claim that ordinary people unreflectively embrace primitive naturalism raises the question of how it is possible for them to be unaware of their commitment. If what I have said so far is anywhere near right, even people who take religious texts literally believe that the world is a unified system of interacting forces. Why, then, do they profess to believe in supernatural agencies, thinking of heaven and hell as discontinuous with the mundane realm? Would they not be aghast if presented with the idea that the natural and the supernatural form a single universe with identifiable doors or transfer points?

In fact, unreflective people are much clearer about what they believe than philosophers make them out to be. They know perfectly well that the realms religion describes are appendages to the world of the everyday; if they were not, heaven would hold no reward and hell no threat. There is an analogy between misbehaving students being sent to the principal for punishment and nasty adults finding themselves on the way to the nether regions. Religious people believe such things unproblematically and they get the ontology right: the natural and what is claimed to be supernatural are equally real elements of the one world in which we live. God is, for such people, a force that can strike you down and a person with whom conversation is possible.

The confusion about the status of the supernatural comes not from people who believe in it but from those who do not. Nonbelievers think that since the world they know contains neither heaven nor hell, believers must have transcendent realms in mind. Yet that is not an accurate depiction of the religious perspective. God-centered people live amid signs and meanings in a world whose "supernatural" regions complement the mundane and rectify its moral failings. But though outcomes in the supernatural realm are just, and hence different from the way things work here, the causal mechanisms bringing them about are identical: companionship and love provide heavenly satisfaction and the fires of hell bring unremitting pain.

Disagreements between religiously and scientifically inclined people concern not the unity or continuity of the world but the inventory of its elements. The former assert and the latter deny the existence of beings such as God and of places such as heaven and hell. Everyone except rationalist philosophers agrees that such matters must be decided by methods that are empirical in a broad sense of the word, that is, by positioning ourselves in the way required to get or fail to obtain certain experiences. Individuals committed to Enlightenment values tend to think that forms of consciousness serving as evidence for the existence of religiously significant entities cannot be obtained. Their opponents charge them with insensitivity to divine signs and impatience in not wanting to wait for evidence that may be presented upon death. When called on to reflect, religious people have no trouble realizing that they are primitive naturalists, even though enlightened spirits want to disallow their claim to naturalism altogether.

A central job of philosophy is to uncover the basic structure of human beliefs. I do not mean, of course, that philosophers are to study the opinions of sundry individuals. They need, instead, to pay attention to the beliefs enacted again and again in daily life, such as the active convictions that food nourishes and that what is lost does not go out of existence. Primitive naturalism is one such deep-seated and frequently verified belief, as is the realism that asserts the mind-independent existence of objects surrounding us. Such an examination of the general beliefs on which people are willing to act keeps philosophy safe from frenzied speculation and the irrelevance of clever moves and hairsplitting distinctions.

I know of only one thinker who has argued that philosophy can make headway by attending to the action-oriented general beliefs of people.

George Santayana proposed to establish a philosophy of "animal faith," consisting of the excavation and critical examination of the beliefs behind what people confidently do. This, he thought, would reveal to us "the shrewd orthodoxy" of the human mind and undermine the contrived problems of professional philosophy. The identification of primitive naturalism as a shared belief we continually enact is a step in the direction of developing the tenets of animal faith. Although various other beliefs implicated in action are also in need of study, this one stands out as a central view that honest philosophies must explore, acknowledge, and adopt.

To be sure, there is dishonesty in action, as when we pretend to be friends with someone we despise. In fundamental matters, however, actions reliably reveal people's beliefs. We cannot pretend for long to get by without food or disguise our habit of situating our bodies with a careful view to other objects, such as trucks that hurtle by. We can say that the trucks are ancient chariots or comets sent by God; such descriptions—picturesque and perhaps symbolic—can usefully call attention to certain features of the objects. But considering what we do, we cannot deny that such things occupy spaces continuous with those inhabited by us and that we believe they have both helpful and harmful causal properties.

Dissembling in philosophy, by contrast, is easy and attractive. We can pretend to doubt everything, maintain that space and time are illusions, invent substances, or announce the discovery of human world–creative categories. All the while, of course, we sincerely believe that our books reach other human beings, take time to lecture in distant cities, find ourselves satisfied with the possession of ordinary objects, and accept the world pretty much as it presents itself, without our contribution. The call for honesty in philosophy is a plea to have our actions serve as the test of our convictions and to give no professional credence to what we cannot enact, that is, to bring our philosophical lives into line with our lives as agents in the world. Honoring the call does not close the chapter on philosophy in the intellectual history of our species. To the contrary, it places the field on a sound footing by setting it a new and clearly achievable task.

The idea that belief is, among other things, a tendency to act has been with us since the days of Plato. Oddly, however, the connected truth that action is or reveals a tendency to believe has escaped the notice of philos-

ophers. Calling attention to it and laying bare the beliefs implicit in ordinary action can eliminate insincere and implausible theoretical views. It
can also establish at last the primacy of action in philosophy. A great
many thinkers have avowed their commitment to this primacy. Kant, for
example, announced that reason cannot gain satisfaction in its theoretical employment; only in the sphere of action can it be fulfilled. Yet his
reason takes no instruction from activity as we know it in this world.
Kant develops, instead, his own idea of what action, properly conceived,
should be. So it is not empirical acts that acquire primacy in his system
but only the idea of action, or action as it is thought in philosophy. The
distinguished thinkers emerging from Kant and reinterpreting his ideas
have not succeeded in establishing more than the primacy of practice *in
theory*, that is, of the *idea* of practice; they have not surrendered themselves to the examination of real-world action and the implications it holds
for the theories we should embrace in philosophy.

Primitive naturalism is an important part of the philosophy that explores the generic beliefs suffusing action in a space-time world. In fact,
it is the central tenet of the philosophical system derived from "empirical confidence." Although Santayana was the first to develop them, it is
important to note that this view of the task of philosophy and this notion of naturalism are independent of the ontology he attached to them.
His categories of essence, matter, truth, and spirit or mind have merits of
their own, but they neither imply nor are implied by primitive naturalism. This means that the weaknesses of the ontology and the current
unpopularity of such conceptual structures leave primitive naturalism
untouched.

There are at least two reasons for the separation of primitive naturalism and its connected philosophy of animal faith from the ontology of
different "realms of being." The first is that though Santayana attempts to
make them a seamless whole, they are nevertheless quite distinct, the
former gaining expression in *Scepticism and Animal Faith* and the latter
appearing only in the later books, collectively entitled *Realms of Being*.
The second and more urgent reason for detaching primitive naturalism
from ontology is that the ultimate issue worth exploring is not the truth,
adequacy, or usefulness of Santayana's system of thought but his proposals for how we might understand naturalism and, more generally, how

we can develop a method by which philosophical thinking might profitably be conducted.

Our age is one in which philosophy has, once again, lost its way. Some believe critical thought can sweep clean the Aegean stables of mistaken religious, popular, and scientific opinions. Others despair of the ability of philosophy to accomplish anything at all, with the possible exception of its own burial. Still others attempt to employ outlandish methods to come, not surprisingly, to outlandish conclusions. At such a time of crisis, modesty and good sense are hard to come by and desperately needed. Examining human actions for the time-tested beliefs they reveal is a promising way to conduct philosophical inquiry. Primitive naturalism as the first fruit of this method reestablishes the social usefulness of philosophy and points in the direction of sensible and lasting results.

# PART TWO

# SELF AND SOCIETY

# SEVEN

# TWO VIEWS OF HAPPINESS IN MILL

The enterprise of reexamining John Stuart Mill's view of happiness may appear abortive. What, after all, is there to say? Anyone who remembers an introductory course in ethics among the blessings obtained from four years of tuition can tell you that Mill has an official view of the nature of happiness. It is a view he embraces with a loving pride reminiscent of the way in which old men talk of their diseases. There is simply no mistaking what he thinks. "By happiness is intended pleasure and the absence of pain," he says, and "by unhappiness, pain and privation of pleasure."[1]

Happiness is pleasure and pleasure happiness: Mill's commitment to this view is public and undeniable. It would be abortive indeed to try to prove that this theory is not his "real" view. The "official view" will always remain his official view, and that largely because Mill wanted it that way. But it may not be futile to ask if the official view is Mill's *only* view of happiness. The vigor of public espousals has been known to vary inversely with the depth of private conviction: many a husband makes a great display of his affection to hide the thought of infidelity.

Suspicion of promiscuity raises its head at once upon the application to Mill of a simple principle of historical interpretation. The principle is that on the whole philosophers are less foolish than their interpreters suppose. This is not to say, of course, that there have been no egregious errors in the history of philosophy. There have been many, and should one ever think otherwise, all one need do is remind oneself that our own efforts will before long be a part of history. But we must not believe that we have found such an error each time a passage yields nonsense on the first plausible interpretation. Instead, we must think it more probable that we have not understood the intent or presuppositions of the arguments than that the philosopher we study is guilty of a blatant fallacy.

This principle was applied with notable success to one of the terrible errors G. E. Moore was supposed to have discovered in *Utilitarianism*. Everett Hall succeeded in developing an interpretation of Mill's design and premises that made his attempt to connect the desirability of ends with human desire both interesting and plausible. To the best of my knowledge, one of the other fatal flaws whose discovery Moore boldly announced has not been similarly treated. I have in mind Mill's defense in Chapter IV of *Utilitarianism* of happiness as the sole end of human conduct.

On Moore's reading we must hold our head in amazement at Mill's argument. Mill's aim is to show that only happiness is desired as an end. Honesty and good sense force him to admit that power, money, and even virtue may be desired for their own sake and not for the pleasure they bring. This, of course, is fatal to the view Mill wants to establish. He attempts to save it by claiming that power and virtue are not ends independent of happiness: "in being desired for its own sake" each is "desired as *part* of happiness."[2] But the idea that happiness has "very various" ingredients, when combined with Mill's official view of the nature of happiness, yields a staggering absurdity. For happiness is pleasure and pleasure is a relatively simple feeling: what could be sillier than to suggest that virtue, power or actual coins could constitute ingredients of this?

So a suspicion of promiscuity is appropriate. Mill is wedded to the view that happiness is pleasure. If he is faithful to it, this important part of the argument of Chapter IV is blatantly absurd. We cannot of course know that Mill was past committing such a blunder. His intentions and capacities are inaccessible to us: they followed him to the grave, if he was fortunate and they did not precede him. But it would surely be unwise to accept the apparent fallacy without a second look. Sound method demands that we search for some hypothesis that will eliminate such gross absurdities. I shall offer just such a hypothesis. At this stage, I shall claim for it only the modest virtues of being interesting and of making some sense of an otherwise senseless argument. To judge its ultimate plausibility is a complicated affair requiring reference to a substantial part of Mill's literary remains. I shall not have an opportunity to do that here, but I shall begin the task of showing what the hypothesis can do to elucidate a difficult problem in Mill's *On Liberty*.

We are not always privy to our thoughts. In the public embrace of a well-loved wife there may be a hug for someone else. The husband may not know whom he adores: he may be stunned to hear himself call his wife by someone else's name. My hypothesis is perfectly straightforward. It is that Mill has two views of the nature of happiness. The first is the official view, which he married out of respect for its lineage and for love. The second is a view much closer to the Aristotelian tradition than to the heritage of Bentham and James Mill. It is probable that Mill was not fully conscious of holding the second of these views. But we can see a hint of its presence even when he thinks he is stating his official position. For he says not only that happiness *is* pleasure, but also that happiness is "the balance of pleasure over pain."

One could be pleased at a given instant, and if pleasure is happiness, we could say that the person pleased is happy. But could one have a *balance* of pleasure over pain at a given instant? The image this conjures up is artificial: one could think of a moment in which a toothache is outweighed by the delight of having one's head caressed while perusing Mill. But surely our internal life is not this atomistic. When Mill speaks of the balance of pleasure over pain, it is not very probable that he speaks of their alignment in a single momentary state of consciousness. It is more likely that he thinks of their balance *over a stretch of time*. The notion of a stretch of time is crucial for it leads us to the idea that in speaking of happiness we speak not of single feelings and states of mind but of persons, their lives, or their condition over a period of time.[3]

Perhaps there is a better way of bringing out this point. To speak of happiness, as though it were something substantive we can have, may readily mislead us. Although it involves feeling, happiness is not something specific that we feel. Lives and portions of lives may be characterized as happy, but even so, happiness is closer to a way of living than to something we possess in life. This suggests that it may be advantageous to cease all discussion of happiness and focus on the notion of the happy man. Mill is saddled with the atomistic focus on happiness because of his preoccupation in *Utilitarianism* with issues related to the rightness and wrongness of actions. He is interested in the calculable, preferably quantifiable, consequences of actions, not the patterns of agents. Although the consequences of actions and the condition of agents are, of course, ultimately inseparable, focus and starting point have a profound impact on the views we take. How true this is does not become obvious in Mill until we reach the famous, and for him difficult, Chapter III of *On Liberty* in which his perspective shifts from the assessment of consequences event by event to the issue of life patterns and personality.

What, then, is Mill's second view of happiness? It is roughly this, that the adjectives "happy" and "unhappy" characterize the lives or parts of the lives of persons. There is a variety of good reasons for calling a person happy, only one of which is what or how he feels. Others may be that he is virtuous or powerful or rich, or that he gets what he wants or at least likes what he gets. Probably none of these *has* to be present for us to call a man happy, and almost certainly we would not be satisfied if only one reason were offered. In any case, that there be a predominance of pleasure in life appears to be neither necessary nor sufficient for being happy in this sense. Perhaps the best way to put this view is by saying that in order to be happy one's life must make sense: it must have an order and organization, a pattern interrelating its elements.

Much of what I have just said is not explicit in Mill. Since he was probably unaware of holding any but his official view of happiness, he obviously failed to work out this second position in detail. What we know of it must be pieced together out of hints, scattered comments, and propositions that, though, not asserted by Mill, he clearly implied.

Now if we suppose that Mill in fact held a view much like the one I just sketched, his argument in Chapter IV of *Utilitarianism* becomes more acceptable. If happiness is a matter of our mode of existence through a stretch of time, it is perfectly meaningful to speak of "parts" or "ingredients" of it. Each of the features of a life I have previously identified as possible reasons for calling it happy may be desired and desired both as means and end. On the one hand, they may be desired because they tend to make lives happy and persons satisfied. On the other hand, typically they can make life happy only by becoming parts or elements of it. "Happiness" (read: the happy life), Mill says, "is . . . a concrete whole."[4] Power and its exercise, to take but one example, are for many both means to this happy life and important elements in its structure. The same is true of virtue and even money.

Let me now suggest the value of my hypothesis for resolving a problem Mill faces in *On Liberty*. Suppose that by rigid controls and the elimination of liberty we could guarantee every, or almost every, member of our society an existence rich in pleasures and exempt from pain. This, I believe, is no more of a utopian ideal today than the elimination of gross physical need was in Mill's own day. The question Mill has to answer is this: Should we sacrifice liberty? It is a hard question, but not an unfair one. My hypothetical formulation is designed simply to sharpen the issue; on a smaller scale, similar dilemmas of choice between freedom and pleasure occur daily in the operation of government. It is to Mill's immense credit, his greatness in fact may lie in this, that in such dilemmas he feels the compelling force of both alternatives. Yet it seems to me clear that in the end he would opt for liberty over satisfaction. I cannot now prove this, and perhaps it is something one could never *prove*. Let me just say that I would feel comfortable with the task of showing that the evidence is heavily weighted in favor of this view. Suppose it is true, therefore, for a moment and ask what reasons Mill has for his choice.

It simply will not do to reduce the matter to a calculus of pleasures. Freedom may in fact be pleasant, but it is very unlikely that the quantity and quality of the pleasures it yields outweigh the pleasures that may be guaranteed by its disregard. Now Mill may fall back, as he frequently does when he faces a thorny problem or senses the need for a confession of faith, on the permanent interests of mankind as a progressive race. It is fairly obvious that this will also not do. If happiness is pleasure and pleasure is the only good, progress can consist only of the appearance of qualitatively better and more enduring pleasures. But why should freedom and education promote this any better than tyranny and propaganda? That liberty is a condition of the improvement of our pleasures appears to me implausible to the point of absurdity.

Does Mill, then, have no reason for his choice? There is an obvious one at hand. If we took the view that happiness is a matter of the life we lead, we could maintain on Mill's behalf that with the loss of liberty, pleasure may increase, but happiness would cease. For on what I have called Mill's second, unofficial view, a man can be said to be happy only if his life or a significant segment of it is ordered and meaningful. What gives the life pattern value is not just the precise mix or succession of its parts, nor the single fact that it is mine. Its worth, rather, is derived from the specific interplay of person and action, the individual, his beliefs and his behavior. Thought and action both express the person and help to create it. This intimate connection of life pattern and personality is an indispensible condition of happiness. The connection, in turn, is impossible without an ongoing process of voluntary self-expression, without the continued generation and appropriation of its actions and acceptance of its fortunes by the self. Without liberty this process could not exist, and with this process no one could be happy. In opting for tyranny, we exclude self-originated, self-expressive life patterns and thus destroy the possibility of the happy life.

I said that this is an argument we could give on Mill's behalf, if we took my hypothesis of his second view of happiness seriously. But strangely enough, this is the very argument he himself gives in Chapter III of *On Liberty*. His discussion there of the relation of individuality, life patterns, and happiness parallels almost exactly the argument I have presented here. The idea of happiness (which he sometimes refers to by the word "happiness" and sometimes by the phrase "well-being"), though not happiness in the sense in which it is identical with pleasure, plays a central role in the argument. For this reason, it may not be too exaggerated to claim that Mill's entire discussion of "individuality as one of the elements of well-being" would be unintelligible without my hypothesis that his official view of happiness is not his only one.

EIGHT

## QUESTIONS OF LIFE AND DEATH

On a cold night in February, our bitch—part black Labrador, part husky, part German shepherd—gave birth to eleven puppies. The litter showed the eclectic taste of our dog: in addition to nine predominantly black pups, we had one beige and one off-white. Eight of the nine black dogs were fine; the ninth seemed smaller, slower, weaker. Within twelve hours, it was also colder than the others, and the bitch rejected it.

Almost automatically, we swung into action. We placed the pup in a heated box, fed it milk from a bottle, listened with concern to its every moan. We were deeply into our lifesaving ministrations before my wife and I looked at each other and asked whether we had any business doing what we did. We were interfering in the operation of a process that was cruel perhaps but overwhelmingly natural. What moved us to act in the first place was a deep sense of the unfairness of it all—ten well dogs and one sick, a weakling ready to pass. Why should he not have a chance to run and play? Why should fate have singled him out for pain and early death?

These, of course, are rhetorical questions. There is no universally satisfying answer as to why; what happens to the embryo, what happens in the formative years cannot be tied to what we do or deserve. These things just happen and the honest ones among us simply admit that from the moral point of view there is a mad contingency to the world—an element of sheer chance we can neither explain nor avoid. And just as misfortune is not tied to a being for what it is or does, so our sympathy with the unfortunate is free of any attachment to specific individuals. We did not feel sorry because *this* black dog was dying; it did not much matter *which* dog was dying at all. The sensed injustice is in *some* being well while others suffer and die.

With dogs, at least it is possible to raise the question of the desirability of intervention with some measure of objectivity. With human beings, on the other hand, our minds get clouded by emotion, by a tacit identification with the victim, the force of which is impossible to measure or resist. We can accept irrational contingency, bitter injustice in nature, but we consider it a defeat if we find it in society. Perhaps we feel that nature is beyond our control. But society is supposed to be our creation so that if it is somehow irrational, we have no one but ourselves to blame.

Our little dog expired within a day despite our substantial exertions. In those twenty-four hours we could reach a measure of peace over the outcome; perhaps it was best this way, and at any rate, we did everything we could to keep it alive. Perhaps the same peace can be reached about humans when they go, especially if everything is tried to keep them here. But what if everything cannot be tried? What if the contingency of being attacked by disease is compounded by the more horrendous contingency of not having enough money to buy the best of care?

There is something abhorrent to many of us that the best surgeons, the best procedures, the best drugs, the best machines may be but a hundred yards away from dying people, and yet they are not available to them. And it is not that the doctors are physically tied up so they cannot come to render aid, nor is there a shortage of drugs or machines. Everyone appears to be in the thrall of an inhuman, disembodied force, of money, which in the end is but bookkeeping entries in a silent book. Persons with renal failure die because they cannot afford the high cost of dialysis; hemophiliacs lead a life of fear or bleed to death because they cannot pay for the clotting factor; children and adults face slow extinction because they cannot bear hospital costs and the fee for lifesaving surgery.

In the face of death, money seems insignificant. Our instant intuition is that all of us have an equal right to health and life. If people do not have the cash on hand, that should not by itself be reason, we think, for denying them treatment. To let a person due when a cure us readily at hand is cruel and morally repulsive. If we cannot equalize natural endowments, we should at least neutralize the social misfortune of being poor. Let us, therefore, provide—we might urge—adequate health care for all, irrespective of the ability to pay.

This is a legitimate perspective and very much in line with one set of our moral intuitions. But it is not the whole story by any means, and it can acquire plausibility only by viewing money in its abstract form as marked paper, as ledger entries or as computer records. But this is not all money is, and the bold intuition demanding equality is not our only one.

Another intuition is less moralistic and more levelheaded. Since the moralist in all of us is known more for intensity of feeling than for dispassionate thought, we may find ourselves vilified even for articulating or seriously considering this alternative. But it is a real alternative, nonetheless, and one that has an element of sensible simplicity to commend it. Why not face the music, we sometimes aver, and accept the natural inequities of fortune both in and out of society? People bested by disease are unfortunate. If, in addition to being sick, they lack the money for treatment, that is a double misfortune. This double misfortune may justify multiple lamentations. It may be the occasion of private beneficence on the part of those more fortunate. But it should never be the cause of compulsory social action, taking money from those who have, to pay the medical bills of everyone else.

This alternative, superficially cruel and inhumane, surely has something to be said for it, if for no other reason than at least because it does not take the naïve view of what money is and does. It is simply not true that money is a neutral commodity consisting of nothing but bookkeeping entries and paper. Money that is not inflated, and therefore progressively worthless, is a measure of social wealth. And social wealth is created by the hard labor of generations. People who die for lack of money, therefore, expire not for the arbitrary or silly reason of not being appropriately plugged into the bookkeeping machinery of the modern world. They die because they have not managed to accumulate their own share of the wealth of the nation. To save them, society would have to use a part of its wealth. And that use must be the result of a conscious decision in the teeth of conflicting obligations and a variety of worthy causes.

And the moment we reach this stage, this second—initially immoral-sounding—alternatives acquires plausibility, even an air of urgency. All the abstract thought and talk favors moralists. Their great rhetorical question about our equal right to health and welfare forces us to agree. Yes, no one has a greater entitlement to live and enjoy life than anyone else. Yes, need must be met wherever it is found and whatever it takes to meet it. From this it is easy to infer that society has an obligation to every individual, an obligation it cannot fulfill without doing everything possible to nurture, protect, and cure us.

This is good abstract thinking, but it is abstract and therefore useless, nonetheless. If our resources were infinite, if social wealth were limitless, we could assume the obligation to create all manner of good. In the delirium of an expanding economy during the 1960s we actually supposed that there was no worthy aim we could fail to achieve, no social program we could not afford. In the best terms of the Protestant ethic, we believed that the only failure was the failure of will. We could accomplish anything we wanted; we just had to set our minds to it. Some theologian or psychiatrist will one day write a remarkable book diagnosing these long past days: the unique combination then of a proud belief in our omnipotence with self-contempt for weakness or wickedness of will invites it.

But there is no obligation to do what one cannot, with the best of will, accomplish. It is simply false that we can do everything. Resources are finite, human energy itself is a fleeting and easily exhausted thing. We cannot combat all the ills of the world; we cannot even combat and overcome all the ills of our own society. We *can* make rational choices, and we can allocate resources in a reasonable way. This may always fall short of what some abstract moral ideal might demand; our being rational does not imply that we can or will overcome the irrational contingency of the world. We should like to push back the limits of misfortune and uncontrolled chance. But we cannot even do this on all fronts. We must make a conscious and rational decision about where to start.

What gives particular poignancy to putting the matter in these terms is the current confluence of several major lines of development. The first is the reality and our growing recognition of the finitude of our resources. The second is the striking development of medical technology, of ever new and ever more expensive ways of prolonging life. The third is the rapidly increasing need for such technologies as the average age of our national population increases. Within the next twenty or thirty years, a historically unprecedented proportion of our population will be in the fifty-years-and-older category. The need for every form of medical intervention, including coronary bypass procedures, renal transplants, dialysis, even heart and liver transplants, along with other expensive procedures as yet in their infancy, will increase dramatically. Conceivably, a substantial portion of the national wealth could be spent on prolonging the lives of the older people in our midst.

Is this what we want to do? The moralist in us, once again, wants to answer with a resounding yes. The egoist in us is also jubilant: many of us cannot afford the lifesaving procedures we may require before long. Yet we must be coolheaded about this. What would a society be life in which the bulk of the social wealth was directed at prolonging life, at wringing another few months of breath out of cruel nature for each of us? More important, what conceivable motivation could we have for focusing our energies on prolonging life?

We have long felt that life is somehow sacred, that more of it is better than less, that we must hang on at all costs for fear of what, or that nothing, comes next. These are time-honored beliefs; if intense and prolonged adherence could make convictions true, they would surely be beyond doubt by now. Yet, let me suggest that they are misleading beliefs. It is not so much that they are false as that they direct our attention away from important truths and fixate it on some compelling but insignificant thought.

I am an unqualified admirer of medical technology. I enjoy freedom from pain as much as the next person and feel as grateful as I feel proud that we are in a position to do all we can to make life longer and more bearable for all of us. Yet, the development of medical procedures, as the development of much of technology, has outstripped the growth of our wisdom. We know how to do things, but we do not always know when it is appropriate to do them. Our ability to prolong life has naturally put the *why* in the shadow of *how*, and many of us feel that in saving lives we have at last found an unquestionable and superior value.

I want to dissent. I want to say that the emphasis is wrong. Life by itself is not a value; it is only a necessary condition of values. The emphasis should not be on who shall live and for how long but on *how* we shall live and why. In the hackneyed phrase, the fundamental question is not the length of life but of it its quality. And even this is widely misunderstood. In the days when selection committees were screening and approving applicants for dialysis and other advanced procedures, they typically looked for persons who could lead socially useful lives. Social usefulness was defined in terms of their value to society, of what they could contribute to the lives of others. To view the life of an individual in these terms is a gross injustice. If there is anything in the world that is an end in itself, a being whose existence requires no justification, it is the human person. To measure the usefulness of human beings is to degrade them to the level of physical objects, of mere things whose only excuse for being is what they can do for us. Our lives and the quality of our lives must be their own justification. The primary question these boards should have asked was concerning the inner life, the emotive conative, and sensory possibilities of the individual applicant. If people can lead lives satisfying to themselves, irrespective of their usefulness to others, they have the minimum qualifications for lifesaving surgery.

Evidently, the minimum qualification is sometimes not enough. My only point is that this necessary but not sufficient condition for surgery is not social utility but the quality of individual existence. This quality is seasonal. In spite of the progressive denaturalization of human life, there is an element of biological and psychological change, first growth and then decay—seasonality—left in all of us. Prolongation of life makes sense only in this context of the acknowledged and all-pervasive seasons of human life.

Childhood, the adult years, and old age all have their unique charms and satisfactions. Extraordinary medical intervention is more readily justified in the case of children whom we can restore to normal functioning so that they may taste the joys of adulthood and old age than in the case of old people who have already enjoyed a full career. What could be the motive for going all out for older people? Only respect for their own misshapen belief that another month or year might make an important difference. If, by contrast, they viewed their lives the way everyone is ready to view the life of a hibiscus flower, they might well be satisfied with less than extraordinary means to keep them among us. When fall comes, the blooms fall, and there is something magnificently natural about it all. That we cannot accept this reality is perhaps a greater misfortune than disease and the inability to pay.

Before long, we shall have to make some rational decisions about how much of our social wealth is to be spent on extraordinary measures to keep the older members of our population alive. We cannot indefinitely add costly riders to Medicare and to Medicaid. When the time of decision comes, we may well find that the amount of money we can plow into making advanced medical technology available for all is more limited than even the most pessimistic among us fear. Should this be so, one of the most promising avenues to a rational decision is the one I have briefly explored. Routine medical care should be available to all. If we place heavy emphasis on prevention and make broad use of paramedical professionals, this should not be beyond the means even of a modestly endowed society. But extraordinary medical and surgical intervention at social cost should be available only to those who are not in their terminal season. We should do what is necessary for children and young adults; progressively less for those well into their adult years; and very little that is beyond the routine management of disease for those whose seasons are done.

This might appear a cruel abandonment of the old. It would certainly be that if it did not go hand in hand with vigorous national education. Such an educational effort should aim at helping all of us think of life as a seasonal career justified in terms of its own rich contents and perfections. This would enable the old to do something that under current social circumstances only very few can achieve: to accept their old age with dignity and to view death as a natural and appropriate end to a satisfying life. There have been cultures in which old people felt and thought this way. We do not, and I find little to recommend our current way of thought.

# NINE

## ON SELLING ORGANS

To those with a diagnostic ear, the question "Should a person be allowed to sell his kidney?" is oddly reminiscent of questions like "Should a ten-year-old girl be allowed to wear lipstick?" Questions of this latter sort, it is good to remind ourselves, used to be asked and debated seriously not so many years ago. Paternalism in government and paternalism in the home are intimately connected. In fact, the growth of parental permissiveness may well be a result of the growing dominance of the public sector: If we let government set our goals and provide our education, why should we not surrender to it the task of defining what is proper and of determining the standards of child behavior?

Yet people who would sell or lease an organ are not ten-year-olds who stay out, ready to be corrupted, after dark. Whose business is it if they freely and knowingly contract to have an eye removed in return for a house or a car or a trip to Rio? Such agreements, as all contracts that involve harm only to the free, intelligent, adult contracting parties, should be in the sacred domain of private decision making. Yet, increasing government interference in all spheres of life has prepared us to accept any stricture and ban as legitimate, if only it is justified by reference to a compelling state or public interest.

How do we know what is in the public interest? We place politicians and judges on the public payroll to help us find out. One could present a plausible argument that many of these individuals do everything in their power to come up with reasonable and defensible results. But there are two problems. Too often there are clear limits to the intellectual power of many of these officials. The pressures are great and time is limited; without a crystal-clear conception of constitutional principles and of the limits of legislation, even the most circumspect of persons can become party to silly or oppressive legislation.

Second, the very notion of a public interest is general and nebulous. There are, to be sure, relatively uncontroversial parts to it: it is generally agreed that individuals must be protected from criminal interference in their affairs and that society as a whole must be protected from external aggression. But it is by no means clear whether tax-financed abortions for welfare mothers are or are not in the public interest. In contested cases we develop our position by resorting to the ideas we have of what man is or ought to be, or perhaps of what our society was meant to be or may yet become. In this way, there is a real danger that the definition of the public interest may be deeply influenced by the unexamined value commitments of politicians and judges.

Why should we think that it is against the public interest to permit sale or lease of the body? Let us make no mistake about it: all we can ever lease or sell in order to earn a living is a part or a function or a skill of the body. Lectures rent a trained larynx properly hooked to a brain; dentists, skilled hands; unskilled laborers, the power of their muscles. In addition to such short-term rentals of a dentist's skill as is involved in filling a cavity, we also permit long-term leasing of certain body functions. Exxon provides contracts to researchers, Harvard to university professors, the local country club to its golf pro, on the basis of the special skills of special portions of their bodies. The law is completely irrational in permitting the long-term leasing of private parts as an element in the contract of marriage while forbidding their short-term rental in prostitution.

Those who claim to have direct access to the public interest argue that legalizing prostitution would place lower classes at an unfair disadvantage. For, they tell is, it would make it too tempting for too many of the uneducated to choose lives of degradation. But this is an incredibly bad argument. It assumes, contrary to fact, that the desire for easy money through fun is restricted to the poor. Moreover, it falls prey to the danger I noted above, of defining the public interest by reference to preexisting and unexamined private value commitments. There is little reason to believe that a deliberately chosen life of whoredom is any more degrading than, say, a life of begging for money or of pumping septic tanks. At least the activities in which prostitutes engage are naturally enjoyable; by contrast, few derive orgiastic pleasure from sorting Amtrak tickets.

Not only would the legalizing of prostitution not harm the poor, it is precisely its proscription that puts them at a competitive disadvantage. For the current ban denies the poor and the relatively unskilled the use of their own asset, which commands a premium. We permit sings and tree surgeons to collect fees for exercising their skilled parts. But we forbid the uneducated to use the skills and organs that could provide them with a comfortable living and perhaps help them escape the treadmill of poverty. My point is not whimsical; the poor do not wish to be saved for morality. They consider it oppressive that their one route to affluence is at once the road to jail.

Perhaps the reason why the sale of body organs is said to be against the public interest is that it involves individuals doing harm to themselves or at least permitting or inviting that such harm be done. But if this principle were consistently applied, it would require us to ban auto racing, football, and the Marine Corps. One might reply that in these professions, all one incurs is the risk of bodily injury, not its certainty. But in professional boxing and in wrestling this risk amounts to a certainty; only the magnitude of the damage is at stake.

What is the magnitude of the damage in selling organs? It clearly depends on the organ sold and on the quality of the medical care employed in the necessary procedures. In recognition of the realities, we have long had blood banks that pay an agreed fee per pint of blood. We also pay donors for their sperm. There is no pain involved in the sale of sperm; to sell blood is at most an inconvenience. To sell a kidney is very much more cosmic, yet most of those who freely give one to a child or sibling have survived the operation and lead healthy lives.

Does the state have the right to deny a person the opportunity to benefit from the sale of his or her most, or only, salable asset. The answer must be no. To deny individuals the opportunity to trade on whatever assets they have is to discriminate against them unfairly. The moralistic point that this would place a dollar value on human health and life is at best naïve. As insurance and workmen's compensation adjusters well know, there are socially acceptable schedules of the financial equivalent of each sort of damage and every organ.

The emotional point that organ sales would enable the rich to survive by buying life from the poor is also without force. The rich already buy life from the poor by hiring private physicians, by employing bodyguards and chauffeurs and security guards. This may be unfortunate. But it is no more unjust than that no one had an opportunity equal to mine to marry the woman I did, even though many would have been happy with her and some will never be happy without.

But what about the poor when they need organs and cannot afford them? The answer to this has to depend on what organs they need and how desperately. If the need is serious and there is a supply of necessary organs, the state may well help those less fortunate to pay for the body parts they must have. The food stamp program and federal funds for kidney dialysis show that such government activities may, within limits, be both practicable and humane. Yet probably there will always be sharp limits to what the government can do to help. Legalizing the sale of organs is not likely to create a flood of transactions. Dismemberment of self will always be a dangerous, unpleasant, and unattractive way to make a living. As a result, the supply of organs is likely to remain permanently low. And this, in turn, means that prices will likely be quite high, a good bit above what legislators will find in their hearts to fund with tax money.

My argument is not that people should give or sell parts of their bodies to others. Under certain circumstances, it may be foolish or even immoral to do so. But we must recognize that people have a right to sell their organs or portions of their bodies, at the least because they are theirs and certainly because no one has the right to stop them from disposing over their assets as they will. Our bodies used to be thought of as God's; this sacred notion has now been replaced by its secular variant, according to which we belong to each other. One day we may break through the radical notion that each adult's body us his or hers alone.

Government has a legitimate role to play, but it is not to stop people from doing what they choose, even if such bands are justified by high ideals of what is in the interest of the race. It must protect all of us from unscrupulous profiteers. In the sale of organs, government should look over the shoulders of the contracting parties not in order to stop them from doing what they want but to be sure that no one is defrauded, that consent is truly informed, that lawyers and physicians do not deceive. The message is so simple and so right that I am embarrassed to say it: the sacred trust of government is to protect us from each other, not from ourselves.

# TEN

## A COMMUNITY OF PSYCHES

*Santayana on Society*

R eaders of Santayana know frustration and delight. To the literate among us, little gives greater joy than to be borne by a rich current of words to insights that burst on us like the morning light. Yet, much in Santayana's fabric of thought dissatisfies. Some think him too poetic, others too deeply devoted to reason and to science. Positivists find him too metaphysical, metaphysicians too positivistic. Stern moralists condemn him for having embraced an aesthetic or spiritual life; religious people bemoan that he is not spiritual enough.

Perhaps one could explain these frustrations as due mainly to our natural hope to find in others what *we* think is right. But there are two areas of Santayana's thought where his readers' pain is too universal to explain away. One is in literary criticism, the other in his social and political views. How can Santayana both condemn Emerson and praise him? How can he celebrate Shakespeare and also consider him a barbarian? And what does he really think about democracy? Which is the best form of government and the best community? How *should* the individual relate to the laws and the state and the international order that may come someday?

I will not discuss literary criticism here, although I think that what I will say about the source of our anger with Santayana over his political theories can also be applied in that area. I will develop Santayana's view of the relation of the individual to the community and do so in detail for two important reasons. The first is that there has been very little serious consideration of this part of his philosophy. More significantly, there is no problem more timely, more pressing, or more difficult than the precise nature and proper form of this relationship. Confusion about it has become a hallmark of American society even while other nations assume thoughtlessly that they have the right idea. I do not wish to flatter thought by saying that if only we had the intellectual answer, it would gain acceptance before long. But it is no joyous task to go stumbling without sight. It may be profitable to see more clearly about matters of such moment.

Why does Santayana seem indecisive about the good society? How can he describe widely divergent social arrangements with equal sympathy, seeing the point of each and refusing to condemn? He has been severely and perhaps unjustly criticized for his ready acceptance of fascist Italy. Yet he deplored his sister's love of fascist Spain, launched a searing attack on imperial Germany, freely publicized his admiration of Britain, and on occasion confessed a quiet love even for the imperfect democracy of the United States. I know no other thinker who could write equally eloquent defenses of a secular, cosmopolitan world order and of a society of fanatical monks.

Are such broad sympathies due to a lack of principle? To the contrary. They are the deliberate and adequate expression of Santayana's most deeply and sincerely held beliefs. For Santayana is a relativist concerning values and this naturally makes him a relativist about social arrangements.

We should not be distressed at hearing the word "relativist." Many of those who believe that values are absolute and unchanging do so because they think of them as relative to or dependent on the will of God. Relativism has received a bad name because Protagoras and selected undergraduates maintain that good and evil are created by what they or anyone thinks. This exalts the power of thought less than it insults the significance of evil and leads to a number of silly consequences. It is not the sort of relativism Santayana has in mind. He thinks values are relative to the established nature of individuals.

If we now ask "Why individuals?" we suddenly find ourselves at the level of Santayana's deepest metaphysical commitments. For he is convinced that value links up with desire, living tendency, and action, and he sees the individual as the only center and source of agency. Of course, the individual is not, for Santayana, some disembodied soul or amphibious person. All motion is in the end physical, and the meanings that convert motion into action are themselves the products of consciousness, which is physically based. The individual, then, is primarily a biological organism, an animal fighting for life and love in a violent world.

Attentive reading of Santayana reveals that the generative image in his mind is that of the single animal attempting by cunning and force to thrive or at least to survive. The world of space and time is a field of action, and substance, he says, is universal food. The best evidence for the unity and continuity of nature is the symmetry of action: all agencies are capable of affecting each other, of aiding or impeding each other's activity. The final reality, then, is to eat or to be eaten, to prevail or to be annulled.

This ultimate rule of existence is converted into value with the emergence of special, self-maintaining vortices in the flux. These organisms, each a controlled and complex set of habits, have the capability of sustaining and restoring their activity. They are enduring, definite beings for whose perpetuation not all contingencies are equally welcome. It is the definite constitution, the established potentialities, the living momentum of organisms that ground value; all creatures seek and avoid, embrace or abhor on the basis of who they are and in what they are engaged.

Humans are no different from other organisms in this respect. Their habits may cover a broader range; they may be more adaptive or more unstable. But in the last analysis, each individual human being is just such a center of selectivity and agency. This swirling center of activity is what Santayana calls the "psyche"; it is simply the individual as a totality of dynamic tendencies. The unity of the psyche is, Santayana readily admits, mythological: it exists only for the observer who wishes to think of immensely complex affairs without having to focus on each complexity. In reality, the psyche is a moving spatiotemporal region that displays a staggering variety of loosely coordinated activities. I see a confirmation of this every time my toenail grows while I think of God.

In this conception of the soul or psyche, as in many other of his philosophical ideas, Santayana draws heavily on Aristotle. The insistence on activity, the language of potentiality (even of first and second act!), the ultimate unity of source of the vegetative, conative, and cognitive functions all remind us of Aristotle. There is one important difference. Aristotle thinks that the individual is a substance that engages in activities. Santayana, by contrast, maintains that the psyche is simply the sum total of its activities. If we insist on using the language of substance—and Santayana is by no means reluctant to do so—only the entirety of the field of action, the sum total of the physical world, is a substance. The psyche is a mode of matter.

But this last claim, while true, is seriously misleading. For although the psyche is a mode of the physical world, in another and very important respect it is a substance. Thoughts and values are modifications of this mode; with respect to them, the psyche functions as source and substratum. This means that the individual is a moral substance; it is the ultimate and only creator of the goodness of whatever is good and of the evil of what it abhors.

I find no significant argumentation in Santayana's works in support of this position. Perhaps this is not altogether surprising. For activity, desire, and consciousness are primary conditions of value-creation. What beings other than individuals can display these properties? Surely not atoms or molecules. The only other candidate is some larger unity, such as the state. The Hegelians made much of this, but throughout the long years of Santayana's productive life, Hegel was thoroughly discredited. Santayana simply did not think it necessary to argue for a position that seemed to him as obvious as the moral ultimacy of the individual.

It is not difficult, however, to reconstruct the sorts of considerations that would have seemed persuasive to Santayana, had he bothered to array them and to develop them in detail. First of all, there is nothing in the state or society that could be read as a valid analogue of desire or consciousness. Collections of individuals simply lack the unity and the biological sensitivity necessary for awareness. Unless one defines consciousness in some excessively abstract metaphysical way—such as multiplicity-in-unity, in which case every modulated belch would have its attendant cognition—society lacks the organ for awareness and we lack all reasonable evidence for supposing that there is anything beyond individual perceptions and thoughts. As to desire, all we can detect in communities is the contagion of seeking and of wants. There is no indication of an added immediacy, of an experience of communal desire in some social mind.

Second, we note that each "action" of every community is in fact an action performed by individuals on its behalf. To say that on December 7, 1941, Japan attacked the United States is shorthand for what a number of sailors and pilots did at Pearl Harbor *in the name of* the Emperor. To be sure, there are many things individuals would not do if they were not in the company of others, or if they did not think that what they propose is sanctioned or required by the rules that unite them. But this constitutes no evidence of agencies more cosmic than ordinary mortals. Whatever is done must be performed by men and women singly or in groups. It is just that one among the factors determining their will may be their perception of what the state or their community demands.

Let me say at once that this analysis appears to be correct. To maintain that Japan attacked the United States *by means of* its sailors and airmen, just as I scratch my nose with my fingers and thumb, is to lose sight of a critical condition of agency. Players in the field must be able to be found. There is no problem in locating me or my fingers. It is not unreasonable, therefore, to say that my fingers were not the ultimate source of agency when they wandered to relieve an itch. But in spite of the fervent testimony of sociologists that institutions are real, who has ever encountered a state? Is there more to General Motors than the patterned activities and possible activities of a large number of people? To explain the supposed efficacy of states, we need have reference to nothing beyond what physical individuals do in the physical world and what meanings they perceive or what rules they find compelling.

I am not denying, of course, that institutions are in some sense real. But the task of the philosopher does not end—in fact it only begins— with this acknowledgment. For reality comes in many forms and it is a disastrous error to identify all of them with power. Mathematical relations are real, yet it would be silly to think that they bend the mind to compel recognition. Physical laws are real, but the *law* of gravity would never keep me tethered on the ground. The joy of sun that lingers into evening is real and beautiful and rare. But it is the rich expression of a healthy life, not the force that makes us carry on. The philosophical task is not to distinguish appearance from reality or truth from illusion. To do justice to the complexity of the world, we must sort out and learn to appreciate the different kinds of reality that surround us. Santayana undertakes this mission in a clear-headed and resolute way that could serve as a model for all of us. He sees the claim and place of every sort of being; concerning reality, he is the greatest pluralist.

Our culture, interested in power without responsibility, is insensibly turning Hegelian. We see power everywhere and want to exercise our own namelessly, as though it were a part of the nature of things and hence could never be called into account. People now widely subscribe to the fiction that true agency, and therefore responsibility, resides in institutions or "the system." As a result, we readily blame government, big business, or the oil companies, while we insist that in our role as employees of these institutions we must not be blamed. If ever there was an inverted moral order, we live it: we say the fictive system does it all, while the true agents hide behind their roles or seek innocence through committees and the collective act. Santayana saw the early stages of this trend and recognized it as a sad inversion. It is time for us to unmask it and to take corrective steps. The trouble with our society is not that we are excessively individualistic, but that we are not individualistic enough. For the individual as single agent carries knowledge of his acts, or at least responsibility for their consequences. Only such persons can constitute a community, a human world that is not a mere social machine.

Santayana's view that values are relative to psyches and his conviction that individuals are ontologically ultimate in the social world should give us at least the beginnings of an understanding of why he appears to be elusive about the good society. For, to him, no society is good simply because of its structures or processes. Such formal features promote the possibility of certain perfections, but all perfections presuppose underlying natural organisms. The value of a community, therefore, is largely a function of the nature of its constituent psyches. Since human nature is neither stable nor uniform, psyches can differ widely, though not indefinitely, within changing parameters. As a result, a society that permits ideal self-expression to one sort of psyche may be the paradigm of evil to another type. There is no one good or best society, because there are many good ones, each best for a certain type of soul.

Let me now develop Santayana's criteria for the goodness of communities in somewhat greater detail and more systematically than he did. His central and most general idea here, once again, has Aristotelian overtones. Psyches have definite potentialities. By and large, it is these potentialities that determine what the psyche desires and what in fact would satisfy it. The notion of the good life is thus the notion of discharging what is latent in us. The good society, in turn, is that which enables or allows all or a very large number of its members to lead the good life. Given the essential interdependence of human beings, the community functions as a condition of individual self-fulfillment.

The matter is, of course, not quite so simple as this would suggest. For there are significant problems in determining the individual's good and there are nagging difficulties in the treatment of minority psyches. The individual soul is not, for the most part, a rationally or even neatly structured unity. Long-term constitutive interests vie for dominance with stray impulses directed upon momentary but very real goods. None but the most impoverished psyche may hope for fulfillment by the satisfaction of all its desires; for those of us in whom life runs hot and thick, internal strife is a daily spectacle. Hence we must distinguish the "real" from the "apparent" good of every creature, and for someone with Santayana's sensitivity for the reality even of the apparent, this can be done only in terms of the contrast between narrow short-range and richer long-range goods. The good life for an individual, then, is one in which he or she is able to satisfy the richest set of most intense desires or attain the largest number of fervently sought compossible goods.

The interest in this harmonious maximization is what Santayana calls "reason." To be sure, there is nothing compulsory about reason or uniform about its products. Those in whom the impulse for harmony is weak may live and die, as did Aristippus, in a golden haze. We can say of them perhaps that they had a good time, but not that it amounted to a satisfying life. There is no legitimate moral criticism of those who opt against reason, so long as we are not asked to bear the cost of their

152    SELF AND SOCIETY

choice. Fortunately, of course, we would not have to criticize for long, in any case: those who steadfastly reject maximization have no reason to embrace the life-enhancing and soon expire of a passing passion.

That reason is uniformly the impulse for harmony may mislead us into supposing that it yields uniform results. But maximization is a formal principle. It orders our desires without determining what they shall be and without creating new ones, which, in some abstract way, it might be better to fulfill or to possess. Reason, like married love, works with what there is. It was reason that shaped the life of Casanova no less than it rules the latest pope. Achilles and the Ayatollah abide by it to varying degrees; in each, it is the gardener that trims natural growths. The man of reason who leads the good life, therefore, is not limited to any one kind of man. It is anyone who brings unity to his soul, no matter what flowers his native soil may grow.

This discussion of reason and the good life gives us the clue to a fuller development of Santayana's view of social authority and the proper treatment of divergent psyches. Ideally, the good society facilitates the fulfillment of all its constituent psyches. Such social harmony has been a human ideal since Plato's time or before. But, once again, it would be a mistake to be rigid about the specific features of such a society. It may operate by inflexible rules and demand unconditional self-sacrifice, if that is what its citizens expect and enjoy. On the other hand, it may be an association of anarchic sybarites, each psyche a lovely note but the whole composing only a loose, uncertain melody. Santayana has no quarrel with the varieties of life, so long as they are authentic and fulfilling to those who lead them.

But such universal fulfillment is an ideal not only in the sense that it would be good to have. It is also beyond the pale of reality. Under the best of circumstances, some souls are left out; even in the bravest new world, deviants and malcontents abound. What will a good society do about them? First of all, it will try to keep their number as low as possible. And second, it will leave them as much room to fulfill themselves in their own way as it can without abandoning its grounding principles. Toleration, the maximal bending of rules consistent with the genius of a community, then, is a necessary feature of any good society. Let me stress at once that no precise or determinate amount of toleration is necessary.

Different social organizations can and should permit differing magnitudes of dissent and deviance. Santayana's point is not that toleration should be infinite, but that intolerance should not be unchecked and gratuitous. His condemnation of militancy is founded precisely on this point. For a militant society is less concerned with assuring the fulfillment of its faithful than with frustrating the will of everyone else. Militancy always involves the effort to impose an alien will. This pursued on a small scale is lamentable; when it becomes a way of social life, it always yields disaster.

But why is a society of total toleration not better than all others? Because the very notion of such a community is a meaningless abstraction. Human nature is so varied that the desires and operations of the people in a community are never completely compatible. Conflicts naturally arise, wills cross in the process of seeking private goods. Those who think that we would grow like flowers without social rules, never had a garden to observe. Without rules, toleration would be restricted to the strong or crafty; everyone else would soon be oppressed or dead. Toleration must therefore always remain a limited and relative matter, for from the standpoint of the leaders of a society there is no difference between tolerating intolerance and perpetrating it.

Must we then suppose that militancy is unconditionally bad? This would at once destroy Santayana's moral relativism. And, I must admit, the deep respect I feel for individual autonomy inclines me to think—better, to feel—that imposing an alien will by force is always evil. But the moment we reflect on the great militant spirits of history and view their actions from their own perspective, the pervasiveness of evil disappears. Attila and the Grand Inquisitor, Stalin and Savonarola all had a perfectly good time attacking or persecuting. But do not let me hang the matter on how they felt. Only an external unsympathetic view can overlook the inner cogency and justification of the militant. We may call his reasons rationalizations, but from his own point of view they are valid and compelling. For the true enthusiast, militancy is not a pose; it is the only form in which his nature gains expression. To condemn him, we must compare his views with ours and find them wanting. Or we must be able to show that his nature is depraved or worse than ours. Such comparisons are not impossible. But they take place in the private imagination, an organ notoriously bathed in prejudice. They all presuppose standards and perspectives that are far from neutral, so that their results become predictable.

Militancy is, indeed, bad from the standpoint of the person overwhelmed. But it is the only form of life worth the effort for some vigorous wills. This is as far as argument can go; the rest is left to physical encounter. For moral—and political—arguments soon come to an end and we face each other with guns or at the ballot box. But preferably at the ballot box? Clearly—for you and me, today. But with guns if circumstances change, if not to impose our will on others, then at least to prevent them from forcing theirs on us.

The outbound militancy of a state is aggression; when directed inward, it becomes oppression. There are good societies, Santayana thinks, that are natively aggressive. They offer their citizens not balanced lives but glorious demise. But no good society is oppressive to any significant extent. For there is a subtle but important difference between not allowing people to do what they want and forcing them to do what we desire. The former is best done by such rules as the criminal law, the latter by force or ruthless terror. A good society, then, will try to make room for deviant psyches. If it comes to the point where deviants must be controlled, it will proscribe rather than prescribe, stop harmful behavior instead of twisting natures.

What renders groups of people true communities is the kinship of their natures or their souls. It is not, of course, that communities are accidents of nature. On the contrary, the native bent of every society carries it to communion. We all tend to create replicas of ourselves in our children. The process of socialization reinforces our similarities. The power of a society in defining wants and channeling efforts, in creating desires and providing for their satisfaction, is unparalleled. The result is a staggering though largely unnoticed uniformity among the psyches that constitute a nation. In spite of individual differences, our habits and values are confined within modest parameters: Jones of Jonestown fame resembles a self-effacing U.S. hermit more than he resembles a mad Ayatollah.

The similarity of psyches, once it is sensed, establishes the foundation of legitimate authority in the state. Those who speak for alien goods receive no hearing in the soul. Authority has a vital basis: only when the voice of our own values calls are we impelled to action or sacrifice. Yet even this voice, spoken through the laws or government, is inadequate to integrate us into a community so long as we think we can do it all alone. Santayana is less eloquent on this point than many of the great proponents of human unity. But he sees it clearly enough: to make a community, we must view each other as necessary friends. This means that each must regard the others as having legitimate claims to fulfillment, and his own welfare as organically tied to theirs. We must see the free self-expression of all, to rewrite Marx, as a condition of the free self-expression of each.

There are many ways in which political philosophies may fail. They have the usual difficulties attendant on description, generalization, and the avoidance of contradiction in complexity. But, in addition, they also face special problems associated with the fact that they have normative elements and stand, as does any theory about society, a good chance of being self-falsifying. In writing of values, Santayana is a devoted follower of Spinoza: he attempts to give a calm, descriptive account of human valuation, instead of telling us how everything should be. Yet we find that with the growth of the organic state, Santayana's claims about the primacy of the individual recede from the descriptive to the normative level. It is as if we found human history bent on convincing us that Hegel was right, after all, that ultimate agency resides in units much larger than the individual. Individual agency is now ever more difficult to trace and personal responsibility is turned away; what used to be obvious fact must now be disentangled by analysis. In a world like this, Santayana's claim that the community is built of single units, that its legitimacy derives from you and me, is more of a call to action than a true account. I agree with the call, but it is important to see how easily even a descriptive naturalist can find himself in the pulpit preaching of threatened values to a yawning world.

Political thought may be self-falsifying, as well. It would be easy to overstate the social impact of Santayana's thought; I certainly do not wish to do so. Yet it has made some small contribution to public knowledge of the cost of relativistic individualism. And this cost is high. A serious commitment to the primacy of the individual puts choice and accountability on our reluctant shoulders. And if we believe in the relativity of values, we rob ourselves of the joy of condemnation. Responsibility without solace is what we face if Santayana and his soul mates are correct; is it surprising, then, that we do what we can to render their thoughts false?

Yet these are not the ultimate problems with Santayana's view. There is one issue that grows out of the essence of his project that presents a nagging, gaping failure. Santayana's attempt is to understand all without passing judgment. This cognitive ideal has been deeply embedded in philosophy. It was profoundly attractive to Santayana, who was by nature reflective, a spectator. But understanding is not the only function of thought; we cannot leave the physical world to brute, untutored action. Santayana's own master, the great Peripatetic, taught that in addition to the pure joys of intellectual life, there is also moral virtue guided by reason through sound habits and the practical syllogism. Here Santayana has little to offer. There is understanding but no guidance for life. If anything, we understand so much that we do not know where to turn. The legitimacy of all styles calls our own in doubt.

Let me be clear about what I have in mind. Schopenhauer thought that all life was equally legitimate. He inevitably concluded that we must never impede the will of any other creature and hence should choose a course of resignation and saintly death. Santayana refuses to draw even this conclusion. For the psyche, he thinks, is primed to live and act; even after, as philosophers, we understand, it is best to leave it to do its thing. But this presupposes that the potentiality of the psyche is fully formed and unchangeable. And it commits us to the view that thought either makes no difference or can create no improvement.

I think these assumptions are false. There is no better way to demonstrate the problem than by focusing on children. Every community's future is locked up in its children and each wants to control it through education. To parents, raising children is a world-creative act. Obviously, we cannot make our children into anything we want. But there are options, there are futures to consider, there are choices to make. In doing so we seek, perhaps more than we ever sought for our- selves, what is rational and good and satisfying. What shall we make of our children? On what principle shall we choose the psyches with which we endow them for life? It is inadequate to say that we must do what our psyches now demand. For in such soul-making we transcend our ken, and as the future opens, our own values lose sacred primacy.

I know that soon enough we learn how we shall have raised our children. But that is not to know how we should do or should have done it. In raising children, the value of our own psyches and of our whole community is what needs to be questioned first of all. How shall we ground our judgment? Moral and political philosophy must have an answer. Santayana's, unfortunately, does not.

# ELEVEN

# THE COST OF COMMUNITY

After the shipwreck, Robinson Crusoe lived alone on his Island of Despair for twenty-five years. He built his own house, made his own clothes, hunted, raised corn, and milked his goats; he did everything necessary to sustain life and to satisfy it by himself. He had to make his own decisions concerning safety and the future; having made them, he had to carry them out. Even the luxury of a comfortable adopted theology was denied him. His interpretation of the Bible and of his own condition, though conventional from the standpoint of the society that bred him, was spun with trouble out of his own brain.

Crusoe's existence, though impoverished in breadth and human contacts, nevertheless presents a picture of extraordinary richness and immediacy. He was in direct and intimate touch with the conditions of his existence. He knew all that was needed for life, and he knew how to obtain it through his own efforts alone. No one did anything for him; the actions necessary to maintain his existence, express his personality, and fulfill his life were all *his*. In this way, he made the island his own. On it he felt at home far more than he had ever felt at home in York. He could appreciate its beauty, respect its seasons, and live by its overwhelming, though largely creative, power. His account of his stay there is framed in pride and tinged with a tender and sentimental love.

The arrival of Friday signaled the beginning of Crusoe's return to the comforts of human companionship. Some might insist that since man is essentially a social being, Crusoe's lonely existence stripped him of his humanity; his return to companionship was at once the return to a human life. There is no doubt some truth to this, though the magnitude of our ignorance of human nature makes it difficult to judge how much. At any rate, the blessings of society seemed so evident to Robinson Crusoe that he greeted the opportunity to resume even a minimal social life with great enthusiasm. Who would hesitate for a moment in his situation?

Yet, the headlong rush for companionship is not all to the good. It may well be an indispensable condition of human life or even of life for humans, and its cost will seem insignificant to the lonely man. The personal cost of social life increases with its complexity until, though perhaps still unavoidable, it can no longer be ignored.

There is both loss and gain in the advent of the second man. Each Friday brings his own Crusoe help and companionship. Work can now be split, resources pooled, and strategies discussed. At the end of the day there is a satisfied hour to eat together and to laugh, to relate all that befell us and boast a little of how we responded. There is also the shared enjoyment of the fruits of labor along with the special joy of seeing how as a result of our work the world is slowly changed to suit our will.

Since the contact between such individuals is cooperative and direct, tasks are likely to be apportioned by mutual agreement. There is, one might say, a direct contract between them: Crusoe offers protection and a share of the island, Friday pledges his labor. Much of what each does is done not only for himself but also on behalf of the other, and on his behalf at his request. As a result, each knows what the other attempts and accomplishes, and each views each action and every result, without difficulty, as his very own.

Some would argue that the inherent problem in such an arrangement is that of inequality. Marxists, for instance, maintain that the class to which a person belongs is centrally tied to the way in which he earns his living, to what he must do to eat and keep a home. Viewed in this light, the relation of Crusoe to Friday may well reveal a basic class distinction. The tasks they perform are not shared equally; Crusoe gives all the orders and reserves for his own enjoyment all the better tasks. Friday's activities are, by contrast, menial and low. Crusoe thinks, and Friday works the ground; he plots strategy while Friday keeps the watch.

The Marxist may well be right in this. Even the miniature society of these two men may not be exempt from the potential for destructive class struggle. The unequal division of tasks and the fact that Crusoe welcomed Friday to *his* island laid the groundwork for future conflicts of interest. The unequal distribution of resources may of course seem sensible in view of the unequal abilities of the agents. This would convince Plato, who thought that each should be given the tasks that suit him best. Committed to a different view of human nature, Marxists would not agree. Some recent psychologists and writers of utopias might argue that such inequality is justified if the parties to it embrace it happily. Strangely, perhaps, Marxists do not accept this, either. They believe that happy acceptance cannot annul the cost of some arrangements.

Is the main human cost of society, then, the unavoidable horror of class, exploitation, and conflict of interest? And is the most fundamental social fact that of struggle to keep the other down? I think the answer is no. There is a more fundamental cost and a more fundamental fact. Marx himself agrees that it is possible to have a society without class conflict. He does so far as to say, in fact, that such a world, which he calls communist society, will necessarily come about. Class conflict, then, is neither inevitable nor universal.

The more fundamental fact I have in mind underlies the possibility of class conflict. It is the present unavoidably, though to differing extents, in all societies. We find it in the rudimentary one of Crusoe and Friday no less than in a Marxist utopia. This fact is that of *mediation* or action on behalf of the other. Without our Fridays, each of us would have to perform by himself all the actions that support his life and express his self. Our companions relieve us of many of these tasks. They interpose themselves between each person and those actions that would otherwise be his. Such interposition is the essence of society and it would be shortsighted indeed to condemn it or to urge that it be quashed. At its best, it is intelligent cooperation and shows that man can rise above the beasts.

The phenomenon of one's actions being performed for one by another I shall call "the mediation of action." The person who performs the actions on one's behalf is "the intermediate man:" he stands between me and my action, making it impossible for me to experience it directly. He obstructs my view of the action and of its consequences alike. All of us have our actions meditated and all, in turn, are intermediate men.

The ubiquity of mediation has three major consequences. In performing our actions, others become the instruments of our will. We tend to view such persons as tools and to treat them as means to our ends. The first result, then, is the growing readiness to manipulate human beings, the tendency to regard people as desireless instruments for obtaining what we desire.

The second consequence is the growing sense of passivity and impotence that infects many of us. It is not that as more and more of our actions become meditated, we cease to do things ourselves. We may, in fact, be busier than ever, performing in a dozen social roles the mediated actions of others. But to do things is not to choose and act; to be busy is not to have the sense of personal accomplishment. What we lack is self-activity, the union in one person of aim, act and achievement, of motive and execution. Even Almighty God would feel a sense of impotence and frustration if, through self-limitation, He found it contingent on others that His will be done.

The third and perhaps more serious consequence of mediated action is the psychic distance it introduces between human beings and their actions. We quickly lose sight of the conditions of our existence and forget, if we ever knew, the immediate qualities and long-range effects of our actions. There appears to be something grotesque or paradoxical about a person failing to have direct experience of his actions. It conjures up the image of a man drunk or anesthetized who can move through life without creating a ripple in his mind. We are clearly no such robots. Yet frequently we do not know what we work, or how it feels to cause what we condone. It is not that our minds have shrunk through willful anesthesia; instead, our bodies have grown lather or more numerous by the expansion of society and by the cementing of those structures and relations that enable us to act on one another's behalf. The responsibility for an act may be passed on, but its experience cannot. The result is that there are many acts no one consciously appropriates. For the person on whose behalf they are done, they exist only verbally or in the imagination; he will not claim them as his own, since he never lived through them. The man who has actually done them, on the other hand, will always view them as someone else's and himself as but the blameless instruct of an alien will.

Psychic distance is a direct result of the lack of direct experience. It shows itself in our unwillingness of even inability to appropriate actions that are clearly ours. It is reinforced by the fact that intermediate men tend to hide from us the immediate and even many of the long-range consequences of our acts. Without firsthand acquaintance with his actions, even the best of humans moves in a moral vacuum: the abstract recognition of evil is neither a reliable guide nor an adequate motive. If we keep in mind the psychic distance between the agent and his act, along with its source in impoverished personal experience, we shall not be surprised at the immense and largely unintentional cruelty of men of good will. The mindless indifference of what is sometimes called "the system" is really our own indifference. It springs from our inability to appropriate acts as our own and thus assume responsibility for them. We do not know the suffering that is caused and cannot believe that *we* are the ones who cause it.

Our psychic distance from our deeds renders us ignorant of the condition of our existence and the outcome of our acts. It fosters what seems to come naturally to most men anyway: blindness to the interconnection of all things, but especially of our acts and happiness. The distance we feel from our actions is proportionate to our ignorance of them; our ignorance, in turn, is largely a measure of the length of the chain of intermediaries between ourselves and our acts.

There is another factor involved in the growth of psychic distance. The longer and more extensive the chain of intermediaries, the less one retains control over them. As power over our actions and the indispensible conditions of our existence slips from our grasp, we begin to feel impotent and unimportant. The less we can regulate the intermediaries, the less we control their actions on our behalf. And the more we lose command of these actions, the more difficult it becomes to view them as our own.

For a hundred years or more now we have known where this syndrome leads: Inevitably, we all end up feeling helpless in an alien world. Drained of spontaneity, we move as in a dream or feel moved by an external, strange and overwhelming force. But for a hundred years or more we have supposed that the syndrome is the result of some malfunction in society. Views as to what malfunction differed widely; some thought it was the excess of struggle in society, others felt it was its paucity. Some convinced themselves that it was the existence of private property. Others claimed that it had to be the breakdown of community, of traditional authority or of hierarchical structure. No one seems to have taken seriously the idea that it is not a special feature of society that causes the sense of psychic distance, impotence, and alienation among its members, but society itself. Yet, if social life is a web of mediation and society a group of intermediate men, this conclusion appears inescapable. The productive question we must ask is not as to cause but antidote. If mediation and its deleterious results are present in each society, the problem is not how some special source begets them, but how some societies manage to counteract them at least in part.

An example might make the notions of mediation and psychic distances a little more concrete. The man left to his own devices to light his house with candle or with wick will learn a practical wisdom that comes only of direct contact with the world. At least within one sphere, he learns the operations of matter, the limits of human intervention, and the cost in pain of every lumen shed. The same man living in an apartment complex in a large industrial society will progress little beyond knowledge of how to switch the light on and off. I thought it a breakthrough when, screwdriver in my uncertain hand, I peeked for the first time in the switching box. I have no quarrel with the benefits derived from the vast system of mediation institutionalized in the power companies. But consider the cost: public ignorance of the methods and costs of providing this central condition of public life, accompanied by defenseless dependence on an obscure though apparently reliable system. One part of the result is false security, which, when destroyed, yields paralysis or a brutal response. More pervasively, we have indifference to cost and consequence, which is the arrogance of blindness, not of power. The apartment dweller is agape but for a minute when he is told that what runs his lights also pollutes his air. Innocently, he backs up to his air conditioner and says, "But I can always clean my air by simply switching this on."

But, some might object, is mediation not just another name for the division of labor? I think it is not. Admittedly, there is a close connection between the two ideas. It is probable that when we act on each other's behalf, we perform divergent and perhaps complementary tasks. In our society, some govern, some educate, and some raise corn. Conversely, when special limited tasks are assumed by individuals, it is probable that some, though not all, will perform acts aimed at benefitting others or relieving them of certain difficult burdens. Frequently, then, mediation takes the form of specialized labor performed for other persons. Mediation, though, need not involve a division of tasks; it can occur between individuals all of whom are engaged in the same activity. Attorneys can represent other attorneys no less than they can act for retired Army engineers. And if this example fails to please, we can readily imagine a society of sustained mediation showing no division of labor at all. We may think, for example, of a religious community dedicated to self-humiliation and service in which each person meets the needs of just one other but none may ever act on his behalf.

My first point, then, is that while the division of labor always involves mediation, the reverse is not true: Mediation does not require that society contain specialist groups. We may view the division of labor as a special form of mediation or at least as a special way in which mediated chains may be constituted. It is, of course, by no means the only form or the only way.

A second and perhaps more important point relates to the difference in orientation inherent in these concepts. The notion of a division of labor is social in character; it focuses attention on the role of groups, the relations of social strata, or the activity of classes. By contrast, the concept of mediation enables us to place activity where it rightfully belongs: on the level of the individual agent. This is not to deny the usefulness of analyses in terms of social groupings or economic interests. It is simply to reassert what seems so frequently forgotten: that all action, all consciousness, and even all problems are ultimately the action, consciousness, and problems of individuals. Mediation is therefore a concept that has immediate intuitive content and applicability for all of us. By employing it, I start from my own actions and how they relate to other persons, and I always come back to see how their actions, in turn, affect my daily life.

One other objection appears obvious. Is not the general use of the notion of mediation dependent on an unreasonable extension of the idea of *my* action? Take the earlier case of the generation of electricity. Can we say more than that the people who work for the power companies provide a necessary service? Their actions are a means to my welfare and may even be an indispensable condition of my life. But why should we call the intermediaries standing between me and my acts? In what sense is the action of generating electricity, in which I am not actually, physically or directly involved, *mine*?

There is no easy general answer to the question of what it is that makes an act one's own. My physically performing an action will guarantee neither that it is mine nor that it is not. What is done by a man while suffering from total, though temporary, loss of memory will not in any important sense be his act. On the other hand, we do not hesitate to lay the blame for distant consequences on persons who did not commit the act. The man who hires a killer, for example, may be physically untainted, yet we think the murder is his doing.

The instance of the hired murderer is significant for at least two reasons. First, it shows that actions not directly performed by a person can yet be clearly his. Contracts, tacit and explicit, expand each person's agency as measured by our readiness to assign responsibility or praise and blame. Second, the case reminds us that sometimes there is an element of convention involved in deciding which action is whose. A full account of the causal antecedents of a given act will rarely if ever answer the question of whose it was. An additional factor involved is a convention, social practice, or explicit decision about how far back we want to trace the causal chain or where we want to lodge the initial agency.

It is interesting to note how mediation, paradoxically, both contracts and expands our agency. On the one hand, few of the actions that sustain or fulfill my life are performed by me. They are done for me—many without my knowledge of what they are or why they are necessary. Yet, on the other hand, these actions are also mine, and mine not only because I would have had to do them or something like them, had there been no others to help out. For there is also a residual act or experience of the self that reveals the action as its own: We pay for services in kind or cash and bear, in any case, the natural consequences of what was done. My taxes and the bombs that fall on me affirm that my nation's acts of war are also mine. If there is anything to the idea of communal guilt, this surely is its conceptual foundation.

It is only by overlooking this interconnectedness of all agency that we can press the narrow question of whose exclusive property a given action is. To ask, "But whose is it really?" and perhaps to limit my acts to those I physically perform is to presuppose the fragmentation of agency typical of the mediated world. A broader perspective suggests that all the actions performed by members of a mediated chain belong to all its members. If actions belong to anyone, they are *ours*. This is one of the central facts awareness of which psychic distance suppresses. With ignorance of it goes ignorance of our social roots and fulfillment. That, in turn, makes it impossible for us to accept—even to see—our share of the responsibility for what there is and for what fails to be.

Of course, I do not mean that my nation's acts are mine no matter what I do. Nor are they mine simply because I benefit by them. They are my acts because I pay for them, not in money perhaps but in reciprocal services. Participants in a chain of mediation are united in mutuality. In making a contribution, each affirms support for the whole and acquires a share of the result. Through social relations we appropriate the act, even if psychic distance makes conscious embrace of its difficult. It is hollow to disclaim responsibility for slaughtered animals if we pay for a coat made of their skins or fur.

To see the conventional element involved in the claim that certain acts are mine, let us consider another case of mediation, one in which one's actions are performed by others far away and without one's detailed knowledge. I have in mind the institution and practices involved in representative government. The sheer size of our society makes the ideal of direct democracy, of the town meeting where each person can have his say, impractical. The next best thing to speaking for ourselves is to elect a person who will speak for us. The authority of the representative to act on our behalf, to act for us even to the extent of committing our funds and lives, derives from our authorizing him. As author of his own acts, each has a right to do certain things, though for or to himself alone; in electing a representative, we transfer some of our rights to him.

Note that the rights conferred are not narrowly specific. We do not send a man to Washington to vote for $10 more in Social Security payments and nothing else. We authorize him to act on our behalf without giving him specific limits or special instructions. There is hardly a law this side of the law of gravity he cannot vote to change; consequently, if his legislative colleagues cooperate, there is hardly a style of life or death he cannot choose for us. Yet, if there is anything to the idea of democratic self-government, we must believe that his actions are not only *means* to our welfare or indispensable conditions of our life. By conscious social decision, we declare his actions ours and live as though the government's deeds embodied our will.

From this perspective, the question of whose property a given act really is does not admit of a simple, objectively true answer. What answer we can give is not discovered; it is something whose truth we help to create.

Such conventional ascriptions and appropriations of acts have psychological underpinnings. Some suppose that the political process of legitimating a government is sufficient to render the actions of the authorities *our* acts. Yet, anyone caught on either side of a credibility gap or a revolution can testify that formal legislation is neither necessary nor sufficient. Underlying the social institution of appropriating the acts of our representatives and setting limits to what they may do is the personal question, "Can we embrace their actions as our own?" The government's acts must be such as to enable citizens to view them as their own or at least not to *view* them as strange or unacceptable. In this sense, acts *are* our own if, but only if, we *see* them as and thus make them our own. When the community or a significant part of it cease to view the actions of its representatives as its own, those representatives no longer have a legitimate claim to act on its behalf. The fragile bond of authority breaks: the government's acts are then no longer binding because those acts are no longer yours and mine.

We have, then, three different procedures by which we may conclude that an act is mine. The first is to trace social interactive patterns. Here acts I perform for others establish a partnership; I acquire a right to what they do, and a responsibility for it, by freely adding my contribution to the social structure or the needed product. These relationships are relatively unaffected by individual grasp of what goes on. Both the law and morality reflect this: ignorance of what one's employees did accidentally in error to another's home is no defense against the claim for reparations.

The second procedure is to follow social conventions. Physical and social interactive patterns are presupposed, of course, by such rules. But it is tradition and our purposes that determine where we lodge agency and responsibility for an act. Such social practices can change; when they do, persons hitherto guiltless find themselves in court.

The third procedure is to see whether the given act was or could be appropriated by me. Though such an appropriation is primarily a matter of *viewing* the act as mine and of accepting its consequences, its limits are set by objective facts. In our society, at least, sincere but mistaken confession to a crime is not a ground for punishment. Yet many people do not think it at all strange for a person to offer assistance to American Indians as atonement for what his great-grandfather may have done to theirs.

In none of these three ways of ascribing acts does it involve an unnatural extension of meanings to say that an action not performed by me is, nevertheless, mine. The cooperative unity of the mediated world makes many distant actions unavoidably mine. But the psychic distance that attends mediation renders it difficult to appropriate them. Our social practices for lodging responsibility could reduce the growing gap between acts that are ours and those we appropriate. But these practices themselves lag behind the growth of mediation and rarely force us to assume responsibility for what unknown others do on our behalf.

Much of what I shall focus on by means of the concepts of mediation and psychic distance is traditionally thought to fall in the category of alienation. The classical literature on the subject leaves one with the impression that alienation is a single, simple concept. In fact, of course, this is clearly false. The notion of alienation has three major flaws. First of all, it is vague, lacking clear rules of application and a procedure by which we could determine which, if any, of its uses is correct. This leaves the referent of the concept substantially obscure.

Once we begin to specify the referent, we run into a second difficulty. The concept has been used rather indiscriminately to designate a variety of different conditions and circumstances. At the heart of this ambiguity is the inadequately appreciated difference between alienation as an objective condition of society or of individuals, and alienation as a subjectively experienced discomfort. Even within the general sphere of objective alienation, there has been a good deal of damaging confusion between alienation as a relation, as a process, and as a product.

The third flaw of the concept of alienation is its hybrid character. It is a notion used not only to describe but also to evaluate. It has descriptive force, in fact, only on condition of an antecedent and usually unrevealed moral judgment. This renders it virtually useless for purposes of objective communication. It is important to agree on the facts prior to judging them; if it is only the judgment that reveals the facts, we shall always be open to the charge of loading the dice and *creating* our evidence.

It is not, of course, that I shall refrain from making judgments. But I will not make them by simply calling an act mediated or declaring human relations to be characterized by psychic distance. For mediation and psychic distance are sometimes desirable and sometimes not, and whether they are or not depends on the context, on their consequences and on our needs. In themselves, they are describable conditions that obtain in society and in the soul. Some of their consequences clearly conduce to a better life. Others are costs. The advantage of these concepts over the idea of alienation is that through them the descriptions and judgments become separable acts. And, while alienation seems an unmitigated evil, more realistically, mediation has both costs and benefits.

It is unlikely that we shall make much headway in understanding the source and nature of our social ailments without abandoning the idea of alienation. The concepts of mediation and psychic distance are prime candidates for replacing it: I hope to show that they can handle in an objective and accurate way all the phenomena that we now group under the alienation label. These concepts are clear, easily grasped, and immediately applicable. They are essentially value-neutral and can thus provide the descriptive groundwork that must underlie responsible judgment.

The moral of Robinson Crusoe's condition is not that we should live in isolation from our fellows and do everything for ourselves. He is but a thought experiment, a limiting case designed to make a point. The point is that the more we are surrounded by intermediate men, the more we live in a cocoon of ignorance, passivity, and sensory deprivation. Our horizon constricts and the world, now strange and distant, reports itself only through senseless rumblings or signals in unintelligible smoke.

The result is a loss of both self and world. Like some modern Jonah, we disappear in the belly of the great Leviathan of mediation. But Jonah had at least Jonah left, though in grievous condition. We have no private, active self, only some tasks, some roles and from to time some fragmentary thoughts.

Community naturally leads to mediation and mediation to a loss of active self. We cannot rid ourselves of mediation. But we can counteract some of its worst effects. If we fail in this, as we have failed so far, the ultimate cost of community will be the impossibility of private fulfillment and public communion.

TWELVE

# PUBLIC BENEFIT, PRIVATE COST

## A Broken and an Integrated World

We live in a broken world and know not how to mend it. People down-town approach in fear; neighbors view each other with suspicion. Parents see their children as strangers in the house, and we are isolated in human company. The sources of power are hidden from almost everyone, and we feel drawn to symbolic, defiant, single acts. The daily life of the nation appears to consist of disconnected events without purpose and lasting issue. No one understands how our efforts unite to make a greater whole and why our best hopes are abandoned or else dashed. In prior years the times may have been out of joint; today they appear utterly dismembered.

We also live in a tightly unified world we are anxious to escape. In our jobs and as members of the state, we are stapled to each other and a common fate. Our movements are monitored, and regulations govern our acts. Others control what we can do, where we must yield, what we must give. Narrow roles in gigantic institutions define us; we are hemmed in on all sides. We march or stumble through a crowded world contributing to acts we never see, helping to cause effects none fully wants or knows. The thought of privacy and hope for self-determination haunt us because their reality is unattainable.

The broken world and the tight crowded world are organically connected. Understanding their relation is indispensable for learning what ails us and for therapy. Yet, we have made remarkably little headway in the last several hundred years in giving a sensible and unified account of the concurrent growth of fragmentation and integration in society. At least one part of the reason for this is the interest in remediation. Social problems tend to be the province of social reformers, and those who wish to bring about change must identify a relatively simple and eliminable cause of our distress. If the problems of social life are the diffuse costs of living in a complex and populous world, for example, improvement in our condition may appear elusive or impossible. The reformer, therefore, naturally seeks a special cause and a unique malfunction: ridding ourselves of this one difficulty promises a resolution of all our problems. Analysis of alienation-phenomena has suffered from this simplistic approach, which has sometimes been disguised by technical language and theoretical embellishments, from Rousseau to Marcuse.

What tends to stand behind the fervor for change is a vision of how things ought to be. This ideal introduces a powerful value bias into what should be a cool description of the bewildering, and perhaps irreducible, variety of social causes and effects. The dispassionate examination of how well our views fit the facts is then replaced by the search for evidence to support our ideas. Frequently, alienation-theorists appear to work by a reverse procedure: they identify the source of our problems as whatever stands in the way of their favorite Utopia, instead of recommending cautious ameliorative steps on the basis of a tentative, empirically responsible account of our situation.

I have no vision to offer of what would be good for everyone. And, though I am by no means uninterested in improving our lot, I firmly believe that a measure of understanding must precede any work for social change. This understanding is not likely to be advanced by theories that attempt to identify supposed special malfunctions, such as the private ownership of the means of production or the breakdown of traditional community values. Our chance for progress in this field will be vastly enhanced if we try to see social problems as natural attendants of social life. Rain makes the flowers grow but also gets us wet; it is perfectly natural, though not logically necessary, that this be so. Similarly, it is best to start with the supposition that social arrangements have both costs and benefits, and that these hang together in some natural, intelligible way. The philosopher's job is to formulate a theory that elucidates this connection. The point is to reduce the diversity of facts to the unity provided by a few concepts. These ideas cannot be expected to explain everything, of course. But their value is proportional to the breadth of the phenomena on which, by interconnecting them, they manage to shed some light. The theory I shall propose is exactly of this sort. I am glad for it to be judged by the measure of improvement it provides in our current grasp of the way in which the benefits of social life are accompanied in the course of things by certain pervasive costs.

Let me begin with a mode of thought natural to the broken world. Analysis into atomic constituents or isolated factors yields excellent results in science. The sequence of happenings in daily life may seem continuous, yet we think it is a flow of discrete, minuscule events. For there are potential turning points everywhere; if only I had not slammed on the brakes when I hit that patch of ice, if only Othello had not believed Iago, if only Nixon had not recorded his conversations, or the recordings had not been discovered, or if at least he had not erased them, everything would be different. In this way, we convince ourselves that our actions have crisis points, small segments or atomic units that constitute their heart.

This tends to make us lose all sense of the unity or continuity of our acts. In fact, of course, intention insensibly flows into the early stages of what we know as physical act and guides its performance throughout. Consequence also is ubiquitous: the act is outcome of the intention and consists of complex parts, the later of which are at least partly results of the earlier. Distant intention and consequences thus define our physical acts. An action, in the full sense of the word, is in fact a unity of intention, physical performance, and consequences. Like the flight of the boomerang, it is an unbroken process; we can distinguish its parts but it is artificial to declare one its isolated heart and wrong to identify any with the whole.

## Complete Actions

In ideally complete or at least maximally intelligible actions, the intention, physical act, and attendant consequences all reside in a single agent. Noting my hunger, intending to relieve it, raiding the refrigerator, fixing a sandwich, eating it, and experiencing the pleasures of taste and then of satiation, is a continuous process; in it I know in a most real, immediate way what it means to do something, what is done, why I do it, and what it takes to bring it about. It is this notion of the individually initiated, performed, and enjoyed (or suffered) act that serves as the generating ideal of human freedom. In autonomous actions desires lead to intentions and we are able to perform what we intend. Those, like John Stuart Mill, who have not embraced metaphysical obscurities in their account of freedom, have always known that it consists of the coincidence of desire and ability to act in a single person. In order to achieve self-determination, we must want or welcome what we do and, in turn, do what we desire. Thinking of it in this way immediately reveals the natural connection of freedom and responsibility. For liberty consists of the continuity or unity of intention and physical act. Responsibility, by contrast, is the undivided oneness of what we do and of the consequences that flow from it. Freedom is lodged in the first phase of a completed action, in the process of converting plan into execution. Responsibility resides in the second phase and consists of the way our action changes the world, of the consequences we must learn to bear as a result of what we did. So long as intention, physical act, and outcome are all centered in the agent, freedom and responsibility remain inseparable realities.

In the broken world, however, the single-agent unity of actions is destroyed. Much of what I do fails to achieve the dignity of a full action, namely, one which I plan and execute, and whose consequences I bear. In much of our lives we have become participants in larger social acts, and in these each of us plays but a minor role. A social act, such as the provision of air service between cities, defines multiple contributory roles. Many individuals provide for its possibility, sometimes without knowing that they do so, by making metal and plastic parts or by assembling planes, by calling in weather data or by refining oil. A relatively few, the presidents of corporations, schedulers, and financial analysts, serve as planners. A large number, such as pilots, mechanics, and baggage handlers, share the burden of actually providing the service. Others, ranging from the customers who fly to those deafened when the planes take off, enjoy or suffer the consequences.

## The Integrated but Dismembered Social Act

In one sense, then, the social act is dismembered. Intending, doing and dealing with the consequences become separate affairs occupying individuals at a physical and psychological remove from one another. And each of these main functions is itself divided into innumerably minute act-fragments, until no one knows what anyone else is doing and none understands how the fragments make a whole. Those in the middle, performing necessary acts, are the most ignorant: shielded from plan and outcome alike, they know neither what they do nor why. People on whom the consequences fall live in frustration. They have access to neither the design nor the execution of what affects them: they feel their fortunes ruled by unintelligible happenstance. The planners appear to be in charge, yet even they cannot control what happens at a distance from them. The reason is that social distance, the presence of facilitating agents between me and what I intend, denies me direct experience of the nature, circumstances, costs, and outcome of what is done. Without direct experience, plans cannot be adjusted to meet reality, preserve ideals, and fulfill even minimal moral requirements.

The lack of firsthand experience is of central importance here. Planners and leaders tend to have little idea of the way their designs are executed. Legislators, administrators, and bureaucrats make rules the application of which is in other hands and whose effects are unpredictable. There is not enough personal contact between decision makers and doers for there to be an understanding by either of the problems, circumstances, and point of view of the other. Executives tend to be so shielded from knowledge of the consequences of their ideas on individual persons that they can have little sympathy for those who suffer from their actualization. Outcomes are considered only in the aggregate and on statistical individuals; the effect of actions on the feeling subject, on the private soul, remains unobserved and hence uncalculated. As a result, those on the receiving end, and in one context or another that means all of us, find the entire process of making decisions and executing them unintelligible or unintelligent. Since it is easiest to explain untoward happenings as due to nastiness, we come to believe that the entire world is bent on frustrating our will. Institutions and those who occupy roles in them begin to be viewed with suspicion and social life acquires an undertone of fear and hatred.

This fragmentation of the social act occurs in proportion to its size and complexity. The more momentous and remarkable human achievements become, the more people are required for their accomplishment. These individuals operate in a tightly organized way, each making a contribution to the larger act, which no one could perform alone. Paradoxically yet naturally, increase in the integration of the social act brings with it a corresponding growth in fragmentation. The disconnectedness is evident when the situation is viewed from the standpoint of the individual; from the social perspective, for a while at least, everything appears to be working effectively and well. The two perspectives, of course, are organically connected. It is precisely the increase in the size of our institutions that reduces the scope of individual contribution, and it is their complexity that submerges us in a sea of incomprehension. The broken world is, in this way, the psychological counterpart of the tightly ordered world of large-scale social acts. This, on first analysis, is the private cost of public good: the great wealth and stability of industrial society are created at the expense of the passivity and psychic impoverishment of its members. The pauperization is not to be measured by the standards of high culture. It is not the absence from our souls of refined taste and clever speculations, but of basic orientation about the world and our place in it. The loss of self-respect and self-understanding—the loss of self—it entails steals meaning and dignity from daily life.

## Mediation

The breaking of the social act into its minute constituent parts begets a world of ignorance and irresponsibility. The dominant phenomenon behind the fragmentation is a social relation we can observe even in the most primitive societies. This is what I call "mediation," the cooperative action of humans on each other's behalf. Mediation occurs whenever someone or something is interposed between oneself and one's actions. The paradigm of such interposition is doing something for another specifically at his or her request. But mediation does not require conscious personal interaction. In its institutionalized forms, particularly in mass society, complex and indispensable social acts are performed on behalf of many without anyone having requested them. No one munching on Wendy's beef has ever asked an Iowa farmer to invest in steers, yet from farm to kitchen many thousands work to keep fries coming and hamburger buns filled.

In its most primitive form, mediation is simply the use of a tool to shield the body or to enhance effectiveness. The gloves I wear when I prune the rosebush are interposed between thorn and living flesh; they are the means used to protect my hands. Carpenters find it advantageous to drill the holes needed for bolts instead of trying to make them by scraping the wood with their nails. What makes these cases of mediation is the placement of a third between oneself and the object one works on or the result one attempts to achieve. The employment of instruments and means—the interposition of such mediating thirds—has served as the foundation of civilized life from its beginnings. Nevertheless, its essential rationality was not fully appreciated until Hegel's wholesale celebration of its virtues. Hegel saw mediation as all-pervasive: it was only the imposition of concepts, of negativity, of developmental stages that made the growth of consciousness—of organized human life—possible. Peirce, under Hegelian influence, declared mediation or Thirdness the category of rationality itself and announced that its increase is the ultimate evolutionary aim of Nature.

## Hegel and Peirce on Mediation

Hegel's vision of the ubiquity of mediation is not without basis. Cooperative labor involves the introduction of empowering others between one's project and achievement. Our institutions are sets of cooperative acts frozen into mediating structures. The language of communication consists of thirds—sounds and written marks or words and sentences—bridging the gap between minds. Inference, the work of thought, is itself a mediating process that attains conclusions by means of rules or interjacent premises. Yet, Hegel went too far in denying all immediacy and, with it, the possibility of a private, subjective life. Peirce, fortunately, corrected Hegel's tragic denial: he saw that Firstness, the qualitative feel of things, is an irreducible and unsublatable element of reality. Thirds themselves, he remarked, have an aspect of Firstness that is, roughly, the way laws and sign-cognitive sequences appear or feel in direct experience.

As a parenthetical remark, let me add that Hegel's rejection of immediacy entangled him in a thicket of mistakes. He failed, first of all, to do justice to consciousness as actually lived, to that flow of unreflective and universalized awareness of which much of everyday life consists. As a result, he left no room in his system for the privacy and individuality that escape description in universal terms, but which constitute the heartbeat of personal consciousness. And because of this misunderstanding of the nature of consciousness, he thought he could assign it to institutions, to states, and to an abstract, cosmic spirit seeking self-realization in history. Finally, misplacing consciousness led him to misplace the source of agency, as well: he thought that concepts, social forces, and such impersonal abstractions as reason are the ultimate causes of whatever takes place.

An adequate theory of mediation must rectify these errors. It must strike a proper balance between mediation and immediacy assuming, at the proper times, the perspective of individual awareness. It must restrict the assignment of consciousness to living animals. And it must lodge agency where it rightfully belongs, on the ontological level of particular persons. Without this, social life cannot be seen to have private costs at all. The truth is that "the litany of lamentations" of which, from the standpoint of suffering individuals, so much of history consists, constituted for Hegel neither loss nor cost. For he viewed the pain in its objectivity, the way scientists observe the death-struggle of flies caught in a spider's web or generals the discomfort of their starving soldiers. But suffering merely seen and described loses its hurt; it ceases to be pain. Without proper attention to the private soul, without deep sympathy for how things feel, theories of alienation remain laughable.

## The Growth of Mediation

When the third I interpose between intention and accomplishment is an inert tool in need of manipulation by me, the cognitive distance between agent and consequence remains minimal. When all is said and done, *I* prune the rosebush and *I* drill the hole; my tools have no independent life. They work when I put them to work, and I know everything that is done, and how it gets accomplished, firsthand. There is, to be sure, a little cognitive slippage: the dentist learns the full nature of what he or she does only when the drill slips from the tooth and strikes his or her hand. But such ignorance of some dimensions of what we do is easily corrected and the co-presence of agent, act, and consequence tends, in the course of events, to provide ample remedy.

The matter stands differently when inert tools become distance-spanning and sophisticated or when our instruments acquire a life of their own. The bombardier, flying in a plane above the clouds, adjusts gauges and pushes buttons. Although his instruments will operate without him as little as a hammer, on its own, pounds nails, they are immensely sophisticated and the great distance they make possible between agent and ultimate effect denies him experience of what he brings about. He knows neither what his machines do nor how, and he is altogether unacquainted with the carnage that results. Such ignorance is sometimes disguised by job descriptions and general verbal accounts. But language itself is a mediating tool that is weakest when used as a substitute for experience.

The psychic distance between agent and consequence is greatest when the instruments that fulfill our will are other human beings. Even a single person acting on our behalf can make it difficult for us to know what he or she accomplished and at the cost of what undesirable side effects. The independent agency of others naturally takes them beyond our intentions and out of our sight. The reports we then receive of deeds performed for us at a distance always lack the richness and immediacy of witness. But here at least we are honored with reports; when mediation becomes large-scale and is institutionalized, no one discloses what is done for us. Of course, in many cases nothing is performed for any one of us uniquely. When I contract for electrical service, people do not set out to make me some power. The thousands of persons employed by the company simply generate electricity, and some of it can be for me if I agree to pay. So although it is not done uniquely for me, it is yet done for me, and there is no significant difference between asking a person to take my photograph and signing up with a company to turn on my lights. In both cases, another person or other persons act as the third required to carry out my intentions.

In large-scale mediated institutions, ignorance of what is done on our behalf becomes endemic. Actions are broken down into their most easily performed fragments and separate individuals are employed to perform each of them. The variety and intricate interconnectedness of these acts is so great as to escape the knowledge of most of us. We live, instead, in an impoverished psychic world in which the benefits of social labor are taken for granted. The paradigmatically individual case of driving a car presupposes mediated chains that beggar the imagination. In addition to design, finance, and marketing, approximately 18,000 parts must be manufactured and assembled. For this to be possible, steel, rubber, and plastic must first be made. Roads must be built with machinery and out of materials created by the coordinated effort of thousands. Finally, oil must be pumped, refined, and delivered to power the car. There is no driver who knows all that was done on his or her behalf or how these things were accomplished and at what human cost. We thus become grossly ignorant of our own actions and of the consequences, many deleterious, we help to cause.

### Whose Action?

But, one might object, why suppose that actions performed on one's behalf are one's own? In simple cases, it is not difficult to see that deeds done for me are, though mediated, mine. If I hire thugs to beat my neighbor's kids, law, morality, and common sense agree that their act is at once also mine. It is obvious, therefore, that physical performance of an action is not necessary for the requisite relation of ownership to obtain. Such direct agency is not sufficient either, for I can engage in bodily activities under duress or in my sleep, which no reasonable person would attribute to *me*. Yet, when the treatment plant dumps my untreated sewage in a pretty stream, the point becomes more difficult to appreciate. I did not dump the sewage, after all, and had I known of it, I would certainly not have had them do it on *my* behalf. It seems, therefore, that the act cannot be mine: not having done it, wanted it, or requested it surely leaves me innocent and unconnected to the harm.

In fact, however, there is no essential difference between hiring a thug or a physician and engaging the services of the sewage treatment plant. In each case, I contract to pay for activities I deem desirable or necessary, and through the agreement and through subsequent payments I acquire partnership in the enterprise. All such undertakings produce a mix of results ranging from the happy to the disastrous, both foreseen and unpredictable. The consequences come in a single bundle: we cannot pick and choose what we want to adopt as our own act and responsibility. I cannot argue that I only wanted to drive at 120 miles an hour, not to hit pedestrians.

To be sure, dealing person-to-person differs from agreement between a person and an institution in the size of the parties involved and the corresponding magnitude of ignorance on the side of the contracting individual. But whenever anyone else helps us with anything, there is a measure of ignorance about what exactly he or she does and how. That nescience, however pervasive it is and whatever portion of it resists correction, is not enough to render the other's action not mine as well, or to absolve me from responsibility.

The illusion of isolation and innocence is itself a creature of large-scale mediation. It derives from the psychic distance at which we find ourselves from acts and consequences in the creation of which we are partners. In institutions, such partnership is established not by specific and conscious consent or physical participation in the questionable deed. Connection to the result through intermediaries is no less real than if I were to cause it single-handedly. I make the larger social act mine by offering even a small contribution to it as member of a mediated chain. Alternatively, I can appropriate it by my support, rendering payment for the benefits I gain. The navigator cannot convincingly use as an excuse that he did not drop the bombs, nor can I claim that I pay only for meat, not the death of animals.

My point is that in the mediated world small contributions to large acts make us partners in their costs and benefits. The acts are ours even if we do not precisely know their nature and cannot control their consequences. They are "bought" with money or through what we do to make them possible. If we gladly appropriate the good that comes of them, we cannot deny connection to the harm.

### Benefits of Mediation

Socially and morally, then, many acts are mine whose nature, or even existence, I do not know and which therefore I cannot appropriate. In our social actions, we belong to the tightly unified world. Mediated chains enable us to accomplish staggering feats: we extract oil from the depths of the sea and send humans into space. As the chains become ever larger and more closely integrated, we manage to achieve hitherto unthinkable control over nature. Human health has improved, life expectancy has grown, comfort has increased in the last hundred years far more than the boldest visionary would have dared to predict. The same advances are achievable wherever people organize themselves to act in mediated chains on one another's behalf. The gains are directly correlated to the size and complexity of the chains: greater social unities can perform more stunning social feats.

I spend time on this reminder of our remarkable achievements and pleasant lives partly because we tend to forget them and partly because I want to relate them to mediation as its desirable effects. Mediation provides social benefits so vast that without it life would yield us mainly misery. But such benefits come not without a cost: the dark side of our growing, integrated chains is the broken world of shriveled selves. The social benefits and their private costs belong together as joint results of mediation in such a way that an increase in one brings with it a corresponding expansion in the other.

## Costs of Mediation

### MANIPULATION

There are five major costs of large-scale mediation. The hungry or heedless manipulativeness we find all around us is the most evident. In mediated chains, we deal with each other in terms of our roles. The roles are defined by tasks to be accomplished; effectiveness and efficiency serve as the structuring values of the chains. There is neither time, therefore, nor natural incentive to attend to our workmates as persons: their feelings, their hopes, their private histories are irrelevant to what needs to be done. We soon learn to view them as instruments, just as we are seen as tools by others in the chain. Everyone's aim is to elicit the desired response, to get what we want or need without regard for those who bear its cost.

The use of people as means to fulfilling our own desires is universally condemned by ethicists. But, too often, discussions of the immorality of manipulation restrict themselves to the individual level. Relatively few writers pay much attention to the social conditions that invite and help to institutionalize the use of humans through the greater part of their lives. Even fewer moralists see manipulation as a natural consequence of these arrangements and circumstances, rather than as the result of condemnable individual choices. I do not deny, in fact I strongly affirm, that even in institutions it is only individuals who do anything: they are the source and center of all agency. But the place to look when we attempt to understand the pervasiveness of manipulation is not greed, nastiness, or the perverted psychology of people, but the patterns of their interaction in large-scale institutions.

Mediation-analysis enables us to do just this. Rules govern our connection with one another in mediated chains and they require impersonal impartiality. The actions we perform become our jobs and our personal feelings must be left outside the office door. Our roles then swallow us and the people we deal with come to be seen as our employees, clients, or customers, that is, as occupants of roles themselves. While such an arrangement has the great value of efficiency and even-handedness, its cost is the disappearance of the personal element from official relations, the reduction of living subjects to rigid, objective roles. Manipulation is a natural result; unconsciously we feel we can all engage in it with the best of conscience, for we use only services not people, and the purposes we promote are not narrowly personal and certainly not our own.

PASSIVITY

Manipulation dehumanizes others; passivity destroys the person inside each of us. By "passivity" I do not, of course, mean lack of assiduous labor. On the contrary, mediated chains keep us constantly engaged, busy with the minor tasks of a driven world. But we cannot feel active if the wellspring of action resides outside us, if we determine neither what we do, nor how, nor when. It is just this self-determination that mediated chains make impossible. When we fill institutional roles, we lack either the motive or the execution: I act not because *I* meant to, or I plan actions *I* will never perform. As a result, we are impelled but rarely motivated and, since contentment comes of achieving our aims, we feel pleasure but are not satisfied.

Such passivity can do more to darken an otherwise pleasant existence than any other single factor. Most of us labor the greater part of almost every day in circumstances over which we have little control. We determine neither the aim nor the content of our work; we must instead be ready, in a machinelike way, to do what bosses or superiors command. The frustration of feeling that we are at the whim of others is exacerbated by the tendency of mediated institutions to transmit communication better down than up. The chains cannot function well without established lines of authority; directives from above must therefore be able to be conveyed rapidly and clearly. Inquiries and suggestions from below, by contrast, tend to be viewed as unproductive meddling. The result is not only that we feel buffeted by the winds of the great social world, but also that we find our cry unanswered. It is not that we who serve in the center of the chains always want things to go the way we imagine. But to retain membership in a community, we must have the sense that we are heard.

## IMPOTENCE

The third major cost of mediation is our gnawing sense of powerlessness, even impotence. We tend to view mediated chains as alien forces that compel and constrain us. The thought that we are powerless is an exaggerated but natural apprehension of reality: in mediated chains, the individual's power is minuscule. "The system" appears to have a life of its own and is insusceptible to personal control. What I do, who I vote for, how much I protest seem to make no difference; even as contributor to the social act, I am but temporary occupant of a position and can easily be replaced. Institutions are vastly more powerful than any individual and if they are seen as the self's antagonist, only paralysis and bitterness result. Even if I view them as my larger, better self, my impotence is not alleviated; as a cell in the body or a wave in the sea, I can only hope to hide or lose myself in them.

The received wisdom is that the way to deal with the powerlessness of individuals is to band together into action groups. Consumer organizations, citizens' lobbies, and grass-roots political committees are supposed to restore the might of the little man in much the same fashion as labor unions were to help us resist the economic muscle of large corporations. And in the formative stages of these associations, solitary agents can indeed make a difference and the lines of communication to the top tend to be open. The extent of the individual's power, though, is at once the measure of group impotence: only organizations of size can constitute a match for large institutions. The result is the inevitable growth of structures whose job it is to protect and enhance the influence of each of us, to the point where no one has much influence even in these structures.

## PSYCHIC DISTANCE

Psychic distance takes at least two forms. The first is self-imposed to combat the effects of frustration and impotence. Since we feel we make no difference, we simply cease to care. We distance ourselves from the affairs of the world and learn to treat our role as but a job. We cease to identify with what we do and become functional schizophrenics in our social lives. In this way, we can protect the self from constant irritation and convert the pain of insignificance into cynical indifference.

The other form of psychic distance is unintentional: it is a natural result of mediation. Passivity comes of not framing the purposes for our actions: psychic distance is the outcome of not knowing their consequences. The persons who mediate my actions serve as a shield: their presence between me and what I help to cause denies me direct experience of my acts and what they produce.

There are some contexts in which a description of what occurs is as good as firsthand acquaintance. For certain purposes, dealing in a cool verbal medium is actually better than the heat immediacy exudes. But when it comes to feeling and moral action, there is no substitute for direct experience; words are imperfect in expressing our joy and pain. Direct presence engages the emotions and sweeps all but the most rigid prejudices out of the way. There is a natural tie between our senses, our feelings, and our acts: the horror we see evokes both sympathy and the tendency to render aid. In distancing the consequences of our acts, mediation cuts off sensory presence and thereby the effective compassion it creates. Psychic distance, as the sensory ignorance of what we work, is at once the reason we lack a motive to improve our deeds, and thus find ourselves at peace with patent evil.

### IRRESPONSIBILITY

The two forms of psychic distance help lay the groundwork of widespread social and personal irresponsibility. This last great cost of mediation surrounds us on all sides and reminds us that alienation is by no means only a matter of how we feel. A crushing sense of impotence about changing anything causes us to retreat into our jobs. Pervasive ignorance of how our jobs advance the social act makes it difficult to see that act as our own. Since we think we neither cause it nor can change it, we simply refuse to take responsibility for what goes on. The irresponsibility is not willful and it is not the outcome of a vicious nature. It is an understandable, innocent response grounded in our inability to embrace the social act as ours. The artlessness of our reaction, of course, does not make it morally right. We are thus faced with the frightful spectacle of well-meaning people supporting by their acts institutional cruelty of a scope they would, as private persons, never dream to cause.

## Increasing Costs

As mediation increases, so do its costs. In addition to the increments in manipulation, passivity, impotence, psychic distance, and irresponsibility attributable directly to growth in the size and pervasiveness of mediated chains, these costs also enhance each other. Being manipulated, for example, fosters passivity, and psychic distance reinforces our sense of impotence. All of them, in turn, make irresponsibility an attractive response, which again aids passivity and appears to make manipulation all right.

At first, it might seem that the benefits of mediation are social, while its costs are borne by private individuals. That is indeed the way many of us perceive the course of the modern world. Improvements in such public goods as sanitation and control over infectious disease appear to be accompanied by an increase in alienation, unhappiness, and the incidence of mental illness. Greater social wealth leads to ever more impoverished personalities. The integration of the social world seems to fragment our psychological unity and we feel as strangers even though we work together every day.

## Private Consciousness

There is a good explanation of these phenomena ready at hand. Cooperative action builds ever greater social unities. Minds, by contrast, cannot be compounded. The growth of institutions is not matched, therefore, by the development of some larger, public consciousness. Private, individual awareness is the only sort there is and that consciousness undergoes, if anything, a curtailment of its scope as a result of mediation. So while the social world expands, the world of private reflection and understanding contracts relative to it. Consequently, the ordinary person comprehends less and less of the interconnections of social reality. The less we know, the more we feel frustrated and shunted to the side. Innocent ignorance is the ground of much emotional disorder, and it is seeing just such disarray that makes us believe that the cost of public good is private pain.

## The Private and the Public

I think that there is a great deal of truth in this explanation. And yet the sharp contrast between public and private will not stand scrutiny. In the final analysis, it is simplistic to say that in the mediated world public benefits are bought with private grief. First, in the strictest sense, there are no *public* benefits. Second, the disorder we face is far from solely private.

There are no public benefits because there is no such being as the public. To speak of it is to invoke an agreeable fiction, or to use shorthand to refer to a collection of individuals. To say that the collection is a community is not to add another entity to the individuals that constitute it but simply to indicate their relation to one another. The public consists of individuals and only the individuals are real. They alone enjoy a conscious direction to life and, therefore, they alone can be benefited or harmed. The point is obvious if we look at it with a clear, non-Hegelian eye. When an infectious disease is eliminated, it is not some faceless Leviathan, the public, that is free of it, but simply you and I. In this way, public benefits are the benefits of many private persons; the good that comes of mediation is no less yours and mine than are its noxious side effects.

The disorder in the world, moreover, is not merely psychological. The inner and the outer, feeling and behavior are not separate chambers without a door. Personal disorder shows itself in what we do, and what happens to our bodies shapes our minds. Passivity is a condition of our souls *and* of our behavior. Psychic distance is a mode in which we experience the world, but it quickly leads to irresponsible action. The fragmented world may have started in our hurting, private psyches, but it did not remain there for long. It has invaded the integrated world and now lives in its heart. Our great institutions are staffed by too few who care and many employees lack initiative. We are cynical of ideals that could move us and treat each other with suspicion or ill will. Public and private are like an old couple: in spite of disagreements, they are never far apart.

## Explanation without Supposed Malfunction

I began with the human act shattered into its minute constituents. Next, I explained how this is brought about in a world where most of our acts are mediated. We then saw how mediation, particularly of the magnitude we find in populous industrial societies, comes with a full package of costs and benefits.

There are three great advantages of an account such as this. First, it makes sense of a wide diversity of facts by the application of a few simple, intelligible concepts. Unification in thought of the multiplicity of phenomena is what it means to understand, and this theory goes some distance in the direction of advancing that difficult task. Second, it does so, I note with satisfaction, without postulating any social malfunction or malformation. Most alienation theories begin by identifying some defective social condition and assign to it a special role in the generation of ill effects. As I have indicated, focus on such a single, preeminent cause, whether it be class struggle or the breakdown of class structure, private property or the desolation of the family, is always misleading. Not only is the world not so simple, this frame of mind also creates the illusion that by eliminating a single social problem, we can be on our way to Utopia.

How can we tell defective social structures from sound ones? This requires a standard of social health and that, in turn, substantial normative commitments. The third advantage of my theory is that it can give a description of the facts without some prior view of what is wrong or right. I am not averse to making moral judgments, but it is best to make them when the facts are in. Values too hastily embraced determine how we view the facts and subtly guide our choice of evidence. In this way, theories are shown true too easily, and yet our understanding of things is not improved.

## Empirical Tests of the Theory

A theory of the sort I have proposed can be made more specific by displaying some of the theorems it generates. A number of these shed revealing light on our current condition.

1. Psychic distance increases proportionately with the increase in the number of mediators. This suggests that populous and highly integrated societies tend to have less immediacy, more ignorance of social function and more irresponsibility than relatively less developed ones. In corporations, it shows sheer size to be an impediment and thus a cost. There is, of course, the possibility of countervailing causes, but the *tendency* I describe should be detectable.

2. Control over the actions performed on one's behalf diminishes in proportion to the increase in the number of intermediaries. This suggests a serious problem for chains of command and bureaucracies, where central direction is viewed as essential and is difficult to attain. Rules of responsibility in the military must be framed in a way that takes this slippage seriously and serves to reduce it to a minimum. Obviously, the quality of communication in the chains is an additional variable affecting control. But the important consideration is that the sheer size of the mediated chain, independently of any special feature of tends to reduce the extent to which central plans can be faithfully executed.

3. Decreased ability to see social acts as one's own (namely, "to appropriate" them) proportionately decreases the readiness to take responsibility for them. This theorem establishes a clear connection between psychic distance and one of its important social effects. The presence of the relationship is a vast and costly reality in socialist countries. But it operates also in large corporations, particularly ones in which employees have little say in the decisions and little understanding of the operations of the company.

4. The extent of the difficulty in approximating full agency in one's work is directly proportional to the effort to find alternative areas of full agency. By "full agency" I mean the unity in one person of aim, execution, and enjoyed achievement. Very few people can attain this in mediated chains. The result is a great growth in gardening, hobbies, and do-it-yourself crafts. Even the more passive types participate: they plan to raise a glass, down the beer, and then enjoy the effects. Our resistance to being told at home is itself a product of being told at work: we stand jealous guard over our self-determination in the evening because we act at others' bidding through the day.

Further theorems can be generated and refined without difficulty. One important feature of them is that they are testable. The theory readily begets a research program and, in addition to the sense it makes of widely diverse phenomena, it also holds out the hope of quantitative empirical confirmation.

## Does It Point to Action?

Yet all of this may not be enough to please those whose interest in alienation theory is motivated primarily by the desire for social change. Such ameliorationists or revolutionaries are likely to view my ideas as pure theory, or perhaps a way of substituting understanding for action.

This view is, of course, unjust. It is true that an analysis in terms of mediation and psychic distance is unlikely to serve as the conceptual foundation of a revolution. But it *can* ground constructive social action to mitigate the costs of mediation. There are two important features of actions so based. They have as their source a confirmed and, I hope, correct theory, instead of themselves serving, in an odd way, as retroactive confirmations of the view. And because the theory makes no moral statement, actions can flow from it only by the way it engages the shared values of the community. If it enhances the self-knowledge of the society and if there is agreement that psychic distance, irresponsibility, and manipulativeness are costs, we can lay plans to reduce them. Such remediation, based in knowledge and free agreement, is the only worthy and feasible course in a democracy.

## Reduce Mediation?

What can we do to reduce the manipulativeness, passivity, ignorance, and irresponsibility that affect us as the result of widespread mediation? Since large-scale mediation entails major costs, it is natural to suggest that we reduce it. This seems an attractive course so long as we do not reflect on the organic way in which almost everything we think good is related. The connection between the astounding comforts we enjoy and the size and productive order of our society is not accidental. Those who wish to turn to some modest Utopia in the name of the principle that small is beautiful must ask themselves how we could feed New York on the product of family plots. If the country were to consist of semi-autonomous small communities, what would become of travel and transportation, commerce and communication, disease control, education, and mass production without which we would find ourselves with ax and spinning wheel?

I am not saying, of course, that mediation could not be decreased a little here and there. There may well be too many mediators in the civil service and there ought not to be any between parents and child in love and moral education. But these are minor modifications in a structure that, because of its benefits, we cannot seriously think of abrogating. People in another day may have felt happy chewing half-rotten meat with wooden dentures; how many today would choose that over corn fed beef? Dealienation strategies must utilize realistic, not romantic, remedies. We must retain the immense benefits of large-scale industrial society—the health, the comfort, the broad scope of choice, the economic and psychological underpinnings of justice it provides—while we effectively mitigate its ill effects.

### Is Education the Remedy?

If mediation yields too much for us to give it up, are we defenseless against its painful costs? Not entirely. But I must warn against the hope for easy fixes. Mediation is ubiquitous and it always causes unwelcome effects. Nowhere in life do we find final solutions; here also, we can look only for constant struggle to keep psychic distance low.

I have indicated before that at the heart of our problems is a discord between private psychological and public social reality. Integrated social acts are viewed by their individual participants as consisting of meaningless act-fragments. The magnitude of the act, when contrasted with the minuscule role single agents play in it, virtually assures its unintelligibility. Lack of direct acquaintance with the plans and outcome of institutional processes keeps ordinary people in ignorance of what is done, how it affects others, and in what ways their activities help in causing misery. The quiet frustration of this ignorance shows itself well in what thought and language do to pretend we understand institutions and their large-scale acts. We endow unwieldy organizations, such as IBM, with unity and causal power, and learn to view them as individual, even personal, agencies. In England people have not yet forgotten to refer to such social structures as "they," ever reminding themselves that institutions are but human beings suitably related. We have lost this wisdom and innocently speak of government and corporation as a single being denoted by an "it."

Since the problem is ignorance, the solution might appear to be education. Yet education, at least as it is practiced today, tends to increase psychic distance instead of reducing it. The reason is twofold. Mediated chains and the attendant division of labor, specialization, and fragmentation are as prominent in the acquisition and dissemination of knowledge as in other activities in our society. And much of education suffers from exclusive reliance on the mediation of words: in this way, direct experience is further impoverished, and thought and sensory exposure become unrelated realms. Education could help us only if it overcame its excessive reliance on the verbal and the conceptual, and devoted itself to the integration of theory and daily life, of schooling and society.

## Regaining Immediacy

When it comes to reducing the costs of social life, remediation must mean reimmediation. The premier strategy for righting the imbalance between private psychological and public social reality and for reducing inhumanity and irresponsibility in mediated chains is to expose every part of the chain to every member of it. More generally, immediate acquaintance with the persons, actions, and consequences mediation hides from us tends proportionately to decrease our psychic distance from them. Such immediacy, particularly when combined with explanations of the interconnectedness of the elements, naturally increases our understanding. But its special dealienating power comes from the way it engages the subjective powers and personal perspective of the individual. There is simply no match for the direct feel of reality conveyed by sensory encounter; nothing mobilizes the resources of the subject more effectively or shakes intellect, feelings, and will into action more quickly and in greater unison. To achieve such widespread immediacy in institutions and in society at large requires the formulation of explicit policies and considerable effort in putting them into effect. Openness in government and inside corporations makes it possible for all interested parties to learn what is being done and why. But passive openness is inadequate. Active steps must be devised to familiarize planners, doers, and those who enjoy or suffer the consequences with one another's situation and work. Chief executive officers cannot be strangers to the shipping room and janitors must have access to those in power. Immediacy and forthright communication allay suspicion, and if we understand what decisions are made and why, we find acceptance of them easier. Conversely, planners tend to be more realistic and more ready to adjust grand designs if they have firsthand knowledge of the problems of implementation and of unexpected side effects.

### Current Efforts at Remediation

We can see the beginnings of a dim recognition that exposing each part of a mediated chain to all the others is a good strategy for increasing both responsibility and productivity. Some management training programs require that young people rotate through all the major job types in the company. More and more chief executives talk over lunch with their workers or visit employees in distant factories. And quality circles break down the communications barriers between production line workers and managers, and thereby not only improve efficiency but also enhance the sense of all that they have a say and a stake in the company. Such activities, when they are sustained and not motivated by public relations posturing, are clearly dealienating in their effects. But we could improve upon them if dealienation initiatives were designed with a better understanding of what they are meant to remedy.

Immediacy within mediated chains improves our grasp of how complex social acts are constituted. When it is mated with helpful explanations, it also shows us the place and significance of our own contribution to such larger public actions. If it is extended to my co-workers in their private capacity, it will reduce manipulativeness by a significant measure. For colleagues outside the workplace reveal themselves as persons, as human beings with needs, fears, and obligations quite like mine. This personal dimension of our relation, even if not intimate, quickly over-shadows narrow role-connected contact in the mediated chain. It is easy to manipulate others if we are strangers to their souls. It is much more difficult to use them without concern for their good or dignity, if we know their feelings, their hopes, their families.

## Immediacy and Education in Political Life

In societies such as ours, where bureaucratic regulation plays a rapidly increasing role, special attention must be paid to immediacy in public and political life. Until some years ago, the president of the United States used to set aside a few hours every week to greet and shake hands with whoever cared to visit. Although these must have been stiff and burden-some occasions, the tradition addressed a need that was real and press-ing even when we had much less mediation. People who feel impotent and lost in the crowd find it of immense significance to be able to meet, to have access to, persons of real power. Political scientists and sociolo-gists may think such desires naive, but their dissatisfaction has a devas-tating effect on the body politic. For access is symbolic empowerment and most of us seek no more. *We* do not wish to be the ones to make the decisions; we want only the opportunity for direct communication, a se-rious hearing, and the frank disclosure of competing views.

A closer look at this communicative immediacy reveals that its es-sence is educational. The hearing afforded ordinary citizens is an oppor-tunity for politicians and bureaucrats to learn. And an honest account of the considerations, pressures, and problems involved in the formulation and administration of policy is a better lesson in civics than any school can teach. Viewed in this light, the central task of government itself is educational: it must organize and orchestrate the reciprocal teaching and learning of the community. The ideal is to have as little power-enforced regulation as possible. As an absolute minimum, government should forgo coercive measures whenever vigorous persuasion or suitable incentives can accomplish the same effect. The vast spread of regulations expresses a loss of faith in the educability of the populace and a stupendous confidence that leaders need not or cannot learn anything from the dialogue that leads to persuasion.

### Accurate Information, Mutual Communication

It is extremely difficult to achieve person-to-person political immediacy in a country as populous as ours. We can go some distance with direct encounter; beyond that, we must rely on technological aids that provide a sort of secondary immediacy. Everyone can spend some time at some point with elected officials and with civil servants. The demand for immediacy is not so stringent that everyone must meet every representative and each new president: an experience or two, occasionally renewed, provides enough general insight. The informed imagination can then take over and render the problems and decisions of other office-holders vivid and easy to embrace.

But in order for the imagination to be informed, there must be a steady stream of accurate advice concerning public figures, problems, debates, and decisions. The media, especially television with its mediated immediacy, are well adapted to providing this. Seriousness of purpose is the high demand: if both media and politicians believe that their function is to educate adult human beings, sensational revelations, bombastic half-truths, and partisan lies will find less favor in their eyes. The other direction in the flow of information is no less important. Through invited complaints, call-ins, public hearings, small group meetings, and questionnaires, but not through impersonal opinion polls, public officials must continually seek instruction from their employers. Such ongoing exchange makes each citizen a full member of the community and enables all to appropriate public decisions as their own.

### Stern Rules of Responsibility

All of the measures I have discussed so far are benignly enlightening. There is also a sterner manner of enhancing immediacy. We are not very clear in our minds about the proper rules of responsibility in mediated chains. After the Second World War, for example, an American tribunal

convicted General Yamashita and condemned him to death for atrocities, of which he was probably ignorant, committed by his troops. By
contrast, the superior officers who probably knew of the My Lai massacre were not even prosecuted. On the one hand, our custom is to consider anonymity in the mediated chain tantamount to innocence. Yet, on
the other, we sometimes pluck people out of the obscurity of the chains
to punish or destroy them in the way of an example. Committee decisions usually mean immunity for the faceless functionaries who make
them. Yet, from time to time, public anger cleans out the committees
and removes even those members who strongly dissented from offending policies.

   If we wish to increase moral concern in our society, we must render
the consequences of our acts immediate. When the acts are institutional
and our contribution to them is minuscule, we do not in the course of
things come to see what we have wrought, and we have no special incentive to inquire. A revision of the rules for holding members of mediated
chains responsible would provide the needed stimulus for them to learn
what they help to cause. The change would have to make the rules consistent and more severe. Each contributor to a social act needs to be made
answerable for its ill effects. The punishment should be proportional to
the damage and to the person's contribution, but it must be substantial
enough to make voluntary ignorance too costly. If people knew the
harmful consequences their apparently innocent mediated actions produce, natural sympathy with the victims would tend to make them question their role in the chain. If they thought they would have to answer for
noxious outcomes, self-interest would cause them not only to examine
orders and procedures but also, when the evil is gratuitous or clear, to
refuse participation.

### A More Humane World

These suggestions for reducing the costs of mediation would, if implemented, make both the public world and our private lives significantly
better. Those who now perform meaningless act-fragments would become acquainted with the others whose agency completes their act. Planners, doers, and those who deal with the consequences would each learn

firsthand what the others contribute, what forces constrain their choice and how it feels to occupy their station. By exposing us to each other as persons, such immediacy fosters sympathy and expands the understanding. It gives each of us a sense of partnership in our joint undertakings. Only in this way can private consciousness apprehend the social act and adopt it as its own. When that happens, suspicion no longer pervades our relations: we are fellow humans equally needy and all caught.

Nothing I have said here is inconsistent with the desire of many and the tendency of some to decrease mediation in their private lives. Greater immediacy with Nature and expanded agency are possible for almost everyone. The first points to the enjoyment of sea, mountains, trees, animals, and the vegetable garden in the yard. The second means liberating competence with tools, with cars, with repairs around the house, and the special delight of immediacy with our acts when we perform them without hope of issue, as ends in themselves. Most important, we could all achieve greater immediacy with each other in dialogue and shared activities. Telephone and television are mediating marvels of genuine usefulness. We need not allow them to deprive us of the ultimate value of our eyes meeting and of hands that touch.[1]

# THIRTEEN

# LEAVING OTHERS ALONE

Imagine a world in which there is only one sort of fruit, say, apples. There are, of course, several types of apples, yellow and red delicious, Jonathan and Granny Smith; occasionally, one even encounters a bad apple. The people in this world learn to appreciate apples, eating them raw and baking them, flavoring them, juicing them, turning them into sauce and making them into filling for wonderful pies. As a result of their cultivation, apples become available in a surprising variety of flavors and as ingredients in a bewildering array of dishes.

What should we say of these people? First, that they took advantage of the possibilities of their raw material, creating something fine out of what, left to itself, would be common and boring. Should we feel sorry for them because they were impoverished, never having enjoyed the glory of a pear? Such feelings seem appropriate when we contemplate our good fortune in having a hundred different types of fruit available year round. But if the apple people lead impoverished lives, so do we because we must get by without another hundred fruits whose names we do not know and whose flavors we cannot even imagine. Just as we can say to the apple people that they would be better off if they could get some grapes, so people from a richer planet could lecture us that our lives without their favorite fruit must be sadly hollow.

What we should tell the apple people is that we are impressed by how much they made of what they had. Their attitude is surely right: we must use what is at hand, enhancing it intelligently to make life a little better. Notice that enhancement consists of diversification; humans tend not to be like cats happy with dry food morning and night. As Leibniz knew, variety is a great good—so great in fact that, without a measure of it, life becomes unbearable. Sensory deprivation, solitary confinement, and isolation in the dark of polar winter can drive people berserk.

Variety in the form of diverse experiences can make existence satisfying, perhaps even exciting. People generally agree that a world in which there are many different sorts of cuisines is better than one in which we have only goulash to eat. The reason for this is twofold. Different tastes add to the modalities of our satisfaction, enabling us to experience surprising delights. Further, the spread of alternatives gives play to choice, so we can enjoy the satisfactions not only of savoring unforeseen textures and tastes, but also of freely deciding what to eat. In such a world, one can still eat goulash every day, but only if one so chooses.

Who could take offense at seeing French, Chinese, and Ethiopian restaurants opening their doors side by side? The more the better, I am inclined to say, even though I cannot imagine ever wanting to visit some of them. Normally, we are happy to let such harmless competitions play out and consider ourselves fortunate to have a choice of where to eat. Plurality does not bother us in such contexts, and we show a commendable readiness to leave others alone. We are simply indifferent in these matters, and that indifference serves as the condition of others pursuing their goals in their own ways.

Not only do I fail to be bothered by the variety of restaurants in the neighborhood, but I also have little concern about what they do in their kitchens. The secrets of kitchens are like the secrets of bedrooms; sensible people do not want to know how their strange neighbors prepare food or for love. Such wholesome distance makes for good relations, enabling us to enjoy fine meals and our neighbors' satisfied smiles. The resultant relationships permit people to flourish on the basis of their own efforts and the voluntary cooperation of others.

Distressingly, when it comes to some matters, the distance is difficult to keep. Some people cannot abide seeing young men with long hair or earrings; others call the police to stop lovers kissing in the park. Individuals dressed in a way deemed tasteless or unkempt earn social censure. Those who voice opinions out of favor or choose unconventional courses of life are viewed with suspicion. Bodies that do not meet prevailing standards are thought to be in need of correction, and people whose religious preferences differ from the norm arouse the sense that they are unreliable.

Xenophobia is a comfortable state; it is vastly comforting if everyone looks the same, feels the same, and expresses common sentiments in a shared language. This enables us to exclude the different as abhorrent or morally flawed or unnatural. If the different should find its way into our midst, we feel entitled to shun it or to stamp it out; surely, it and it alone must be responsible for whatever misfortune befalls the community. Generosity soon comes to consist of saving people from their awful selves; we spare no effort in criticizing, correcting, and converting them. But conversion may be too kind or impossible; women cannot readily be turned into men, nor blacks into whites. As a result, oppression and obliteration appear, from time to time, as justifiable ways of dealing with minorities of race, religion, and ethnicity.

We can see an important difference between the apple people and many closed communities: The former work to diversify their meager supply of fruit, while the latter do everything in their power to limit diversity to a few acceptable forms of the same general type. One is hard put to think of a society that has promoted a plurality of values among its members. On the contrary, by design or unconsciously, communities shape young people and immigrants in their own image, heaping rewards on those who conform and making deviance a source of pain. Even when the United States was wide open to immigration, it thought of itself as a melting pot in which new arrivals would burn off their foreign trappings and, through education in English and in a new way of life, could soon become indistinguishable from the locals.

Why do we gladly diversify our food but avoid the different in people, values, and behavior? The reasons are many. The unfamiliar is uncomfortable and the strange makes us feel out of place. Seeing people do what for us is taboo may be threatening or, precisely because of its attraction, a source of resentment. Moreover, the different heralds a possible need for change, and even in a society such as ours, given to the veneration of the new, change is kept within narrow limits. In the case of religion, sexual practices, and family life, differences are disquieting and touch the deepest recesses of our being, evoking visceral responses and sundering the world into "them" and "us."

Historically, the most powerful factors in developing an antagonistic attitude toward the different have been a desire and a conviction. The desire is to exert power over others and thereby to put our stamp on at least a small portion of the universe. The justifying conviction consists of the claim that our values and our ways of behaving are natural and right. The desire is familiar to all of us, though rarely acknowledged. The conviction seems innocent and therefore unsuspected, yet it structures much of what we think and do.

Controlling others is actually more than a desire; it is a burning urge. Its source may be evolutionary: in this dangerous world, those who can channel the aggressions of others or can at least enlist them to their aid improve their chances of survival. But the drive is generalized and roils behavior long after ordered social life makes the struggle for physical existence unnecessary. Accordingly, parents want to make their children "behave," the police often exercise overweening power and bureaucrats take delight in forcing everyone to obey their rules. Salespeople want us to buy their goods, solicitors maneuver donors to give more than they wish, and neighbors often seek to impose arbitrary limits on what their neighbors can do with their land.

The desire to exercise power over others is so great that children find it difficult to escape the domination of parents even after they grow up, politicians resist term limits with all their might, and individuals who built businesses want never to retire. That people seek others to tell them what to do, paying fortunes to hire interior decorators, personal trainers, and consultants of every sort may appear as evidence against this view. In fact, however, it is further confirmation: In hiring them, they do our bidding and, though we listen to them, *we* determine what we want, and thus the last word is always ours. They let us wield power over them for a fee.

The conviction that seems to justify our lording it over others is that what we, and people like us, do is natural and right. The customary defines the natural; the food we ate as children has not only the warmth of familiarity, but also an astonishing appropriateness. Some think that goulash is a dish invented by God, and it is only perversity that keeps people from eating it; others believe that the paradigm of food is pasta or lamb kidneys or the lungs of cows. We tend to feel the same assurance about clothing, table habits, raising children, sexuality, ambition, profit, the treatment of women, the range of acceptable life plans, and religion. We grow into thinking that our tradition articulates the requirements of nature and that we do things exactly as it has ordained. I was raised to believe that God spoke Hungarian, as did everyone else uncorrupted by the misfortune of being born and raised in foreign lands.

I cannot overemphasize the significance and power of this innocent social egocentrism. "Innocent" in this context means the unintentional or unreflective intuitive embrace of a certain way of life, which happens to be the only one offered as a model. Anointing our ways as natural, however, loses its innocence when it begins to serve as the foundation of xenophobia and illusions of grandeur, leading genders, tribes, classes, races, and nations to develop a hierarchy of worthiness, each awarding itself the top spot. That way lies the history of humankind, which has certainly not been an innocent affair, spread out over millennia of injustice and exclusion. The cruelty and the horror of it far exceed what animals do to each other in response to the call of hunger; humans crush one another not as a result of justifiable need but in the name of establishing the natural order of things.

Schopenhauer saw as clearly as anyone that will seeks to overpower will and that it takes a relatively high level of moral culture to resist getting one's satisfactions that way. His recommendation of universal sympathy as the antidote to this cruel self-seeking, however, goes too far: we have no business cheering on oppressive wills and it is, in any case, too much to ask that we invest ourselves in every failing cause. Something much less strenuous and therefore much more doable is adequate to make the world a better place: we have to learn to leave people alone. Although this sounds like an endorsement of moral isolation, it is not. Leaving others be as a pervasive moral disposition is perfectly compatible with living in a community with them, caring for them, and responding to their needs. All it forbids is uninvited interference in their affairs, that is, making them do what we want, even if we think it is justified by being good for them.

Philosophers have not been excellent at acknowledging the importance of leaving others alone and reducing our obligations to a sensible level. Josiah Royce declared that "there is no rest in Zion": the moral person must be engaged in doing the Lord's work without cease.[1] We must right all wrongs, meet every need, and vanquish the evil that surrounds us. We are familiar with the hyperventilation to which this gives rise; it defines the moral tone of the reformer. We would have to be gods to meet such Herculean tasks and, indeed, Royce knows that the work is infinite. That is why he avers that God completes what in our finitude we must leave undone, making the gradual perfection of the world the joint venture of the human and the divine.

The introduction of God is at once the recognition that the task is too great for us. Since the task is infinite, without God we face moral despair. But if God picks up the slack, we might as well leave him a little more to do and thereby make our lives a lot more comfortable. Caught between the demand to exhaust ourselves and the temptation to throw in the towel, we face the problem that however much we do, we know we accomplish much less than we should. The magnitude of our duties makes guilt a certainty, and such certain failure weakens moral resolve. William James, even though he believed in the importance of what he called "moral holidays," did not do much better. He thought that every conscious need imposes a demand on all the world, and in particular on anyone who can help, to meet it.[2] Here again, the resultant obligations are potentially infinite, with only finite resources to discharge them.

The contemporary version of certain moral failure and unavoidable guilt is James Rachels's view that there is no relevant moral difference between failing to aid people in a distant famine and killing them on the spot.[3] If that is true, our duties never end; tithing to Oxfam still leaves us murderers. All the moral marvels for which we are responsible, of course, must be done in accordance with our own ideas of what is in the interest of distant ad deeply different others. Our aid to them is wrapped in our values; in availing themselves of it, they see their desires, habits, and traditions beginning to change. Worse, we find ourselves rushing around in the futile attempt to intervene everywhere, attempting to fix what cannot be corrected, or what cannot be corrected by us, or what we have no business trying to correct. The frustration and mischief that arise can be eliminated only if we embrace our finitude, respect the integrity of others, and allow people to conduct their lives as they see fit.

Letting others pursue their goods according to their own lights is a vital condition of autonomy. But even those who value self-determination or liberty tend to think of leaving others be as a special duty imposed in certain circumstances, rather than as a pervasive moral disposition. The better view is to conceive neutrality with regard to others as the foundational moral attitude of which obligations constitute a temporary suspension. The justification of this attitude and the grounding assumption of freedom is that human beings are self-moving agents capable of recognizing, seeking, and attaining their own good. If we deny human intelligence, drive, and competence, we will naturally wish to take over the lives of others to help them along. But this assessment of human ability is scurrilous and flies in the face of facts. If even dogs in heat know what is good for them and often attain it, there is little reason to suppose that humans do not and cannot.

Of course, those who speak of the good tend to have high standards in mind, explaining to all why they should seek what, left alone, it would never occur to them to desire. This, however, is but another case of imposing values on people who may well want to have no part of them. I do not wish to deny that under special circumstances others may know more about one's good than one knows oneself. But this is exceptional and rare. For the most part, being oneself day and night gives one a privileged view of what satisfies; there is little basis for substituting the judgments of others for our long experience and considered opinions. What appear to some as errors in valuation may in fact express the deep, authentic, and internally justified commitments of different others.

Establishing the disposition to let others be as a fundamental moral attitude is not capitulating to selfishness. Egoists typically maintain the dominance or the sole legitimacy of a single good. People who gladly leave others alone tend to do so, admittedly, to pursue their own projects. Their focus on their plans does not imply, however, that only their own projects are worth pursuing. On the contrary, the attitude makes sense solely on the assumption of the legitimacy of a plurality of goods. This multiplicity of values, each centered in a feeling agent, is what makes the need not to interfere in the lives of others compelling. For each life has a native judge and advocate; each person is in the best position to determine his or her interests and to devote energy to their pursuit. People who let others work for their own good unimpeded simply act out their respect for the self-defining agency of which personhood consists. Claiming to know what is good for others and attempting to make them live up to it look much more like the work of selfishness than does keeping ourselves benignly at a distance.

Distance from people may be motivated by indifference to them. I am perfectly happy to leave the lake alone, because it simply does not matter to me. I do not rush over to tend it when a speedboat slashes its face, and I do not grieve when it freezes in the cold. An attitude of this sort toward human beings, however, strikes me as horrendous; connected to one another from cradle to grave, we cannot be indifferent to one another's fates. The distance I advocate has its source not in cold unconcern but in caring. Humans tend to do particularly well when they can make their own decisions and enjoy enough operational space to carry them out. If we wish others well, we let them flourish as they will, cheering them on from a distance. Good wrestlers and runners need no help from us; all we need to do is stay out of their way.

Leaving others alone because we want them to do well has as its flip side helping them when the need arises. If we wish everyone well, we must be ready to aid them in emergencies or when obstacles are overwhelming. The wise wait until the desire for help is obvious, if not through overt request then through crushing circumstance or pleading eyes. To give true help is to become an instrument of the other's will, honoring the integrity of what the needy want, instead of telling them what they ought to have. Moral wisdom consists largely in knowing when to leave people alone and when to help them and, when helping them, how not to subvert their aims.

In addition to being morally suspect, taking over other people's lives is also strategically unwise. The bears of Yellowstone Park got used to tourists bringing them food. As any intelligent creature would, they quickly abandoned foraging and took up favored spots near the highway, rendering themselves dependent on the kindness of people. We can find a trace of this tendency in human beings, some of whom raise no objections to being provided with what they need. Those wishing to interfere in the lives of others must therefore be ready to acquire permanent dependents who require continuing attention. The social welfare system operates in disregard of this fact of human nature; instead of helping people over the hump, it offers ongoing support, tempting individuals to surrender responsibility for their own fates.

Helping others, therefore, is a far more complicated affair than it may at first appear. It must not be done in a way that impedes acknowledgment that people are intelligent choosers and independent agents. Paradoxically perhaps, providing for others may be of no help to them; it may invite them to surrender their independence and throw themselves on the mercy of strangers. The consequent inactivity, vulnerability, and collapse of self-respect interfere with even minimal satisfactions and make for a disconsolate life. The art of helping others begins with the recognition that giving does not always help. Just as courage does not mean tackling every danger, so caring does not demand that we answer every call.

But, it can be objected, is this not substituting our judgment for that of needy people and, if so, do we not wrongly interfere in their lives? The answer is no to both questions. Although refusing aid has important consequences for the people seeking it, it is primarily a decision about the activities of the donor. Such decisions are exercises in self-determination; in making them, we form an opinion only about how we ought to act and say nothing about what anybody else should do or aim to be. One's actions determine, first and foremost, one's own life. To leave others alone is simply to keep one's distance, and not a subtle way of exercising power over them.

Permitting others to seek their goods in their own ways tacitly acknowledges the existence of multiple perfections, that is, of many ways in which good lives may be led. Since all these lives seem natural and appropriate to the people attracted to them, it becomes easy to recognize any claim of exclusive naturalness as a local illusion. Like each language, every life is natural when viewed from the inside, but alien to the unfriendly observer. The ubiquity of the natural destroys extravagant assertions of universal normativity. If natures differ, so must the values they seek and the experiences that satisfy them. We can match aims, values and fulfillments to natures, but there is no independent standard in terms of which natures can be ranked.

Curbing our desire to rule over people and abandoning the error of supposing that ours is the only natural or worthy way to live would go a long distance toward making this a more decent world. There is an attitude to life that makes attainment of these difficult goals a little more likely, though it is itself not easy to sustain. The attitude I have in mind expresses the conviction that though some things matter intensely, most things do not much matter at all. In its current state of development, the human psyche is easily riled. Powerful emotions are released by relatively trivial events and observations: good looks engage our sexual machinery and earrings worn by a male child can subvert peace within the family. Deviations from the customary evoke disproportionately violent responses, as when gay-appearing gestures lead to physical assault and casual criticism plunges sensitive people into deep despair.

We live as universal sensoria tuned to react to everything untoward in the world. We seem to have preferences about all things and get "bent out of shape" whenever things do not go our way. We seem never to ask the question "What is that to me?" and in good conscience to remind ourselves that a host of things are simply not our business. We like it better if we can feel outrage or at least anger, and minimally worry and concern, about the ways of the world. We do not like to admit that there is much we cannot change, and, even if we could, it would make little difference to us except to please our prissy sense of order. Why should we want the world to line up the way we imagine it right? The conceit that we know how people should behave, events work out, and the stars align themselves is laughable, yet we never seem to find it hilarious.

I want to be sure I am not misunderstood. There are plenty of things that should concern us in the most profound way. Suffering and joy matter, as does the humaneness of human relations. Undeserved ill, cruelty, injustice, and early death should engage our efforts. We must be ready to take a stand against activities that threaten to harm humans and other living creatures. But many of the things that most exercise our minds are as nothing compared with such serious business. What religion others choose to practice, their private sex lives, their eating habits, their manner of speech, the way they click their tongues and roll their eyes, the veritable cornucopia of their peculiarities amount to less than is worthy of mention, never mind of outrage and retaliation. If someone chooses not to bathe, we have the option of distance; if people want group sex, we can decline to join the crowd. The joy of choice is that we can look the other way. Instead of trying to crush those of a different persuasion, we can affirm our own values by clinging to them tenaciously as the right ones for us.

We cannot calculate the harm that has come from the conviction that everything, or a large number of things, matter for our welfare, and that therefore the world should operate just so. Yet how can it affect my good if others worship the wrong god or the right god in the wrong way? Is it really a disaster if my neighbors enjoy open marriages and members of some political parties closed minds? Does it make sense to fight over what to eat for dinner, where to put the couch and whom never to invite again? These and many other issues have no significance and, in any case, whatever arrangement prevails soon passes away. But even nonexistence fails as a haven; some couples cannot leave their history alone, rehearsing old hurts in the quest to wound again.

If anything does not matter, it is the past. A modest amount of reflection is adequate to learn what one can from old mistakes; for the rest, we need to liberate ourselves from concern over the unchangeable. Yet we find it difficult to forgive even those we love, new wars are started to settle old scores and people who were never masters are invited to pay those who were never slaves huge sums in reparation for what happened to individuals long dead. The impulse to view everything as significant and hence demanding rectification will not let go of our minds, converting us into restless souls grotesquely busy with the attempt to reform, adjust and regulate the world. The result is frustration and pain, without much headway in making anything better.

The commitment to leave others alone and the conviction that many things in life do not matter are connected but they are not the same. We may decide to get out of the way of other people even though we think that what they do is both significant and annoying. Conversely, we may believe that many things do not matter, yet invade the autonomy of others out of wickedness or as nihilistic entertainment. Nevertheless, the commitment and the conviction go naturally together, each reinforcing the other in the quest for a sensible life. Thinking that only a relatively few things should be allowed to disturb our equilibrium invites us to let others explore their own concerns. In turn, the more we see others busying themselves with their own lives, the less we are tempted to believe that what they do is of significance to us. The result is improvement in the moral tone of society and a corresponding increase in human happiness.

My discussion of what cuts against appreciation of the different can serve as an outline of the obstacles in the way of a generous pluralism. Is fostering a variety of values, styles of life and types of person worth the price? I have already indicated that leaving others alone and believing that lots of things that happen hold little significance for us would yield important benefits. But many people love the comfort of belonging and the exhilaration of persecuting the different much more than they delight in sympathy for the alien or a just distribution of happiness. Therefore, it may well be that individuals in tightly knit, intolerant communities live more satisfying lives than those who have to deal with the disquieting challenges and demanding sensitivities of strangely different people in their midst.

That this is not a far-fetched conjecture is amply displayed by the internal concord of Spartan society and by the unproblematic calm of religious communities and of medieval Japan. Such little worlds can have their own problems and crises, but they are not typically due to the disintegration of their value-consensus. What attracts people to them is that the rightness of their customs receives reinforcement from all sides; no one defies the prevailing powers or denies the truth of shared ideas. Revealingly, we think of such agreement as a hallmark of heaven, where we enjoy praising the Lord in unison. Isolated fishing villages share this unanimity with the afterlife; in spite of their poverty, they provide a satisfactory social life due to concord about everything that matters.

Such uniformity of opinion and action is not a matter of choice for us, and it is quickly becoming unavailable for other communities, as well. The mobility of people, the easy accessibility of vast stores of information and the secularization of the world make it impossible for any nation to be a closed religious community or a modern Sparta. In some places, dissent and deviance are crushed and a coerced conformity appears to prevail for a while. But before long, imposed customs begin to crack and individual choice reestablishes alternative values and discordant modes of life. Despite efforts to control immigration, much of the world is now America, mixing races, religions, and ethnicities in ways that both break down and enrich original cultures. In the United States, the pluralism of values, religions, lifestyles, characters, customs, and preferences is a fact to be dealt with, not a choice to be made. It makes no sense to ask if we should opt for a homogeneous or a widely diversified society; pluralism is simply unavoidable.

This suggests that wisdom lies in tolerating the pluralism we find, permitting African Americans, Hispanics, gays, people of underappreciated ethnicity, transsexuals, and pacifists to carve out what existence they can in a society no longer overtly antagonistic toward them. The principle of leaving others alone recommends this passive attitude to what others do; accepting them and letting them do what they wish is tantamount to welcoming them into the community. Anyone who knows the history of exclusion will think this not a small matter. Historically, minorities by choice or nature have faced insuperable obstacles to full participation in the benefits of social life. They have been denied schooling, the vote, the right to hold property, the choice of occupation and of marriage partners, free movement, medical care, and sometimes even existence itself. The moral improvement of the human race has rendered these cruelties exceptional and unacceptable events. They still occur here and there, but the weight of public opinion and the might of civilized nations militate against them. A passive pluralism, tolerating a wide variety of values and allowing people of all sorts full social participation should be enough to fulfill the requirements of moral decency.

What duty demands, however, is inadequate for flourishing. Even the apple people sought to diversify the one fruit that fell to their lot, and they did so with good reason. Comforting as uniformity may be, in the end it does not satisfy. Boredom with the same is an attractive alternative to insecurity in times of stress, but when things settle down, we start searching for the excitement only the different can provide. This desire for variety may be inscribed in the curious, that is exploratory, nature of humans and animals. But even if it is not, we find it everywhere, suggesting that its satisfaction is a vital element of the fulfillment we seek. And, indeed, there is ample evidence that people who enjoy a combination of stability and change are more satisfied than those who enjoy either one without the other.

For this reason and for others, therefore, pluralistic society is, on the whole and within limits, more conducive to human flourishing than one that is uniform and inbred. I say "on the whole" because living in the midst of competing values is not an unmixed blessing; for people of rigid habits and firm convictions, putting up with what they may well think is wrong can entail distress. Only on balance, after factoring in the pain, is it appropriate to judge pluralistic societies to be better. And I say "within limits" because diversity can be so great, though that is certainly not a problem in our country today, that it destroys the shared values on which a society is based.

The positive pluralism to which this points requires not just the toleration of diversity, but also its encouragement. Different cuisines, divergent ways of relating to family, a variety of religious practices, and multiple conceptions of self and occupation serve as Mill's "experiments in living" without which many of the best approaches to dealing with our problems may well go unexplored. There is much to learn from the accumulated experience of other cultures and divergent traditions, and there is a special lesson in seeing that ethnic groups that were in their original homes mortal enemies can peacefully coexist in a country that

values them all. Variety provides us with choice, and choice with the opportunity to develop ourselves in directions we could not have imagined
on our own.

The pains attendant on positive pluralism are easier to bear if we keep
in mind the principle that many things in life do not matter much. Gay
marriage, for example, evokes visceral responses from many people.
This may be a battle over words, in which case it could perhaps be resolved by calling legally sanctioned gay lifetime commitments "unions"
instead of "marriages." But to the extent it is not, we could sensibly ask
ourselves what it is about single-sex relationships that matters so much
that we are prepared to throw generosity to the wind and deny them the
protections of the laws. How does it affect me if two men in Seattle or
two women on a Florida beach pledge to each other their eternal love? I
realize that deeply felt religious beliefs play an important role in the refusal to permit such things. But does it weaken one's religious resolve if
others do not agree with it and if worldly authorities do not enforce its
edicts? Conversion is of value only if voluntary; conformity achieved by
force cannot please a decent deity.

The same holds for many of the other fierce battles in the so-called
culture wars. The bitterness and intensity of the conflicts reveal that they
are struggles for power, that is, attempts to make others do what we want.
Very little in the way of substantive human welfare lies at the bottom of
these controversies: no one's life or happiness hangs on whether we may
display the Ten Commandments in a courthouse or outrageous paintings in a museum. For the most part, the source of the trouble is bruised
sensitivities. People take offense at seeing what they do not like in public
spaces, and launch campaigns to stifle harmless expressions of opinion.
One of the heartening moral developments of the past fifty years is
growing sensitivity to the sensitivities of others. Unfortunately, however,
sensitivities seem to expand in direct proportion to the willingness of
people to respect them. If we recognized the readiness to act hurt as an
instrument of controlling others, a calmer moral tone might begin to
suffuse our public conversations.

Positive pluralism opens us to the joy of diversity. Once we overcome
our dread of the different, the richness of the world engulfs us as a wave
and leaves our cleansed souls with gratitude and amazement. We become

like the apple people when they stumble upon a garden of bananas, strawberries, and grapes and realize for the first time all that they had missed. With them as with us, variety gives life; the multiplicity of values serves as food to build strong selves. We could never be the people we are if other people were not delightfully, resolutely, and in some cases radically different.

# PART THREE

# PLURALISM AND
# CHOICE-INCLUSIVE FACTS

# FOURTEEN

# RELATIVISM AND ITS BENEFITS

Perhaps it is our animal urge for security that turns us into dogmatists in manners and morals. As dogmatists, we live in glorious and safe ignorance of alternatives; we find it not unlikely but actually inconceivable that a style of life and a form of behavior—perhaps even a mode of dress and a fashion of wearing hair—different from ours could have any legitimacy or value. Being essentially insecure, the dogmatist pounces with fury upon each innocent change and contrary current; he senses danger, opposition, or conspiracy everywhere, and fights each deviation from his norms as if his life depended on it. The steadfast dogmatist is, therefore, immune to external change. He may be destroyed, but he will not change his mind; he would sooner lose his life than his illusions. In putting his life on the line in their defense, he will fancy himself the defender of all that is good and wholesome; the collapse of his cause and his inability to impose his will on the rest of this restless world will seem to him a tragic defeat of everything true and noble.

The dogmatist's faith in the universal moral standards he holds can survive every external test. Only the great internal crises of the human soul can shake the foundations of such deep and instinctive commitments. The sensitive dogmatist may someday find that judging by inflexible moral rules he must condemn the person whom his heart adores. This conflict of abstract principle with love may bring the whole edifice of his verbal morals tumbling to the ground.

The disintegration begins when he first demands a justification for his moral stance. How could one justify condemning a friend or one's mother for lying? We could syllogize: All acts of lying are bad, and this surely was an act of lying; hence, it was clearly bad. The dogmatist could wipe his hands of the matter at this point and never give it another thought, were it not for his nagging conscience. Why should we believe that lying is always bad? Lying is a form of deception, he might answer, and clearly all deception is bad. But this is no place to stop. That deception is bad itself stands in need of proof. How shall we demonstrate it?

Perhaps deception impedes the development of human faculties or interferes with their operation. If he cannot stop here, the dogmatist can perhaps maintain that such interference is bad because it causes pain or fails to create pleasure. Or because it fails to maximize the social good. Or perhaps even because God may not approve of it.

But will the previous question not recur? What is wrong with not creating pleasure when we could, or with letting the social good take care of itself? And why not try to enliven a dull eternity by refusing to obey God's will? Here we have come to ultimate values. There is no further principle to appeal to: reasoning ceases and the wheels of justification grind to a halt. Polite disagreement is abruptly left behind; ultimate commitments unfurled, we ride into combat for the true and good.

Faced with the need to show that his own ultimate values are universal and defensible, the dogmatist can rely on two strategies. He may say that certain ultimate values stand in no need of being justified; they are self-evident and shine by their own light. Alternatively, he may admit that every moral judgment must be vindicated. Specific ones can be supported by showing their relation to more general principles we hold. General principles, in turn, are justified in terms of some being or attitude or nonmoral state of affairs.

Will these strategies work? Not much can be said for the first of them. It is reassuring to think that there are universal moral, standards that can be known merely by reflection. If there were such principles, self-evident and knowable by mere intuition, moral disagreements could result only from haste in judgment or a clouding of the moral sense—nothing, surely, that sound education and a clear head could not cure.

Bishop Joseph Butler, the great eighteenth-century British moralist, writes as if he believed this when he recommends that to be sure our judgments are right we reflect on them "in a cool afternoon." But is the matter quite so simple as that? We are all familiar with what it is like to be totally convinced of the legitimacy of a value or the universal applicability of a moral standard. Yet, the very firmness of the conviction makes it suspect. Could it not be the expression and result of our gullibility? Does it really have the marks of objective truth?

What response can the defender of such ethical intuitions make to the man who is unable to see the self-evidence of some principle? What reply is possible to the philosopher who, after many earnest attempts, cannot see the universal truth of *any* moral judgment? What we want to say is that persons, actions, and consequences are good or bad as objectively as physical objects are red or green or blue. The colors are there for everyone to see. Similarly, the moral features of things are open to every sensitive person's scrutiny. Those who cannot recognize them are simply blind to the moral hues of life.

The analogy of color vision is striking and inventive. But in reality, it does not work to the intuitionist's advantage. The color any given object appears to have is only partly the result of its objective properties. The light in which we bathe it and the nature and condition of the sensory mechanism involved are equally indispensable determining conditions. The color varies with changes in any one of these three factors, at least one of which is the psychological and physiological condition of the subject.

This is sometimes countered by the claim that although an object may appear to have a variety of colors, its *real* color is that which an observer with normal sense organs operating under standard lighting conditions will perceive. This objection is, of course, worthless. The very fact that we have to stabilize the variables of lighting and sensory organs by calling them "standard" and "normal" constitutes an admission that all color determinations are relative to them. And what we shall call "normal" is perfectly arbitrary. Standard lighting conditions are those that resemble sunshine. But what if our sun were a red star? Normal observers are those that can see a "full" spectrum of colors, including red. What if the bulk of the population were red-green color defective? We simply cannot talk of colors without tacit or explicit reference to the nature and condition of the perceiver. The shrill insistence of the majority cannot make the color they see the *real* color of the object. Though I may have to heed their view, it will always remain a fact that the object appears red to many but a rich brown to me.

The case of values is analogous. What appears good is only partly a result of the objective features of the action or event. The principles or categories in terms of which a given culture or subculture views an action are in some respects similar to the lighting conditions we may use on an object of perception. And the nature and condition of the sensory mechanism is paralleled by those of the mechanisms of desire and preference in the agent.

Pleasure may appear good to some and evil to others. We cannot infer from this that one or the other side must be right though, as G. E. Moore generously conceded, it may be very difficult to establish which one. If disagreement is genuine and ultimate, as in morals it often is, pleasure will seem as genuinely good for Aristippus as it is bad for Cotton Mather. The natural conclusion to draw is that "good" and "bad" are relational terms: as with colors, we cannot meaningfully speak of the value of persons, actions, and consequences without reference to the categories of a culture and the standards and commitments of the man who judges. The moral hue of the world of action will change with changes in our social milieu and in the organ of our moral sight.

It is clear, then, that there are no self-evident objective—that is, universally true—moral principles. But if absolute values are after all, in need of justification, where shall we look for the principles that might support them? There are four areas to which we may turn for the foundation of morals: (1) society with its rules and attitudes and institutions, (2) human nature with its structure and laws of operation, (3) nature and its purposive constitution, and (4) God as the Infinite Lawgiver of creation.

Let me remark at once that if social rules and attitudes were to serve as the foundation upon which the structure of morality is erected, we could not legitimately say that values are absolute and unchanging. Persons, actions, and consequences would then be good as a result of their relation to socially established norms. While every society would have *some* values, there is no reason to suppose that the values of any one would coincide with those of any other.

One might attempt to argue for the universality at least such generic values as social cooperation and the survival of the members of the group. Yet this is a verbal gloss: It is a way of reading identity into diverse views and values by the expedient of calling them by the same name. "Social cooperation" among traditional Eskimos involves different values and fundamentally diverse modes of behavior from what is required for it in a tour group from Hoboken or in the Pentagon. Even today, "survival of the members of the group" means radically different things in Washington and Peking. Generalities sometimes reach the stage of becoming vacuous and verbal: there is no better example of this than the claim that all societies share a single vision of the good. Values, if social in origin, vary with societies. If they do, the similarity of societies is the measure of the uniformity of the good.

A similar observation should be made about the view that locates the source of values in human nature. If the view is true, values are uniform only to the extent that individual human natures coincide. It is clear, therefore, that absolute values could not be grounded this way without the ancillary tenet of a shared and unchanging human nature. Questions about the nature of man are notoriously difficult to handle. In any case, this would be no place to handle them, even if I could. There are a few things, however, that need to be said. They can be said briefly and with a reasonable degree of certainty. The question of what we shall be satisfied to call the nature of man is partly a definitional, and hence conventional, and partly an empirical matter. We always have the option of permitting our definitions to be guided by our preconceptions or our changing whims. We can go so far as to take the heroic course of disregarding most of the empirical evidence in our steadfast conviction that many of those who appear human do not properly deserve the compliment. If, however, we allow the suggestions of good sense to guide our concept formation, we shall find ourselves overwhelmingly committed to the view that human nature is no constant and that what we are dealing with is, at best, a wide spectrum of resembling individuals who do not share a single common essence. If human nature is to serve as the foundation of morals, the more reason we have to doubt the uniformity of man, the more we are entitled to deny the existence of universal values.

This leaves us with only two possible foundations for absolutistic morals. The first is the possibly infinite realm of facts we call Nature. Our dogmatist might take a cosmic perspective and assert that the world is saturated with potentialities that demand actualization. It is a law of nature, we might think, that beings with specific potencies must strive to reach fruition: Perfection consists in having what is latent discharged. Actualized being is both the aim and the result of potentiality; without it everything would be frustrated and incomplete. Thus value is or is grounded in the actuality that lures matter to create it.

The lawlike and natural connection between fact and fulfillment would amply suffice as the foundation of morals, were it not for the fact that it does not exist. The view that Nature is replete with potentialities aiming at self-realization and values that, although they do not yet exist, charm the world to make them actual is perhaps the most colorful of human fables. There is struggle and striving in the natural world. But who would want to say that each of a plenitude of beings aims at achieving some minor element of the cosmic good? We *can* look at things this way, just as we *can* see shadows as giants and each frog as a metamorphosed minor royalty. But in doing so we commit a great blunder: tacitly, we impute aim and consciousness to every natural impulse. The flux of nature has direction and frequently results in the production of some value. To suppose that direction implies an aim, that motion requires an underlying love of the beautiful and the good to generate it, is to view simple physical fact as if it had an element of mind animating it at every turn.

If we examine the facts calmly and free of the persistent drive to find more rationality in the world than it in fact displays, we will be struck less by the remarkable adaptation of means to ends and the direction of every impulse at its own actualization than by the spectacle of the mindless impartiality with which nature fulfills or frustrates its own potentials. There are millions of acorns for every tree: the phenomenon of discharged potency is the exception rather than the rule. Why should we disregard the wide compass of dysteleology and the plenitude of crushed potentials in nature? If we must see purposes in the flux, we might agree with the disenchanted Schopenhauers of the world that perpetual frustration of the will is the rule in nature and actualized good is for most a rare and furtive joy. In any case, to ground the concrete values of the moral life in some hypothetical cosmic principle that reads vestiges of mind into a mindless flux is as implausible as it is ill advised.

Let me finally speak of God's decrees as a possible support for human values. It is obvious that in grounding the good in divine commands we are presupposing the existence of a God who can make laws, proclaim rules of behavior, and create values as he sees fit. The existence of such a God seems highly dubious to me. I say this not as a person who believes in the existence of no deity at all, nor as one who refuses to accept the reality of a Christian God. My objection to the conception of God as an untrammeled creator of values and laws is precisely that it is not Christian enough, that it introduces the disturbing and religiously unacceptable element of arbitrary power into the concept of a Being of pure love.

One could dwell on the grave philosophical difficulties of such a concept of God. But that is another story. For now it is enough to make two points. If God is the source of all values, in one important sense they are not objective or absolute. At a minimum, they are binding values only because God chooses them. It is, to spell this out, only because of their relation to God that they are values at all. This should incline those who object to everything relative to mend their ways or at least to realize that it is not relativity they quarrel with but its terms. They think it all right for values to be relative to the whim of God, but not to the will of man.

Second, what are the conditions requisite for making the commands of an Infinite Being relevant to our finite lives? No command, whatever its source, could be binding on a person who lacked the intelligence to grasp it or the capacity to act on it. One cannot command a stone, or an Eskimo in Latin, no matter how elegant or fluent. Commands and values must suit the station and the circumstances, the nature and the capacities of the person who is to act on them or adopt them. Hence, even if all values have their source in God, their uniformity is not guaranteed. If human nature is varied, commands and values relevant to one man may be unsuited, perhaps even unintelligible, to others. The uniformity of

God's effective commands thus becomes dependent on the uniformity of human nature.

Was Protagoras, then, right in the end and is nothing good but thinking makes it so? There are a few things farther from the truth, but not many. We do not think or act as if mere thoughts and feelings could make much difference to what is good or bad. And if Protagoras were right, we could never be mistaken in our aims and values: Whatever we desired at any time would then be good, *for us.* Yet what could be a more painful or pervasive fact of life than moral error in choosing our goals? Inadequate self-knowledge frequently makes us adopt ends that do not satisfy. And who has not chosen the lesser over the greater, the nearer over the remote, the apparent over the real good?

Such shortsighted and inhumane relativism could never account for the bitter complexity of moral experience. But there is a relativism that many candid and tolerant minds spontaneously believe. Human nature is various; this variety, due to biological, social, and psychological conditions, must be construed not as a threat or an evil, but as a God-given bounty of being. A variety of natures implies a variety of perfections. Only the egotist, committed to seeing pale replicas of himself everywhere in the world, would want to impose the same values and the same mode of behavior on every living soul. Sanity and toleration demand that we allow each person to pursue his own, possibly unique form of fulfillment; if we had even a vestige of Christian love, we would rejoice in seeing the growth of any man toward his goal.

Values vary with the individual's nature. The good, therefore, is not a question of what we think or how we feel but of who we are. A person's nature, though not unchanging, is perfectly definite. This makes it possible for him to progress in self-knowledge. It also renders the goals that would fulfill him definable and his values precise. These values may differ from the ideal of the next man, but they are not less vital or legitimate.

Would moral or social anarchy not flow if we acted as though this view were true? Not in the least. If the nature of the individual determines his values, similar natures yield similar commitments. The fact that human beings live in cooperative societies is the best evidence that their natures are similar or at least compatible. This is assured by processes of socialization which are, on occasion, so successful that even people left free to do precisely what they want continue to do their usual, useful tasks. What little self-realization there may be that interferes with the fulfillment of others can be readily controlled by threats or a measure of force. In an orchestra each instrument plays its own tune; is this reason for saying that there is anarchy in the pit? The fact that values are individual does not entail that people must fail to agree on common goods and goals.

From the time that God or Adam called the first two philosophers into existence they and their descendants have argued about the ultimate source of values. Argument can go on too long. Even now, the interest of too many philosophers in the relativism I propose would be limited to developing it in its technical details. They could then discuss it and suggest minor changes in its formulation. One feels intellectually clean after such an exercise; by using the training we have in drawing useless distinctions, we think we justify it.

I earn my living by chopping my share of logic, so I cannot consistently denounce the procedure. In reality, it has an important role to play: We must explore and appraise what precisely is worthy of belief. I welcome that sort of hard-nosed inquiry into this view. But there is another task that is no less important. At some point we must announce results and go to the public to convince. The intellect's obligation to pursue truth is no greater than the demand on the will to disclose it. Philosophy must have its own technology: if science yields refrigerators and the Salk vaccine, philosophy should give us the tools for wisdom and an improving public mind.

Consider the benefits that would accrue if we could make this relativism generally accepted. The view is a secular variant of the beautiful thought of many theologians that even the least of his creatures has dignity and justification in the eyes of God. If sincerely believed, this thought could transform the soul. It would help allay our suspicion of all things alien. It could render us more modest and loving by showing the monstrous egotism displayed in judging another. As a result, we may develop a more tolerant and helpful attitude toward lifestyles and values different from those we like or admire; we could then begin to appreciate moral variety or the bounty of fulfillment and perfection open to humans. The personalities shaped by such beliefs and attitudes would be attuned to the beauty and harmony of life. The vast energy we consume in hate and in trying to shove our desires down reluctant throats could be harnessed to enhance our appreciation and joy. If such attitudes were dominant in it, human personality may for the first time reach the stage of not being disgusting.

If private improvement would be extensive, public benefits would likely be immense. Children could be brought up with fewer useless precepts and damaging attitudes. Education, both of intellect and of character, could at last lose some of its rigidity. Human relations could be infused with an element of humanity and understanding, and cooperation may well take the place of blind antagonism. Condemnation of other persons or nations becomes difficult in proportion as we see the legitimacy of differing ideals. Moral pseudo-justifications of much hatred and war would, therefore, at once be closed off to those who take the relativity of values seriously.

The greatest beneficiary of the universal acceptance of moral relativism would, without doubt, be human liberty. There is a shrill, constrictive tone to many of our laws. They impinge on fields where compulsory social prescriptions are inappropriate. Most of the laws we loosely group as designed to enforce the uniformity of morals would be seen as unjustified, if we were all relativists. This would increase the scope of human choice and render all manner of human action free.

Evidently the firmest social or state controls are necessary to protect persons from the real harm others would do them. But due allowance must be made for the difficulty of generalizing about what is to count as harm. The experience that would be harmful to a child may well mean fulfillment to an adult homosexual. If we forbid that children be tempted into such actions, must we also forbid it to consenting adults? And what is the imaginary public interest requiring that monogamy be the sole law of the land? Attention to differences in desires and temperaments would reveal such restrictions on human interaction as intolerant, if not insane.

Society would not collapse if we were to let a hundred flowers bloom. To be sure, it would be different in structure and operation from what it is today. But I cannot count myself among those who think there can be no improvement of the way things are.

But if believing and acting on moral relativism would have such profound impact on the nature of men and society, is it a mere accident that we have not yet accepted it? I cannot think so. Our beliefs and acts surely express our nature; what violates the integrity of our being or would tend to change it is difficult to embrace. Instinctive dogmatists will find it hard to see the merits of relativism on intellectual grounds alone.

Our best hope to escape egotism is by appealing to it. The individual's choice of making the world or even a small segment of it live by his values is negligible. With the increase in social regimentation and the growth of large impersonal institutions each person finds, in fact, ever more trouble in freely conforming even his own conduct to his ideals. A cutback in scope promises increase in intensity: sound self-interest demands that each attend to his own life and leave the moral state of others their sole business. The alternative is to lose control even of one's self, a frequent condition of ambitious egotists.

At stake is the eternal hope to tame human nature. Benevolence may be too high an ideal. Toleration of others would be enough or, as an absolute minimum, indifference to how they shape their fate. If we could only believe moral relativity, we would have the intellectual foundation of such indifference. Our nature could then be changed enough to merit being called human. We might even render our lives joyous and our survival assured. When shall we go to work?

# FIFTEEN

# THE ELEMENT OF CHOICE
# IN CRITERIA OF DEATH

Death is easier to undergo than to understand. It comes unbidden, or we can attain it with minimal effort. Yet, the willfulness of human nature makes it difficult for us to settle for the easy; we want understanding of it, not the experience.

Thought begins with the silent assumption that words reveal the world; the unitary noun "death" must, therefore, be the name of a single phenomenon. Since we can readily distinguish living persons from decomposing bodies, it is natural to suppose that death is something interposed between these two, a happening that rends the smile of life and reduces us to a heap of cooling cells. But if "death" denotes such an event, it must occur at some precise moment between the time we still thrive and the hour our remains are interred. Lives terminate at some point, we all seem to agree; there must therefore be a simple and correct answer at any time to the question of whether given people are then alive. If they had been born and have not died, they are still with us; if they died, we should be able to determine how long they have been gone. Death, then, appears to be a point-event that separates us from the dark. It is a single, simple, irreversible happening that has temporal location but no temporal dimension: it occurs at a time, yet it takes up no time in occurring. It is an instantaneous affair.

This is not only where thought begins; it is also where it ends for many earnest people. Physicians tend to conceptualize death in this way and find support for their view (when they think confirmation is needed) among certain philosophers. Even the President's Commission for the Study of Ethical Problems in Medicine and Biomedical and Behavioral Research endorses this idea in drawing a distinction between the temporal process of dying and death as an instantaneous event. It quotes with approval the view of Bernat, Culver, and Gert that "death should be viewed not as a process but as the event that separates the process of dying from the process of disintegration."[1] I readily acknowledge the attractiveness of this approach. We are, after all, either dead or alive, and which of the two appears to be a matter of empirical fact. If so, it should be possible to articulate the correct criteria of death, which the Commission promptly undertakes to do.

We should note, however, that such simple and attractive views carry a danger. They seem so right, they tend to paralyze the mind. They stunt critical inquiry and thereby make it difficult to uncover their hidden commitments. Since even the simplest views are based on assumptions, the result is inadequate self-understanding on the part of those committed to them and general inability to give them a just appraisal.

The theory that death is simply an event in nature has its own central assumptions. For if it is a purely biological phenomenon, our proper cognitive relation to it is that of discovery. Its status then resembles that of America before Columbus's arrival: It is there ready for the light of knowledge to fall on it, ready to be detected and explored. To be sure, our continent was not *called* America before the Europeans arrived. But discoverers add only the name; they do not create the lands. So it seems to be with death also; it is a natural phenomenon we discover and then name. We contribute nothing to its existence; on the contrary, its prior reality makes our inquiry possible and useful. Our initial, natural view commits us in this way to a realist ontology concerning death.

## Three Sorts of Cases

To see how much of an unjustified presumption is involved here, we need to distinguish three different sorts of cases. There are some instances, such as that of the Pacific before Balboa beheld it, in which objects enjoy existence independently of any cognitive or conative human act. In a radically different set of cases, existence is totally the outcome of our activities. The meeting of a board of directors, for example, is an occurrence altogether dependent on human acts and practices. For no one is a director except in a complex social context, and no meeting of those who are directors is a meeting of the board unless its scheduling and convening follow established rules.

There are also intermediate cases in which human choice and action build on preexisting things or conditions to create a novel object. No person is fat apart from human judgment, yet corpulent people are not created by our perception or our whim. There is an underlying physical reality: the distribution of weight among the population. This continuum, ranging from those who weigh less than one hundred pounds to individuals who tip the scales at over five hundred, then receives a human contribution that breaks it into the loose categories of the thin, the average, and the fat. Such categorization, based on taste, tradition, and social purposes, is by no means trivial. It establishes new objects, namely, groups of people judged to be deserving of differential treatment medically, socially, and in our personal relations.

In the human world, there are a very large number of cases of this third variety. The law and our social practices frequently call on us to draw relatively sharp lines to separate phases of an otherwise continuous process or to stress the differences among remarkably similar conditions. Such differentiations represent human contributions to physical facts: they express our choices and embody our values. The person who wants a fine lawn needs to kill noxious growths. But in its physical constitution, nothing is a weed. Weeds are physico-social objects, namely, broad-leafed plants that grow, undesirably, in the grass. The combination of independent existents and selectivity expressing human interests and purposes is evident here, as it is when we call someone smart or beautiful, or when we set the time at which a young person can begin to drive, or when we fix the end of the Middle Ages.

In which of the three types of cases does death belong? Although some people, Christian Scientists perhaps, view it as a human creation or illusion, it is unlikely that death lacks objective basis. Does this mean, however, that it is an exclusively physical event that "separates the process of dying from the process of disintegration"? Although this is the currently favored position, I do not think that it is right. Persons of scientific sophistication should have long had their suspicion aroused by the notion of death as an instantaneous point-event, for such presumed occurrences resemble humanly contrived termini much more closely than they do the unbroken temporal processes we find in nature. The function of determining the *exact moment* of death yields another bit of evidence against the purely physical view. Our interest in this is largely legal, not scientific: We want to know in order to establish criminal liability or, as in the case of multiple deaths in a family due to a single accident, to clarify the pattern of inheritance.

### Death a Physico-Social Reality

The role this notion of the death-event plays in our common practices provides added confirmation that the object it identifies is not a purely physical reality but a physico-social one. Our primary purpose in applying the concept of death to people is to indicate a very important point of change in our relations to them. So long as people are alive, certain activities are obligatory while others are forbidden with respect to them. If we are members of their family or of the team that cares for them, we must, for example, attempt to communicate with them, to ascertain their wishes, and to aid them when appropriate. On the other hand, we are not permitted to open their safety deposit boxes and read their wills, to perform autopsies on them or to cart them to the cemetery for burial. The relations and the activities that embody them change in a radical way once death has taken place. It then becomes acceptable for us to treat our patients and loved ones in the ways our society deems appropriate to the dead.

No one would want to deny, of course, that there are important differences between those alive and the dead. These divergences constitute the objective foundation for distinguishing the two. But how much difference there must be and which traits or activities of the living must change in order for us to say that they have died are matters of judgment. Since the concept of death functions as a trigger or an indicator to alter our activities with respect to those to whom it is applied, it must involve a social standard of decision about when such change of behavior is proper.

In developing criteria of death, then, we must do two things instead of the one usually supposed. On the one hand, we must attend to the facts of organic decline; this is an empirical inquiry about independently existing biological phenomena. On the other hand, we must also formulate a socially acceptable decision about precisely where in the continuum of decay to draw the line between the living and the dead. This is essentially a normative activity in which we bring tradition, religious and moral values, and social utilities to bear on important human relations.

## Value Elements in the Choice of Death Criteria

The current line of thought sheds new light on the conflict between the whole-brain and the neocortical criteria for declaring a person dead. Advocates of each position tend to view the controversy as factual, namely, as a disagreement about when or under what circumstances death *in fact* occurs. It should be obvious by now that there is no factual solution to this debate and that both sides, when they insist on one, betray inadequate self-understanding.

There can be no objective solution because there is no empirical disagreement; neither side offers an alternative biology. The real opposition, though misleadingly couched in factual terms, is conceptual, and that conceptual conflict is grounded in incompatible value commitments. Advocates of the neocortical view tend to think of humans in terms of the category of persons and thus regard death as the cessation of such higher activities as feeling, consciousness, self-consciousness, and reflection. Proponents of the whole-brain thesis, by contrast, adopt the ancient and perhaps more inarticulate idea that humans are intimately connected with or inseparable from all of their integrated bodily acts.

This conceptual disagreement is but the cognitive expression of divergent valuations. Champions of the neocortical view prize consciousness and the activities it makes possible. The vehemence of their affirmation that a life lacking awareness (and related acts) is worthless sometimes takes the form of refusing to call biological existence without neocortical function "life" at all. Their reasoning proceeds not from the objective recognition that cessation of higher brain functions is tantamount to death. Instead, though often only tacitly, they move in the opposite direction: initial commitment to the all-importance of certain activities makes them choose destruction of the organs supporting those activities as the indicator of death.

Advocates of the whole-brain criterion think in a similar fashion. But their devotion, no doubt traditional and religious in derivation, is to integrated bodily acts. Factual considerations come in only when they try to establish the biological foundation of those acts. Cessation of the integrative work of the entire brain, then, is not the sign of when death *in fact* takes place; it is where we must place the point of death if we have an antecedent commitment to the importance of integrated bodily function.

We cannot, therefore, adjudicate the conflict of criteria in anything less than frankly normative terms. The question to ask is not when death *really* occurs but why we should draw the line between life and death at the higher cognitive rather than at the lower integrative activities. Recast in these terms, we can develop a better understanding of the differences between the criteria and hope eventually to resolve their conflict in a socially acceptable way.

### Biological Facts, Social Decision

The essence of my claim is that formulating a criterion of death involves, in addition to factual considerations, a social decision. Whether the heart beats is an empirical matter susceptible of factual determination. Whether when the heart stops beating death has occurred involves the application of a social standard. This standard is not written into the nature of things and, accordingly, cannot be read off from the facts of biology. It is established by taking biological realities into account and then making a more or less conscious communal choice. The choice is not dictated by what we know of the operations of the body; religious, social, moral, and technological considerations also play a part. That, for example, we insist on the *irreversibility* of the cessation of heart, lung, or brain function is not a matter of recognizing what death is; it is an expression of our interventionist values. What it means is that we refuse to view anyone as dead so long as there is something we can do to sustain or restart the biological machinery.

In other cultures, the normative and religious milieu make cardiac resuscitation unthinkable; when the gods stop life, such people might believe, it is sacrilege for humans to interfere. Those who respond by claiming that our practice is superior yield the point at issue by moving to the normative plane. For then they agree that criteria of death are far from being purely factual: if irreversibility, for example, is not a part of them, then it ought to be.


## Other Societies

If I am correct that locating death along the continuum of organic decline involves a social choice, it is likely that different societies place it at different points. And that is precisely what both history and anthropology show. People in some societies have, not unreasonably, decided that no one is dead until the next sunup after spontaneous movement ceases. In other cultures, expressing different values and divergent natural constraints, death has been pegged at the point where people get sufficiently weak to consume more social goods than they can produce. Traditional Eskimos might have had something like that in mind when they invited infirm old people to lessen the community's burden by walking into the blizzard or the night. Cruel and unacceptable as this might seem to a society in need of consumers, it was clearly reasonable and legitimate under then prevailing circumstances. I note that even there death had a physical basis, but it was supposed to occur relatively early in the process of decline and disintegration. The act of walking out into the snow was not suicide but proper acknowledgment of the fact that in the eyes of the community, one was already dead. Along with whatever weaknesses it displays, this view has an intriguing and beautiful feature. In industrial society, our last act is an involuntary movement of the heart, lung, or brain. Eskimo culture permitted many the privilege of a last act that was not only voluntary but also virtuous and noble.

My point is not to urge the superiority of Eskimo ways. I use their example to underscore the fact that the point of death can be situated at a number of places along the continuum of organic decline. Where we put it is a matter of choice determined by the beliefs, values, and circumstances of the community. The naively realistic view of death obscures this centrally important element of choice. Yet even the most fervent belief that death is something the criterion of whose occurrence can be discovered or read off from the facts cannot eliminate the element of social decision involved in formulating it. The naiveté of the realistic view, well exemplified in the report of the President's Commission, succeeds only in keeping the choice unconscious and hence uncriticized. The thought that we can *discover* the point of death conceals from us what we really do and thereby makes an intelligent examination of our activity impossible.

## Death a Biologically Based Social Status

My argument shows that we have reason to think of death not as a simple organic condition but as a biologically based social status. Since the status is social in nature, there are public and community-wide standards for determining it. This is the truth behind the claim that the decision of when one is dead cannot be left to personal whim. The choice of which I speak is not, therefore, that of the individual physician or of the patient. It is a choice the community must make, or has made, as displayed in its rules and practices. The physician merely applies this customary or statutory standard.

We need to remind ourselves that the presence of human decision does not remove generality, only the comfort of supposing that our ideas are replicas of reality and hence our beliefs accord cozily with the nature of things. The choice, moreover, is obviously less than unconditional or absolute: no society is free to set as the sole criterion of death a sneeze or a strong itch under the left armpit. The line of death must be drawn at some significant point on the continuum of personal decline. But such disintegration involves the change or cessation of a multiplicity of activities; societies have considerable leeway in pinpointing death at the stage where functions of particular interest to them become impossible to perform.

*Activities and Costs*

If the line between life and death is drawn on the basis of a social decision, what factors influence this choice? Two considerations appear to be always present. The first is, as I have just indicated, the identification of important activities that, when one can perform them no more, is a sufficient reason for thinking one dead. Declarations of death are, therefore, at once (though tacitly) statements about what the individuals involved are no longer able to do. The second consideration is the assessment of our responsibilities to declining people and of the cost of carrying them out. We have many duties to people who are alive; declaring them dead instantly eliminates a host of these obligations, imposes only a few new ones, and makes hitherto unacceptable acts appropriate.

Lest I sound cynical in mentioning the cost of locating death at one place or another in the biological continuum, let us remember that societies hard-pressed have always set the point of death on a cost-benefit basis at the early stages of nonfunctionality. In many contexts, elderly Eskimos could still function reasonably well. But the cost of supporting them through debility and disease was thought too high for the meager resources of their community. When Europe suffered from the plague, individuals with the first signs of the disease were treated in ways appropriate to the dead: the health costs of providing treatment or even the comfort of companionship were judged intolerable. The long-term maintenance of numbers of humanly nonfunctioning biological wrecks is a luxury open only to rich and stable societies. I hesitate to infer from this that none but the very wealthy can do what is morally right.

The growth of technology and the rapid increase in the number of old people in our own society may make cost considerations paramount again. If the number of individuals with severe neocortical and other organic damage but functioning brainstem were to increase dramatically, another President's Commission may well find the cessation of higher brain activity an adequate criterion of death. As an absolute minimum, escalating healthcare costs are likely to cause a reconsideration of the current requirement of the irreversibility of the cessation of key organic functions. Our actual practice of refusing resuscitation to significant numbers of terminal patients, clearly at odds with the Presidential Commission's criterion, already shows recognition of the deeper wisdom that although some heart stoppages may well be reversible, from a human standpoint they are not worth reversing.

It should be clear from these comments that the cost of what we would have to do for certain groups of people if they were judged to be alive is a factor, and sometimes the decisive factor, in formulating a criterion of death. But in many, if not most, cases the primary consideration in the social decision underlying the definition of death is what individuals at different stages of organic disintegration can do. The issue is in part one of technology: with the aid of suitable devices, we can now do more over a longer period than ever before. But for the rest, it comes to a question of our beliefs, values, and needs, or they shape our view of the hierarchy of human activities.

What are the acts and achievements absence of which has been supposed to render one dead? Even if we leave out the personal and idiosyncratic failures of function for which individuals have rendered themselves dead, we find a bewildering variety of activities. I have already mentioned relative economic unproductivity and the early signs (with minimal loss of function) of contagious disease. We can add loss of rational control over one's life, loss of strength sufficient to prevail in combat, permanent loss of consciousness, loss of pulmonary function, loss of cardiac activity, and loss of the integrated operations of the entire brain. At the spiritual end, we find irreparable damage to the proper work of the soul or to one's relations with God. At the other extreme, death is supposed to occur only when all biological activity, down to the cellular level, has ceased or when putrefaction sets in. There is hardly any significant human activity that some society or subculture has not thought crucial to life and whose loss has not been supposed to signal death.

## Is Death Not a Biological Fact?

An objection is likely to be urged, perhaps quite impatiently, at this point. Those who insist on the pure factuality of medical science may indicate displeasure with the way I seem to mix the social and the biological, what to them appears as the optional and the compulsory. This tends to blur the distinction between ostracism, traumatic or destructive community practices, metaphorical senses of "death," self-sacrifice and suicide on the one hand, and the stubborn reality of the cessation of biological function on the other. Modern medicine takes little interest, I may rightly be reminded, in odd social rituals. Its gaze is fixed on the natural process that underlies human interaction and whose end destroys its possibility. Whatever a community does to or requires of its members, their actual death does not occur until their bodies give out. The definition of death should therefore reflect this primacy and ultimacy of the physical.

This is a serious objection, and although much of my discussion so far has been devoted to showing the dubiety of its assumptions, it deserves a straightforward response. I begin by happily granting the importance of biological process. My concern is only with our current supposition of its all-importance. Life is a very large collection of activities; the cessation of some, many, or most of these constitutes death. I want to stress that not *all* the operations of life cease at any point where death is supposed to occur: some residual activities and relations go with us to the grave. There is, therefore, significant selectivity in deciding which activities are central for life and which are peripheral. The President's Commission, for example, maintains that brain integration of biological function is essential; its absence is a sure sign, or is even the very nature, of death. By contrast, apparently on the theory that cellular activity is necessary but not sufficient for organized life, its continued presence is declared irrelevant to the death of the organism.[2] Those who favor cessation of neo-cortical function as the criterion of death, on the other hand, insist on the centrality of the cognitive and conative activities associated with consciousness. To them, continued organic process, even if system-wide, is insufficient to keep persons alive.

## The Choice of Which Life Activities Are Central

How are the "essential" operations selected from among all those that compose human existence? All choice presupposes interests or purposes or values. The focus of physicians is the biological substratum of life, its roots and not its flower. Understandably, therefore, they give preference to causally central, capacitating processes. Are these, in fact, the crucial operations of life? Almost certainly, if we identify life with organic existence and thus adopt the biological perspective of medicine. But if we seek the fruit of life and not its sustaining causes, the view of medicine may well appear reductivist and inadequate. The activities selected as central to life will then be thought, emotion, and the other higher functions; their termination will constitute death just as really as cardiopulmonary failure does for the physician.

We can see, then, that the selectivity necessary for identifying central life activities inevitably carries us past the factually empirical. It introduces a set of interests and a system of correlated values. The biological perspective common to physicians is itself a social creation with its own underlying purposes. It is largely the collective possession of an entire, important subculture in our society. And this society permits, encourages, even fosters the predominance of the biological perspective in the medical subculture because of the immense health benefits it provides.

None of this presents a problem if it is properly understood. But the precise factuality of science and vast success of medicine tend to make us forget about the interests and the selectivity that underlie them. Expertise is easily converted into truth: insensibly, we drift into thinking that biology and biochemistry and medicine provide an accurate, literal, and complete account of human reality. Medicine becomes, in this way, the final arbiter of life and death: we look to it for precise information, for solutions to our problems, even for reliable standards of when life, and not merely its biological support, ends.

### Standards of Health and Death Socially Established

When we convert the results of this important but conditioned and limited enterprise into unconditional truth, we lose sight of the vital role social decisions play in establishing it and shaping its structure, and in setting the standards of health and death. This inattention is the source of the false idea that death is a purely natural terminus that involves no human activity other than the attempts of the health care team to retard or to reverse it.

In fact, we cannot understand death and cannot even hope to establish rational criteria for it without putting it in its proper historical and social context. If we do that, we see at once the omnipresence of human activity, the way in which our choices and values surround, frame, structure, channel, establish, accelerate, and in some cases eliminate natural processes. The best way to remind ourselves of this centrality of human purposes is to call attention to the diversity of social practices. The absence of this cross-cultural or anthropological perspective renders much contemporary discussion of the criteria of death one-dimensional and the deliberations of the President's Commission sterile and unsatisfying.

My response, then, to persons who charge that in discussing death I mix social and biological considerations is warm congratulations. They have detected my strategy; I hope that at this point they can even see my arguments for it. If they do, they may come to agree with me that we are unlikely to make progress in this field without due attention to the social and normative context, that is, to the deliberate choices we must make and the reasons for them.

### How to Choose a Death Criterion

How does paying heed to choice and value help us in assessing the relative merits of the whole-brain and neocortical views of death? First, it protects us from the misleading suppositions, fatal for inquiry, that the primary issue between these competing theories is either factual or conceptual. It is, of course, absolutely essential to get the relevant facts exactly right. And conceptual clarity and precision are equally important. But these are initial requirements only; without agreement that is hammered out of the traditions and beliefs of the community and that takes due account of social utilities, they are inadequate to establish the line between life and death.

In our society, the agreement is pursued and achieved within the confines of the political system in its broadest and most inclusive sense. This system can operate only if public discourse is free and enlightened. Such discussion of community policy, in turn, presupposes accurate information and an educated citizenry. The role of physicians is not to inform us of when death *in fact* takes place but to provide reliable knowledge of the stages of organic disintegration. And the job of philosophers is not so much to resolve thorny ontological problems about the personhood of human beings as to focus public discussion and political decision making by the critical examination of our beliefs and of the consequences of the values we embrace.

The report of the President's Commission was political in just this sense: It offered itself as a voice in the social dialogue, presenting a criterion of death that might be generally acceptable. But lacking a clear understanding of the central role of values in any such proposal, it attempted, erroneously, to pass off its results as supportable by scientific facts. Such a naively realistic approach may be thought to be rhetorically effective: who, after all, would want to contradict what physicians say about the objective realities that fall within their domain? Yet the conclusions of the Commission have succeeded neither in enlightening public discourse nor in stilling the controversy surrounding the conditions under which a person should be viewed as dead. Lasting agreement will not be achieved until we develop a reflective and public consensus of the relative strengths and weaknesses and of the costs and benefits of rival positions.

## Whole-Brain or Neocortical View?

### THE WEIGHT OF TRADITION

This is obviously not the occasion to work out the details of such an assessment. I will sketch only its outlines, calling attention to the sorts of considerations we must take into account. I have already indicated that these fall into three broad categories. First, any attempt to establish the line of death must reckon with our habits, traditions, and established practices. These appear to be a mixed bag: some favor the more conservative whole-brain criterion, while others are readily compatible with the neocortical view. We have, for example, the deepest devotion to the human body, caring for it and treating it with respect well past the point where such regard can do the person inhabiting it any good. We also have habits of optimistic intervention that make it difficult for us to admit that anyone is past hope and nearly impossible to feel released of the obligation to continue to benefit them.

Such practices support the view that death cannot be thought to occur until centrally controlled organic activity ceases, or perhaps until even later. But other established forms of behavior point to permanent loss of the higher conscious functions as the proper dividing line between the living and the dead. Our spontaneous attitudes to people do, after all, undergo radical change when we find them unresponsive in a deep coma. And those closest to patients so afflicted, the members of their family and of their health care team, tend to deal with them in a way that is clear-eyed and unsentimental. This is amply displayed in the widespread practice of denying resuscitation not only to comatose individuals but also to those in advanced stages of senility and to terminal patients in drug-induced stupor.

### THE ROLE OF ESTABLISHED BELIEFS

Our shared beliefs show the same ambiguity as our practices. On the one hand, we have such a strong commitment to the value of individuals that the possibility of false positives—the survival, reversal, or misdiagnosis of the loss of higher conscious functions—makes us suspicious of the neocortical view. Although nineteenth century fears of burying people who seem dead but are somehow alive are no longer with us, we are reluctant to believe that individuals who appear physically intact and may even breathe on their own could, nevertheless, be irremediably dead. On the other hand, we also believe that people who have permanently lost consciousness have undergone a profound change and that respectful treatment of their bodies is largely the expression of residual respect for who they had been. When such treatment becomes protracted and burdensome, the people directly involved with it, who tend to understand the situation best, generally agree that though the body may linger, the person is no longer there.

Our beliefs in these matters were formed under the influence of our religious heritage. But the Judeo-Christian tradition is itself of two minds about the significance of the body for true life. It invites us to consider our physical nature as but the earthly shroud we should be happy to shed or as a prison we must be eager to escape. At the first reliable sign, therefore, that the human (not the vegetative) soul has fled, we should be comfortable in disposing of the body as we would of any other piece of unneeded matter. Yet, another powerful element in the tradition insists that the connection between person and body is far more intimate. If, in this world at least, the soul is inseparable from the body, respect for people is respect for their earthly forms. Moreover, it is not for us to decide when the physical tenure of persons comes to an end: We must support them without fail until God's will is made manifest by the total ruin of their bodies.

The line of death we draw should be conservative in the sense that it agrees, to the greatest extent possible, with our practices and beliefs. My discussion so far makes it clear that neither of these clearly favors the neocortical over the whole-brain criterion. The deliverance of the third central consideration—social utility—is, however, almost univocal. In every respect but two, drawing the line at the total cessation of the integrative activity of the brain entails vastly more cost than its rival. Of the two, one is purely economic, namely, the employment by the hospital industry of a significant number of people for the purpose of caring for permanently comatose individuals. Given the availability of more productive, alternative employment, this is not a compelling consideration. The other cost of a neocortical criterion is the possibility of error it presents. After all, it is conceivable that people who appear to have lost all higher conscious functions may at some later time astoundingly regain them. But additional vigilance readily reduces or eliminates this cost; the criterion must be so phrased and applied that the recovery of anyone about to be declared dead is only a logical, not a clinical, possibility.

For the rest, the neocortical view is vastly preferable. The suffering of patients who are capable of feeling pain but not of taking or asking for countermeasures, the protracted torture of their families, the sensed impotence of the health care team, and the unproductive use of social resources all point to the unwisdom of the whole-brain view. As any observer of the current scene knows, social choice between the two criteria is not easy. But if they are our major alternatives, rational assessment favors destruction of the neocortex as the better place to draw the line of death.

## The Individual-Centered Multiple Criterion View

Are these views, however, the only major contenders? There is another one that has, for the most part, escaped the notice of philosophers. That it enjoys broad support is demonstrated by the spread of legislation permitting people to write living wills. Because we tend not to think of the criterion of death as chosen, we have failed to recognize the remarkable fact that such laws empower people to adopt their own criterion. The multiplicity of criteria from which persons can freely choose is necessary for the good death and particularly appropriate to the political system we have adopted. The matter is complex, so here I shall only sketch the nature of, and the arguments for, this individual-centered multiple criterion view.

If our exertions are mere motion without consciousness, there is no such thing as the good life. Similarly, if departing this world is a clinical point-event, there can be no good death. Although there are clear asymmetries between the good life and the good death, there are certain important similarities due, in large measure, to the presence in each of what makes for the good anywhere. At any rate, the good life and the good death form an integral whole. This is well expressed in Aristotle's view that a timely and fitting exit is necessary for the completion of a rich and satisfying existence. It is difficult to think of happiness as constituted by less than just such a structured and meaningful life. The sensible conclusion to which this leads is that death is a part of life (even though it may well be the last part), and that the good death is an indispensable element in the happy life.

## The Good Death

Innocent as this view may sound, it has important political consequences. For combined with our inalienable right to pursue happiness, it implies that we have a similar right to seek the good death. Mindless legislation banning suicide violates this right. It is astounding that the President's Commission, though entrusted to deal with ethical problems, shows no awareness of the distinction between death and the good death, of the relation of the good death to the good life, and consequently of the right of individuals to self-determination in the matter of when, how, and under what circumstances they shall expire.

For those who do not favor the rhetoric of rights, the same point can be made in different language. In our country, it is established public policy to promote such central values as liberty. Freedom cannot exist, of course, without limit. But the spirit (though not always the letter) of our laws, well supported by fundamental moral principles, is to restrict the liberty of each only where it infringes on the liberty or welfare of others, and to leave it unabridged in matters relating to the individual alone. Since death is paradigmatically a private matter, it follows that its determination should be left open to individual control to the greatest extent possible.

In a very general analysis, the good life has three basic conditions or ingredients. We must have desires and purposes, we must be fortunate enough to live in circumstances where they can be satisfied, and we must have the capacity and energy actually to achieve them. Without the convergence of will, luck, and power, the good life is impossible; even Stoic control and Eastern resignation presuppose certain aims and, if nothing else, the luck of having the internal strength to crush worldly desires. The lack of power yields envy and bitterness; the absence of will makes existence meaningless; without luck, life remains a frustrated quest.

The good death has the same conditions as the good life. First and foremost, we must be fortunate enough not to pass away before our time. We must avoid extravagant cravings, such as that for endless physical life, and frame sensible desires about the time and manner of our demise. Finally, we must have the power to achieve what we want either by taking direct action or by causing others to respect our will.

The coincidence of will and power makes for effective autonomy. The role of the state is to respect and to safeguard this autonomy in the choice of death no less than in the decisions of daily life. To afford people control over their own death amounts to giving them power to determine how they are to be treated. Autonomy in the choice of conditions under which we no longer wish to live, therefore, requires our legal and social empowerment to decide when members of our health care team are to cease their labors and begin to treat us in ways appropriate to the dead.

## Choice of One's Own Death Criterion

If my earlier argument that death is a biologically based social status is correct, to say that someone is dead is partly to affirm that the person has reached a certain stage of organic decline and (most important) partly to indicate a change in our relations to that individual. As a signal, the declaration is meant to shape our expectations and to revise our obligations. Such statements must not be made lightly or without warrant. What justifies them is an assessment of which significant activities the individual in question can no longer perform. Who is to determine what these valued activities are? The decision is best left to the persons involved; only they can judge what is of paramount importance in their lives and when their existence is no longer worth its cost. In a pluralistic democracy, we can acknowledge this sovereignty of individuals over their lives and leave the timing and manner of death to personal choice. Instruction by competent individuals of their fellows about the circumstances under which they no longer wish to be treated as living persons does not require an instant funeral. There are stages in our dealings with the dead; the initial declaration, though it precipitates complex social and legal changes, may demand only the cessation of treatment or, more controversially, active steps to bring a recalcitrant heart in line with its owner's will.

There must, of course, be limits to such self-determination. The decision about the timing of one's death, though not irrevocable, must be serious and sincere. And there has to be an appropriate biological basis for the choice: those suffering from sinus colds or impacted wisdom teeth must be barred from the decision. But persons even in the early stages of terminal or degenerative ailments clearly qualify: cancer patients, for example, and those afflicted with Lou Gehrig's disease should be free to determine the criterion, fulfillment of which is an adequate sign that they are dead. We should, in other words, leave it in their hands to decide where in the natural process of disintegration life no longer serves their human purposes. The time at which heart, lung, or brain ceases to function is not, then, for those who decide otherwise the moment of their death; in their cases, these customary signs serve only as the physical confirmation of what took place before.

### Where Autonomy Is Impossible

The individual-centered multiple criterion approach is obviously inapplicable to microcephalics, accident victims without living wills, and those in a persistent vegetative state. This third view focuses on the good death, and for people in such unfortunate circumstances, the good death is not possible. In their cases, the autonomy principle cannot be applied because they are not in a position to will anything or to act on their desires. For them, all we can hope for is an institutionally made humane decision.

The best place to draw the line of death in such cases is the cessation or, in some cases, the irreversible cessation of neocortical function. Our ability to sustain bodily processes beyond the point where they are of any conceivable personal benefit has generated a desperate need to distinguish between biological and human life. In view of the success of medicine and the sciences, we must make extraordinary efforts to remember that biological processes serve only as the support and substratum of human existence. When we unalterably lose the ability to will and do, to think and hope, to feel and love, we have ceased existence as human beings. The only humane course then is to declare us dead and to treat us accordingly. If the diagnosis is careful and accurate, we need have no fear that this harms anyone: once the human person is gone, in the faltering body no one is there.

# SIXTEEN

# HUMAN NATURES

If I drive south from Nashville, Tennessee, in less than ten hours I will run upon a large body of water. The existence of this sea is an objective fact: It was there before the first human being swam in it, it is there when no one beholds it, it will likely be there when we evacuate the earth and move on to pollute other planets. Even if, following some bizarre conception, a mad dictatorship denied its existence, its waves would continue to wash its shores, its fish would still frolic over oyster beds. I offer no comprehensive theory of the nature of objective facts. For my purposes, it is enough to note that some things do not owe their existence to human thought or effort.

The body of water I run upon is called "the Gulf of Mexico." This is a conventional or choice-determined fact, a fact that depends on intersubjective agreements. We could refer to it by one of its old, Indian names, or call it "the Gulf of Contentment," or even, simply, "Sam." The water neither implies nor requires any particular name. Viewed from its perspective, therefore, what we decide to call it is not only contingent but also arbitrary: Social, political, and geographic considerations conspired to establish it as the generally accepted one. Yet, it continues to be a hostage to human decisions. The Florida Department of Tourism may well launch a campaign to rechristen it "the Gulf of Florida," and succeed in convincing everyone to use no other name.

It is not very difficult to identify objective and conventional facts. The distinction produces classes that are mutually exclusive and appear conjointly exhaustive. Many people, therefore, think that every fact is either objective or conventional and none is both. This unfortunately overlooks a third, intermediate class of facts, whose central significance has in any case been inadequately appreciated by philosophers. I have in mind facts whose constitution involves both objective elements and human decisions. Let us call these "choice-inclusive facts."

Since the days of Kant, the idea of realities constituted by human beings has been commonplace. The facts to which I wish to call attention, however, are not transcendental but quite ordinary and empirical. They are determined not by the nature of human cognitive faculties but by contingent and reversible choices. Everyone is familiar with such facts although, because they masquerade as objective, their proper nature tends to elude us.

How, for example, should we view the claim that the body of water I run upon is a gulf? Objective facts set our parameters. We are dealing with a certain volume of salt water located in a specific geographical area. Shall we call it a sea? This is clearly what its size suggests. It is, in fact, larger than most seas and much larger than many. Its geographical peculiarity, however, is that land bounds it on three sides, making it appropriate for us to call it an inlet or a bay. But, though Hudson Bay and the Bay of Bengal are large, bays on the whole tend to be relatively small bodies of water. This makes it acceptable for us to classify it as a gulf, which is a relatively large part of an ocean or sea extending into the land. Yet, if it is a gulf, the Sea of Japan and the Baltic Sea, which are smaller and more bounded, should be gulfs also. The Gulf of Guinea, on the other hand, since it is much smaller and is bounded by land on two sides only, should not be a gulf.

The conclusion of this line of thought is obvious. It makes no sense to ask, "What is this body of water *really*? Is it *really* a bay, a gulf or a sea?" Within limits, it is what we decide it is. The limits are imposed by its physical features: We cannot, without being silly, class it as a mountain range or as a coffee pot. But we have good reasons to classify it as a sea, as a bay, and as a gulf, and which of these carries the day is a matter of choice. The right question to ask, therefore, is "Which is the best way to classify this body of water?" And this is a question to which there is no unambiguous, or even meaningful, answer without a prior account of what we want the classification to do. In the case of the Baltic, with rival nations inhabiting its shores, it may well have been in everyone's interest to secure universal rights to navigation by declaring it a sea. Classification as a gulf, on the other hand, may have accomplished for the Gulf of Mexico the opposite desired effect conveying to colonizing European powers the idea of a private American waterway.

There are several types and many instances of such choice-inclusive facts. All of then-involve objective facts along with some decision, normally a social one, about classification. Some choices concerning how to categorize the objective facts are inappropriate or wrong no large body of water is a flowering mimosa plant. But there is no single classification that is exclusively right. The facts allow flexibility in our concepts: Depending on what we wish to accomplish, widely divergent ways of sorting and grouping the bounty of nature may be appropriate and useful.

In saying that someone is fat, for example, we do not disclose an objective fact about the person. There are, to be sure, objective facts involved: the body weight of the individual and its relation to the weight of other people in the population. But we can also detect a decision, such as that to be fat means to exceed by twenty percent or more the average weight of people of one's height. We could, of course, decide to draw the line elsewhere, say at exceeding the average by only five percent, or by fifty. There may be good reasons to incline us in one direction or the other. But in no case do we accurately capture what it is *objectively* to be fat, for the simple and conclusive reason that there is no such thing.

Adulthood is another choice-inclusive fact, since it involves both the age of individual and the decision, recently revised to the chagrin of young people, concerning where to draw the line (among other things) between those who can drink and those who cannot. Nothing is large, hot, or heavy, and no one is poor, smart, weak, generous, tall, a failure, retarded, or even dead[1] as a matter of objective fact. The reason is not that the application of these terms involves tacit comparisons between members of a class, but that the comparison does not by itself justify the application. We also need a decision to specify the point in the relationship of the compared items where we first wish to permit the term to apply.

Such decisions are, of course, not arbitrary. Normally, they are public, subserve some shared ends, and involve a variety of formal and informal social mechanisms in their formulation. The decision about where to draw the line between the living and the dead for example, is now being made through the political process. The traditional distinction cast in terms of the cessation of cardiopulmonary function, had been rendered inadequate by the development of advanced techniques of resuscitation and life-support. A presidential commission was appointed and made the novel suggestion that the irreversible cessation of whole-brain function be designated as the criterion of death. The new standard addresses some broad social concerns and is more clearly in line with technological realities than the now antiquated, traditional criterion. Accordingly, in the last dozen years or so, nearly thirty state legislatures have adopted the recommendation. With additional support, the new social decision about the point of death will be clearly in place, generating, as physicians declare people deceased, an indefinitely large number of choice-inclusive facts.

The continuing abortion controversy is also best seen as disagreement concerning the social decision about the beginning of life. There is no novel objective fact to be discovered in this sphere: no biological research or abstract philosophical reflection can tell us when human life begins. What we need is a generally acceptable decision about where, in the continuous process from fertilization to birth, it would be best to draw the line between merely biological and genuinely human existence. Too much is at stake for this determination to be groundless or arbitrary. The religious beliefs, personal values, and established lifestyles of people must all be taken into consideration, along with economic interests and the broad social implications of each proposed decision. The fact that consensus has eluded us for so many years is a result not of having failed to *discover* what we seek, but of the intensity of the feelings involved and the complexity of the balance among values that we must achieve.

The currently popular categories of biology are also choice-inclusive in character. The full continuum of plant and animal life serves as the objective foundation of the facts their application creates. In addition, however, there is also a tacit choice to cut up the continuum in a certain way and not in innumerable others. We could, for example, classify porpoises by their habitat and method of locomotion, in which case they would be a sort of fish, or by their weight, in which case they would be related to cattle, or by their intelligence, in which case they would belong in the same group as humans and the great apes. Viewed in this light, our current classification, based on method of respiration and reproduction, loses its apparent privilege. Each of these arrangements is legitimate and useful; each focuses on some interesting features of the animals and highlights some of their significant relations to others. To say that one and only one of them captures the way things really are amounts to a slanderous impoverishment of the world. All of them illuminate a bit of reality, though not necessarily the corner into which we wish to peer.

Biologists might respond, however, by contrasting our changing purposes with the enduring value of truth. Some classifications are simply better, they might argue, for learning the truth about animals. If we focus on the respiration and reproduction of porpoises, for example, we are more likely to discover their evolutionary origin than if we study the ways they use their tail. The right classification is like a key that opens the door to nature's secrets; when the key fits, we know that our idea is not only useful but also true. If this is so, our ordinary quests are not on a par with the search for the right classification, the pursuit of truth. Among other differences, their satisfactory termination presupposes that we get what we want. In the scientific search for truth, by contrast, there is no room for private whim or ulterior public purpose. When we operate under the constraint of objective facts, the only permissible desire is to ascertain the way things are.

This line of thought is impressive. It plays on our suspicions about our motives and appeals to our hunger for heroes. It depicts scientists as selfless devotees of truth and the rest of us as slaves to the shabby designs of daily life. I, for one, do not have the problem many philosophers experience today with acknowledging the independent reality of facts and truths; I even take pleasure, when summer approaches, that the Gulf of Mexico is there waiting for me. Nevertheless, it is worth remarking that not all truths are of the objective variety: choice-determined and choice-inclusive facts are also appropriate objects of the search for truth. And the rigors of this search have been much exaggerated. In fact, nothing is more plentiful and easier to get than truth. We are surrounded by truths on all sides; if we permit it, their sheer number will numb the mind. My car is made of roughly eighteen thousand parts. This gives eighteen thousand truths, if I care to enumerate them, along with millions more about how the parts are related. A colleague concerned about his record of speaking the truth told me that whenever he finds himself asserting too many dubious propositions, he quickly recites the multiplication tables to raise his daily truth-average.

It is not truth we want, obviously, but relevant truths, general truths, novel truths, or interesting truths. Inquiry must be guided, therefore, by objectives and values beyond promiscuous curiosity or else it will drown in truth. These values express the multiplicity of our concerns and enterprises; they identify the corners of the world where we want to look, the sorts of things we want to find, the kinds of uses to which we wish to put our results. The scientific enterprise is not a detached, indiscriminate search for truth. It is an organized human activity, governed, like all others, by our needs and interests. The aim of at least portions of it may be purely epistemic: some scientists may want to identify those characteristics of objects that are central in the sense of connecting and concomitantly varying with the largest possible set of their other features. Such systemic objectives however, express the long-term, deeply entrenched, need-based concerns of the vulnerable animals we are no less than do our more immediately practical interests. An omniscient God would pay no heed to central, unifying features; gods secure from injury would find their curiosity easily satisfied and consider the relentless search for knowledge an embarrassment. That porpoises breathe by means of lungs is no more of a truth than that they weigh about as much as cows. And the desire to determine their evolutionary origin is no less a contingent human purpose than the craving to study the engineering of their tails However we relate and classify things, we will find some truths. Whatever choice-inclusive truths or facts we find, they will always have some purpose behind the decisions that give them structure or definition.

Now that I have angered those who believe in fixed and natural species with my comments about the choice-inclusive character of biological categories, I might as well proceed to infuriate the friends of human nature. The statements we like to make about what is and what is not a matter of human nature, about the identity of the human essence in everyone and about the endurance of human traits are also all based on choice inclusive facts. Since the facts are choice-inclusive, they have an objective component that imposes constraints on what can be called a human characteristic and who can be classified as a human being. But the element that is independent of our choice establishes only the outer, and rather fuzzy, boundaries of appropriate categorization. Within these parameter the facts that surround us do not mandate any particular classification; they are rich and flexible enough to permit a variety of organizational arrangements. How we order then therefore, cannot be determined simply by what they are. Their features and relations provide a jungle of opportunities for the mind. Consciously or without awareness of what we do, we must resolve to focus on certain relationships and to disregard others.

Whom shall we classify as human beings? Primitive tribes tend to be notoriously exclusive, many of them reserving for themselves alone the distinction of being human. Even the civilized Ancient Greeks were tempted to view only themselves as properly human and called outsiders uncouth and imperfectly human "barbarians." Although the story of Adam and Eve suggests a single origin and a single nature for us all, the Old Testament account of the struggles between the Israelites and surrounding tribes leaves no doubt about who were and who were not to be considered true sons of God. The history of humankind is at once the history of denying human status to selected groups: to women, children, blacks, Asians, Jews, Indians, Slavs, infidels, Saracens, Christians, and Huns. The more civilized parts of the world have now reached consensus on the undesirability of such exclusiveness. But this humane agreement has emerged not as a result of the general recognition of a single human essence, but due to the decision to stress certain telling similarities among us and to dismiss our differences as irrelevant.

The twin facts that acknowledgment of the humanity of all promises significant benefits and that the campaign for this concession has been waged with such passion should have alerted us that this is an area not of objective but of choice-inclusive facts. Important values are at stake and these values give shape to our decisions about what similarities to stress and how to classify. The objective facts underlying the classification permit us to call everyone from Albanians to Zulus human no less than they allowed the exclusion of idiots and infidels. But they are not infinitely patient. Clouds and waves and slices of apple pie cannot reasonably be considered human beings, nor can home runs and the stars in the evening sky. So it is possible to be wrong about such matters, though not as easily and as often as philosophers suppose.

In certain other cases, it is not clear what the facts will allow. In such fuzzy borderline situations, the centrality of the decision presupposed by classification is plain to see. There used to be earnest philosophical discussions about whether humans could be but sophisticated robots and whether advanced machines could one day become human beings. Such questions masquerade as queries about objective facts. They cannot be resolved, however, on the basis of observation, of clever argument, or even of what a native speaker of our language could appropriately say. The fundamental flaw in the discussions is that the question generating the inquiry points in the wrong direction. It is unproductive to ask whether human beings might not, after all, *be* machines, and how complex a machine would have to be in order for it to *be* or *become* a human being. These are not matters of objective fact, of how things are. They are, instead, matters of conscious or unconscious human decision. The proper question to ask, accordingly, is concerning the circumstances that would have to obtain in order for us to decide that, for purposes of classification, the obvious differences between human beings and machines can be overlooked.

What might such circumstances be? We must note, first, significant similarities between humans and machines. The leprechauns that were supposed to have driven the gears of old clocks were sufficiently like us to enable us to call them small human beings. The gears were not, nor are internal combustion engines and hair clippers. Next, something about machines might engage our concern or sympathy. We might, for instance, be struck by the fact that they are very intelligent or that they act as if they could suffer pain. This would activate our value commitments and, as a result, certain of our general beliefs, such as that intelligence is worthy of respect and that gratuitously inflicted pain is evil, would gain extension to machines. We would then examine the consequences of classifying machines, or at least some machines, as humans. Such classification would have important social results: as human beings, computers and robots could no longer be sold and would have to be treated as employees or independent contractors rather than as inanimate tools. They would fall, moreover, under the protection of all labor laws, guaranteeing them lunch hours, overtime pay, periodic vacations, and workmen's compensation benefits. At some point, advanced robots may even launch a campaign for recognition as beings with rights. Faced with such a situation, we might well decide that it is better to classify them as humans, with all the costs that involves, than to endure the consequences of continued differentiation.

Might it not be, however, that such a decision is merely the political acknowledgment of a reality? Perhaps machines of a certain complexity just *are* human and have been all along while we were trying to decide how to classify them. We do, after all, tend to believe that blacks were fully human before they were accorded that status with the abolition of slavery. Why should the humanity of machines at a certain stage of their development be any different?

This view has some initial plausibility. For, should we ever decide that machines are human, some people are likely to say, "I have noticed for a long time now that they are *so much* like us." And others may well announce, "I have *always* thought of them as human beings dressed in metal." But shall we consider this intuitive plausibility adequate to convince us that when we classify machines as human we merely note an objective fact? This decision depends at least in part on the similarities between the circumstance; surrounding the two situations. Does the process that issues in the announcement that machines are human resemble acquiescence in objective realities more than it resemble decision making?

On any careful and sensible examination, the answer to this must be no. Objective facts, such as the existence of the body of water we call "the

Gulf of Mexico," are relatively easy to recognize. In such cases, we have little need for collecting evidence or for lengthy deliberation: the realities tend to impress themselves on us. Some earnest religious person might predict, for example, that the world will end on a specific date, say at 9:00 o'clock in the morning. By one minute after nine, it will be blindingly clear to everyone that judgment day has not arrived: that the world continues on its merry way in an objective fact. Of course, there are some independent realities we cannot ascertain so easily. The presence of a planet beyond Neptune, the identity of Dwight Eisenhower's wartime lover, the whereabouts of Bonnie Prince Charlie were at one time or another all surrounded by uncertainty. But even in such cases, something other than a decision is required to settle the matter. Once we catch Pluto in our telescopes or the general in the boudoir, the controversy is resolved. Stubborn inquiry graced by luck suffices to get straight about these objective facts. Choosing the outcome here is not only inappropriate but also disastrous, because it obstructs the needed investigation and makes what we want a cheap substitute for what there is.

This is not at all the situation with the question concerning the humanity of machines. Humanity is not a feature that stares us in the face, but a designation we award on the basis of complex criteria and shrewd assessments. When the question is whether we should award it to machines, inquiry can reveal no additional facts adequate to develop an answer. To be sure, getting straight about the similarities of machines and humans is an indispensable element in moving toward a resolution, but the structure of the problem makes it impossible for this to suffice. For even if what machines do closely resembles our own activities, the issues of origin and ingredients remain. Machines, after all, are manufactured, while human beings are the results of more private and more pleasurable acts. And manufactured objects consist of nonliving components, instead of the cells and organs that constitute our parts. The question of what level of resemblance in behavior, if any, is enough for us to overlook these obvious dissimilarities cannot be answered by reference to facts. It requires a decision and with it the assessment of purposes, desires, context, likely consequences, costs, and benefits. If someone declares, therefore, that machines cannot be human unless they are capable of falling in love or of liking strawberry shortcake, he is not stating objective facts but affording us an insight into how high a value he places on such things as caring in a sexual context and fresh fruit with whipped cream.

These considerations reveal that there is no compelling similarity between accepting or rejecting the humanity of machines, on the one hand, and recognizing, noting or accepting objective facts, on the other. Might we not have compelling reasons, however, for deciding to treat questions concerning who is and who is not human as though they were queries about objective fact? We might, indeed, and we frequently do, though this can give no comfort to the objectivist. Making one's view appear to have a warrant in the very nature of things is an excellent strategy for convincing others and stilling one's own doubts. Declaring certain values natural rights, for example, puts us in a more powerful position than if we simply announced our intention to fight for them. Asserting that certain social structures, political arrangements, or modes of behavior are direct outcomes of the nature of man makes them appear weightier than if we merely said that we favor them. If we should ever decide that machines of an advanced design are really human beings, we could therefore greatly facilitate public acceptance of this changed state of affairs by insisting that they have been humans all along and that we are only paying our belated respects to an objective fact. Obviously, however, neither our objectifying tendency nor the decision to treat certain choice-inclusive facts as if they were objective changes the nature of the facts. Although choice enters into the constitution of some classes of facts, to which class any given fact belongs is not a matter of choice.

The complex and variable criteria and the shrewd assessments involved in promoting certain groups of beings to the rank of humans were present throughout the long history of expanding the boundaries of our race. Little by little, we, or influential groups among us, made decisions to overlook the differences due to class, race, sex, religion, national origin, intelligence, drive, and physical endowment, and to treat a very broad selection of individuals as equally entitled to consideration and respect. The objective facts permitted these decisions without compelling them. Slaves, for example, resembled their masters as closely before emancipation as they did afterward, but resemblance is insufficient for classification as a human being. Accordingly, to say that they had been human before they were set free is a misleading, ontological way of stating the moral truth that they should have been classified as humans long before.

It is precisely the moral context and the value-consequences of such reclassifications that justified expanding membership in the human family. Clearly, we are all better off for having decided to treat blacks, women, members of different religions, the handicapped, even our enemies, as full-fledged human beings. The benefits of this increase in the range of the concept of humanity, however, have been mitigated by two powerful trends. One is the failure to recognize that the facts about human nature are choice-inclusive, rather than objective. This has left a simplistic ontology in possession of the field, in whose terms we continue to believe that all of us share a single essence and that granting people rights and respect is just a response to noting the presence of this independently occurring form. The second trend is supported by the first. Since we think of our concept of humanity as identifying a natural kind, we have failed to introduce into it the diversity needed to keep pace with the increase in its scope. We have admitted to membership in the human community a wide variety of individuals whose nature is at odds with established conceptions of what is properly human. Not having loosened these traditional standards, we now face a situation in which we fervently wish to continue calling such individuals subhuman and their practices unnatural, yet we cannot do so without revoking their newly gained status. This is the source of a fundamental ambiguity at the center of the modern world: We have come to accept the legitimacy of lives we cannot but condemn.

Important and valuable as it has been to embrace the idea of a single human nature uniting us all, we must therefore supplement it by the conception of human natures. The facts permit this manner of classification, and our needs and our purposes amply justify it. The human landscape is adorned by variety; vast differences frame our similarities. Philosophers interested in generalization tend to overlook the full range of this diversity and resist being reminded of it by shunning empirical observation. In fact, however, humans differ significantly in feelings, values, and activities. The commitments their lives express vary not only from society to society and from age to age, but frequently from individual to individual, as well. Moreover, some (such as the severely retarded) lack the capacity for higher mental functions, while others are virtually unable to experience emotions, Some alter their responses unpredictably and without cease, while others (such as catatonic schizophrenics) are unable to change much at all. Some probably perceive the world in ways the rest of us cannot appreciate, or lead internal lives rich in private images and meanings. Some are incapable of significant communication, and some that we unhesitatingly classify as human (such as hydroencephalics) share with us none of the activities supposed differentiating of our species.

We must be careful not to suppose that every divergence among us is suitable as the basis of an irreducibly different human nature. The variations must be wide enough and central enough to enable us to avoid trivializing the notion. We certainly do not want to suppose that short and tall people, beer drinkers and teetotalers, individuals with 20/20 vision and with 20/40 vision are different by nature. The purposes that underlie our choice to distinguish human natures revolve around appreciating our dissimilarities and tolerating those who live by divergent values. Accordingly, the differences we seek must be generic disparities in the commitments and in the lives that express the commitments of groups of human beings.

Such differences are not difficult to find if we focus on the desires, activities, and satisfactions of people. A desire is a wish gone active: It occurs when, as a result of prizing something, we develop a tendency to take steps to obtain it. These steps constitute the bulk of the activities of daily life: They are the seekings, the searchings, the habit-bound purposive routines, the dexterous moves, and the secret rituals that fill the everyday. It is a mistake to look for them only at the dramatic junctures of life. They constitute, first and foremost, the elements of our microbehavior, such as the adjustments of eye and hand when we reach for a slice of pie and the movements of jaw and tongue as we chew it. Focusing on microbehavior makes the connection between action and satisfaction particularly easy to see. For even simple activities consist of action-segments, each of which is carefully monitored to determine what change may be needed to move closer to the desired end. If the action-segment is satisfactory, the activity proceeds apace, as when I continue to turn to respond to a voice behind my back. The unsatisfactoriness of the action-segment, on the other hand, leads to rapid correction, as when I note that, in whirling around, I have managed to turn too far.

Desire, action, and satisfaction constitute, in this way, an unbroken and interactive chain. In our grand passions no less than in microbehavior, desires generate activities and satisfactions ratify the action. When our exertions yield no fruit, or produce it at too high a cost, we tend to question and eventually to revise both our desires and our activities. The early hankering to fly by spreading one's arms, for example, is abandoned because of futility, while the hunger for throwing baseballs through large windowpanes (an easily performed and highly satisfying task) is surrendered only with the worldly wisdom painful consequences produce. In an ongoing process, therefore, desires, actions, and outcomes exert a determining influence on one another. Whatever we choose to believe about the nature and justification of values, this process is in fact their birthplace and their testing ground.

Human natures vary according to significant differences in the desires, activities, and satisfactions of people. That there are such differences is a matter of objective fact; that each defines a divergent human nature is a choice-inclusive fact. Stress on what is unlike about us must not, of course, be permitted to obscure our similarities. The differences, however, are so broad, so neglected, and so important to the growth of decency in the treatment of others that it is appropriate to dwell on them at length. Dissimilarities in desires, activities, and satisfactions make for different sorts of values that structure different sorts of lives. In honest moments, many of us quietly admit that it is unintelligible how others can act on the values and be satisfied with the lives they embrace. We know, however, that on reflection we must add that they surely feel the same way about us.

The desires, activities, and satisfactions, for example, that full-fledged membership in an acquisitive society requires render us human beings of an identifiable sort. The relentless drive to work, the incessant accumulation of new and old products, the savage haste make leisure as brief and rare as birdsong on a cloudy day. Even in universities, where life is supposed to afford reflective distance, people move in a swirl, or haze, of exertions, devoted to serving the needs of the moment, chasing name and visibility, not antique perfection. Such a life, viewed from the outside, might seem impoverished or wrapped in frustration or lit only by feeble pleasures. Yet, many of us choose it eagerly and find happiness in nothing but its movement.

We can contrast such desires and activities in the flux with the lives of people who seek peace and rest in monasteries or under the bridge. A human nature passive in the face of contingency or resigned to the will of God operates by different values and seeks dissimilar satisfactions. The large houses, fancy trips and car phones that measure meaning for the person on the make are, to this soul, ashes in the mouth. Acquiescence replaces drive and will; what desires remain aim at a simple and wholesome mode of life. Attempts to manipulate people and the world recede and the person, at one with nature, learns to move without motion, like a still bird carried by the wind. Some small percentage of the homeless, of welfare recipients, and of deeply religious people may well be such dropouts from acquisitive society. Spirituality and the simple life remain powerful ideals even in the worldly postindustrial age.

Adopting the view that there are multiple human natures removes one important line of support for dismissing unpopular values and alternative forms of life. It makes it impossible for people to claim that one and only one style of behavior is natural and right or that certain desires and activities and satisfactions are unnatural. To the extent that who we are determines what we value and how we ought to act, it constitutes the theoretical basis of a wholesome pluralism. In this way, we can at last secure the full legitimacy of our fellows; so long as they cause no harm, their differences from the majority in economic, religious, social, or even sexual values, or in the relative ranking of these values, will not justify their differential treatment. We will simply ascribe what appear to us as odd behavior and unfathomable bent to innocent differences in our human natures

Modernity has taught us a double lesson. We have come to recognize that much in the world is contingent and that much of what is contingent can be improved. These discoveries were first made in relation to the physical world; only recently and gradually have we come to think of traditions and social and political arrangements as optional an open to intelligent control. It appears that we have not yet fully extended this recognition to our own thoughts and conceptual schemes. We continue to believe that there is one and only one correct or best way to think about things, and philosophers, unburdened by historical knowledge, tend to identify this with our current mode of thought. This is unfortunate. We must learn that our opinions, our distinctions, even the terms of our reflection lead conditional lives and may need to be replaced. In many areas of thought, we enjoy vast flexibility and vast power to adapt our ideas to our broader purposes. On intelligent and imaginative variations in how we think can help us achieve our epistemic goals and do justice to the astounding richness of the actual.

# SEVENTEEN

# PERSONS AND DIFFERENT KINDS OF PERSONS

Among the neglected treasures of American philosophy, Borden Parker Bowne shines with the regal color of the amethyst. The color mix is rich, pulling hues from divergent parts of the spectrum, but always warm, favoring humane, even spiritual, interests. It was not by accident that amethyst became the symbol of spiritual authority and found its way into the rings of bishops. Its message is that the ordinary world of physical existence and a deeper, personal, moral reality intersect. We live at the crossroads and must choose. Even if we reject full ecclesiastical hierarchy, as Bowne was apt to do, the power of the amethyst confronts us with a hierarchy of values and invites commitment to what are in any case our birthright and our destiny.

Our birthright and our destiny, I say, because we are persons and personhood immeasurably transcends everything in the mechanical world. We are persons—the idea satisfies, even if it is not clear. How can we give some content to it? Bowne obliges: "The essential meaning of personality is selfhood, self-consciousness, self-control and the power to know."[1] This is, of course, terribly general and Bowne himself denies that we are abstract intellects or abstract wills. In a more concrete vein, he offers this description: "We are living persons, knowing and feeling and having various interests, and in the light of knowledge and under the impulse of our interests trying to find our way, having an order of experience also and seeking to understand it and to guide ourselves so as to extend or enrich that experience, and thus to build ourselves into larger and fuller and more abundant personal life."[2]

This is an excellent description—it connects with a great deal in my experience. We all know a lot of people just like this, though, of course, not everyone answers to every part of the description. Some persons I know, for example, make no effort to understand their experience. Others wish neither to enrich nor to extend their lives. And how many in this culture, never mind the South Seas, take no interest in making their personal existence "larger and fuller and more abundant"?

Should we call folks persons even if they do not show all these marks of personhood? What if they lack some of the more abstract features, such as self-control? What about those who are neither self-conscious nor enjoy the power to know because they are in a permanent vegetative state? These problems pale, however, by contrast with a devastating fact: Bowne's concrete account provides a perfect description of my dog, Lou. She knows me, members of my family, and the woods around the house. She has feelings of joy, sadness, and perhaps even shame. She has "various interests," focused largely on playing, eating, and being loved. Her experience is ordered—perhaps rigidly so—taking her from morning naps to afternoon meal and the evening chase. She tries to find a way to extend and to enrich her experience by acquiring better control of the petting hand. To do this, she must understand what works best: grateful licking from finger to wrist combined with uncontrolled wagging of tail. I have no doubt that she wants to achieve a more abundant personal life. Why else should she constantly ask for more food and love, lie in the deep leaves in the fall, and roll on her back to turn her belly to the sun?

Lou is unquestionably a person, then. Actually, even without such philosophical warrant, I have always believed this. Occasionally, in a mood of wonderment about wild metamorphoses and reincarnation, my wife and I ask just who Lou really is. The answer to that, however, is obvious: she is Lou, the sweetest and fattest black lab–like dog we know.

Bowne would not be satisfied with this promiscuous readiness to call dogs persons. But what reason could he offer to deny them the designation? "Personality and corporeality are incommensurable ideas,"[3] he says. Perhaps so, but if that means no one with a body can be a person, both Lou and I will fail to qualify. In fact, Bowne himself shrinks from such an implication: he is happy to talk about the bodies and souls of persons and thinks that they can interact. So a more promising line is to explore what justifies us in assigning personality to humans and to contrast that with how we relate to dogs.

Bowne asserts that we are "quite sure of one another's existence and of our mutual understanding."[4] How do we achieve this? "Our thoughts of our neighbors arise within our own minds as a mental interpretation of our sense experience,"[5] he says. Sensory clues must be taken to reveal a deeper, nonsensible reality. This is what we do with speech when we construe sounds as disclosing the presence of other minds.[6] Communication with these minds justifies the belief that the beings to whom they belong are intelligent, living persons.

This account of how we come to ascribe personality to perceived others strikes me as generally correct. We enjoy sensory contact with objects, observe their behavior, and, when it meets certain standards, declare them to be or to be closely associated with persons. The sensory clues, the necessary interpretations, and the relevant standards are complex and subtle. Speech or communication of some sort doubtless plays a central role in the ascription. None of this means that only and all humans are appropriately designated persons. For whatever conduct marks the presence of self and mind, that conduct is there in Lou. And if intelligent exchange (of which what we think is speech constitutes an unduly restricted form) is the ultimate criterion, my communication with her is richer, more precise, and far more satisfying than anything I can achieve with a baby. I readily grant that when I discuss philosophy or the stock market with her, I get only a lick and a stare. Concerning such matters, however, I do even worse with humans: they stare just as much, but they never lick. I also admit that though I speak English to her, she does not respond in the same tongue. Nevertheless, she and I share other languages: those of expressive sounds, meaningful looks, and a wide variety of bodily attitudes and motions.

I conclude that Bowne faces the following difficult situation. What-ever criterion or set of criteria is chosen for ascribing personhood, some humans will not qualify under it, but some animals will. Some very young and very old people are neither self-conscious nor self-controlled, for example, while—after a moment of indiscretion—Lou appears to re-flect on what she has done, determines that she got too excited, and will exercise more self-control from here on. One response Bowne might make is to convert his American personalism into Native American per-sonalism by extending to dogs some of the respect and courtesies, such as a place in heaven, normally reserved for humans. This, however, will not really resolve the problem because dogs are by no means the only animals that qualify as persons, nor are all that qualify animals. If we read the sensory clues, machines of a high degree of sophistication must also be classified as persons. Even without *Star Wars* fantasies about the future, we can say that some of our advanced, self-moving, intelligent mechanisms give signs of knowing, feeling, and seeking in a controlled way to "extend or enrich" their lives. If this is so, however, how can per-sonality and corporeality be incommensurable or even incompatible ideas? With this step, Bowne has to give up too much for his position to remain intact or even identifiable.

Problems of this sort are, of course, not unique to personalism and to Bowne. Similar issues arise, for example, in the abortion controversy, where the personhood of the fetus carries a heavy ideological burden. This is not accidental, but grows naturally out of the concept of person itself. For this idea is neither like that of being present nor like that of the timeliness of filing an appeal. Whether a student is present or not is a purely objective question. It is easily answered by calling the roll or by looking around. Nothing is a matter of choice in such cases: if, once the door is shut, Susie cannot be seen among the students eagerly taking notes, she is simply not present.

The question of the timeliness of an appeal, by contrast, cannot be resolved by reference to objective factors. To be sure, issues of objective fact arise: we need to know, for example, when the documents were actu-ally delivered. But this becomes relevant only when placed in a context of conventional decisions. We or designated individuals in the legal system must determine what shall count as an appeal and decide how many days to allow for it. These are matters of choice and agreement; nothing about them is objectively right. Thirty days for appeal is no more correct than sixty or ninety-five; delivering them to the Clerk of Court is not more nearly right than sending them for redistribution to a post office box in Seattle. The point is that here decisions create the reality: without the rules we make, nothing could be an appeal and no appeal could be timely or otherwise.

Someone's being a person is not an objective matter along the lines of his or her presence in class. It is also not a conventional matter of the sort timeliness of appeals constitutes. Interestingly, it appears to fall between these two categories, involving both choice and significant objective considerations. That certain types of beings are persons is not discovered; hence, it is not a simple objective fact. It is also not created out of whole cloth, however; hence, it is not a fully choice-determined, conventional fact. In such intermediate situations, we make choices about how to carve up a continuum of objective cases we find.

Following Bowne, we may begin by observing the conduct of a range of living creatures. In doing so, we are certain to find striking parallels, continuities, and similarities. Some of these will recommend themselves for special attention because in our own case we find them associated with particularly valuable or painful experiences. We may wish to highlight a few of these by establishing a group to which only those who display such similarities may belong. The purpose we have in classifying in this way is frequently, though not always, practical. We may wish to protect or to promote certain traits or else to stamp out or at least to reduce the incidence of others.

An example of what I have in mind is the way we classify certain birds. We note a number of them tend to roost in city parks and by their noise and droppings make a nuisance of themselves. We generalize that, by and large, any bird that behaves in this way is undesirable and we take action on this judgment. This classification of birds expresses a purpose, let us say the control of pests. In doing so, it may subvert or disregard other purposes, such as that of scientifically correct classification or that of categorization in terms of aesthetically pleasing colors and shapes.

I have called the facts that result from the imposition of optional categories on objective continua "choice-inclusive facts."[7] A significant number of the facts we distinguish in the world are of this sort. There are at least two elements of choice involved in such facts. The first is to stress some feature over others by creating classifications on its basis. The second is to determine the degree of similarity necessary to gain a place in the group. The first thus establishes that there shall be a certain sort of class; the second defines the range of its membership.

The recent history of the concept of person strongly suggests that its application creates choice-inclusive facts. For it has come to function as a term of commendation or of congratulatory contrast between humans and animals. Humans (according to some, even human zygotes) are supposed to be persons; animals can never reach this lofty status. How do we know that we are persons? Is this something that a careful examination of our experience of ourselves discloses? Is personhood something that, if only we manage to look in the right place, we can find? Certainly not. To call ourselves persons is simply to express our resolve to set ourselves apart from the rest of creation as somehow special and precious.

How do we accomplish this? By focusing on some high-level accomplishments of human beings, such as knowledge, self-consciousness, and self-control, and declaring these to be defining traits of personhood. We choose these particular features rather than irritability, year-round sexual appetite, and predisposition to weather-influenced mood swings precisely because we want to maximize our distance from animals. But is it reasonable to suppose that all humans enjoy or are even capable of these rarified achievements? Of course not. Once we declare that all humans are persons, however, we no longer have to demonstrate the presence of these traits. Instead, our possession of them is assumed and thus assured, and we can proceed to find reasons why their display is inadequate or altogether absent in some cases.

If special purposes did not motivate our ascriptions of personhood, we would be satisfied with empirical findings. It is perfectly clear, for example, that people in advanced stages of degeneration and in permanent comas lack knowledge, self-consciousness, and self-control. If this fact were taken at face value, we would simply concede that such folks are no longer persons and thereby remove a powerful obstacle to treating them and their families compassionately by helping them out of their misery. Many of us refuse to do this, however, because we think—

mistakenly—that their personhood is an ontological or objective fact about them, rather than a temporary status that is socially conferred.

If we understand the personhood of people as a choice-inclusive fact about them, we can lay bare the way such predicates are ascribed. We are confronted with a continuum of individuals, both human and nonhuman, that display a variety of types and levels of knowledge, self-consciousness, and self-control. Those, such as C. S. Peirce, who show these features in abundance qualify preeminently as persons. Others may qualify to a greater or lesser degree, requiring a decision on our part concerning whether they resemble Peirce and others closely enough. That some qualify more or less does not mean that being a person is a matter of degree. Whoever is judged to be a person is a person completely, with all the benefits and privileges that status confers. But his or her qualifications for personhood may be partial or weak and it is a matter of social decision as to where we draw the line between those who are persons and those who are not, that is, how weak a qualification for personhood we shall consider enough.

How do we know where to draw the line? In answering this, it is important to remember that there is no right place. Depending on our purposes, we may want to be restrictive or expansive. The history of the concept of person shows that we started out in a fashion that limited the application of the idea sharply. Over the last several hundred years, we have become more permissive, admitting into the human race and to personhood large numbers of people who do not look, do not think, and do not behave the way we do. In the West, we have long thought of God and of God's angelic companions as persons, but we have not been able to get ourselves officially to confer personhood on the likes of Lou and on machines.

Are these limits justified? Not if people in comas are honored as persons. But circumstances may arise in which we may want to restrict the notion to intelligent and sophisticated human adults. Alternatively, the contingencies of life may occasion us to expand it to several species of mammals and perhaps even to certain types of manufactured objects that show machine intelligence. Such expansions and contractions would be justified by the circumstances and the purposes we wish to accomplish. None of them is just right, though they can be good or bad and they can achieve or fail to attain our purposes. Can we ever be wrong in such matters? Of course, and in many ways, though not in the way in which it is wrong to say that Susie is present when she is not. We can embrace the wrong purposes, choose inept means to attain them, and be inconsistent in our application of the concept. We can also extend the idea too far, assigning personhood to everything that moves, or not far enough, retaining it for the two of us and seven balding friends. The point, however, is that we are never wrong in that we fail to recognize personhood where it exists or see it where in fact there is no trace of it. We are not wrong, in other words, in a recognitional way, though we can be wrong in how we think and what we want and how we go about things.

One vast advantage of viewing personhood as a choice-inclusive fact is that it demythologizes an area of concern that now suffers from fuzziness of thought. The fuzziness derives, at least in part, from the sense that we tread on hallowed ground, and therefore a careful examination of claims is inappropriate. In celebratory discourse, pickiness constitutes bad form, so we stand back, swallow hard, and learn to live with inadequate thought. As a result, we extend the notion of personhood too far and not far enough, and few dare to challenge such traditional confusion. We extend it too far, because we seem to think that personhood is an essential possession and thus even those humans reduced to mere biological existence continue to enjoy it. We fail to extend it far enough by overlooking the obvious similarities between humans and higher mammals and thus categorically rejecting the possibility that the likes of Lou can qualify. Misery and cruelty flow from both errors: humans who would be better off dead are forced to live, and animals who need protection are denied all standing.

The fundamental idea that needs to be assailed is that personhood is an ontological condition invariably attendant on humanity. Such a species-specific and species-limited idea is not likely to have an empirical origin or to be responsive to empirical counterevidence. The proper antidote to it is recognition that even belonging to a species is a choice-inclusive fact. At any rate, if being a person is a choice-inclusive fact, we are reminded that the criteria for ascribing personhood are not only contingent, but also within our power to adjust. Moreover, we are then constantly led back to daily experience to determine whether any given individual or group actually displays the characteristics we require for personhood.

There is no need to be concerned about the moral consequences of the possibility that one's status as a person may with time be lost. Sensible criteria of personhood and fair application of them should safeguard the values we hold dear. The argument that if we yield an inch about the humanity or personhood of people on the far edge of life, then no one's rights or existence will be safe again has always struck me as tendentious and exaggerated. Contingency and security are not incompatible; the fact that the criteria of personhood are open to choice does not mean that they are arbitrary. And the fact that at some point we may cease to qualify by them does not place our lives in constant jeopardy. In any case, absolute proscriptions themselves have not had a distinguished history of success in protecting people; it is too easy to declare those unlike us or our enemies nonpersons and as such beyond the reach of sheltering rules.

On the contrary, recognition that ascribing personhood is a decision should be an energizing and empowering act. It empowers by enabling us to take conscious and critical charge of activities we had performed without full understanding before. It energizes by the realization that, without our input, such important decisions may not go the way we want. Conscious, critical, and energetic contributions to the social choice of criteria of personhood and to their fair application provide far greater assurance of personal security than rigid adherence to an absolute code.

The stress on security achieved through control of consequences raises the issue of the relation of personalists to pragmatists. These two remarkable systems of thought constitute the pride, the most original elements, of American philosophy. It is noteworthy, moreover, that pragmatists and personalists share commitment to the central value of the individual, to the democratic creed, and to many of the highest spiritual activities developed in the history of humankind. It is unfortunate that these two philosophical currents have never combined their flow to make better progress toward their common sea.

The reason for this, I suspect, is that pragmatists tend not to be realistic enough and personalists are too deeply devoted to a transcendental order. My own version of objective and choice-inclusive facts should remedy the pragmatic abhorrence of realities that are unconnected to human activity. Personalists, in turn, need to give up their transcendent ontology, along with the disparagement of ordinary experience this involves. It is not that they must abandon the beautiful idea that much of human life occurs in the "invisible realm."[8] The moral and communicative relations that obtain between us are, indeed, invisible and they constitute the most important facts about human beings. But is there a reason to suppose that this invisible world is different and more real than the one we normally inhabit? Do we gain anything by supposing that the personal world of consciousness is incompatible with or at least distanced from the physical realm in which we suffer and thrive?

I suspect that these views constitute the Kantian and idealistic residue in personalism, which is a historical and dispensable accretion. If they were dropped, nothing required for personalism in the full sense would be lost. The primacy of the invisible world would simply become the primacy of moral and communicative relations among us in this one. Our minds, our freedom, our purposes would be resettled from transcendent exile and would become central, meaningful aspects of our natural lives. All it takes to accomplish this is not to view the natural world in the worst possible light. If this world is completely mechanical, we simply do not belong. But we are here, so it cannot be just an inhuman machine.

# EIGHTEEN

# GRAND DREAMS OF PERFECT PEOPLE

Male cats mate happily with any female in heat in the neighborhood. Something similar occurs in colleges as nearness and availability overwhelm all other considerations. So we see young men and women marry people who happen to be at hand when the time is ripe.

Yet, there is an important difference between cats and humans. Even young people in a hurry to mate select those they view as the best among available partners. This suggests that they take an interest in their future and often even in that of their offspring. The standard by which they measure what is best may be quixotic or questionable, but there is no denying that they are engaged in a rudimentary eugenic quest. The ineffectiveness of the process renders it harmless and the earnestness of the young lovers swept along in it makes it all charming.

But the charm evaporates with the ineffectiveness. When individuals make a science of finding mates and succeed in raising smart, hardworking, and beautiful children, their neighbors are quick to cry foul. The undeserved good fortune of others can be borne with a wistful sigh, but their ability to master circumstance and control the course of their lives evokes suspicion and resentment. There is something terrible about seeing others go about life with rational deliberateness while we continue to bumble around.

The promise of genetics to introduce universally available improvements in future generations does not suffice to allay our concerns. The idea of having healthier, lovelier, and happier children with no effort on the part of parents is attractive, but people are gnawingly skeptical that it can be accomplished. In any case, at least a part of the charm of children is that they are like us; if they were radically better, we could not have the cozy sense of their being *ours*.

Parents dote on children who look and act like them. Being prettier or a better athlete is welcome if the increment does not interfere with recognizing ourselves in the next generation. Purging our offspring of our imperfections, though, makes them at most admirable strangers, not our beloved own. It makes it hard for us to believe that we had anything to do with begetting or raising such exquisite little people.

What, after all, are our imperfections? The little mole above the curl of lip that makes a woman's smile mysterious? The tendency to dream that leads to surprising inventions and enterprises? The habits of excess that lurk behind great achievements? Most husbands and wives do not agree on the traits of which their children should have more or less. For every family in which they do, there are five others that dismiss its ideals as grotesque or lamentable.

The diversity and peculiarity of what we want our children to be reveal profound disagreements about values. Of course, we all want them to be wonderful. But our conceptions of what it would mean for them to prosper or to excel show striking dissimilarities. Soldiers and preachers do not hope for the same traits in their offspring, and hard-drinking couples are unlikely to wish dull respectability on their young. The desires of those who live in other societies or in other historical times differ from ours in ways difficult to assess and perhaps impossible to approve.

Such differences are anything but trivial. They call our attention to the vast range of human nature and demonstrate the hopelessness of attempts to attain universal truths about what people prefer and what is good for them. Yet, philosophers have always been in love with such sweeping ideas. For more than two thousand years, they hoped that their methods of investigation would lead them to incontrovertible insights into the essence of things. When the wiser among them realized that this was never to be, they switched their allegiance to physics, elevating it in their thoughts to the science of sciences.

The failure of physics to develop into a unified science of the world has not discouraged these thinkers of grand thoughts. Recently, they shifted their hopes to genetics. The Human Genome Project, they believe, will at last provide us with a definitive and objective account at least of the portion of reality that constitutes human nature.

In one respect at least, this represents an advance. The focus on human nature carries us past the naïve view that we can examine objects without any reference to observers. In another respect, however, we are back where we began. For genetics attempts to study the observer in just the simple-mindedly objective way in which physics approaches particles and forces. Investigators promise us insight into the real essence of human beings and think they have to attend neither to the structuring conditions of their own values and purposes nor to the pervasive selectivity that underlies their choice of facts.

Love of the universal and the objective is easy to understand: They offer certainty and unlimited scope. Those captured by this love search for finality in knowledge, forgetting the humbling lessons of anthropology and history. Genetics is supposed to tell us not only about the facts of our constitution, but also about the values proper to us. The hope is that in discovering who we are, we will at once learn what we need. And laying bare the mechanisms of preference will presumably enable us to distinguish proper choices from those prompted by error or disease.

Some think such lofty achievements are beyond the scope of genetics and yet look to the biological sciences in general to tell us about the proper function of human beings. Their hope is that diseases at least are objectively determinable facts. A study of organ structures may clarify their optimal operation and that, in turn, reveal the parameters of natural activity. Even if such knowledge is inadequate to guide us in personal choice, it can be parlayed into public policies that promote favored values.

Make no mistake about it: The connection between the growth of knowledge and changes in public policy is anything but casual. New knowledge often yields new technology that promises a variety of benefits. We want magical cures for our problems, and such desires create a universal demand for what science can provide. This raises the question of how expensive benefits can be provided on a large scale, mobilizing the champions of justice to search for justifications to shift the burden of funding new programs of distribution and of treatment to taxpayers.

What justifications work when the cost of benefits is momentous? That the lives of beneficiaries would be improved clearly does not, because the lives of donors may well suffer corresponding damage. Every demand to fund a public program reduces the opportunity of individuals to improve their condition in their own way with the money they earn. Possible benefits are, moreover, potentially infinite, expanding with the availability of money to fund them. The process may result in the virtual or mediated enslavement of productive citizens to those who declare themselves to be in need, without hope of significantly reducing the number of demands.

Another possible justification for large publicly funded programs of enhancement might be built on the intuition of the champions of justice that it is terribly wrong for innocent people to suffer from disability and disease while others no more worthy flourish. This feeling is clearly right, but it can be converted into an argument for social initiatives only if the actions it prescribes could meet with success.

Unfortunately, however, such programs of large-scale amelioration are hopeless. We cannot equalize talents, endow people with will, or undo the ill fortune of those not favored by the natural lottery. More, the exquisite interplay of the conditions of individuals with their desires and aspirations renders it impossible for us to determine which changes are desirable and which might destroy the delicate balance of a coping life.

This places the advocates of wholesale justice in a precarious position. People of good feeling agree that we must do what we sensibly can to help our fellows. But philosophers in search of closure do not want to leave the limits of such benevolence to be drawn from time to time in the concrete contexts of life by a caring community. They want some sweeping principle on the basis of which we could decide, pretty much once and for all, what everyone has a right to expect. A principle built on human nature would be best, providing a stable foundation for the allocation of publicly funded treatments and function enhancements.

Norman Daniels thinks he can ground such a principle in what he calls "species-typical normal functioning." The range of such functioning is supposed to be ascertainable by the biological sciences in a way that is "relatively objective and non-evaluative."[1] Disease and disability constitute adverse departures from this norm. Those who suffer from them cannot do what others can and hence lack fair equality of opportunity, a condition the community must find ways to overcome.

If Daniels succeeds in establishing the idea that disease must be treated and disability minimized through enhancements of capacities, we will have to find ways to fund a variety of costly new interventions. On careful reading, it is not clear what exactly Daniels hopes to show. On the one hand, he speaks of disease as a scientifically verifiable objective condition, so that those who once thought that masturbation is an illness were simply wrong. But, on the other, he seems satisfied to present the account of species-typical functioning as political in nature, designed to generate consensus for publicly funded health care initiatives.

What looks like an innocent ambiguity can easily grow into a slippery move in persuasion. Political proposals must be assessed on the basis of their costs and consequences. The appearance that one among them carries the sanction of science confers on it an unfair advantage over its rivals. The advantage is all the more unfair if its claim to scientific objectivity cannot be sustained. So anyone who subscribes to the standard of species-typical normal functioning must be particularly careful not to characterize it to biologists and philosophers as a useful political proposal, while presenting it to the public as objective science.

There can be no hope of neat general closure on issues of what treatments and enhancements the public is willing to underwrite, so long as they remain open to political negotiation. For reasons partly sound and partly idiosyncratic, some treatments—such as kidney dialysis—will receive funding and others—such as cosmetic surgery—will not. Philosophers devoted to the rule of principles find such halfway solutions and halting compromises objectionable. But nothing more can be expected in the real world, in which any advance can be reversed and grand projects tend to remain unfinished.

So the hope for closure must come from some knockdown moral or scientific argument that would make our obligations unmistakable and hence perhaps unavoidable. Can Daniels's idea of species-typical normal functioning serve as the basis of such a decisive moral or scientific consideration? It could certainly not; in fact, it would be difficult to detail all the points on which it falls short. Let me just speak about the most obvious.

It may be possible to describe the species-typical function of oysters, though I suspect our success in doing so may be due at least in part to the distance from which we view the lives of mollusks. With us humans, at any rate, differences of culture and history make it impossible to identify any activity that is uniquely and universally our own. There are, of course, the generalities of biology and anthropology. What we share biologically, though, such as the need for food and the activities of metabolism, fails to distinguish us from other animals and especially from other mammals. Such anthropological similarities as cooperation and the search for meaning are too encompassing and hence empty to provide useful insight.

What, then, will count as a species-typical function of humans? One can hardly resist the temptation to select some local characteristics and elevate them to the level of universality, or to anoint the statistically normal distribution of traits as the norm. Neither one of these procedures can encompass what everyone does. They also cannot give us an account of what we *ought* to do or what, if we do not or cannot do it, will render us ill. Worse, in isolation from local values and practices, they cannot even identify which activities or disabilities put us at a competitive disadvantage.

At first sight epilepsy, for example, looks like an impairment of normal function. Would we consider it that if the vast majority of people experienced epileptic episodes? Under those circumstances, it would be an illness just as little as periodic sleepiness is a disease. Similarly, if the number of those suffering from chronic depression in the United States increased tenfold from the current 17 million, it would no longer make sense to identify depression as a disease. Generally, what appears as a disability if only some people have it fades into the background conditions of life once its incidence becomes widespread.

Moreover, even when illness appears to be a matter of biological mechanism, involving for instance elevated glucose levels in the blood, it is not a simple affair of objective measurements. Such situations frequently involve continua of possible readings, and we have to decide which readings are acceptable and which constitute or betoken disease. How do we know that, in the absence of compensating factors, plasma glucose concentrations in excess roughly of 140 mg/dl indicate diabetes? This is not a discovery once made about diabetes but a thoughtful decision concerning when intervention is appropriate that continues to be enacted by conscientious physicians.

Since we must *decide* where to draw the line between normal operation and disease, both notions include an element of convention. The construction of diseases and disabilities is, of course, anything but arbitrary. We use extensive observation to put us in touch with the details of people's lives. And we are careful to distinguish illness from acceptable forms or levels of activity by reference to a host of considerations, including the frequency of the problem in the population, our ability to intervene in its course, the undesirability of leaving it untreated, and the way in which it connects to a variety of social practices and religious values.

These considerations suggest that Daniels is wrong not only in thinking that species-typical function is a scientifically objective notion, but also in supposing that it is a positive idea by contrast to which we can define disease. More likely, the ideas of illness and disability constitute the foundation of thought in this field, and we construct the notion of normal operation by contrast with such adverse conditions. The unproblematic tends to fall below the level of explicit consciousness; attention is engaged only when things go awry. We note sickness and disability first and seek to bring people back to normal functioning, which we understand as the relatively indeterminate range of activities and conditions that do not display such trouble.

The idea of illness is, at least in our society, not a theoretical or a cleanly cognitive one. In addition to the value judgments and the social and religious significance built into it, the notion of disease is also deeply practical. It serves as a demand for action or at least as a notice and perhaps as a commitment to intervene. This is further indication of the primacy it enjoys over the notion of species-typical function and of its superior specificity to that nebulous idea.

Daniels's account of illness and of its connection to species-typical normal functioning thus appears open to disabling objections. Even if it were defensible, the invariable connection he asserts between illness and impaired opportunity could not be demonstrated. The tie between disability and opportunity is not the simple natural one suggested by the idea that those who have no legs cannot run the marathon. The relation is mediated through social values and practices that may convert what appears as an obstacle into a grand source of achievements. Epilepsy, for example, may come to be viewed as a sacred condition and those suffering from it can be exalted as priests or rulers. And many societies consider the devastatingly simple-minded as spiritual people free from the constraining rules of everyday life. Moreover, often though not always, disabilities create opportunities for the development of different, compensating abilities. Many blind persons show exquisite sensitivity to sounds and smells, and those born without arms can attain remarkable skill in operating with their toes. Surprisingly, some who fall far below the average in cognitive capacity may enjoy particularly creative or emotionally rich lives. In these instances and in many others, human ingenuity and perseverance succeed in converting misfortune into victory. So the connection between disability and opportunity is mediated not only by social practices, but also by individual values and achievements.

Viewing the situation from a great distance, one can of course intone that it would be better if people did not have to struggle against such misfortunes and obstacles. This is idle talk, however, that valorizes the common and shows a deep misunderstanding of the role of challenges in life. No one but affected individuals can choose between ordinary and heroic compensatory abilities, and it is by no means clear that, given the chance, they would hasten to embrace the everyday.

There is a deeper way of putting this point. In one sense, fair equality of opportunity must operate in abstraction from the values and the peculiarities of individuals. In another sense, however, such equality remains meaningless and empty unless it takes into account the conceptual frameworks and value structures of affected individuals. Equality of opportunity for concrete, historically situated persons is very different from how it might operate for bloodless agents of abstract rationality. The critical difference is that the natures of persons with disabilities play a central role in determining what counts as equality of opportunity for them.

A part of the reason for this is that lived disabilities are not accidental afflictions of people whose rational substance remains ever untouched. Chronic disease and permanent disability function as structuring conditions of personhood for those who must live with them. What Alcoholics Anonymous wants to do for its members happens naturally to persons with quadriplegia and even with juvenile-onset diabetes: they come to view themselves as individuals whose choices must and do reflect their conditions.

To choose treatments or enhancements that may provide fair equality of opportunity by bringing them closer to the species-typical norm is, therefore, to opt for selves other than the ones they have become over the years. The difficulties attendant on such courses of action (suppose I choose to become Mother Teresa or Attila the Hun!) are easy to overlook or to understate. Even if people with disabilities embraced such self-changing courses of action and even if the treatments and enhancements worked, it is not at all clear that their lives would be improved. At the very least, they would face periods of painful adjustment and instability.

This train of thought leads inevitably to the conclusion that what we owe humans who suffer from chronic ailments and disabilities may have very little to do with equalizing their opportunities. Nothing is an opportunity unless a person thinks it is both possible and desirable, and opportunities can be equal only if they are commensurable. The differences among people make it impossible to measure what one values against the commitments of another, and hence unthinkable to equalize their chances of pursuing what they want. We are left where people of good feeling have been from time immemorial: We must do what we can to help where we can, both on an individual basis and by social policies that take individual differences seriously.

Whether it is *hubris* or foolish hope, we wish to fix everything in the world. Nearly daily reports of progress in mapping the human genome assure us that, before long, we will identify the genes for every desirable and undesirable trait. Then we will obliterate or at least shut down the "bad" genes and enhance the operation of the "good" ones to create human beings who will live long, happy, and moral lives. In the meantime, we launch imposing social programs to eliminate injustice by equalizing opportunities, and if not outcomes, then at least income. Nothing but grand schemes suffice, nothing but final solutions attract.

What happened to the recognition of finitude? How can we overlook the fact that we are mired in the details of daily life and that perfection has always been a destructive dream? Is the human race not old enough to recognize the eternal gulf between the ideal and where we are, and to learn to satisfy itself with a little advance here and there in the direction of decency and self-improvement?

Our ignorance is vast and necessary. It is vast because we are not likely to learn everything we need to know and do not really need to know everything we learn. It is necessary because we can never uncover the secret loves burning in the hearts of others or understand their private hopes and satisfactions. But in all our sensible moments we know that it is best to care for individuals in their individuality and to meet needs where we find them, one at a time.

To aim for a little improvement in our children and for some small growth in caring takes the human condition seriously and stands a chance of success. Initiating large social programs and re-engineering the genome will fail as surely as every holy war. We can walk and sometimes even run, but flapping arms will never make us fly.

# NINETEEN

# PHILOSOPHICAL PLURALISM

Philosophy is the only human enterprise that has created a field of study out of puzzlement over its method of operation. Nearly from the time of the earliest practitioners, philosophers wondered about how they could do what they were doing and frequently even about what they were doing in the first place. Of course, there always were unselfconscious souls who pursued what was of interest to them without concern for method or the arbitrary limits of fields of study. But such people tended to be labeled amateurs and dismissed as lacking technical sophistication. This left philosophy in the hands of professionals who crafted novel concepts, gloried in minute distinctions, and spoke in a torrent of neologisms.

Uncertainty about the nature, scope, and value of philosophy was, in the history of the discipline, often combined with arrogance based on its purported excellence. People supposed that since philosophy may accomplish nothing in particular, it must be good for doing everything in general—that is, for serving as the thought behind or the self-understanding of all human endeavors. In graduate school, I was taught that, as philosopher, I needed to learn no facts; I had only to think. The reason offered for this remarkable luxury was the sheer power of philosophical thought: by means of it, my professors seemed to agree, we can understand, criticize, and improve the meager cognitive output of everyone else.

This extraordinary combination of self-doubt and swagger played a central role in the social history of philosophy. Groundless haughtiness tended to suffuse the attitude of philosophers not only toward those who worked in other fields, but also toward fellow practitioners who used different methods of reflection or reached unfavored conclusions. The intellectual history of philosophy is therefore as much a story of summary dismissals as of respectful controversies. Lucretius dismissed Plato and was in turn disregarded by almost everyone in the Middle Ages. Hegel and his followers paid no heed to Schopenhauer, and many philosophers—including Heidegger—failed to take Spinoza seriously. Nearly all twentieth-century analytic philosophers thought and wrote as if idealists from Hegel to Bradley and Hocking had never existed. By no means least, for a long time, Nietzsche was considered a literary figure unworthy of philosophical attention.

As if being overlooked were not enough, thinkers who do not take the starting point or fail to follow the procedures currently in vogue are denounced as not doing philosophy. There is hardly a greater insult to philosophers than to be denied the benefit of standing as a respected colleague. Yet such exclusion has become standard in the profession in the twentieth century, supported by such movements as logical positivism that declare much of what philosophers say literally nonsensical. Even those who manage to move past such juvenile charges are quite prepared to relegate much philosophy to psychology and literature, and treat colleagues who think in those ways with condescension.

Philosophers who deride other philosophers typically believe that there is a royal road to insight and that that road is paved with the latest technical innovations. For decades, people believed that doing philosophy without the language of *Principia Mathematica* was futile; at the other end of the spectrum, phenomenologists maintained that only language descriptive of human experience enjoyed any warrant. Even postmodern thinkers who are closely attuned to the pains of exclusion refuse to take seriously philosophers who do not use such words as "excess," "normalize," and "decenter" a sufficient number of times.

Minimal attention to the history of philosophy is enough to see that the hope for such a royal road is illusory. Platonic dialectic, Cartesian doubt, the geometrical method of Spinoza, Kant's transcendental method, Hegel's historical dialectic, and Nietzsche's genealogies, among countless other preferred ways of embarking on the philosophical enterprise, hold out hope for incontestable results for a short time only; soon, relentless critique wilts the promise and proponents of the great new invention find themselves as but another party in factional disputes. There is not a single proposition of philosophical substance on which professional thinkers agree, and it is highly unlikely that such a proposition will surface anytime soon.

I hasten to say that I do not think the world would be a better place if philosophers agreed in their views. Agreement is of value when its absence leads to armed conflict, bitter resentments, or divorce, but it avails little when critical dialogue is the only vehicle on the road to truth. Philosophy deals with the most difficult of human problems; there is no reason to suppose that we can attain final insight or even general agreement on matters of such depth and significance. The point, however, is that absent that insight, no philosopher has a right to look down on the efforts of others. In philosophy, we are simply not in a position to know who is closer to the truth. Every thesis has some arguments to support it, yet each is open to criticism, and none can be established conclusively. Accordingly, the proper attitude of philosophers is to let a hundred flowers bloom and make only modest claims about their own achievements.

Such relative unproductivity does not compromise the value of philosophy. Physics and biology move cumulatively toward truth; their sidelined theories tend not to come back to life, and when they do, it is only because new evidence clearly supports them. Philosophy, by contrast, offers no compelling evidence for any of its captivating views. Its value lies in expanding our minds by developing imaginative new ways of looking at things and in sharpening our critical skills by offering rigorous objections to every theory. Examining the human condition suggests that we cannot give final or universal answers to questions about the meaning of life, the existence of God and the nature of the good. This does not mean that such questions are meaningless and should be avoided, only that their function is to occupy and agitate us perennially, instead of leading us down a road to satisfied, harmonious belief.

Not all worthwhile activities yield results. Like playing cards and kissing, philosophy is intrinsically delightful. As part of the flower of life, it needs no product to justify its existence; partaking in its movement is a spontaneous joy. Understanding the conceptual moves of the great philosophers, discovering the connection between seemingly unrelated events and seeing through the bluster of human self-importance are permanent sources of satisfaction. Drawing distinctions and defending conclusions engage all the active parts of the mind. The dialectic of ideas offers exhilaration at every turn, and a vigorous argument over some philosophical claim constitutes, for those in the know, one of the finest experiences of life.

Although philosophy is not useful in the way of the physical sciences, it can nevertheless result in desirable consequences. Not all lines of inquiry yield the same sort of fruit: Some establish bodies of knowledge, others create better inquirers. Philosophical work makes humans more skeptical, more conceptually nimble, and therefore more discerning as thinkers. Generally, better thinking makes for better life. The benefits of intelligence are not only private and psychological; they are on display in hospitals and businesses, where philosophers lend their trained sensitivity to the cause of more responsible and more humane practices. The recent vast growth of applied ethics aptly demonstrates the value of philosophical education: the critical examination of proposed courses of action, the detection of dissembling, the unmasking of lived contradictions, and the presentation of alternative perspectives clarify our social decisions and move us closer to a world of caring.

That metaphysics and epistemology are unlikely to generate a flood of new truths is therefore perhaps not such a great loss, after all. Although there may be little progress in philosophy, philosophers can grow greatly as they learn from the mistakes of their predecessors and develop their conceptual sophistication, their perceptiveness, and their critical skills. This is one of the reasons why the consideration of past thought is vital for philosophical education. The remarkable history of philosophy, including its recent chapters, is a vast storehouse of ideas that provides rich material for the critic. Students raised on the thin diet of the latest controversies, by contrast, may actually suppose that they stand a chance of developing decisive arguments for some final truth. This denies them a sensible view of their activities, and their inevitable disappointment, later in life, may turn them into people who cynically live off a profession whose value they silently dismiss.

Alternatively, individuals devoted to a single way of doing philosophy tend to retain their partisan zeal and compensate for their lack of final results by a sense of superiority. As all things intellectual, this claim of transcendent excellence does not have a purely cognitive basis; the school of one's training, the fame of one's teachers, and the reputation of one's university all contribute to the impression that some professionals and their methods are much better than others. The appearance is supported by the fact that the standards of the profession are approach-specific. If argumentative prowess and analytical ability determine the quality of philosophers, Continentalists do not even rate. If the practical import of ideas is not a proper interest of philosophers, whoever focuses on James and Dewey must be a charlatan. And in the opinion of those who start from Peirce's way of making our ideas clear, analytic philosophers cannot avoid irrelevance.

The contempt philosophers feel for colleagues who do not share their values and techniques is nothing short of bizarre and has served to undermine the honor and integrity of the discipline. In serving on National Endowment for the Humanities committees, I noted that members of the panel from English and history and anthropology tended to support applicants from their fields. Philosophers, by contrast, could not wait to light into their colleagues; they tore research proposals apart, presenting their authors as fools or as championing out-of-date, inferior ideas and methods. As a result, scholars from other fields garnered much of the money that under normal circumstances would have gone to philosophy. These gatekeepers to our profession thought their actions were justified by the imperative to maintain high standards; in fact, they often undertook to judge work they did not understand, and condemned styles of thought and topics of investigation simply because they had no sympathy with them.

Something similar was occurring in the American Philosophical Association prior to the pluralist revolt of 1978. In the Association's dominant Eastern Division, disciplinary exclusivity was wedded to institutional nepotism in such a way that it became nearly impossible for philosophers who were not analytic in orientation and who did not serve in Eastern seaboard graduate schools to break into the power circle or even into the program. As if there had been a dearth of talent in the Division, the same person from the University of North Carolina was tapped to chair the Program Committee twice within five years; the second time, he found room for no less than seventeen individuals connected with his university on the notoriously small and limited program in December. The system of exclusion worked perfectly with regard to the presidency and the other offices of the Division, as well; one by one, the senior members of the Harvard and Princeton departments took turns in leading the Division, leaving room for one or two colleagues from Pittsburgh only as an accommodation to the provinces.

The stranglehold on elective offices was made nearly unbreakable by the voting procedure. Officers were elected at the Eastern Division business meeting in northeastern cities. Home institutions defrayed the cost of attending these meetings only if their faculty gained a slot on the program. Since members of the Association from colleges, from inland schools, and especially from the South rarely found themselves on the program, they were effectively disenfranchised. A tiny minority, consisting largely of those the leadership put on the program, determined the next set of leaders year by year.

The astonishing thing is that people some of whom contributed to the development of political philosophy and who were therefore sensitive to the nuances of democratic participation never saw anything wrong with this system. The uncritical assumption of these acutely critical thinkers was that all and only philosophers distinguished enough to be elected president could lead the Association effectively. It seemed not to matter that there was not a shred of evidence for this view; the untenable conflation of philosophical excellence with practical sense and institutional savvy was never challenged and remains an operating principle of the Association even today. At least a part of the reason for the persistence of this illusion was the absence of a clear idea of what the APA was to do beyond organizing three national meetings a year and responding to issues in the life of the profession that it could not skillfully dodge. There was no agreed understanding then, as there is none even now, of how the Association might advance the good of the profession. Its committees rarely escaped being ineffectual, its national office staff was skeletal, and its Board seemed for the most part satisfied with the celebration rather than the active encouragement of philosophical achievement. As a result, it lagged far behind its sister organizations serving other academic fields in the effective promotion of the discipline. There is no better indication of the enduring power of philosophy than that it managed to survive these decades of institutional neglect.

At least since the 1970s, the APA fancied itself the guardian of philosophical standards, which rendered it so conservative that it lost contact with new developments in the field. The explosive growth of the group meeting program connected with the Eastern Division, for example, took the APA leadership altogether by surprise; the widespread interest in historical figures, practical issues, Continental thinkers, American philosophy, and interdisciplinary topics could not have been predicted on the basis of the papers featured on the "official" program.

The growing distance between the APA and many of its members was one of the reasons for the revolt that culminated in the election of John E. Smith as vice president and president-elect of the Eastern Division in 1978. There were, of course, many other reasons, including social, political, economic, and geographical ones. The vast majority of APA members felt that paying dues earned them no say in the affairs of the organization. The Northeastern graduate school power elite held the keys to advancement in the profession by nearly exclusive control over grants, publications, and program participation. National Defense Education Act fellowships swelled the number of excellent graduate students in philosophy; since job creation in central graduate schools did not keep pace with the production of PhDs, many fine young scholars had to take jobs in small colleges and provincial universities. This upgraded the quality of philosophy teaching across the land, but left students from even top-named schools abandoned by their teachers and stranded in forgotten small departments.

At the same time, a number of universities began offering new doctoral degree programs. Avenues to distinction were largely closed to faculty and students in these schools; judgment of the very legitimacy of the programs was left in the hands of reviewers from long-established departments. Small colleges from the South were particularly hard hit by haughty neglect: when it came time for committee assignments, Eastern Division Executive Committees could hardly ever think of anyone in the South capable of rendering worthy service. The revolt of 1978 offered an outlet for these and other frustrations. There was talk of founding an alternative organization, but it quickly became clear that taking over the existing structure would be easier and more efficient.

To be sure, there was also an ideological element in the revolt, though its significance can be overstated. The departments with a stranglehold on the profession were analytically minded and professional or technical in their approach. The anger of those wanting reform, however, was directed not so much at the analytic style of doing philosophy as at the arrogance of declaring analysis the only proper method of thought. This exclusivity represented a danger to the small but quickly growing band of Continentalists, as well as to those serving in Catholic institutions committed to speculative metaphysics and the history of philosophy. The revolt aimed not at defeating or eliminating analytic philosophy but at establishing the legitimacy of alternative methods. It wanted to introduce a wholesome pluralism into the profession, and a look at philosophical activity today shows that in this it clearly succeeded.

Two additional developments chipped away at the hegemony of analytic philosophy. By the time of the revolt, its research program in epistemology—its central discipline—was nearly played out. Rorty announced its demise in 1976, and for this he was reluctantly honored with the presidency of the Eastern Division. Further, philosophers found that they could not fill their classrooms and retain the attention of their students in small colleges and provincial schools by presenting the abstract topics and dry distinctions of analytic thought. They responded by reaching back to the humanly more interesting figures in the history of the discipline and by tackling pressing moral concerns. The history of how much of the current boom in applied ethics is due to the necessity to fill classes and the opportunity to publish in journals not under the control of narrow professionals is yet to be written.

The success of efforts at institutional reform is notoriously difficult to assess. The pluralist revolt elected some presidents of the Eastern Division and placed a stream of individuals on the Executive Committee. Most important, it called the attention of the APA leadership to the level of disaffection of its membership and to the luxuriant growth of interest among philosophers in new fields, new topics, and new methods. The organization is more open now than it was twenty-five years ago, but each liberalizing concession had to be wrung out of it. For this reason, it is fair to say that it neither led the profession nor served it well; instead of stimulating or at least welcoming new sorts of work, it made room for them only grudgingly and when the pressure became too great to resist. That the pluralization of philosophy was accomplished by the spontaneous activity of thousands of practitioners who lacked organized institutional support constitutes convincing evidence of the vitality of philosophy. The pluralist revolt served as the voice of thinkers who were experimenting with the new.

Many of the narrow political goals of the pluralists were never achieved. The hold of rich and established graduate departments on the Board of the APA has been weakened but not eliminated, APA divisional presidencies are still viewed as rewards for excellence unconnected to practical sense or the ability to lead, and elections continue largely as popularity contests based on name recognition and current assessments of technical publications. Yet it is clear that academic philosophy is profoundly different today from what it was a couple of decades ago, and of this change ongoing pluralist agitation was both symptom and part cause.

The question of how pluralistic philosophy should be is easily answered: as pluralistic as its practitioners want it. There are, of course, limits to pluralism in the curriculum. Since faculty salaries are paid largely out of undergraduate tuition, instructional offerings must attract a sufficient number of students. Although the correlation between offerings and enrollments is loose, no department can afford to devote the bulk of its efforts to teaching marginal, arcane, or highly specialized courses. This does not mean, however, that the research programs of instructors must be restricted to what they are asked to teach; they are and should remain free to pursue any line of philosophical investigation and use any appropriate method in doing so. This leaves room for the intellectual development of tenured faculty members, who can—at least in principle—determine what they read and think and write.

Obstacles to pluralism often arise, however, in the hiring practices of departments. During the early stage of the pluralist revolt, Professor Burt Dreben spoke to an audience concerned about the openness of the profession and allowed that he was puzzled why the Harvard Department was considered narrow. "We have both Quine and Rawls," he said. "Isn't that pluralistic enough?" The wonderful naiveté of this comment reveals the fact that pluralism is a matter of degree. A department that features Quine and Putnam is clearly pluralistic in one way: the two of them hold divergent opinions concerning at least some shared issues. Having Quine and Rawls introduces greater pluralism by diversifying the issues, though not nearly as much as adding Rorty would. Yet Rorty, Rawls, and Quine agree with each other on topics and modes of thought far more than any of them does with Derrida, John McDermott, or Irigaray. A department in which American, Continental, and analytic approaches to problems coexist, moreover, is not nearly as pluralistic as one that also features some of the concerns and techniques of Indian, Native American, and Chinese thought.

Departments tend to diversify within the range of their interests. Communities largely analytic in orientation may insist on having someone who covers the early Wittgenstein, while departments of Continentalists feel satisfied only when they can add a specialist in the late Heidegger to those who publish on *Being and Time*. In places where ethics is the center of gravity, emotivism and moral realism are thought to require separate champions; if the stress is on political philosophy, liberals, communitarians, and members of the Frankfurt School all need representation. Such hiring priorities have their ground and justification in value judgments about what is of significance in the profession. For the most part, these judgments are unconscious or have not withstood challenge, yet they serve to exclude large numbers of talented and highly trained philosophers from even consideration for employment.

A more vicious form of the same sort of selectivity occurs when members of a department agree that what some professionals in the field do is not philosophy or at least not philosophy of a type that deserves to be done or taught. Those who derive their inspiration from the great philosophers of the past may be devalued as mere historians, thinkers who read Plato or Kant from a Continental perspective may be declared unintelligible, and individuals who take Dewey and James seriously may be denounced as charlatans. As a result, departments tend to hire young people closely similar to those already on staff and thereby perpetuate a narrow and stagnant culture. Philosophy is not like physics in which a research paradigm is firmly in place; we live in a sea of criticism and can progress perhaps only by permitting our deepest assumptions to be challenged.

No department can make room, of course, for every fashion of doing philosophy. But every department can avoid a monolithic orientation that makes for the cozy agreement about approach and method of all its members. We are also well advised to avoid tokenism of the sort I observed in one distinguished department, in which a large staff covered a collection of then-urgent analytic topics, leaving the history of philosophy, aesthetics and all of Continental thought to a single unproductive and overworked pariah. What may appear as institutional obstacles to pluralism in philosophy are in fact roadblocks constructed by philosophers in deciding not to hire, retain, reward, and promote professionals whose philosophical convictions fail to match favored or established patterns. The tendency to exclude the different is widespread and affects Continental departments no less than analytic ones. It is fed by the suspicion that if one or two individuals of another persuasion gain a foothold, they will want to turn the entire department into an enclave to their own liking.

Pluralism in philosophy, as elsewhere, is possible only if people approach each other with trust and show themselves worthy of it. Above all, it requires a fallibilistic attitude committed to the idea that since we may well be wrong, others can legitimately disregard our efforts and pursue their own. Philosophy is not alone among academic disciplines in suffering, or profiting, from lack of a single method; literary criticism, political science, and psychology are, to different extents and in differing ways, in the same situation. But no field of study shares the ambition, scope, and consequent uncertainty of philosophy. Making room for widely divergent approaches is therefore even more important in philosophy than in other contested disciplines.

The argument that the quality of methods other than one's own is not high enough to warrant representation in one's department does not stand scrutiny. Without extensive acquaintance with philosophical methods, it is impossible to judge their power. The frequently heard analytic objection to Continental thought that it is unclear cannot be taken seriously unless it is the outcome of long and sympathetic study. Kant is unclear to those who have not spent time examining his aims and technical terms, and *Principia Mathematica* remains obscure to people who refuse to attend to the details of its elegant structure. Even the claim that philosophers must present arguments in support of their views is questionable unless made on the basis of thorough familiarity with the works of religious thinkers and those who write interestingly and persuasively in the wisdom tradition.

Such casual arguments supporting a dismissive attitude toward alien or novel forms of thought do not do their proponents proud. Instead of succumbing to them, departments need to ask themselves if they do all they can to serve their field and their students so long as they refuse to make room for the out-of-fashion and the new. The image of merely accepting the different is, however, far too passive. Departments have an obligation to seek out not only promising young people, but also promising new lines of thought, no matter how strange they may at first appear. Such casual arguments supporting a dismissive attitude toward alien or novel forms of thought do not do their proponents proud. Instead of succumbing to them, departments need to ask themselves if they do all they can to serve their discipline and their students so long as they refuse to make room for the out-of-fashion and the new. Only in that way can we be sure that philosophy remains vital and fertile, and that we escape the ossification resulting from narrow and unchallenged programs of research.

The APA must play a central role in opening philosophy to a variety of fructifying influences. It must welcome diversity in the profession and throw the gates of service and acknowledgment open to all its members, regardless of their philosophical method or position. This requires elimination of the attitude, still prevalent today, that some professionals do serious philosophy, while others play in the sandbox. It also demands expansion of the program of the Eastern Division, whose traditionally limited size makes inclusiveness difficult to attain. Program committees need to be large enough to accommodate people knowledgeable about and sympathetic with all major contemporary trends. By no means the least, instead of the yearly ritual of passively waiting for committee nominations, the National Office should aggressively seek out members highly qualified to promote the Association's purposes.

Most important, the APA should at last devote itself to engaging the broader public that is the ultimate employer of its members. The personal value and social usefulness of philosophy are not widely known in this country, even though our daily choices, our social customs, and our public policy debates are in desperate need of intelligent critique. In spite of this need and of the benefits to our profession of meeting it, distinguished thinkers subscribe to the preposterous view that philosophers get attention when they do good philosophy. They do, indeed, among the few dozen people who work in their narrow fields, but they and their writings remains unknown beyond the choking confines of the academic world.

There is no reason and no justification for restricting philosophical education to young people enrolled in classes; the out-of-school public is, if anything, more anxious to obtain it and more likely to make immediate use of it. As the premier national organization of philosophers, the APA must shoulder the task of fostering this audience and encouraging the profession to address it. Historians are untiring in their drive to educate the adult public; economists have persuaded the president to appoint a Council of Economic Advisors; half the world beats a path to the door of psychologists to gain self-understanding or at least some useful advice. Only philosophers seem satisfied with the safety of academic isolation, abandoning a historic mission of the discipline and surrendering its only means to increased influence and appreciation.

Pluralism in philosophy does not imply the elimination of standards. On the contrary, it means, as it does in social life, the structuring presence and legitimacy of multiple standards, each appropriate to a different method of inquiry in the field. A discipline as modestly endowed with generally accepted results as philosophy must be open to divergent approaches. Without such wholesome pluralism, we will continue to suffer the sequential hegemonies that dragged philosophy in the past century from Hegelian idealisms to positivist games and, beyond that, to a variety of failed analytic experiments. Philosophy is perhaps more pluralistic now than it has been at any time since the founding of the APA. Our task is to secure respect and toleration for this bounty of energetically different investigations and to help philosophy overflow its academic banks so that it may become a full participant in the intellectual life of our country.

# PART FOUR

# MEANINGFUL LIVING

# TWENTY

## TO HAVE AND TO BE

In an incident Aesop did not record, three animals were lamenting their fate. "If only I had more to eat," said the pig, and he imagined himself buried under an avalanche of fragrant victuals. "If only I had shorter hours and less work," complained the ass as he rubbed his aching back. "If only people had more things and I greater skill to steal them," whispered the fox, for he did not want to be found out.

The God Zeus, known for his cruel sense of humor, heard their complaints and decided to grant the animals what they desired. The pig's larder was overflowing with food; he had so much that he had to ask the fox to store some of it for him. But soon the pig could no longer enjoy these good things. Eating too much had caused indigestion, and he could not even think of cooking or of food. The ass's workday was reduced; his master bought a small truck to do his heavy work. But soon, instead of concentrating on all the important things he had said he would do, the ass fell asleep and spent his day in a stupor. The fox did not fall asleep, but once the initial glory and excitement of plucking defenseless chickens had abated, he grew indifferent to the charm of pillage. He was bored.

The fable has, of course, no moral for anyone who thinks that boredom, stupor, and the glut that comes of overconsumption are integral parts of a good and human life. No good has ever come of the fanatic claim that only one's own ideas are right and only one's own values authentic. If there is anyone who wishes to adopt the fabled pig's desires or share the fox's fate, I will be glad to have him try. The ultimate test of living by the right values is satisfaction or equilibrium, and satisfaction is an individual matter. It is possible that undisciplined consumption is the good of some, while others find happiness in the indulgence of their orgiastic passions. Nothing could be farther from my intention than to censure such behavior. Nature continues to laugh in the face of those stern moralists who strain to set bounds to the plasticity of man.

I will not condemn a way of life, then, and I will not categorically reject the set of values that it embodies. Nor will I recommend the universal acceptance of another, possibly quite dissimilar, set of principles or aims. I will restrict myself to a critical appraisal of some of the values by which some men in our society live, and for which too many may be willing to die. A critical approach need not lead to criticism: it is merely the dispassionate attitude of the investigator who attempts, in this instance, to determine the value of certain values. As sympathy can only be aroused in men who share a certain concern and possess imagination, values can be discerned only by persons whose natures coincide and who are endowed with sagacity and insight. For this reason, my conclusions will have no validity at all save for those whose nature—being similar to mine—prescribes for them a similar way of life, who are able to achieve the self-knowledge that is required to recognize this, and eventually perhaps to muster the courage to carry it out.

If the values of the pig, the fox, or the ass satisfy you, I will not argue: surely, nature will out. Your satisfaction implies that in truth you are a human pig, or a human fox, or an ass. But what of the rest of us who live amidst the ruins of values that were our fathers'? Tossed in an ocean of conflicting obligations and alien pressures, many of us survive by makeshift, impermanent adjustments: we live without settled principles, with a private attitude to life, without a planned pattern to our being. We are not trained to divine the demands of our individual nature, and as a consequence many of us lack the inner unity that is the unmistakable feature of a *person*. There is nothing mysterious about this inner unity. Morality is a kind of hygiene: it is a cleanliness and unpromiscuity of mind. As the child learns the simple facts of animal hygiene—to eat only that which nourishes and to reject whatever does not agree with his nature—the adult has to learn, sometimes through tragic experiences, the importance of acting by a single principle and living by a single plan, assimilating and dismissing as his nature commands. A healthy conscience is but the inner demand for consistency, which makes one's life the history of a person instead of a disconnected series of events.

There is a current fallacy whose prevalence I do not feel called upon to discuss. This specious but unuttered principle is best expressed in the phrase, "To live is to make a living." All the values of our consumer age are implicit in this phrase. "To make a living," of course, means to earn enough to be able to purchase the goods necessary for life. But what are the goods necessary for life? According to what I shall, for short, call the Consumer's Fallacy about the Ends of Human Life, enough food to avoid hunger, and enough shelter and clothing to keep warm, are not enough to *live* in the full sense of that word. Implicit in the Consumer's Fallacy is the claim that we do not even begin to *live* until we have the right or approved kind of food bought in a good store, fashionable clothing, and a cave as good as our neighbors'. This, of course, is only the beginning. For there are characteristically human needs, such as the need for fast cars, the need for heartshaped bathtubs, and the need for the envy of one's fellows. We *live* when we have as many of these and other goods as our fortune will allow or our stratagems create.

The possession and the use of manufactured physical objects have become primary and fundamental facts in our culture and in our lives. They have penetrated our thought to such an extent that the attitudes appropriate to ownership and use have come to serve as the model for our attitudes to the world at large and to other human beings in it. Our attitude to almost every thing we have or wish for is the attitude of a consumer. We use not only cars and washing machines, but also reputation and the goodwill of our neighbors. We possess not only typewriters and television sets, but also security and the loyalty of our children. It is, of course, natural for the human mind to reify the intangible: to substitute images for attitudes and concrete objects for abstract relations. But when such conceptual aids cease to be merely that and begin to penetrate our mental life and to govern our actions, when human beings begin to be considered physical objects and human feelings things to be consumed, the result is that the good life becomes a life filled with goods, and our attempt to live it culminates in a rage of possessiveness.

At the basis of the Consumer's Fallacy is the supposition that a man is what he has: that happiness is a function of the goods we possess and the things we consume, that it is the result of urges satisfied. Thus Hobbes, an early exponent of the Consumer's Fallacy, writes: "Continual success in obtaining those things which a man from time to time desires, that is to say, continual prospering, is what men call FELICITY."[1] If this is true, the introduction of mass advertising and of credit buying are the two greatest steps ever taken to promote the happiness of man. Advertisers create new desires, and consumer credit makes it possible for these desires to be readily satisfied. The unbroken cycle of desires and satisfactions guaranteed amounts to that "continual prospering" which men call "felicity." Continual success, which is happiness, is the share of the American who desires, purchases, and consumes in proportion to the installment payments he can meet. And lest my point be misunderstood: What is purchased need not be a manufactured object, it may be love, and the installment payment need not be a sum of money, it may be time to listen to a woman's troubles, or a promise of security.

If Hobbes and his contemporary soul mates are right and happiness is but the satisfaction of desires on the basis of wisdom in trading, I wonder why so many Americans, shrewd businessmen at work as well as in their private life, remain unhappy. If Hobbes's analysis were correct, the successful consumption of physical objects and of human emotions should suffice to make us happy. How is it then, that so many of us are successful as owners and consumers, even as consumers of human feelings, but unsuccessful as men? The answer to this question is not to be found by an examination of the means we utilize to achieve our ends: it resides, instead, in the nature and inadequacy of our current ends. Similarly, the cure for human dissatisfaction is not by concentrating on increasing our possessions, nor again by concentrating on combating the natural urge to have, but by relegating possession and consumption to their rightful and limited place in a comprehensive scheme of human values.

The Consumer's Fallacy and the accompanying tendency to treat human feelings as commodities and human beings as serviceable objects, is closely connected with our current veneration of progress. Progress is a kind of motion: It is motion in the direction of some desirable goal. What differentiates progress from mere movement or change is its directionality. Direction, in turn, implies a fixed point of reference: some state of affairs for which we strive, an objective that is deemed worthwhile. I do not wish to assail the apologists of progress on the issue of mistaken standards; that some of the objectives in terms of which we measure our "progress" are insignificant or worthless is too obvious to require emphasis. It is as easy to suppose as it is barbarous to assert that the possession of two radios per family or the development of wash-and-wear, warm-yet-light, no-ironing-needed underwear is the yardstick by which human advance is to be judged. My immediate concern here is not with such mistakes, but with two even more fundamental errors that the indiscriminate veneration of progress promotes.

The first blunder is best expressed in the scandalous slogan, "Progress is our most important product." Progress, in fact, is a movement, not a product, and its sole importance derives from the importance and the value of its goal. No progress is valuable in and of itself; only the end of progress is of any worth, and it is only by reference to this end that a change may be called "progressive." The value of progress is, in this way, entirely derivative: it is wholly dependent on the value of the fixed objective at which progress aims. This single reflection should eliminate the mistake of supposing that progress can or ought to go on indefinitely or, in other words, that progress can be its own end. Like all forms of transit, progress aims at a destination not at its own self-propagation: Its object is a state where progress will no longer be because its goal will have been achieved. I am not denying that progress is a "good thing" in some sense of that ambiguous phrase, of course. But good things are of two sorts: those we want for their own sake or as ends, and those we want for the sake of other things or as means. Comfort and pleasure may be things we want in and of themselves; if they are such *ends,* they are valuable. Coal and electrical generators are a *means* to these ends. They help to bring about our comfort and pleasure and while not intrinsically valuable, they are at least useful. Now progress is at best useful; it is not intrinsically valuable. It is good as a means but not as an end: It must have an end or objective other than itself. Hence, progress can never be the goal of progress and no progress can be indefinitely sustained. Progress makes no sense at all without the possibility of fulfillment or attainment, and the more fervently we desire the attainment of our goal, the more we look forward to the time when progress, having got us our aim, will have ceased to be.

The sharp separation of progress from its goal is the source of the second mistake to which I alluded. We believe that it is important to progress and pride ourselves on being a "progressive" nation. We tend to overlook the fact that progress is not a term of unqualified commendation. Progress is movement in the direction of that which we do not have and which, at the same time, it would be good to have. Its existence implies a current lack along with the hope of future consummation. For this reason, any society committed to progress is at once also committed to the future, and whoever is committed to the future ceases to live in the present. But it is impossible to live in anything but the present. The person who attempts to live in the future ends up by not living at all: his present is saturated with a heavy sense of impermanence, worthlessness, and longing for the morrow. His concentration on what is yet to come blinds him to the satisfactions that are possible now. His desire to come closer to his goal makes his present a chamber of horrors: by hastening the passage of the days, he wishes his life away. Not only is his longing agonized, but after such fierce desire each attainment is also an anticlimax. Unreleased emotion paints in hues reality can never match. The object of desire once possessed is only a pale replica of what it was to be.

The meaning of life is not to be found in the future and the characteristically human malady of trying to find it there leads only to disappointment and despair. Caught between the incompleteness of striving and the essential insufficiency of the possessions that flow from desire and hard work, the future-directed man lives with a pervasive sense of insecurity, anxiety, defeat. The paradigm is the grotesque figure of the man who works so hard to provide for his retirement that he dies of a heart attack when he is forty-two. I will call the belief, fostered by our veneration of progress, that the means and the end must be distinct and separated by time, the Fallacy of Separation. The combination of the attitudes of ownership and use implicit in the Consumer's Fallacy with this Fallacy of Separation issues in disastrous effects on the attempt to lead the good life.

The Fallacy of Separation is so deep-seated in our thinking that it is difficult for us to conceive and almost impossible to admit that means and end may coincide. But this admission is the foundation of all sound ethics and, accordingly, it is found on the first page of Aristotle's great work on the subject. There Aristotle says, "A certain difference is found among ends; some are activities, others are products apart from the actions that produce them."[2]

As a result of our commitment to the future and of our interest in "products apart from the actions that produce them" the concept of *activity* has been virtually lost to Western civilization. An activity is a deed, any deed, that is performed for its own sake. It is an action done not as a means to obtaining some ulterior end or producing some product. Let me make my point with unceremonious simplicity: to engage in activity is to keep doing things without getting anywhere. But why should we wish to get anywhere if we are satisfied with whatever we are doing? The desire to get somewhere, our everlasting restlessness, betrays a sense of dissatisfaction with what we have and what we do and what we are. If we find something worth doing, it is reasonable to enjoy doing it and to ask for no more. If we are satisfied with what we do and are, it becomes unnecessary to look to the future and hope for improvement and progress.

Because the concept of activity is alien to us today, we tend to think that whenever change ceases, stagnation sets in. If this were true, no one would be more stagnant than the Christian God, who is free of desire and eternally changeless. However, to be without the striving that characterizes the infantile romantic mind is not necessarily to be static or inert. Striving might come to an end not only out of exhaustion or disgust, but also because the condition of all striving, the separation of means and end, the sequestered sleep of the impotent: it is, instead, achievement unfailing and instantaneous, because in it alone the human act is its own reason for existence. I readily admit that all activity is useless, and hasten to add that this uselessness of activity is the best indication of its great value. The useful merely *produces* good things without being one.

Activity, on the other hand, is good in and of itself. Too often our actions are useful to bring about ends that are worthless. When these actions cease to point beyond themselves, like poisoned arrows, when they begin to function as ultimate ends, they acquire a worth that places them in the category of what is useless but because of its intrinsic value also priceless.

If the good life is a happy life, the pig, the fox, and the ass are guilty of two fundamental errors. The first is an error of attitudes, the second an error of aims. The Consumer's Fallacy prompted the animals to extend the attitudes of ownership, use and consumption to areas, such as leisure, happiness, and the emotions of human persons, in which they are inappropriate. The Fallacy of Separation prompted the infelicitous beasts to look for aims and goals that are other than activities, for products of the human act instead of the enjoyment of the act for what it is. In short, the pig, the fox, and the ass all wished to *have* and not to *do*. But human beings are built to be bustling engines: They are agents, and only action can satisfy them. Possession is not action; it is a passive state, and as such at best a substitute for activity.

There is no clearer instance of a possession that functions as an activity-substitute than what is now commonly called a "status-symbol." To *be* a developed person is to engage in characteristic activity. Nothing is more difficult than this, since it involves self-knowledge, spontaneous action, and self-control. Thus, the majority of us settle for less, while we wish to appear as if we had not compromised. If we cannot *be* someone, we can do the next best and *appear to be*: and this is done by acquiring the possessions that seem to go with being a man of distinction or a developed individual. On the level of the popular mind, the confusion is even clearer. Each status symbol reveals an attempt to substitute having for being, ownership for activity, possessions for character: Each is a visible manifestation of our endeavor to be someone by having what he has.

A question spontaneously arises in my mind, and I am sure it has already arisen in yours. What cure can we prescribe for the three beasts? My answer to this is as simple as it is disarming. I cannot prescribe a cure for animals. If satisfaction attends their life, I congratulate them: if they do not interfere with mine, I will at least tolerate them. But how could I prescribe a mode of life for forms of life that are as alien from mine as oysters are from migratory mice? I can only speak for myself and for anyone else whose similar nature demands a similar fulfillment.

For us my counsel is to be. Life itself is an activity, and we should not approach it with the attitude of the devourer of experiences or with a possessive violence. We must develop attitudes appropriate to activity, to self-contained, self-validating human action: nothing short of this can make a life happy, spontaneous, and free. Finally, we must engage in appropriate activity. Which activities are appropriate for us is determined by our nature and may be discovered by self-knowledge. The two rules of the personal hygiene of the mind are to know oneself and to concentrate on the exercise of human powers for its own sake and not for its products or its usefulness. By knowing ourselves we will do the right things, by concentrating on the exercise of human powers for its own sake we will do them for the right reason. In this way, each moment of life acquires meaning and inalienable value. In this way, death cannot cut us off or leave our lives dismembered. For under these conditions each moment of existence shines like a total crystal: Each is an appropriate, meaningful, and completed human act.

# TWENTY-ONE

# DRUGS: THE FALLACY OF
# AVOIDABLE CONSEQUENCES

Why not use drugs? If mescaline makes life more interesting or more bearable, if marijuana gives please and enhances personal relations, if even a tiny amount of LSD opens new vistas for the mind and creates undreamed intensities of awareness, why should we refrain from their judicious and controlled use?

There is a growing consensus that, our hysterical laws on the subject notwithstanding, we have a right to use drugs, even if they are lethal, so long as this results in no harm to others. In a pluralistic society, each man must be allowed to determine his own good and plan his private life. The state's role must be confined to the minimization of other-inflicted harm; it cannot be permitted to establish itself as the arbiter of values and to minimize suffering and maximize satisfaction universally, even against the wishes of its citizens. Viewed in this light, the private right to private damage is but the negative side of our inalienable right to the pursuit of happiness.

Whether we have the right to take drugs is one question; whether it is right for us to take them, however, is quite another. An example might help to make this clear. If I harm no one else in the process, I surely have the right to kill myself. In the prime of a happy life it may not be right to do this; sometimes it is wrong to exercise a right. What I mean when I say that in a certain case it *is not right* to do what one *has a right* to do is simply that doing it under those circumstances would not lead to the most desirable results. Killing oneself in the prime of a rewarding life would not lead to the happiest consequences; the achievement of all desirable ends would then be rendered impossible by one's end too hastily desired.

To determine whether it is right to take drugs, whether taking them "makes sense," we must weigh at least two things. First of all, we must consider their probable consequences. Second, we must be clear in our minds as to which consequences are desirable. Both of these are hard requirements for the prospective drug user to meet. The latter, however, is particularly difficult, for it amounts to the demand that he be clear about his values, about the ends he wishes to achieve. It is obvious that he must be clear about them: Without knowing what is of value (at least to him), he cannot determine if the states of consciousness drugs create are truly worth having.

Now many who use drugs do so precisely because they are not clear about what to value. Confusion and apathy about meaningful life patterns, ignorance or skepticism concerning what would truly satisfy, lead to experimentation that has no explicit aim. A significant if not overwhelming proportion of drug users drift into the habit; for them neither the initial employment nor the continuing use of the chemicals is a part of the rational pursuit of worthwhile ends. It may begin on a dare or as an attempt to see what it would be like and continues, fed by frustration and, perhaps like masturbation, for a lack of something better to do.

It would be idle rationalism, and hence not a rational ideal, to demand that all human action be the deliberate pursuit of desirable ends. Some experimentation is both inevitable and good in human life. But there is a feature of drug experimentation that gives one pause. No one has his toe cut off for the experience; the consequences of such an experiment would be blatant and immediate. In the case, however, of some other human actions—sexual intercourse, for example—their most striking and lasting effects may be delayed. Few mortals have the imaginative power to endow such distant consequences with the glow of reality. In addition, our culture particularly discourages this imaginative act. Since we have acquired a measure of control over nature, it is easy to suppose that her efficacy may be contravened and her processes reversed. Our technology and much of our social life foster the impression that the natural consequences of our acts are optional and may at will be rescinded. Pills and operations appear, to the casual observer, to go a long way toward undoing the ravages of nature. We routinely convert the damage wrought by catastrophes or culpable acts into the calculable medium of cash and feel that when the insurance pays off the injury is erased. Our sense of the openness of the future makes it difficult for us to admit being bound by what we have been or done; we think of human contacts and contracts not only as voluntary in their inception but also as permanently terminable and tentative.

The result is an unspoken fallacy embodied in our attitudes and actions. The error, which we might call "The Pill Syndrome" or "The Fallacy of Avoidable Consequences," is the easy supposition that human actions are not attended by long-range or irreversible consequences. A young woman of my acquaintance who is known for her eclectic taste in men had two abortions before she reached twenty. She was surprised, even indignant, when she became pregnant for the third time. She viewed her condition not as a natural result of her activities but as a special calamity in need of explanation over and above what common sense and simple biology could provide. The same surprise and indignation were registered by the student who walked into my office to report that tests made on him revealed permanent brain damage as a result of the protracted use of drugs. The ultimate shock, of course, is to realize that the very pills we take to avoid the unwanted consequences of our actions have unwanted and unavoidable effects. The thalidomide disaster is but one instance of what I have in mind: from aspirin through birth control pills to morphine, the chemicals in our pharmacopeia are the sources of much incidental harm. In counteracting the consequences of our actions, we incur new consequences to counteract.

Drug experimentation is particularly dangerous because the fallacy of avoidable consequences is so deeply enshrined in our minds. Many of the most serious effects of drug use are delayed and in any case are not so easily open to public inspection. Eventual brain damage is not as striking, though vastly more disastrous, than an ugly spurt of blood from a severed toe. It is difficult to believe that actions that seem so right or at least harmless may return to haunt us through our lives. We may know nothing of consequences and may in any case believe that whatever the effects, they can be dealt with later. The trouble is that such beliefs are frequently quite false. The fact that the world does not come crumbling down after the first puff or the first injection may yield a sense of security or relief. It does not mean that ruin will not follow.

What rational purposes could the use of drugs subserve? The desire to conform or to excel by the bold contempt for consequences is not rational. Nor, contrary to considerable sentiment, is the attempt to escape the world. The reason for this is obvious. Reality simply cannot be evaded. If to escape us to flee and leave behind (the way we flee the smoke of towns in driving to the mountains), then death offers no escape. No one leaves this life unscathed: would we call escape that upon whose completion *there is no one* who escaped? But suppose that I could somehow survive the dissolution of my body. Even then, death is too great a change for us to say that the tainted soul that dies and the purer one surviving are the *same*. And if they are both same, would the rebellious spirit who is oppressed by this world not find the next more rigid and oppressive?

If death is no refuge, drugs can offer no solution to the man whose spirit longs for freedom and release. He must turn to the oppressive world for the drugs he needs to escape it. The more he relies on them to make life bearable, the more he is at the mercy of the forces he feels he must elude. They may produce in him a sense of freedom but in reality they do not liberate. Elation and the feeling of free flight conceal a helpless, tragic slavery.

Could we not use drugs for gaining better insight and new perspectives on life? That is, presumably, why many of them are called "mind-expanding" chemicals. What purpose could be more rational and more significant than the enhancement of understanding? If drugs are useful for this, their use is justified and should perhaps be urged in all our schools.

It is here that our much-vaunted drugs disappoint us the most. The "mind-expansion" they yield is not measured in new ideas or an increase in the depth of our grasp. They do not make our judgments saner or our thoughts more accurate. They increase the intensity of consciousness rather than its scope. The net gain is one of pure sensation: the flow of sentience is speeded up and everything seems more vivid and exhilarating. The subtlety of our discrimination is not increased; there is not even emotional growth while the influence of drugs endures. We may sit in front of the TV set overwhelmed by the colors or laugh uncontrollably at the sound of our laughter. The sensations are indelicate and overpowering—a type that might have been enjoyed by dazed dinosaurs. The "mind" these drugs expand is that shared by men and flatworms: It is what we more properly call mindless sentiment.

What is wrong, one could well ask, with sensing to excess if it gives pleasure and makes life bearable? Why should we not wallow in beer or pot in front of TV sets? I have no quarrel with delight, even though the pursuit of cheap pleasures is not a pleasing life. If a martini is consolation, a whiff or a puff or a pill may help more. But here the man eager for instant joy must be careful to weigh the long-term cost. Just as controlled and limited experimentation with drugs may be a good thing for the curious, chemical euphoria may be of value to the man whose alienation makes other satisfactions difficult to gain. In the case of both, though, ultimate self-interest demands careful attention to possible disaster. The price in health and sanity, in hope and missed opportunities, may be too great to pay. No experiment is worth the experimenter; and if it is enjoyment we want, there are alternative avenues that involve less damage and much less danger.

# TWENTY-TWO

# LOVING LIFE

## Young Dogs

Young dogs, sniffing and tumbling at the entrance of a mall, quickly attract a crowd. Full of energy but uncoordinated, they crash into shoes, lick the fingers that scratch them, stumble off the curb. Dignified businessmen catch a glimpse of the delight and smile as they move on. Young girls stop to hug the balls of fur; salesclerks watch the squirming puppies and the girls. The dogs are so alive that their vibrancy transfixes everyone. Seeing such innocent, unreflective bliss blots out all worries and fills us with joy in life.

Up and down the street, throughout the city, everywhere in the world, people delight in their activities. They talk and swim, build houses and see the sunrise from them, make music and make love. They hug their children, argue about politics, and move to the beat that comes from passing cars with self-forgetful intensity. They plan and play and eat and work and even reminisce with fire in their souls. Their energy cannot be contained, their spirit animates everything they think and touch. Humans live at white heat; they are aflame with life and love.

We love life in others and in ourselves; we are in love with life. Like good lovers, we embrace it with total devotion, commit all of our being to its service. We guard it jealously and caress it with a passion we cannot understand and hardly believe we can feel. When our love is reciprocated and life is good, we feel joyously fulfilled. We need nothing beyond such happiness. When life threatens to leave, we act like wounded lovers unable to see why our beloved should abandon us. Summoning all our energy, we acknowledge no rules and no morality in the fight to make sure that life remains.

Some think that we merely like to live or that we consent to life only grudgingly, in light of the alternative. Those who speak of a struggle for survival depict existence as a series of grim fights that prepare us only to fight some more. The German philosopher Schopenhauer views eating as but a way to avoid death by starvation and the modern British thinker Hobbes maintains that in its natural condition life is nasty and insecure.

Common human experience does not bear out such descriptions. Children throw themselves into their activities with self-forgetful glee. Adults and even old people delight in doing whatever they can do well. The search for new thrills and challenges constitutes a significant theme in human history. The pain of living of which the great Greek thinker Aristotle speaks is typically restricted to the sick; for the most part, as Aristotle himself knew, pleasure accompanies what we do, so long as we do it voluntarily and well.

If we merely liked life, we would be satisfied with however much or little we may get of it. But loving it means that we seek without cease the activities of which it consists. This is the surest mark of love: lovers never get enough of their beloveds. They create new opportunities for togetherness, new activities to share. They feel satisfied in their union but never sated. More of it, they think, is always better and an infinity would be just right.

Even those who complain a lot love much of what they do. The sick welcome improvement not only as a release from pain, but also as a glorious sign that life is returning. When healing is far away, hope is enough to give us bursts of joy. And when even sensible hope has fled, encouraging words from the doctor suffice to cheer the soul. We do not just *like* to live, we are *in love* with life, in deep, passionate love. To be in love with life is to love being alive.

I offer no theories about whether this love is unique to humans. Generally, less is the special possession of our species than we like to think. When we watch young dogs at play, can we believe that they do not find life joyous? Yet, when puppies turn into dogs, they are satisfied to sleep much of life away, while many humans stay up at night looking for challenges or meeting them. It is possible that the energy of life burns more brightly or for more hours a day in humans than in other animals. This is a mixed blessing, of course; being in love is exciting, though not without risk and pain.

Our love of life may be a madness, as perhaps all passions are. But for us it is, in the American philosopher George Santayana's words, a normal madness. On some reckonings, slow, sleepy animals may well be better off than humans. Equanimity is a great revenge on a world we cannot control. The energy of humans makes them care intensely, and those who care give hostages to fortune. Yet letting things matter makes for an especially rich life: living at white heat has its compensations.

I also offer no theories about whether love of life is universal among humans. I do not wish to say that members of other cultures want to live less or that they live less passionately than we do. But I note that the intensity with which modern Westerners throw themselves into the activities of life and the wide range of these activities suggest that we enjoy (or suffer from) particularly powerful drives. Though perhaps people in all ages and in all societies have experienced passion, not all cultures have the concept of being in love and certainly not all share our enthusiasm for the wonderful variety of life. I leave cross-cultural judgments of who is better off to those who think we are not doing well.

### Loving What We Do

What does it mean to be in love with life? First and foremost, it is to love the activities of which life consists. Obviously, not everyone loves every activity. This is why the opportunity to choose and wisdom in choice play such central roles in the good life. But everyone loves some activities and, given a chance, can learn to love more. Much of this love is spontaneous: eating, playing, rubbing each other, making happy noises, watching the dance of light, building things up and knocking them down delight us as soon as we start doing them, without the need for a training period.

Under normal circumstances, even infants enjoy their activities as soon as they are able to engage in them. They do not value them for their use: They like cooing and gurgling just as much as they love to eat. They draw no distinction between activities they start spontaneously and those that are responses to external circumstance. Everything seems to be done with total involvement: Crying and laughter engage the entire body, bottle or breast call each part of the little being to attention and exertion. Even the smallest tickle evokes delighted grimaces, giggles, and the waving of arms.

Children at play may be the best example of self-forgetful love of life. Worry is a sign of maturity, an expression of concern that nothing is as it seems. We learn it when we first suspect that we must look beyond the pleasure of the moment or that the good is about to be ambushed. Children are, of course, perfectly aware that nothing lasts forever; even the longest day of play ends when it is time for supper. But fortunately for their peace of mind, they do not worry about the end when they are in the middle. Their happiness is sustained because it never occurs to them to focus on anything other than what they do at the moment.

Absorption in well-loved activity is what makes childhood the best-loved season of many lives. Not having to do much one does not want to do is a great privilege, a luxury permitted only to lucky children and irresponsible adults. No careful observer can doubt that young people love life by loving their activities. Even when their days are filled with illness or misfortune, a moment's respite is enough to throw them into single-minded concentration on some beloved game. Adults who can imitate this improve their lives to an astonishing degree.

We are born as squirming charges of energy seeking release. Education and social life direct our energies to suitable objects and objectives. The activities we learn are indefinitely various; left alone, most of us would never have thought of most of them. Would watching gauges in a boiler room or stitching the upholstery of cars have occurred to anyone as a good thing to do? Yet, we find ourselves doing such things to make a living or to meet our obligations. Can we suppose that we love these activities and, through them, our lives?

We clearly do. Many of the activities social life teaches are easy to enjoy. It takes little to see the point of kissing and conversation, of driving cars and driving with a basketball down the court. But life becomes hard when much of it is filled with things we have to do to make ends meet. Going to work when we do not like what we have to do there requires bitter discipline, perhaps the discipline of hunger as the alternative. Philosophers have long worried about the sadness this involves and the waste of human lives. Karl Marx, who never did a stitch of such unwanted, fragmented work, denounced it as forced labor. The American philosopher, John Dewey, thought long and hard about what structural changes we would need to make in society to eliminate it.

The truth of the matter is that human psychology is constantly in the business of reducing misery. Perhaps out of self-defense, even the most obnoxious activities acquire a fringe of pleasure. At first, we may enjoy the satisfaction of a challenge met, and later, the predictability of a habit. Even bad jobs afford companions-in-misery, to whom it becomes a pleasure to complain. The most devastatingly boring routines establish expectations of regular sequences that confer small satisfactions as they are met.

Society also hurries to our aid, heaping honor on all gainful employment. Most important perhaps, the delight of what we obtain with work, even if it is only money, spreads to the activity to make it bearable. A friend of mine who fights and haggles over trades for eight hours a day used to hate his job when he was young. He must have been good at what he did because he made a lot of money. He recently confessed that now he cannot wait to return from his vacation; he has come to see the insults and the haggling as delightful means to wealth.

We love life because we love the activities of which it consists. When the activities are indifferent or painful, we render them acceptable and even good. The great problem with retirement is that the activities at work we so love to hate define us and give us a hundred reasons to live. When they are removed, fishing is inadequate to take their place. It is not surprising that many of those who retire soon die. Having little left to love, they have precious little to live for.

There is no reason to suppose, of course, that we love everything we must do. But we love much of it and certainly more than we let on. Our passivities bother us a great deal more than our activities: We like least not what we do, but what happens to us. And there are terrible things that happen to people, some as a result of what others do. But even there, working to overcome handicaps, ill fortune, fear, and disease leads us to activities we can love and enjoy.

Without the opportunities to improve our condition that the problems of life present, our minds would be simpler and we would have less to do, less to be proud of and much less to love. To say this is not to justify the human condition, only to describe it. And such a description, in turn, does not justify imposing additional burdens on ourselves and others in the name of increasing opportunities for improvement and for love. The problems nature does not impose on us, human nature creates; there is no need to add to them by deliberate design.

### Loving the Good Life

Loving life also means enjoying what life provides. The history of humankind is, among other things, the history of self-abnegation. Puritans want to have little to do with the pleasures of the body and ascetics reject the allure of worldly goods. That they have to demonize these otherwise desirable things is testimony to the unnaturalness and difficulty of what they try to do.

The body is the source of varied and largely innocent pleasures. Excess and careless perversion can, of course, subvert the happy life. But trying to make sure that we enjoy nothing physical is a task our nature frustrates at every turn. If we fast to assert control over the body, the first bite gives exaggerated joy. If we suppress the sexual urge by day, it finds an outlet in the middle of the night. The body overwhelms our resistance to its pleasures or tricks us into enjoying them in disguise.

The reason early moralists cautioned against enjoyment of physical pleasures is precisely because they are so powerful and alluring. Uncontrolled devotion to them does, indeed, interfere with social life and common responsibility. If we do not civilize these impulses, human existence can quickly descend to a level below that of animals.

The rule that waste should be sprayed only in special places in the house and not in the kitchen or the dining room, for example, is not an arbitrary repression of urinary freedom but the sensible attempt to separate importantly different functions. In the name of living well with each other, we must learn what can be done with whom and how and when.

Many of the customs that in time grow into taboos are, from a distant and disinterested perspective, adjustable. Whether sexual relations should be confined to marriage and whether marriage should be restricted to heterosexual, single-partner unions are questions we can abstractly debate. But it is clear that we cannot allow sexuality to serve as the only, and hence unimpeded, value in human relations and we must devise some social structure for nurturing the young.

Changing established customs is often desirable or unavoidable. Technological, economic, and social circumstances constantly modify our ways and values; we feel their effect more keenly today than perhaps ever before. But total liberation from custom is either impossible or the road to madness. We must have some established ways of doing things, some structure of values, some order in our lives. If the order that represses bodily pleasures leads to terrible consequences, we are justified in revising it. But we fool ourselves if we think that lifting every prohibition solves all of our problems.

One of the great drawbacks of despising the body is that it removes not only the problematic excesses of physical life, but also its rich rewards. This is a severe loss: it reduces the variety of what we can enjoy and the intensity of our love. The world is full of marvelous things that even puritans can appreciate. But the marvels of nature are not unconnected to the magnificence of the senses by means of which we note and embrace them. The human body, when tied to the imagination, becomes a vibrant sense organ by which we can participate in the beauty that surrounds us.

This mode of enjoyment is as different from cool objectivity as swimming in a moonlit pool differs from noting distant light shimmer on the waves. Those who do not love the body are at a distance from the world. Being uninvolved has its advantages, but the loss it represents is devastating. Involvement means being interested in everything and taking pleasure in every process and change.

The seventeenth-century thinker Spinoza and a number of more recent writers feel overcome at how natural—how fascinating, how surprising, and yet how natural—everything appears. This is one of the feelings that permit us to leave behind our concern for ourselves and for the narrowly local. It opens the past and especially the future as objects of our concern, as things to be interested in and to care about. People who identify their interests with the future of human life and with what is beautiful in the world, live better and find it easier to die.

There is another great advantage to loving and fostering the body. Those who do, double their pleasure. Everything we see or touch has an objective presence in the world, but also an immediate life in our senses. Objectively, planes are splendid devices of convenience and power. Kings would have offered their empires for an hour of what they enable us to do. But they are also silver birds and shimmering specks in the sky. Their vapor trails make them arrows that fly at thirty thousand feet. At a distance, they look like tiny toys; closer, they reveal intricate shapes and bulges that reflect the light. We can appreciate them both for what they do and for the splendid variety of their appearances.

The same is true of every other object. The plum bought at the store is also the ravishing taste as it bursts cold sweetness in the mouth. The CD is also the sound of Mozart as it fills the soul. The waves at the sea are also a rhythmic rumbling and something dark that flowers into white.

Even obnoxious objects can, in this way, be converted into beauty: the annoying wall my window faces can suddenly resolve into an intriguing pattern of colors and lines. A few heroic thinkers even claim to have extracted the pure shape of pain from the body's complex reaction. They say that, focusing on it hard, they have been able to overcome or overlook their suffering. Natural childbirth may present a related phenomenon: It replaces the pain of wrenched muscles with the more agreeable feelings of effort and control.

For reasons not easy to understand, many people sing the praises of antique virtues. They mean by these not the sort, such as courage and generosity, that Aristotle happily endorsed, but the austere ability to make do without what the modern world provides. It is better, they suppose, to take no medications, use no fertilizers and buy no newfangled machines.

They view computers and fax machines not just as unnecessary luxuries, but also as positive impediments to a simple and wholesome life. They prefer old telephones to new ones and bicycles to cars. They think that home-canned vegetables are better than what can be bought at the store and that if only we could rid ourselves of the unnatural offerings of new technology, we would enjoy better and more satisfying lives.

There is not a shred of historical evidence to support such beliefs. We all know that new technology brings new problems; toxic chemicals bothered no one until we started generating them as by-products of industrial processes. But, on balance, technology is a potent life-enhancing force. It has made life richer, longer, and more painless than ever. Romantic fascination with the past can be sustained only at the cost of invincible historical ignorance.

Such ignorance is promoted even by the great, live educational exhibits of history. Colonial Williamsburg, for example, has a unique opportunity to show daily life in Jefferson's and Washington's day. Yet visitors to the restored city see neatly kept houses, clean streets and newly made furniture of old design. Air-conditioned restaurants serve wholesome food prepared in immaculate kitchens.

Is this how it used to be? I doubt that the smells of the old city could be reproduced; if they could, tourists would leave at once. Food was cooked in filthy kitchens, guest rooms were infested with roaches, and rats and mice roamed the unpaved streets. Nearly all the inhabitants carried parasites, many died young, and most of those past thirty suffered from tooth problems and gum disease. The world then was a dirty and dangerous place in which people were rarely safe from illness and almost never comfortable.

If that be wholesome life, give me chemicals and air-conditioning, and by all means instant communication with my loved ones far away. If a machine could take our romantics back in time, they would beg to return to the safety and comfort of our civilized ways. The closest we can actually come to time travel is a trip to some less developed corner of the globe. So let whoever wish to condemn the benefits of technology live in a small village in New Guinea or Ecuador as an experiment for a year or two. Would they not wish to come back at the end of the first week? Even those who enjoyed their Peace Corps experience were delighted to return to civilization.

To love life is to love all the good things it offers. The marvelous new products and stunning opportunities of industrial (and now telecommunications-based) society are among the best of these. To go for a week to Hawaii may seem hedonistic, and to fly over the South Pole has been called superficial. But they are experiences ordinary people could never have had before. They are exciting and enriching and enjoyable; do those who stay home profit more? I celebrate the modern world in all its glory, with all its machines, its conveniences, and its comforts. To love life is to drink up all of it, to do it all, to hug it as our own.

Sometimes the attack on modern life masquerades as a sort of spirituality. But such holiness can define itself only by the war it wages on convenience. There is a deep undercurrent of such feeling among intellectuals in this country who declare the goods of industrial society, our opportunity-enhancing machines, and the fineries of life unnecessary, even wicked luxuries. In their attack on the benefits of technology, however, they never explain where to draw the line. If electronic mail is harmful to the soul, are letters also if they move by truck? Is there something wholesome in communicating by smoke signals that is lost when we turn to CNN? If dishwashers are unnecessary, shall we abandon soap as well, and clean water later in the year?

The truth is that religion does not forbid us to live well. In his great work on religious experience, the American philosopher William James wrote, "life, more life, a larger, richer, more satisfying life, is, in the last analysis, the end of religion. The love of life ... is the religious impulse." Sensible people enjoy life in all its pleasures and helpful products. Without ideological baggage, we choose every convenience we can afford and embrace every life-improving, opportunity-creating invention.

Life really is better today than it had been hundreds of years ago. One reason is that we have learned greater respect for our bodies and take better care of them. Another consists in our having developed marvelous devices that enable us to do with ease what we could never have done before. Not only are we in love with life, life now is more worthy of our love.

## Wanting More Life

Not the least, loving life means wanting more of it. Dread of death is not the outcome, as the poet Walt Whitman thought, of imagining the world going on in our absence. It is rather the unspeakable grief of having to cease the activities we so enjoy. The dying we do in the process of aging is just such a surrender of activities: Little by little, we become unable to do the things we like. Death in its finality just completes this retreat, closing the door on all voluntary activities.

To want more life is, therefore, not to want the blank of mere biological survival, but a continuing sequence of things we can do and achievements we can enjoy. Even for those unattracted to infinite Faustian craving, the appetite for activity feeds on itself and lifts only slowly with the loss of energy in the last season of life. Nothing shows the importance of doing things more than the worrisome idea of heaven. What would it be like to spend endless time in a place where everything is right? What would we do eon after eon? We recoil with horror at the idea that our only activity would be to sing the praises of the Lord. With *my* voice, day after day, to eternity?

Holding onto life can be the pathetic expression of fear. But normally, it is the lusty sign of an uncompleted agenda or of a surfeit of energy. Like a person shot who continues to charge ahead, the momentum of life carries us along. The eighty-year-old who persists in traveling because there is so much to see and the cancer-riddled mother who refuses to die because there is a child to raise serve as exemplars of what it means to want more life and why. They and the rest of us move on because important things remain to be thought and said and felt and seen and done.

An elderly man once started coming to my classes. We went to lunch, and Bob told me that he had recently sold the store to which he had devoted his life. He said that, at seventy-two, he felt he had not lived at all. Over the following years, he threw himself into activities for which he had not had the time or money before. He took college classes, went on a long trip to China, and developed a circle of friends with whom he could discuss economics and history. He and his wife traveled to Europe several times to see what life there was like and what centuries of faith had built. At what became regular lunches, he told me what he was thinking and what new things he had learned. The world was a new and wonderful place for this man, who had lived long but was not old.

Bob's first bout with cancer was a war. He vowed to beat the disease and cheerfully submitted to every invasive treatment his doctors recommended. I admired him for his uncomplaining fortitude. And he was rewarded with several years of travel and friendship, even though in a weakened condition. Then the cancer returned, and Bob was no longer willing to fight. His friends urged him on: Another operation and more chemotherapy might yield six months more life, perhaps a year. I was disappointed in his decision to fight no more. I could not understand how someone who had been so full of life could ever call it quits.

Only long reflection on Bob made me realize what an important lesson he had taught me. He was in love with life, and he was willing to fight for his love. But one must not want anything at all costs; sometimes the price is too high for what you get. The first course of treatments had weakened him; the second would have made most of the activities he enjoyed impossible. Travel would have had to be given up, and the cancer, growing at the mouth of the stomach, would have made lunches with friends an embarrassing torture. Bob had had enough. The few more months of life in a room or bed could not justify the suffering and the sense of loss.

The lesson is clear. Love life so long as there is something worth loving; for most of us, just breathing for another year is not. As we age or suffer from disease, we learn to sacrifice a lot for diminishing returns. So long as we can continue to do and feel and think and say, it is foolish to give up. But at some point, wanting more life runs into the stark reality that the sort we can get is no longer worth the cost. This does not mean that we surrender our love of life. As in a broken love relationship, we give up the loved one, not the love. With a tragic sense or with quiet resignation, we face the fact that the days of love are gone.

# TWENTY-THREE

# ARISTOTLE AND DEWEY ON THE RAT RACE

Aristotle put his stamp on the history of Western thought by inventing the concepts of activity and process. That is not the only way in which he exercised a formative influence over much subsequent philosophy nor are these the only novel concepts that flowed from his fertile mind. But these ideas became cornerstones of a distinguished series of metaphysical systems. They also came to articulate a vision of the good life or the life proper for humans.

The observation underlying the distinction between activity and process is that some actions appear to be complete while others seem to point beyond themselves for their completion. In digging and pouring foundations, for example, we find that the acts make sense only by reference to further things to be accomplished in the process of building. Foundation work is, in this way, intrinsically incomplete: it requires a significant sequence of additional performances to render it meaningful or whole. A moment or two of pleasure, by contrast, demands nothing further: It is experienced as complete and satisfying simply by itself. Extension of the feeling is, of course, welcome but it is not necessary to render the initial pleasure a complete and self-contained moment of joy.

On careful inspection, this incompleteness is revealed as not a random or accidental feature of some acts. Complex physical performances, in particular, appear to be rent by a sort of fragmentation that renders them imperfect and unsatisfactory. The reason is their integrated complexity itself. Within such processes, each part is tied to the rest, and none makes sense alone. Pouring the foundation is incomplete without building the basement, nothing can be a basement without a first floor, and before the structure can become a house, we must build each of its parts in its proper place and in the right sequence. This seems neither surprising nor altogether bad, and we may well decide that such processes achieve completeness only when finished: They are whole in the totality or whole of their existence, but always fragmented in the parts. This whole, however, never actually exists because the parts that constitute it are successive. Past and future infect the entire process; all the parts necessary to make it whole never coexist, and paradoxically, at the moment when it reaches completion with its last constituent act, all of it has sadly ceased to be.

Sequential actualization is, in this way, essentially imperfect since it is structured by time: it must always rely on the dead or the yet-to-be for its completion, which means that it can never be complete. Its fate, both as human action and as metaphysical event, is expectation and grief. It is a yearning after what is to come and the sadness over what is irretrievably gone. Aristotle and others have, therefore, concluded that it can serve neither as a foundation for our understanding of what *is* nor as a design for how to lead a satisfactory life.

In sharp contrast with this, activities are complete at each moment of their occurrence. Their simplicity assures that they can be actualized at once. In this way, they liberate themselves from the tyranny of time; even when they exist for a while, as when happiness endures for a precious hour, they are complete and self-contained at each portion of that stretch, gladly accepting continuance, but losing nothing if it fails to be granted. Activities constitute, therefore, human acts that are gems: they are meaningful, self-contained achievements free of the corrosive influence of time, of all expectation and sadness. They are eternal not in the sense of lasting forever, but in that they transcend or defang the temporal to reach perfection in a moment.

This notion of timeless actuality became the foundation of our understanding of the divine. Aristotle himself thought of his odd god as consisting of just such an eternal act in which the timeless tunelessly contemplated itself. Thinking of God as being constituted of activity assures divine completeness and perfection. One of the ideas of substance—that of an existent in need of nothing beyond itself in order to be or to be complete—captures this notion of a being shielded from time, growth, decay, need, desire, and imperfection. This manner of conceiving the ideal being permeated not only theology: it became the grounding notion of many of the great metaphysical systems. It has a remarkable history through the Middle Ages and was memorably introduced to the modern world in Spinoza's *Ethics*. It haunted German metaphysics after Kant, as a long series of system builders struggled to work through their love-dread relation to Spinoza. In one form and context or another, it has survived to ground much of the metaphysics of the twentieth century.

Despite this distinguished past, the idea of activity would not command the interest it does if its use had been purely theoretical. Conceptions of God, however, typically also articulate ideals for human life. Activity was viewed precisely in this light from the first. Aristotle thought of it not only as a way of understanding God, but also as an ideal to which we needed to aspire in order to actualize the best in us. He knew that, as temporally embodied, we could never escape the world of labored processes. But contemplation of the changeless beckoned to him as at least a momentary completion of imperfect lives and, therefore, as a manner in which we could be godlike. The same ideal, in typically exaggerated form, was present in Spinoza, who saw absorption into eternal, pure act as the only life worth living.

A fundamental disagreement separates Aristotle and Spinoza. The resolutely sensible Greek could think of no way of breaking down the distinction between process and activity and of thereby escaping temporality and death. As natural creatures with minds, we always remain both temporally fragmented and, potentially at least, eternally complete. The Stoics showed Spinoza a way to avoid this undesirable ambiguity in human life. Their belief in the power of the mind convinced them that the distinction between process and activity was not absolute: by taking the correct attitude to what we do, they maintained, we can convert any process into an activity. If what renders an action a fragmented process is that it is performed to obtain an ulterior end, all we have to do to change it into an activity is to do it, and each part of it, as an end in itself. This breaks the process into a sequence of activities, each of which is meaningful and complete without reference to anything beyond. The Stoic insight suggested to Spinoza that a life in the eternal was really possible. His account of how passive emotions can be converted into active ones was his version of the transmutation of process into activity and his explanation of how, though finite, we can completely fade, or rather brighten, into the eternal.

The ideal of self-contained activity, of life in the eternal, has remained powerful to this day. Some people advocate attitudinal adjustments to unpleasant tasks; others continue to draw a sharp line between the realm of means and those things that are of intrinsic value. Many condemn commercial and industrial life because of its endless cycle of fragmented acts and trivial demands. All of these critics tacitly assume the process/activity distinction and embrace pure act in some form as our only hope of satisfaction.

A fine, though perhaps surprising, twentieth-century philosophical articulation of the same ideas can be found in the work of George Santayana. Although he studied with William James and found himself in sympathy with some of the central ideas of pragmatism, when it came to thinking through the nature of the good life, Santayana reverted to Aristotle's time-honored distinction. He viewed the physical world as an endless sequence of events and animal life within it as a cycle of needs and fleeting satisfactions. Nothing caught in this web of the tenuous, not even the temporarily successful life of reason, could escape the ultimate inadequacy of all processes.

Santayana was more explicit than Aristotle in identifying process with the material world and activity with a phase of consciousness or mind. Accordingly, he maintained that nothing is of ultimate value except conscious feeling. But even the realm of mind is permeated by the anxiety and incompleteness characteristic of temporal process: Since, referring to what is beyond, neither belief nor emotion shows itself satisfied with the immediately present content of consciousness, they cannot constitute self-complete moments of activity. We reach fulfillment only in the spiritual phase of awareness, which is free of all restless striving and of all reference to the absent or the beyond. Santayana deliberately identified this "spiritual life" with activity in Aristotle's sense.[1] It consists of a string of pure intuitions (contemplative acts of consciousness), each complete in itself and presenting some form for cognitive grasp or direct enjoyment. Placid aesthetic immediacy is thus the only thing perfect in the world, the only act whose performance does not in the end dissatisfy.

The broader context of Santayana's theory of the spiritual life was naturalistic. He thought that absorption in the given constituted a perfection open to certain animals, and that it required the continued support of a living body. Nevertheless, the view amounted to a reaffirmation of the supremacy of mind and, in the form of aesthetic immediacy, of a sort of cognition. It also identified time and its attendant imperfections as the enemy. We could not hope to defeat this antagonist but, by momentary escape, we could cheat it of victory.

This depiction of Santayana's view of the perfection open to us reveals its remarkable similarity to Schopenhauer's theory of art. Schopenhauer thought of the aesthetic intuition of universals as one of only two ways of escaping the ravages of an ever-hungry and never satisfied will. The ultimate form of escape was denial of the will-to-live; if resolutely executed, this terminated life. Contemplation of the beautiful offered a less radical, and therefore less permanent, solution to the problem of endless frustrated striving. It enabled one to eliminate desire for a moment by providing absorption in a pure, uselessly beautiful object.

The resemblance is important to note because it shows the close connection between application of the process/activity distinction to the question of how to live well and the deepest, most devastating pessimism. So long as we think that time is the enemy and set ourselves an ideal of godlike, eternal act, we cannot avoid seeing much of life as worthless, if not positively evil. In such a sea of imperfection, with nothing but momentary glimpses of beauty to redeem us, we can readily decide that life is without hope and significance.

If we think of divine perfection in terms of activity, we can hope to achieve a state similar to God's blessedness by engaging in activity ourselves. Our inevitable failure to sustain such pure actuality need, then, not plunge us into ultimate despair; with God, we can have the promise of another life in which eternal activity will go on unabated. The pessimism of Schopenhauer and Santayana becomes unavoidable if we retain the process/activity framework but eliminate the theocentric metaphysics that has been its historical partner. Contrary to what some philosophers think, Schopenhauer and Santayana were not pessimists simply because they failed to believe in the existence of God. Their hopelessness was due to rejecting God's existence and the promise of a future state while, for purposes of elucidating the ideal human life, they retained the very concepts that, employed in metaphysics, lead at once to God. The lesson may well be that we end up paying a high price if we refuse to employ a set of concepts in one area while we retain their related use in another.

The process/activity distinction rests on the claim that there is an essential incompatibility between ends-in-themselves and means, between ultimate value and utility. Philosophers since Aristotle have, accordingly, maintained that whatever aims at some goal beyond itself cannot also carry intrinsic worth. Astoundingly, no one challenged this idea until the twentieth century. Much in Hegel hinted at its wrongheadedness. But Dewey was the first to bring it into question and to develop an alternative conception.

In *Experience and Nature*, Dewey acknowledges that much of what we do "in home, factory, laboratory and study"[2] is devoid of intrinsic value. The ends we prize, by contrast, are "spasms of excited escape from the thraldom of enforced work."[3] Labor is merely useful while enjoyment is good in and of itself. Its value resides in our being satisfied with it independently of where it may lead or precisely because it leads nowhere beyond itself. It appears, therefore, that work is intrinsically incomplete process, enjoyment luminous and perfect activity.

Dewey, however, is quick to dispel this appearance. In reality, work can be seen as useful only if "we arbitrarily cut short our consideration of consequences"[4] by focusing on the commodities it produces to the neglect of its cost in the quality of human life. Enjoyments, in turn, approximate ultimate ends only if we detach them from the full context of their conditions and consequences and thereby convert them into passivities devoid of meaning. The process/activity distinction applies, therefore, only to life fragmented by improper institutional arrangements and to events we abstract from their place in experience. The extent to which it applies is a measure of how far "experience fails to be art."[5]

To speak of experience as art is to say that in it means and end, the useful and the valuable all fully coincide. This sounds at first as a restatement of the idea of activity: since such divine acts are performed for their own sake, they display no distinction between means and end. The reason, however, why we can see no such distinction is that activities contain no means at all. Means are realities not in themselves desirable that tend to bring about what we seek. We turn to them for their causal features or for their mediating role in leading us where we want to be. There is no such mediation in activity; we perform what is wanted directly, for its own sake. In activity, we transcend time and achieve perfection by refusing all contact with the merely useful.

Dewey speaks of the genuine unity of means and end, not of the absence of means. This demands rethinking the traditional notion of means, which is the "coerced antecedent of the occurrence of another thing which is wanted."[6] Such causal conditions, serving as external necessities, appear to have nothing in common with the ends they help bring about. Dewey rejects this as the only, or the proper, idea of means and introduces in its place a notion according to which the means is an intrinsic element of the end. In addition to being a causal condition of the end to which it leads, a means must meet two criteria: (1) to be freely chosen and used to bring about a consequence, and (2) to be an integrated portion of that consequence.[7]

It is generally agreed that if they are not chosen and used, causal antecedents result in effects without being means to them. Dewey goes a step beyond this and notes that, under normal circumstances, the love for the end extends to whatever helps us attain it. Achieving results by control over the generative conditions of things and events is a characteristically human endeavor. Such deliberately and intelligently caused consequences are, in Dewey's language, "meanings." The need for meanings runs deep in our lives; their attainment constitutes art.[8] The first criterion connects means, therefore, with the prized and enjoyed ability of humans to take control of their lives, or at least of important portions of them.

The second criterion amounts to a rejection of the separateness of causes and effects. Affecting the tone of an exasperated instructor, G. E. Moore thought he wreaked havoc with Mill's wayward attempt to show that music, virtue, and money could have both instrumental and final value.[9] Dewey picks up Mill's mantle and maintains that nothing can be a means *unless* it is both useful and a part of the desired end. He presents telling examples of means that are, at once, elements of the whole to whose creation they contribute. Flour and yeast, he argues, are both means to bread and ingredients of it. And a "good political constitution, honest police system and competent judiciary, are means to the prosperous life of the community because they are integrated portions of that life."[10]

Dewey's alternative to the notion of activity, of what can be done as an end directly, is the idea of action that is both means and end. Events in experience present this double face: They play a role in the sequential (causal) order, and they display qualities we can immediately enjoy. Dewey does not think that these divergent features of actions are matters of perspective. Everything actually has both relational and intrinsic, both instrumental and consummatory, properties. We need neither adjustment of attitude nor act of will to gain access to them; a growth in sensitivity is enough. Such growth, if Dewey is right, enables us to realize that instrumental and final values are not incompatible. Accordingly, intelligent human beings will seek satisfaction by participating fully in both the labor and the delights of life.

This notion of means-end integrated actions is a far more worldly ideal than Aristotle's. It abolishes the supremacy of the cognitive and the contemplative, and opens the entire range of human activities to the legitimate search for satisfaction. It eliminates the prerogatives of the eternal and turns attention away from the age-old fixation on transcending time to the use of the time available. It restores the dignity of everyday activities and establishes them as proper elements in meaningful human lives. It refuses to view the totality of our condition as flawed (along the lines of the idea, for example, that we are rational beings tied to absurd bodies in an irrational world) and looks, instead, for concrete ways to enhance enjoyment in the present and to increase it in the future.

Dewey's claim that we can perform actions both for their own sake and for the sake of what they bring is heartening. If true, it would make life richer and satisfaction in it easier to attain. By redirecting our efforts in accordance with it, we could engage in actions that are both fulfilling and useful; we would not have to sacrifice pleasure to service. But is Dewey's claim true and his ideal workable?

Utopian thinkers have an easy way of sidestepping these questions. Dewey himself readily admits that many of our current practices fall short of being both means and ends; they include "much of our labors in home, factory, laboratory and study."[11] A single easy step from here could take him to the declaration that means-end integrated actions constitute an ideal in the sense of what defines how things would be if humans were rational, the world sufficiently pliable, and social arrangements optimal. Such standards beckon from afar; nothing need live up to them now or at any time until the millennium or some astounding change in human nature. This insulates the ideal from criticism as impractical; its function, it might be urged, is precisely to articulate a standard that is difficult, if not impossible, to meet.

Such an approach has satisfied framers of abstract ideals throughout the history of thought. To his great credit, Dewey sees no appeal in it. His denotative method requires him to anchor all his views, including his ideas of the good, in actual experience. We must, therefore, be able to find cases of action that are valuable both as means and as end, and that we undertake to do in order to secure both sorts of good. Such actions, Dewey asserts, must be both instrumental and consummatory simultaneously "rather than in alternation and displacement."[12] Moreover, much of the rest of what we do should be reorientable so that it approximates this ideal of the coincidence of utility and intrinsic value.

At least two sorts of ordinary practice qualify by Dewey's criteria: love and play. Kissing, done in the right context, clearly displays both instrumental and final values. Unquestionably, it is pleasant and tends to lead to additional fine activities. As enjoyed for its intrinsic qualities, it is an end; as freely chosen to bring about a larger, more orgiastic, consequence of which it is an integrated portion, it is a means. Persons engaged in it may, moreover, be reasonably viewed as initiating and continuing it for the double reason of how nice it is and what exciting things grow from it. It is, therefore, both instrument and consummation, as is every other element of the act of love.

The same holds for games and for play. Dribbling the ball down-court is not a coerced antecedent of going for the layup. It is an activity enjoyable for its own sake, but also for the sake of the basket that may come from it. As freely chosen instrument of scoring and as an integrated element of the larger scoring drive, it is a means; as fun experience and display of ball handling skill, it is an end. People who like playing the game, moreover, dribble for both reasons: they enjoy fast movement with control of the ball, and they look forward to the opportunities for scoring it creates.

Unfortunately, not many other examples of human conduct appear to qualify as optimal by Dewey's high ideal. Some ends we seek, such as entertainment and beer-soaked highs, lack useful outcomes. The majority of actions we perform as means can be enjoyed only by idiots or by those sufficiently unconscious not to note or object to repetition. Means and ends are, in this way, fragmented and sequential, and we pay a high price for fleeting satisfaction. At first sight, therefore, Aristotle's view of the human lot as pervaded by incomplete and ultimately unsatisfying processes appears more accurate about the bulk of life than Dewey's more optimistic assessment.

Two well-known psychological phenomena operate to reduce the onerousness of means. The pleasure of attaining the objective tends to spread to the instruments that helped us in the quest. Shaving, an otherwise unpleasant or indifferent act, can in this way become suffused with excitement if it is a condition of morning love. Brokers on the floor of the stock exchange report that long train rides to work cease to be objectionable when their trading goes well. Such anticipatory pleasures do much to make life bearable, even if the delight they offer is bittersweet or ambiguous.

The second psychological mechanism of relief is the remarkable human capacity for acceptance. Unavoidable, debilitating routines can become bearable with the years. Their assurance and predictability offer comfort, and the force of habit makes them expected, even essential, parts of life. Boring and menial work may seem a depressing way to earn one's living. But vacations reveal how much even such miserable routines can come to function as important elements of at least acceptable days. Given a choice, perhaps only a few would opt for such lives, but swallowed up in them we do all we can to make the pain subside.

Although these mechanisms render existence centered on unpleasant instrumentalities a little better, they fail to achieve satisfaction beyond the compensatory. They fall far short of endowing instruments with intrinsic value or of making dehumanizing tasks a pleasure to perform. So long as there are disagreeable but necessary actions, they are, therefore, inadequate to attain Dewey's ideal of means that are at once consummations.

Must we, however, always face disagreeable necessities? We face them now and, if they are to disappear, it will be either because we refuse to view them as unpleasant or because they will no longer be needed. The former leads us back to the attitudinal adjustments of the Stoic and is unlikely to gain Dewey's support. The latter points to increased control over the conditions of our existence and thus to applied intelligence and technology.

We find that many onerous tasks have been eliminated in the last few hundred years. We no longer have to gather wood for heat, haul our own water, or take an oxcart when we visit friends. In many respects, we live in what James called a "wishing-cap world" in which:

> We want water and we turn a faucet. We want a kodak-picture and we press a button. We want information and we telephone. We want to travel and we buy a ticket. In these and similar cases, we hardly need to do more than the wishing—the world is rationally organized to do the rest.[13]

In such a world, we have to do much less, or at least much less that is objectionable, to attain our ends. One part of the reason is that we have reduced the amount of human labor necessary to meet our desires; the introduction of machines, for example, makes our efforts more efficient. Another is that much necessary work has been shifted to others who, since they are specialized and have access to the right equipment, can do it more easily or better. Very few people raise their own food, for example, and few could even think of making their own cars.

These vast and, on the whole, beneficial changes appear to favor the view that industrial life moves us in the direction of Dewey's means-end integrated actions. The appearance, however, is deceptive. Industrial society makes life more comfortable at the cost of a momentous separation between means and ends at the workplace. The tasks we perform in huge organizations are routine and restricted. As the sheet metal worker in the airplane factory, we make small and anonymous contributions to large social products. Our actions constitute the means, or fragments of the means, to ends we have not intended and may not understand. These means may well be "integrated portions" of the ends, but they are not freely and intelligently chosen by the individuals involved. Even if instruments and products stand in a consummately rational relation in the institution, those who work there cannot easily connect their efforts with the objectives they subserve.

The gulf between means and ends is widened by the fact that necessary specialization makes tasks narrow and repetitious. Competition with others generates internal pressure to work relentlessly, and the demand for productivity causes haste. Under these circumstances, it is difficult to view fragmentary tasks as intrinsically enjoyable ends. Perhaps the work of those who shape metal sheets does have an intrinsic quality that, if only they could focus on it, would give them satisfaction. Their situation at work, however, is not well adapted to promote such focusing. And even if they succeed for a day or two, their need for work will outlive their ability to see it as meaningful or fun.

All of this may, of course, be true only because we are at an intermediate stage of industrialization. In another hundred years, all jobs unworthy of humans, all routine, repetitive, and boring tasks, will possibly have been eliminated. This could leave for us only acts, such as love and play, in which everything is both means and end. All the rest of the work of the world may well end up being done by intelligent machines.

If we do not destroy the human race and the planet in the process, this is a plausible scenario. Suppose that it comes about. Would human life then consist only or largely of means-end integrated actions? The likely answer is no. For the mechanization of productive tasks does not substitute pleasurable means for unpleasant ones; instead, it trivializes means or eliminates them altogether. The development from raising, killing, and plucking a chicken and then cooking it on a wood-burning stove to warming prepackaged microwave fowl makes the point obvious. In reading, we have to move the eyes and turn the page; television requires little more than a grateful stare. We do not have to go to science fiction accounts of electrically stimulated brains in pleasure vats to know that people gladly choose and often dream of passive sensuous delights. The mechanization of the world is propelled by this desire and serves it. The promise and ultimate reward of such a society is to convert much of life into enjoyed ends. This is closer to Aristotle than to Dewey, with the difference that such ends are passivities, not activities. A large additional increase in technology offers, therefore, little of benefit to Dewey's ideal.

It may be better to look for the growth or distribution of means-end integrated actions by starting from the example of professionals and their work. Physicians, presumably, do not have to engage in disagreeable routines. The actions they undertake are freely chosen, and the treatments they administer (especially in preventive medicine) are integral parts of the sustained health of their patients. It appears, therefore, that doctors have the privilege of performing only or mainly those actions that feature both instrumental and consummatory value. Perhaps we could all be like doctors and other professionals and thereby enhance our enjoyment of what we do.

This picture of physicians is, unfortunately, selective and therefore inaccurate. It romanticizes their work by overlooking the everyday context in which they operate. In reality, doctors can enjoy what they do only because they hand over much of what is unpleasant or routine to nurses, orderlies, assistants, bookkeepers, and secretaries. And even with these tasks delegated, it takes a wild stretch of the imagination to see their daily work as similar to making love. Particularly is this true after the fifteenth Pap smear or when examining, late in the afternoon, the fiftieth baby with colic. Even love, I suppose, loses its allure when there are too many customers.

The key, then, is to do what one wants for as long as one wants to do it. This is not a bad, brief account of freedom. Most people know the connection between freedom and pleasure because they find that they tend to enjoy what they choose without constraint. If we keep this in mind, we may conclude that the first criterion a means must meet according to Dewey, namely, that it be freely chosen and used, may be adequate by itself to assure a significant improvement of the human condition. If only all of us could do what we wished, embracing ends and choosing means without external interference and without the demands of necessity, we would be able to experience each means as at once a consummation.

What is there to stop us from growing in this direction? Dewey himself stresses the importance of freedom and sees it as indispensable for a satisfactory moral and political life. What we need here, however, is radical freedom for the individual. Each person must be in a position to decide what he or she wants to do, even if the decision disregards legitimate social needs. Can a society operate with this much liberty? Only if it finds a way to make people want what is needed. This is excessively difficult to accomplish. We can force individuals to do the socially necessary—to pay taxes, for example. We can train people to do what is useful (to take care of their parents, for instance) by creating in them a sense of obligation. Human beings get used to having to do such things and accept them as unavoidable parts of life. But they do not come to like or to enjoy them and they certainly do not seek them out. Socialization has its limits. Although some psychologists claim that they can make anyone like anything, it is clear that no one can make enough people like enough unpleasant things to enable a society to run on the basis of free choice alone.

Friends of Dewey must by now be anxious to set me right. Since the search for large-scale or Utopian improvements in human life did not appeal to Dewey, it is unfair, they might assert, to saddle him with a view that requires us to turn most of the actions of the largest number of people into meaningful, means-end integrated acts. This is a good reminder, even though it misses the point of what I have done. Of course, Dewey is a meliorist looking for incremental change. Of course, such change is possible: we can reduce the unpleasantness of means a little here and there by making life more like love, by selective advances in technology, by modeling more jobs on the professions, by expanding the sphere of freedom. Those, however, were not the questions we set out to examine.

Dewey presents his idea of means-end integrated actions as an alternative to Aristotle's notion of activity. As such, the conception articulates an ideal of human conduct in the most general terms: although it does not tell us in detail what to do, it gives precise instructions on how to do it. I have been examining the warrant for this ideal and its scope. I had little trouble identifying its source and instances in experience. Its range, however, gets Dewey in trouble. For he advances it as a condition at which human action in general should aim, bemoans the fact that such action falls short of it, and attributes this failure to current institutional arrangements.[14] This suggests that there are some strategies we can pursue to bring much of our conduct significantly closer to the ideal. I have explored what these strategies might be, but found none that offers significant relief.

Aristotle was satisfied to note that some things we did were by nature processes, others activities. The Stoics developed this distinction into a technique useful for dealing with the rat race. To maximize satisfaction in life, they admonished, we need simply to convert processes into activities by doing each element of them for its own sake, as an end. This requires only a change in aim or attitude, and that, they believed, is always within our power. If we followed the Stoics, we would perform whatever actions were needed without concern for their ultimate success. Such focus on the present would, presumably, make our personal lives and social actions meaningful at least for the moment.

Dewey's ideal, more robust and less resigned about the future, provides a better expression of the modern temper. But how can we turn it into a useful strategy for dealing with the pressures and the meaningless necessities of existence? Can we hope to spend our days as though we were making love to life? Having Marx before him as a failed example, Dewey shied away from recommending revolutionary social changes to institutionalize means-end integrated actions. Unfortunately, even if he had wanted to advance such recommendations, my discussion shows that it is not at all clear what they might have been.

There is one sure way in which we can all enjoy the intrinsic qualities of otherwise objectionable means. We can simply perform the acts of which they consist as ends-in-themselves, for their own sake alone. All this takes is a change of attitude or a firm resolve to focus on the immediate. The only trouble is that it is the Stoic gambit, and it converts means-end integrated actions into activities.

# TWENTY-FOUR

# IMPROVING LIFE

In an otherwise astonishingly abstract and tedious essay, Harry Frankfurt argues for the interesting thesis that the unidirectional relation between means and ends is insupportable.[1] He points out that Aristotle, the father of the Western tradition of thought concerning means and ends, maintained that means are valuable only for their tendency to bring about desirable ends, while ends are valuable in and of themselves. The relation is asymmetrical because means derive their value from the ends to which they lead, but ends gain no benefit from the relationship.

Frankfurt argues, by contrast, that even if ends do not profit from having certain means necessary for their attainment, people do. For the actions in which one must engage to bring about certain ends endow one's existence with meaning by providing purposive activity that is complex and "radiates extensively within the person's life."[2] So just as means have instrumental value because they lead to certain ends, ends have instrumental value because they require certain activities as means. Further, ends have "final" value because we care about them and they are worth having on their own account, and means have final value because they are worth having as necessary constituents of a meaningful life.

This point appears remarkably similar to Dewey's idea of what is sometimes called "means-end integrated actions."[3] According to that view, human actions are at their best when each one of them is both means and end, that is, useful for what it produces and enjoyable for what it is. Is this "coalescence"[4] of instrumental and consummatory value what Frankfurt has in mind? If it is, Dewey has at last made his much-awaited appearance in the precincts of analytic philosophy. Unfortunately, however, his arrival continues to be delayed. Frankfurt's ideas are different from Dewey's for at least two reasons. First, he speaks of ends acquiring instrumental value because they require certain means that have final value. The means obtain such intrinsic value, however, only because of their relationship to a meaningful life. Frankfurt says that the means are necessary for such a life, but not that they constitute it. This indicates that the means lack intrinsic value, after all. They simply serve as means to two desirable ends instead of one: They are useful for obtaining the specific final goods at which they aim and a meaningful life of purposive activity.

Frankfurt could amend his view, I suppose, and say that the connection between means and meaningful life is more intimate than he initially implied, for such a life is constituted by purposive activity rather than being merely brought about by it. But this still keeps him a distance away from Dewey. The hallmark of what Dewey calls an "external means" is substitutability.[5] Working as a waiter is an external means to earning the money necessary for life, for nothing about earning a living specifically requires it. This is but another way of saying that working as, say, a taxi driver can easily and adequately replace it. Similarly, what we need for meaningful life is not this or that specific purposive activity, but only some purposive exertion or other. So means acquire final value not for what they are but for the sort of thing they represent. This is at odds with Dewey's commitment to the value of individual activities and events, and also with what we treasure and how we treasure it in everyday life.

The second difference between Frankfurt's and Dewey's views is closely connected to the first. Frankfurt is satisfied to talk about generalities of the order of meaningful lives, suggesting that some activities acquire intrinsic value for contributing to them. With characteristic common sense and commitment to the denotative method, Dewey avoids speaking of such totalizing abstractions, restricting his account of the coincidence of means and ends to specific activity-sequences. Instead of arguing that nibbling one's lover's ears contributes to something as nebulous as a meaningful life, he points out that such small bites are both intrinsically delightful and truly helpful in getting where one wants to go. This strikes me as a far more interesting and promising approach to the improvement of life than anything Frankfurt has to offer.

How far can Dewey's ideal of means-end integrated actions take us in the quest to improve human life? I examined this question once before, but there is more to say than I had a chance to develop there.[6] Here, I first explain why this topic and Dewey's response to it are of great significance. Then I outline historically important alternative approaches. Finally, I examine Dewey's proposal in detail and evaluate it against the background of these alternatives.

Since the beginning of the historical record, humans have enjoyed the pursuit and possession of valued experiences. Unfortunately, the pursuit was often painful and the possession disappointing. But even when the enjoyment was deemed worth its cost, it could be attained only at considerable labor or sacrifice or pain. The Bible testifies to this element of the human condition and identifies it as a consequence of original sin. God's punishment of Adam and Eve's transgression condemns women to bearing children in pain and all of us to earning our daily bread by the sweat of our brows. The situation has not changed much since those early days. Although life today is immeasurably easier than it must have been thousands of years ago, we still face having to delay gratification, having to do much that we don't care for and having to submit to the discipline of enduring painful means to obtain satisfying ends.

Perhaps the first systematic response to this lamentable condition was the establishment of class structure, shifting all onerous activity to large groups of unfortunate slaves or laborers. This allowed the tribal chief or king or lord to devote his time to the enjoyment of the goods of the world. Hegel describes this strategy well in the master-slave dialectic, noting the struggle by which the lord attains control over the lives of his slaves.[7] The result is that the slaves work the ground to produce the necessities of life, while the lord retains for himself the negation, that is the consumption and enjoyment, of things.[8] Whether the lord ends bored, dependent on his slaves or desperately in search of a challenge, it remains true that he does not have to do much he does not want, and lives with far fewer demands on him for unpleasant exertions. Since his happy self-indulgence is gained at the cost of great misery to others, this procedure solves the problem only for a few, while it exacerbates it for everyone else.

Another strategy to deal with unavoidable misery, as Hegel aptly points out, is the slave's. He has no opportunity to shift the burden of the painful cost of delight unto others and thus no choice but to face endless labor with equanimity. The Stoic solution is to accept whatever comes one's way without complaint and to do what one must as though one wanted to. "Do not seek events to happen as you want them to," Epictetus, himself a slave, says, "but instead want them to happen as they do happen, and your life will go well."[9] Such control over desires or refusal to acknowledge the unpleasantness of the unpleasant can presumably be attained by anyone. But its cost is too high, requiring the extinction of natural human preferences and feelings. Indifference to the painful quickly turns into indifference to all things, exacting loss of the joys of life as the price of subduing its pains. If the lord lives at the expense of others, Stoics hardly live at all: they despair of our ability to improve the human lot, abandon all hope and satisfy themselves with changes to their attitudes even when the drive for objective changes would succeed.

Aristotle's famous distinction between processes and activities is a highbrow variant of the class-structure strategy. Processes involve the usual separation between potentially painful means and desirable ends. Their hallmark is that their ends are external to the means used to attain them, and the ends can be attained only with effort and over a period of time. In activities, by contrast, means and ends coalesce or else means simply drop out. Each activity is pursued for its own sake and we can engage in it directly, without having to perform any antecedent acts. This means that activities involve no instrumentalities at all. They are ends-in-themselves that require neither preparation nor time for their performance: They are instant accomplishments, and hence transcendent moments of delight.

The way to eliminate the painful labor of life, then, is to concentrate on those experiences that are possible without it. Such experiences tend to point away from the material underpinnings of life, consisting mainly of the higher achievements of what Aristotle calls "intellectual virtue." Thinking and seeing and contemplative enjoyment are activities in the required sense: to do them, he says, is to have done them,[10] meaning that, in them, doing and deed, process and product are indissolubly one. Small wonder then that the life of the philosopher is second only to God's. Thinkers know how to engage in activities and thereby to liberate themselves from the dissatisfactions and drudgeries of life. Free of the incomplete acts to which we are condemned in the temporal world, philosophers can live, at least for a few moments, in the eternal.

Aristotle's plan for bettering life is not as harsh as Hegel's lord's, but it is just as elitist. The difference is that class divisions rest on discrepancies of power, whereas Aristotle's strategy relies on divergences of taste and training. In reality, though, a division of labor underlies Aristotle's proposal as well. The material needs of life do not disappear while we contemplate; only when they are met, in fact, can we enjoy the leisure necessary for thought. So the shift from processes to activities does not solve the problem of unavoidably painful instrumentalities. It redistributes the pain to those who must produce the goods of the world and to those times in the lives of the educated when they are not busy contemplating.

A variant of the Stoic slave's strategy has for long enjoyed popularity among morally serious people. The approach is reminiscent of Kant and is, in at least one version, powerfully supported by the promises of religion. Instead of recommending indifference to joy and suffering alike, this strategy isolates necessary but undesirable labor and designates its performance a matter of moral obligation. Calling it duty removes such misery from the realm of what we could expect to like; that what we ought to do should be no fun is unsurprising and irrelevant. Kant sums it up neatly by asserting that morality has nothing to do with happiness. Its austere edicts derive from reason and bind us to obedience through respect for a law we impose on ourselves. Whether we like it or not is never to the point; it would be not only hopeless, but also wrong to try to change the course of things in such a way that duty becomes less onerous or, God forbid, something we can happily embrace.

Self-development, for example, is a duty we must not avoid.[11] Boring teachers, endless practice, and painful self-control must be endured without complaint. That we experience them as torture testifies to the fact that they do us good; they could surely not be as beneficial if they were fun. Pain, therefore, is a natural, inevitable, and wholesome signal that we take our obligations seriously. In the *Critique of Practical Reason*, Kant goes a step further and converts the traditional promises of Christianity into philosophical support for the view that we must overlook the painful instrumentalities of life. For those who put up with them and do what duty demands are entitled to heavenly rewards.[12] Over the infinity of our immortal lives, God will adjust happiness to match virtue and thereby compensate the upright for their pains. Evidently, this does not erase the suffering in this world, but it holds out the hope that things might go better in the next.

A central characteristic of modernity is the unwillingness to leave it to God to set things right. For the last five hundred years, Western civilization has been in the business of showing God how He might take a more active role in bringing improvements to the world. What I will call "the technological strategy" consists in identifying undesirable features of reality and launching intelligent efforts to change or to eliminate them. This has been a hugely successful enterprise, enabling us to extend human life, defeat disease after disease, and make daily existence vastly more comfortable than earlier generations could have imagined. Many of the pains previously thought unavoidable no longer plague us. Machines have taken over much undesirable labor and resort hotels testify that social life is organized so that at least some people can enjoy stretches of time as uninterrupted series of ends.

Intelligent industrial and commercial activity have been so effective in dealing with human problems that we hear more and more sanguine appraisals of its ultimate promise. Various forecasts predict an end to wars, the expansion of life expectancy to a hundred and fifty years, the elimination of hunger and all disease, and mastery over both depression and aggression. Manipulation of the genetic material of our species is supposed to enable us to create problem-free individuals whom we can clone into societies of happy and responsible people. Distinctions of class, race, and gender will melt as we educate or breed prejudice out of people. Everything unpleasant will be recognized as unnecessary or at least as unworthy of humans, to be accomplished by metallic or silicon machines. Utopia, in brief, is just around the corner, offering ever greater benefits at diminishing cost.

The promise of such unclouded days is curiously at odds with the reality of industrial and commercial life. No matter how much better off they are than prior generations, people today seem no more happy. The incidence of mental illness is increasing, and suicide, especially among healthy young persons, is a baffling and distressingly common phenomenon. Even the best adjusted find themselves engulfed in a whirl of immediately pressing but otherwise meaningless activities. Our workdays are filled with busy preparations for consummations that are fleeting or that never come. Most important, the tedious labor we used to have to expend to secure the necessities of life directly has been replaced by equally tedious but different service to huge institutions.

This last point is crucial. We do not have to go hunting each day; we do not even have to fertilize the garden and kill and clean a chicken for lunch. But we do have to go to work and serve in whatever ways our employers direct. Many of these activities are of little interest and carry no intrinsic reward. They involve pushing paper and attending meetings on issues of momentous indifference, or moving physical objects from one place to another, or attending to things that are difficult to see as anything but insignificant. No matter how many external means we succeed in eliminating, others no better rush in to take their place. The servant of modern corporations may enjoy fewer satisfying ends-in-themselves than the hunters and farmers of old.

This brief look at historical alternatives highlights the importance of Dewey's idea of means-end integrated actions. His view promises permanent improvements to the human condition. Instead of solving the problem of how to dispense with undesirable labor for a few people only, as do class-structure arrangements, Dewey offers a strategy that is universally or at least generally applicable. Instead of proposing a subjective, attitudinal adjustment, as do the Stoics, or a trick of reclassification, as does Kant, he presents a way of objectively reconstructing our relations to our activities. Although he strongly favors intelligent improvements in the material conditions of life, he has no difficulty in seeing through the excessive optimism of the devotees of technology to the travail that underlies the achievements of civilization.[13]

Dewey's view of means-end integrated actions consists of the following three general ideas:

1. Each event and action has an intrinsic quality that can be enjoyed;
2. Each event and action is connected to others by means of causal or sequential relations;
3. Events and actions can be arranged in sequences so intimate that their earlier and later phases are united.

Although Dewey was deeply indebted to Hegel, he learned from Peirce not to be satisfied with mediation or thirdness alone. Peirce's category of firsts reminded Dewey that there is an inexpressible immediacy in all of experience. Enjoyment or suffering of the qualities of what happens is the outcome of paying attention to them for what they are, independently of the relations connecting them to other events. I am satisfied that experiences have such qualities and that, in a stance of immediacy, it is possible to enjoy many of them. I am by no means sure, however, that all of them can be enjoyed rather than suffered, but I will wait to discuss that issue until Dewey's position is clear.

Dewey's second claim also strikes me as unproblematically correct. What he calls "the sequential order"[14] consists of naturally connected events, that is, of processes or natural histories. These orderly connections make it possible for us to achieve some measure of control over the environment. I may note, for example, that sunflower seeds falling on the ground tend to germinate and grow into new plants. I can exploit this connection and place sunflower seeds where I want the plants for decoration or maximum yield. The procedure works equally well in situations in which we wish to prevent a natural process from prevailing. I may notice, for instance, that rain soaks my head when I am outside, but not when I have a roof over my head. I can then design a small roof, called an umbrella, to carry with me to prevent nature from having its way. Such useful interventions presuppose no special theory of the nature of causation; all we need to do is observe sequences and find the time or the place to direct, abort, or redirect them.[15]

The first idea affirms the possibility that each experience can be enjoyed as end; the second points to the fact that every event is instrumental in bringing others into existence. Important as these claims are for Dewey's view, the characteristic feature of his theory is the third idea, addressing the way earlier and later events must be connected in order for a sequence of actions to be means-end integrated. In general terms, the relation needs to be one of unity. Dewey seems to have identified two different sorts of unity that may obtain between means that are not external and the ends to which they lead. The weaker condition for escaping the status of being an external means requires that means be enjoyable as ends-in-themselves and that ends be useful for further attainments. This suggests that such processes must exhibit unity at least in the sense that their elements are similar in being both useful and intrinsically valuable. This condition, if met, would be adequate to eliminate the drudgery of life by rendering means inherently and not only instrumentally valuable.

The stronger condition for a means being "intrinsic" demands an internal relation between means and ends. According to it, sharing final and instrumental value is inadequate for means-end integrated actions. There must also be a more intimate connection, which takes one of two forms: either the means must be a part of the end, or the end must be a completion of the means. Dewey explains the first version of the relation with great rhetorical power, returning to it again and again. He attacks the view that means are antecedents that must disappear before our desires are fulfilled. On the contrary, he says, they are vital ingredients of what will come about, in just the way flour is both a means to and an element in the bread we bake. He uses a variety of other illustrations to make sure his point is clear: he notes that sound institutions are both means to an orderly society and elements of it,[16] bricks and mortar are both necessary instruments and valued components of houses,[17] and paints are means to the pictures they constitute.[18]

The second version of the relation is a little more difficult to explain than the first. Dewey suggests that means and ends must be related in such a way that the means foreshadow the ends and the ends complete the means. An example may make this relation clearer. Baking an apple pie is an activity united by the identity of purpose and outcome. When all goes well, my objective and the eventual object produced are the same, and the entire process is directed by what I want to attain. I may begin by looking for apples to peel, rejecting squash and carrot; I buy pie shells instead of cheese pizza; I place the unbaked pie in the oven rather than in the disposal. Dewey insists that such intimately interconnected processes occur in nature even without human intervention. He has in mind sequences the ends of which are fulfillments and not merely cessations.[19] The mating of animals and the creation of islands as a result of volcanic activity may be instances of such fulfillments, though the question of whether they are or not is irrelevant to what Dewey wants to say about means and ends and, accordingly, does not need to be decided here.

In perfect accord with his method, Dewey developed the weaker and the two versions of the stronger account of how means and ends may be unified by observation of experiential sequences. He may not have realized that he was dealing with three independent requirements for means-end integrated actions or he may have thought that any one of the three involves or entails the others. I see no obvious or simple connections among them. One could subscribe to the demand that all elements of an experiential sequence be both means and ends while rejecting the idea that means must be parts of ends or ends fulfillments of means. Similarly, even if a means is eventually incorporated in its end, it need not be an end on its own account when experienced as an early element of a process. However this may be, meeting three criteria, even if interconnected, is a heavier burden than Dewey needs to bear. For this reason, I will examine them one at a time, and credit Dewey with a significant advance if even a single one of them can be generalized enough to help us improve human experience.

What sort of generalization do we seek? We want to see if by using Dewey's criteria of nonexternal means we can convert displeasing experiences into ones that satisfy. Such conversions cannot be matters of adjusting attitudes alone. They require reconstructions of experience and possibly even significant institutional changes, albeit none that is utopian. Such a test of Dewey's ideas is clearly in line with his meliorism and expresses in concrete terms his commitment to philosophy as the critic of social practices.

The idea that ends are fulfillments of purposive processes is, among the three requirements, the one most expressive of Dewey's commitments. His notion of purposive process connects to his ideas about meaning and intelligent control. Viewing ends as completions of human efforts, therefore, amounts to placing them in the context of our desires to bring about outcomes favorable to life. Careful attention to the conditions of what we do enables us to achieve the consequences we want, and outcome controlled by our own actions is what Dewey calls "meaning."[20] He adds, "The characteristic human need is for possession and appreciation of the meaning of things."[21]

For ends to be fulfillments of means, they must be meaningful and therefore humanly constructed outcomes. Dewey's idea is that anything so constructed involves effort and victory, and he finds it impossible to believe that such successful activities could fail to be joyous. His prescription, then, is to make the employment of means intelligent so that we can take delight in the effective exercise of human powers. This is thoughtful observation of what pleases us and generally good advice. As early a student of human nature as Aristotle remarked that unimpeded activity directed upon worthy objects is naturally accompanied by pleasure.[22] The joy of possessing the end spreads to the means used to attain it and is reinforced by the exhilaration of experiencing our power. What we have to do to carry the day is then not an alien necessity, but an affirmation of what we want and who we are.

The obvious problem is how we can experience means-end sequences as self-controlled exercises of our power. Clearly, most of the ends we enjoy are fulfillments resulting from our intelligent efforts, if "we" and "our" are taken to mean "human" or "social" or "institutional." "We" manufacture airplanes and fly them all over the globe. "We" build skyscrapers and fill them with corporations that bring goods from the far corners of the world to satisfy our cravings. "We" create systems of communication that enable us to know what happens in Australia or in outer space. Modern life is full of stunning institutional achievements of which we, if we manage to identify ourselves with the human race, can be genuinely proud.

The difficulty resides in the relation of the *we* to the *I*. Normally, the grander the fulfillment, the more people are required to secure it. Participants in such social acts must be organized in chains of mediation,[23] with a clear division of labor between those who plan, those who execute the plans and those who enjoy or suffer the consequences. An astonishing level of ignorance pervades these chains: though everyone is busy contributing to the ultimate result, very few understand how what they do is integrated into the larger whole. This means that even the people whose direct agency attains the end find it difficult to see the achievement as their own. They are familiar with but their own small fragment of the means; control of consequences is not in their hands.

We find, therefore, that agents in our highly mediated society experience themselves as instruments of causes they do not adopt and may not even approve. Contributing but an insignificant ounce of power to the megawatts needed for large-scale social acts, they cannot adopt the end as the fulfillment of anything they know about or labor to achieve. Their alienation is an outcome of the magnitude of institutional acts and the multitude of people required to carry them out. For this reason, it is very difficult to overcome. Eliminating large-scale mediated chains sacrifices the attainments of industrial civilization. Quite apart from Dewey's abhorrence of psychological manipulation, the last hundred years provide ample evidence that increasing social-mindedness or identifying the *I* with the *we* in peacetime cannot be achieved for long by propaganda.

How could individuals come to see the ends they help attain as meaningful fulfillments of their own efforts? Three conditions would have to be met. They would have to understand the social acts in which they participate much better than they do now. They would have to be partners in the decisions to undertake such acts. They would also have to share equitably in the benefits such acts generate. This is but another way of saying that our society would have to be organized to provide effective and universal education, openness in institutional, social, and governmental decision making, participatory democracy in all human interactions, and social justice for all. Human life indeed would be immeasurably better if we lived under such circumstances. But no one can seriously contemplate such developments outside the realm of dreamy utopia.

Is the other, simpler form of Dewey's strong criterion for nonexternal means applicable to much of human experience? The wide range of Dewey's examples suggests that means that both generate their ends and become parts of them constitute the rule and not the exception. Flour certainly is both instrumental to and an ingredient in bread, bricks are necessary for houses and also parts of them, and colors are required for paintings and also constitute them. If this relation obtained generally in experience, means and ends would be at least partly identical, recognition of which would tend to transfer to means some of our enjoyment of ends. Instead of viewing means as oppressive necessities, we could welcome them as early, incomplete appearances of what we hope to achieve.

Unfortunately, convincing as Dewey's examples may seem, they all share a common, limiting feature. The means he selects for attention consist of enduring physical and social objects. Bricks are not used up when we build a house and flour does not pass out of existence when we convert it into bread. The cultural objects he identifies tend also to persist: a "good political constitution, honest police-system, and competent judiciary"[24] are continuous patterns of activity. These examples overlook all the elements of means subject to the destructive power of time. Bricks must be carried to the masons, and they must fit them in the wall hour after tedious hour. Flour must be mixed and kneaded at night by a baker who would much sooner be home sleeping with his wife. The integrity of institutions is achieved by the agonized self-control of those who could abuse it, and must be safeguarded by painful vigilance.

All of these activities disappear with the doing, and most of them involve undesirable labor. None of these elements of means can be retained and raised to glory as parts of what in the end satisfies. They torture us with their boredom, their repetitiousness and their unavoidable pain, filling our days with what no one wants and no one can escape. The long, uncomfortable journey does not end up as part of the fun of visiting distant places. A sonata beautifully played does not incorporate years of youth lost in involuntary practice. The starving person's anguished search for food is best forgotten when the meal begins. Even if some elements of means survive and reach fulfillment in their ends, most of them do not; they remain as the bitter costs of getting what we want.

That leaves us, alas, only with Dewey's weak criterion of means-end integrated actions. This conception presents means and end as a continuous process each part of which is useful, on account of its relations to other events, and enjoyable, because of its intrinsic qualities. Dewey thinks so highly of this coalescence of means and ends that he employs it to explicate the nature of the esthetic. His point is that artistic creativity aims to produce works each element of which is delightful and yet leads seamlessly to the rest. Symphonies are like this and our lives can be lived this way, as well, if we do not permit enjoyment and utility to be separated.

The Enlightenment dream was to make life rational. Dewey adds to it the Nineteenth Century hope of making it a work of art, as well. This creates a grand ideal that we can, here and there, approximate for a time. There are activities every element of which is rich in consequences and rewarding to experience. The play of children comes to mind, as does the sexual play of adults; sports qualify, as do good conversations. I discussed this at greater length elsewhere, and I continue to think that having such experiences suffuse one's life would make for an exceptionally satisfying existence.

The problem for those of us wishing to improve life is that some of our experiences are already means-end integrated actions and it is not clear how the bulk of those that are not can be reconstructed on that pattern. Giving a cat a pill, having a rattle found and fixed in the car, and preparing one's tax forms are just not joyous activities, and there is nothing we can do to make them that. One can bribe oneself with rewards for undertaking such tasks, and if one is gullible, one can make oneself believe that they are fun. Such psychological manipulation, however, is not what Dewey has in mind. His idea is that every experience has a quality intrinsic to it that, if we focus on it properly, can be a source of joy.

There is no denying that careful attention to the details of things elevates the human spirit. Intricacy of pattern and richness of involution still the human mind with grateful amazement at the actual. But such resolute focus requires leisure and peace of mind; interest in the utility of the perception tends to negate concentration on the immediate. Many qualities, moreover, are not agreeable to experience. Attention to the distinctive features of agony, of foul smells and of human failure is not rewarding, and it is best to move through such deserts without looking long and hard.

We can, of course, imagine the world without deserts, but that is utopian. For Dewey, rightly, the issue is how to make incremental changes, improvements that in the end add up. And that is just where the notion of means-end integrated actions is supposed to help, but does not help enough.

But how much is enough? In spite of occasional statements that demand and promise more, Dewey himself seems satisfied with modest progress in the affairs of life. Perhaps no one should hope for more. Difficult problems have no grand solutions; it may be wise to settle for ideals that leave us a little better off here and there. Combined with the power of technology to relieve us of the worst suffering and of the most inhuman labor, Dewey's idea of means-end integrated actions may help us achieve some, though by no means all, the little improvements of which the human frame is capable. Not wishing for utopia, or even for universal improvement, is a sign of maturity. Yet it is a sad sign: Relinquishing the hope for more decisive and more permanent betterment of our condition leaves a living wound in the human soul.

# TWENTY-FIVE

# STOIC PRAGMATISM

Whatever specific beliefs pragmatists share concerning experience, knowledge, value, and meaning, they generally agree that a central part of the business of life is to make life better. James speaks of the ideal of meeting all needs, Royce of defeating evil, and Dewey of making experience richer and more secure. They are at one in thinking that human intelligence can make a vast difference to how well we live, and they extol the possibility of improving our circumstances. They tend to be dissatisfied with the status quo and see indefinitely sustained amelioration as the solution to our problems.

Stoics, in sharp contrast, are quick to call attention to the limits of our powers and recommend accepting them without complaint. They tend to think that only our beliefs and attitudes fall securely in our control. Epictetus, Seneca, and Marcus Aurelius agree that anything we would consider an improvement of the human condition is temporary and that, in any case, fulfilling our desires accomplishes little. The key to living well, they maintain, is control over self, not over circumstance, and they embrace inner calm in the face of whatever misfortune befalls us.

Even such a brief characterization of these two great philosophical traditions makes it clear that pragmatic ambition and stoic equanimity appear to be incompatible values. Pragmatists and stoics seem to occupy opposite ends of the spectrum, with the former busy trying to improve the conditions of life and the latter adjusting their desires to the course of nature. Much as Dewey's language is grating to contemporary ears, he comes close to capturing the apparent difference between the two sets of beliefs and practices in his famous contrast of the civilized and the "savage" attitudes to life. He writes:

> A savage tribe manages to live on a desert plain. It adapts itself. But its adaptation involves a maximum of accepting, tolerating, putting up with things as they are, a maximum of passive acquiescence, and a minimum of active control, of subjection to use. A civilized people enters upon the scene. It also adapts itself. It introduces irrigation; it searches the world for plants and animals that will flourish under such conditions; it improves, by careful selection, those which are growing there. As a consequence, the wilderness blossoms as a rose.[1]

I think that this radical distinction between the stoic and the pragmatist is misleading and inaccurate. My argument is designed to bring the two views closer together than it has been supposed possible. First, I will try to show that there are times at which the pragmatic attitude is inappropriate and good sense requires that pragmatists believe and act like stoics. If intelligent pragmatists have to be stoics from time to time, then pragmatism and stoicism are not incompatible, after all.

The second stage of my argument aims to connect pragmatic and stoic attitudes more closely by showing that the usual distinction between them as active and passive is ill conceived. In fact, if we pay careful attention to the writings and practices of stoics, we recognize that they are disposed to undertake action and improvement no less than do pragmatists. The difference between them is not primarily in what they do, but in their motivation for doing it.

Finally, I will proceed to connect stoic and pragmatic ideas even more intimately. I will want to show that in every case in which we wish to improve something, we have to accept the conditions that make amelioration possible. We must be satisfied, among other things, with the tools at hand, the skills with which we handle them, the circumambient situation, and the range of our prospects. In this way, every improvement relies on what cannot at the time, or perhaps ever, be improved, but must be embraced without complaint.

None of this means, of course, that there are no differences between what pragmatists and stoics believe. On the contrary, there are important disagreements, but they are of a sort whose presence does not make the constructive combination of the two views impossible. I want to show that a view we might call "stoic pragmatism" is not only possible, but also desirable, and that it provides a better attitude to life than either of the two views alone.

## I

Pragmatists tend to maintain that the good is some process rather than an end state, however desirable. Dewey, for example, argues that the ultimate value is growth, by which he means progressive enrichment of experience and improved control over circumstances. This is a brilliant move, eliminating such narrow or final-state values as pleasure, happiness, self-realization, and doing one's duty as contenders for the top spot. Their place is taken by a unitary value with variable content: what counts as growth depends on where we are in life, what we need, and what is possible.

Growth is an appropriate value for children and for adults ready to tackle new challenges. Even older people continue to grow in some respects: They can learn to drive an RV after retirement and increase their knowledge of highways that lead to Florida. In the twilight years, however, the modalities of growth become restricted. Increase of forgetfulness and other disabilities impoverishes experience and so has negative value. The areas in which positive development can occur slowly recede until the old find themselves bedridden, dependent on others and barely conscious. At that point or before, all opportunities for growth disappear, and life offers only exhausted ineptitude made bitter by the memory of better days. At such times, seeking growth is unintelligent; we are better advised to accept what cannot be changed and thereby reduce frustration and pain.

The wisdom of seeking acceptance rather than growth is by no means restricted to extreme old age. Quadriplegics undergo a period of growth after their accidents: they learn to cope with their grievous physical condition. But soon, they master the meager repertoire of actions possible for them and, at least in that important respect, acceptance of limits must take the place of trying to do more. The same is true in innumerable other contexts in which people or circumstances restrict our operational range. Children who want to be adults have no choice but to wait. Unrequited love, unattainable ideals, the permanent absence of means, and hopes out of season, among many other conditions, leave room only for acquiescence, making continued attempts at amelioration futile and thus irrational.

People who think growth is always possible could object here that, if all else fails, we can at least increase our ability to accept circumstances without complaint. But acceptance does not work that way. Some activities and features of activities admit of degree: one may, for example, make one's responses in dating people more and more intelligent. Other doings are of the all-or-none variety, and that is clearly where acquiescence falls. We can accept one thing and not another, and some people accept fewer things while others accept more. But in the case of any event or circumstance, we either accept it or we do not. Growth in acceptance is possible only by adding to the things to which we accede, and not by increasing the degree of our acquiescence.

Moreover, exploration of the condition in which we find ourselves is typically followed by acceptance of its limits as a totality. Quadriplegics can wish for improvement and hope that the harsh restrictions on what they can do will one day melt away. But intelligence demands that they resign themselves to the confines of their ability completely and as a whole. In this, all humans are like quadriplegics: we must accept the operational constraints imposed on us by who we are. We cannot lift ourselves out of three-dimensional space or deposit ourselves in a different epoch of history. More specifically, we cannot fly by flapping our arms, cannot become prosperous by thinking we are and cannot avoid the damage wrought by age. We can of course try to sidestep some of these inabilities by finding alternative means to accomplish what we want. If our arms will not fly us home, there is always an airline willing to sell tickets. But the very attempt to employ other instruments presupposes that we recognize and bow to what we cannot do.

If we turn to James now, we see a closely similar situation. He thinks that desires and needs are demands for satisfaction: the ideal is to leave no such demand unmet. Ameliorative work consists, therefore, of doing everything we can to fulfill our desires and to help others fulfill theirs. But James recognizes at once that desires—a "howling mob"[2]—are tragically disorderly and miscellaneous: the satisfaction of some of them is incompatible with the satisfaction of others. Whatever desires we favor, some others will remain out in the cold; they will have to be, as James says, "butchered" in the name of constructing the most inclusive set of satisfactions possible. The best world we can create in this way, the best world *possible*, is not the *best* world; we have to make choices, and the exclusion of otherwise legitimate desires makes the choice tragic no matter which way we proceed.

James does not say in so many words that this awful and unavoidable loss is to be endured with stoic equanimity. But clearly, our actions must be directed at bringing about the most inclusive order, that is, the largest compossible set of satisfactions. This is as far as amelioration can go. For the rest, we must learn to accept the price of such achievements as inescapable. What we have to give up is rather more than opportunity costs, for those include things we cannot do but may well not desire. The price of satisfying some desires is to surrender others equally or more fervently sought, and therefore to yield to the sad inevitable. Throwing our support to other wants changes only the desires to be crushed; the "pinch between the ideal and the actual" requires that we always leave "a part of the ideal behind."[3] The proper attitude to this feature of the world is to accept it and to learn to live with it. Acquiescence measures the distance between the best we can do and the truly best.

There are two significant differences between Dewey and James concerning the need for acceptance rather than ameliorative action. The first is that Dewey says little about circumstances in which growth is impossible and must therefore be supplanted by a less activist value.[4] James, by contrast, clearly announces that loss is unavoidable, and points in this way to the limits of amelioration. Further, given Dewey's structuring value of growth, the need for acceptance is not ubiquitous and tends to surface especially in the aftermath of tragic events and in circumstances near the end of life. James, on the other hand, detects tragic loss all around, and sees no way in which it can be stemmed.

## II

The most notable feature of pragmatists is their commitment to bring life under intelligent and effective human control. This activism contrasts neatly with the supposedly passive attitude of stoics to anything outside the self. Epictetus epitomizes this frame of mind when he says, "Do not seek to have events happen as you want them to, but instead want them to happen as they do happen, and your life will go well."[5] One way to draw this contrast is by noting that pragmatists look for technologies that help them change the world, while stoics want to develop technologies to change the self. If the primary aim is to achieve equanimity, it is best to desire nothing and to learn to live with failure and misfortune. The attempt to bring the world in line with one's wishes is, for the stoic, a fool's errand, offering only distorted values and perpetual disappointment.

Pragmatists, on the other hand, view the diversion from energetic engagement with the world to inward-turning manipulation of one's wants as compensatory. Surrender of the task of mastering circumstances in times of social upheaval is a natural and understandable response, but it leaves individuals vulnerable and societies without hope. Since control is necessary for life, stoics restrict the field of their endeavor to what they can surely command: their attitudes, desires, and values. But pragmatists can charge that this bargain is both illusory and unwise. All control over the external world cannot be relinquished: life demands that we breathe, find food, and sleep in safe places. Moreover, stoics underestimate the intimacy of the connection between the physical and the mental; in abandoning the struggle for control of at least some parts of the external world, we leave ourselves powerless to defend even our internal autonomy.

Depicting pragmatists and stoics as in sharp opposition, the former active in the attempt to transform the world while the latter passively accept whatever comes along, plays well until we look more deeply at stoic texts and practices. Even Epictetus declares, "Appropriate actions are in general measured by relationships."[6] "Appropriate actions," Cicero's *officia* or duties, are roughly the obligations we incur as a result of the natural relations in which we find ourselves. Epictetus explains the idea by reference to having a father: the son's relation to the father "entails taking care of him, yielding to him in everything, putting up with him."[7] This demands not only self-control, but also a variety of physical activities. Taking care of a father may well involve paying for his support, feeding and clothing him, and making sure that he gets medical help.

Such natural relations extend well beyond biology. On account of his heritage, Marcus Aurelius found himself in line to be emperor. He did not seek the job and, when his turn came, he did not spurn it. Pursuing it would have committed him to valuing power and riches, which are unworthy goods. But, given his family background and the long-standing customs that governed the selection of Rome's rulers, rejecting it would have meant denying who he was. Stoic indifference in the deepest sense suggested that whether he did or did not become emperor mattered little in the cosmic scheme of things and should therefore have been of no consequence to him at all. Shirking obligations, however, would have mattered intensely, as it still matters to stoics today, because it touches on internal control whose absence denies us self-respect. Freedom from concern over external, contingent events is thus not at odds with shouldering responsibility; on the contrary, the inability to master the world turns stoics to the task of mastering themselves, the heart of which consists in accepting what comes their way, *including obligations*.

Meeting one's responsibilities and keeping one's promises, especially in the teeth of contrary inclinations, is a source of quiet satisfaction. This "rational self-contentment," as Kant called it,[8] arises not from *achieving* what is expected of one, but from *choosing* the right course of action and doing one's best to carry it out. The central issue is the integrity of the person, that is, the unity of the agent as it exerts control over its desires. This normative structure of the self serves as the foundation of stoic virtue, which consists of living in accordance with nature. The invocation of nature, however, does not justify doing whatever comes naturally: right action is restricted to what meets the demands of reason, our highest faculty. Reason does not normally counsel inactivity; on the contrary, it requires that we bring our actions, no less than our attitudes, in line with its commands.

The active political lives of Seneca, Cicero, and countless other Roman stoics do not violate their philosophical commitments. They embrace action as a necessary part of the full life. They believe it important to be engaged members of their communities, to criticize irrational habits and to educate both the public and its leaders about what is of permanent value. Seneca's essay "On Clemency" is addressed to the Emperor Nero. Elsewhere, he writes "your first task is to judge a thing's value, your second to assume a controlled and tempered impulse with reference to it, and your third to harmonize your action with your impulse."[9] Intelligence can make a difference in our lives. Seneca advises to "apply good sense to your problems; the hard can be softened, the narrow widened, and the heavy made lighter."[10] In places, he is indistinguishable from a pragmatist. He remarks that "the man who laughs at the human race deserves more gratitude than the man who mourns over it, for he allows the hope of amelioration, whereas the foolish weeper despairs of the possibility of improvement."[11]

These considerations make it obvious that the contrast between active pragmatists and passive stoics is simplistic and will not stand scrutiny. Pragmatists are just as vitally interested in habits of self-control as stoics are committed to appropriate social ameliorative action. The similarity is so close that if we observe only their non-linguistic behavior, we may find it difficult to tell the two groups apart. This does not mean that their likely reactions to every event and circumstance would be identical, only that systematic differences between them are hard to find. But even though stoics may well do what pragmatists advise, their motivations for closely similar or identical actions are sharply different. Stoics seek nobility of mind and tranquility of soul, and view actions as either indifferent or merely means to internal self-transformation. Dewey, by contrast, values the consequences of our acts both as means and as ends, never shying away from satisfying desires and enriching the material aspects of life. Perhaps oddly, therefore, the difference between those who stress the significance of external achievements and those who focus on the internal life is internal or motivational.

*III*

Perhaps we should not be surprised at the similarities between such apparently different philosophies as stoicism and pragmatism. Both are, after all, comprehensive views of how to live well and both extol the value of intelligence and control. Here is yet another important resemblance between these systems of ideas: each captures only about half the truth about the human condition. Pragmatists stress the alterable elements of our situation, stoics the features of life that cannot be changed. In focusing on its central insight, each overlooks the valid points of the other and exaggerates the scope of its own. Pragmatists are so taken with all we can do to make life better that they tend to say little about our circumambient impotence. Some stoics, on the other hand, are so impressed with the uncontrollability of external events that they declare all attempts at amelioration futile. Only by correcting these oversights and overstatements can we hope to develop a philosophy that adequately reflects our situation and our prospects.

Epictetus draws a sharp distinction between matters that are within our power and those that are not. The former include only "internal" conditions, such as belief, attitude, and desire.[12] Everything else falls in the other category: Reputation, money, social standing, physical health, and the very actions of our bodies are beyond our ability to affect. This is an extraordinarily bold claim that flies in the face of everyday experience. For most of us, attitudes and desires are much more difficult to control than the movements of our hands. Moreover, it is simply false that defrauding people does not harm one's reputation even as it helps one's finances, that smoking does not tend to impair one's health and that we are unable to walk, drive cars, and chatter endlessly about all the things we cannot do.

Epictetus hints at but does not develop a distinction between what is essentially and what is only accidentally in our power. This way of presenting the matter avoids the foolish suggestion that we never have control of our bodies and affirms only that we can readily lose it. Desires and attitudes, by contrast, even though we may choose not to rein them in, are presumably always within our orbit of influence. The essential/accidental conceptual frame helps to make clear what Epictetus has in mind, but in the end it is not defensible. For starters, as all references to essence, it has its foundation in values embraced rather than in facts observed: in this case, it serves as testimony of the stoic commitment to view self-control as a permanently accessible good. In reality, however, our power to think and feel as we wish is more tenuous than our ability to move about and see, and is sometimes largely dependent on it. Rule over the internal environment is a rare and difficult achievement; physical control, by comparison, is often effortlessly easy. Further, integrity of bodily action persists through much of life, but many people are haunted by ugly thoughts and quickly lose their temper. The sharp contrast between what we can and what we cannot control is a fiction designed to bolster stoic resolve to be high-minded and steely-willed.

In any case, why should the impermanence or fragility of social and physical goods militate against their value? If anything, short-lived and rare satisfactions are especially desirable on account of their scarcity, and there is nothing ignoble about social pleasures. Much of what is uniquely admirable and distinctively human derives from the way we cherish and support each other. The stoic injunction to be as independent and invulnerable as the gods may speak to us in times of abandonment, but as a plan of life it is grievously truncated. To give up on creating a full human existence out of the contingencies that swamp us amounts to a sad, if not cowardly, escape. The rich life of which Dewey rightly speaks includes satisfactions appropriate to circumstances and sufficiently diversified to touch every element of our being. Though control may slip out of our hands at any moment, there is no reason to believe that a strategy of minimizing commitments and retreating to the citadel too soon makes for a nobler or better life.

Just as stoics overlook the positive contributions of pragmatism, pragmatists underrate important stoic insights. The reason is understandable: humans have acquired awesome power over nature and their circumstances since the beginning of the Industrial Revolution. Improvements in healthcare, travel, communication, and the production of food have changed life dramatically. Growing respect for rights and increased concern for the welfare of all have rendered existence generally safer, longer, and richer in worthwhile experiences. Those who extrapolate from these developments now speak of gaining control of human nature itself so that we may cure all its diseases and eliminate its flaws. Pragmatism is the consciousness of this burgeoning power, the happy conviction that things never thought possible will soon be achieved with ease. At their best, pragmatists do not forget the counsels of finitude: they know there are limits to what we can do. But it is difficult to preach fall in the summer of achievement and not to be blinded by love for the grand technologies of change. Without a sober assessment of what is possible, we tend to forget how situated, local, limited and perhaps even passing our accomplishments remain. This is the point where stoic reminders may help.

Consider what we cannot change, no matter what we do. The inexorable passage of time is beyond our ability to affect: Youth comes but once, loss is irreversible, every action excludes a hundred alternatives, and each inaction exacts a toll. The unforgiving properties of space are no less past change: absence and distance haunt us, presence makes us vulnerable. The physical features of things must be reckoned with: that gravity tethers, weight crushes, and steel penetrates must be accepted. We do not control where we were born and in what century, even though such facts set the parameters of life and opportunity. How can we reverse the damage of being born without bowels, with failing immune system or lacking a supple brain? Who can counteract the influences of poor upbringing, awful teachers, and cruel events? The failures and misfortunes of which some lives consist cannot be undone.

In some of these cases, someone at some point might have made a difference; in others, nothing ever could be done. But even where there is room for intervention, the opportunity soon passes and it is too late for remedy. That is how all of us live, bearing the wounds of the undying past. Why is it that people, drowning in impotence, do not despair of their condition? A few do, of course, and live in quiet grief. But for most, limits and disabilities recede into background conditions of existence: They become things we cannot help and must maneuver around. And finesse and maneuver we do, declaring that what we cannot change must not matter much, that we are fortunate to be as well off as we are and that disabilities are really opportunities. These may be effective strategies for coping with what fortune casts our way, but they disguise our true condition, as shopping takes one's mind off bankruptcy.

The scope of things beyond control and thus inviting acceptance is even broader than this. When I want to have my car fixed, I have to operate with what knowledge I have of its problems and with the mechanics available. I could, of course, seek additional knowledge of the combustion engine, but the growth of my understanding would then be dependent on my intelligence and on the information that can be obtained. Or I could search out better mechanics in a distant town; but then my success would turn on useful contacts, access to transportation, and my ability to judge people who are in the business of fixing cars by the promises they make. The same situation would replay itself if I wanted to increase my information, enhance my contacts, obtain transportation, or improve my ability to judge. Amelioration has definite conditions whose existence must be presupposed unchanged; each time we improve something, something else closely connected with it must remain unimproved. The ambition to make the world better in some particular requires that we accept it in many others.

This shows the intimate connection between the need for acquiescence and the possibility of amelioration. The two are indissolubly wedded; we simply cannot have one without the other. I must accept the hammer as it is if I want to drive a nail and the razor available when I need to shave. We do not improve tools when we use them,[13] and even the general properties of space and time that serve as conditions of action are embraced unchanged, eagerly though perhaps unconsciously, as we avail ourselves of them. If acceptance is the price of improvement, we readily see that stoics and pragmatists call attention to different sides of the same coin: The former stress all we must take for granted, the latter the useful changes we can make.

## IV

The last consideration points to the appropriateness of a new stoic pragmatism. This view combines the accepting modesty of the former with the search for improvement championed by the latter. The theory reflects the attitude of human beings who seek a better life but feel ready to face reality when all else fails. It reduces the boundless ambition encouraged by the success of science and offers a sensible account of our prospects as

individuals and as a species. It neglects neither sound counsels of finitude nor the vigorous assault on life essential to making it better, supple-
menting guarded optimism about the future with a realistic sense of the
limits of achievement and the possibilities of failure.[14]

Stoicism and pragmatism enrich and complete each other; in combination, they can serve as a valuable guide to social planning and individual life. On the social side, we face the temptation of supposing that
existence can be rendered not only richly enjoyable, but also safe and
free of accident. Heady advances in controlling nature and overcoming
injustice have made us believe that our power can be extended without
limits. Human cooperation in science, engineering and global commerce
promises a golden age of happiness for all. New discoveries in genetics
and neuroscience hold out hope for a world without disease; eternal
youth, with coquettish smile, seems to beckon to us from just around the
corner. Huge government investments in research by armies of scientific
investigators create expectations of daily progress and frequent breakthroughs. The growing repudiation of exclusionary practices and enhanced commitment to the good of all enables us to say that never before
in the history of humankind have things looked so good for so many.

These perceptions and hopes are not illusory. The values of the Enlightenment are alive and well in pragmatism and in our daily practices.
Sustained effort guided by intelligence has made the world a vastly better
place for us than it has ever been. The key to improving things further is
not to abandon the faith that energy and smarts can advance us. But
important as it is not to lose momentum, it is even more vital to guard
against crushing disappointment. The probability of frustration and consequent disenchantment is directly proportional to the immensity of our
expectations; the more we want to accomplish, the greater the chance
that we will fail. Accordingly, stoic pragmatists tend to scale down their
hopes even as they increase their efforts to make life better. The attitude
with which people approach their tasks is a central part of the welfare of
the community: if they feel amazed and grateful that we have come so
far, they are not likely to ask for the sky or cease their efforts in the face
of difficulty.

The stoic in stoic pragmatists reminds them of the contingency of life,
the vastness of the universe, the finitude of everything human, the tragic

cost of whatever we do and the possibility that our efforts will be of no avail. Stoics whisper *"memento mori,"* as religion used to but perhaps no longer does, calling the attention of communities to the larger, historical cycles over which they exercise no control. Without a cosmic perspective, we cannot present a just assessment of our situation; with this prospect clearly in mind, we can never place ourselves at the center of the universe. Stoic detachment is a powerful antidote to the hype that elevates science to the level of savior and social effort above natural limits.

On the personal side, pragmatism teaches drive, stoicism surrender. Both are necessary for living well; the former so that we may develop what is latent in us, the latter so we do not become slaves to our success. The Protestant ethic puts many people in overdrive and makes it difficult for them to abandon effort and let go. We may become fixated on an activity or fall so deeply in love with life that we never reach the moment of equanimity that enables us to quit. How long should we pursue people we adore but who show no interest in us, or a profession for which we have no aptitude? Too often we tend to persist, believing that continued work will win the day. Although we cannot succeed without effort, there is no assurance that effort always pays. Wisdom consists in knowing how far to push and when to hang it up.[15]

This is perhaps the most valuable contribution of the stoic. Consider decisions about the end of life. Sooner or later, almost everyone must join the battle with old age or disease. The pragmatist advises all-out war: let the fur fly if the prize is more or better life. Initially, or so long as there is something of substance to gain, this surely is the right attitude. But at some point, combat becomes futile: another operation and yet another round of untested chemotherapy amount to torture and gain no result. Nature checkmates us in the end, and when that becomes plain, it is unbecoming to knock over the board in anger and pointless to play out every move. At that stage, the stoic teaches us to smile, to say it was a good game and now goodnight.

# TWENTY-SIX

# PRAGMATISM AND DEATH

The ameliorative strategy to life that is the hallmark of pragmatism fails, critics say, because it cannot deal with the ultimate fact of death. It is not altogether clear what "dealing with death" means, that is, what critics expect pragmatists to do about the termination of life. Stoics supposedly know what to do about death, namely accept it without complaint. Deeply believing Christians also know what to do when it comes time to die: they make a last confession, commend their souls to God and pass away in the faith that they will meet their maker face to face.

Neither one of these strategies is open to pragmatists because they are committed to the improvement of life here and now. Their theory requires completion in practice, and this suggests that critics expect pragmatists to attain a decisive victory over the end of life, a victory to establish once and for all that "death shall have no dominion." Short of such a mighty achievement, pragmatism seems to offer only Band-Aids for the wound of life that permit us to bleed to death.

It is understandable that critics should hold pragmatism accountable for what it says about death. Its central interest is in the improvement of life or, in Dewey's version, in the growth of what is precious. The upward trajectory this celebrates suffers abrupt interruption in death; from the subjective standpoint, the termination of one's existence counts at once as the loss of everything. To be sure, individuals may make some contribution to the flow of life or introduce some changes to the culture of their day. But these achievements tend to be small to the point of insignificance, leaving what is of genuine value unpreserved; in death, the record and distillate of a lifetime of experience disappear without a trace. The termination of life leaves nothing of the skills, memories, judgments, perspectives, and unique ways of savoring the world that constitute a person.

Some philosophers have attempted to address this momentous loss by reassuring us that it is either not final or not real. Religious thinkers call upon God not to permit any created value to lapse by guarantying our immortality or by letting His memory serve as the guardian of everything good. If, as Saint Thomas, Kant, Royce, and innumerable others suggest, our subjectivity will never perish or, as Whitehead and other process thinkers insist, it will at least be remembered by God, we can go about developing our personalities in the sure knowledge that what we create represents a permanent addition to the total value of the world.

Such answers to our anxieties are clear and, even if untrue, count as significant suggestions. The argument that the loss of personal life is of no significance, on the other hand, lacks plausibility. Hegel, for example, maintains that an inner life that is inexpressible amounts to nothing and that its supposed extinction—normally viewed as utter personal ruin—is therefore of little moment. This explains Hegel's cavalier attitude to the death of individuals, but it is of little value to people in immediate contact with their private values and feelings. Hegel may be satisfied with whatever small contribution persons can make to their cultures, but such objective immortality is cold comfort to those whose intense personal lives convince them that they are more than wavelets in the stream of life.

Pragmatism is primarily a secular view, so it cannot offer assurances that we are immortal or that nothing of real value is ever lost. One could imagine pragmatists agreeing with Lucretius that, though death is final, it is nothing to fear because we will never experience it. But this is an attempt to deal with the dread surrounding the end of life rather than taking aim at death directly: it counsels calm acceptance of the inevitable instead of offering a strategy to sidestep or delay it. As such, it is insufficiently proactive for the pragmatist who seeks concrete measures to stem the tide of death that forever surrounds us.

That death can and must be defeated is a view embraced by a growing number of scientists and physicians today. Some maintain that death is a disease of which we can be cured. Others, more modestly, believe that the human lifespan can be extended to 150 years soon, and indefinitely beyond it if we are inventive and make the right investments. One might suppose that these thinkers are the true pragmatists, setting their sights on the endless improvement of the human condition and foreseeing a time at which we will be essentially immortal. Yet, I find it difficult not to view such ideas as a parody of pragmatism. There is, of course, nothing wrong with extending human life by a year or a decade. That, in fact, is what has occurred in a spectacular way in the last hundred years. Life expectancy in the United States increased from 47.3 years in 1900 to 78.4 years in 2008. We can reasonably expect further modest increases unless pandemics, natural catastrophes, or large-scale armed conflicts intervene. To suppose, however, that we can extrapolate and look for such explosive growth to continue is baseless.

There are natural though relatively indeterminate limits to growth of every sort. If we extrapolated from a child's first five years of life and supposed that it will grow an equal number of inches in each five-year period, we would expect to see thirty-foot giants at retirement. The limits are difficult to gauge but they are nevertheless real. Plenty of protein and some growth hormone can make individuals grow taller than they would otherwise, but good food and chemical enhancements can do only so much, and people who grow too tall tend to suffer, in any case, from poor coordination and unpredictable organ failures.

The situation is likely to be similar with those who live for a very long time. We already see that the gradual deterioration of body and mind leaves the elderly shipwrecked in nursing homes. Hitherto rare diseases beset them, and, like everything else in the world, parts of their bodies wear out. The dream of indestructible physical objects must have had its source in our frustration at seeing everything decay; it gains support from the apparent imperishability of the hills and the buildings we raise to crown them. But the permanence is illusory: neither hills nor magnificent structures survive the ravages of nature. Is it not odd that all of us know this and yet serious people declare that of all the physical objects in the world, human beings can be made the most durable?

The ambition verges on madness when scientists announce that aging is a disease. Because what is debilitating illness in one society may be viewed as the touch of the divine by another, no one has yet succeeded in developing a satisfactory account of the notion of disease. If illness is simply an undesirable biological process, some pregnancies could be seen as diseases, as could instances of hunger. This conceptual weakness aside, the belief that aging is a sickness confuses the basic processes of life with their impediments, condemning everything we do and everything that happens to us as noxious and in need of change. This is the latest scientific version of what used to be called original sin, with biological researchers taking the role of Jesus Christ, our advocate, who relieves us of our rottenness.

There is a totalizing impulse behind this drive for everlasting life, driving us to believe that if an extra year of life is good, an infinite number of them must be vastly better. Our Faustian love of infinity makes us want it all: youthful vigor when we are a thousand years old, a supple mind at age five thousand, and love in the afternoon on our ten thousandth birthday. The social changes necessary to accommodate this crazed vision of life cannot even be imagined. The endless existence of the first generation to achieve immortality would leave no room for the young; the wholesome decline of the weary would be replaced by hoary men and women bubbling with the energy of Shangri-La. The subjective consequences of guaranteed survival would be equally devastating. Without finite compass, lives could have no trajectory, leading to the growth of boredom and the desire to die. How long would it take to explore the possibilities of life if our development were arrested to keep us forever eighteen years of age? Beyond that, we would face only repetition and the weariness that comes of enacting the same script day by day.

Finitude is a condition of the architecture of life; we can build ourselves into striking structures in a limited time, but would lack motivation to do much in an endless life. The lesson is constraint, leading to effort and achievement. The wholesome message of finitude is that we do not have all day, that time will run out, and that we just cannot do everything we want. Endless life eliminates the regimen of choice and labor and makes us habitual procrastinators. Rejecting the desirability of an endless noon does not mean, of course, that adding a year or two to how long we live is a trivial advancement. To the contrary, that way lie good sense and the foundation of a satisfying life. It is emphatically not the case that the shorter the life the more it is to be valued. As with salt and sex, more is good up to a point but loses its attractiveness when we face a glut. Aristotle was right that there is a natural range of optimal performance for many behaviors. The range falls between what is too much and what is too little, as determined by enlightened experience. Something like this also holds for length of life. The appropriate range may be broad (say, from sixty to one hundred) and with the improvement of medicine, health, and nutrition, it may creep up over time. But we know that some deaths are premature and others, fervently hoped for, are too slow to arrive.

Pragmatists do not have to deny that there are limits to what humans can accomplish and to the number of their days. Accepting the fact that our lives and powers are finite is consistent with their gradual expansion. This is the belief of a pragmatism chastened by ultimate acquiescence, a pragmatism with a stoic correction for the times when intelligence and effort fail. Such times arrive in everyone's life, and when they do, quiet surrender is appropriate. But pragmatists will not yield without a fight, to test if there might not be a way to avoid checkmate. They know that we need two sorts of wisdom in leading a good life. The first enables us to invent ways to attain our ends; the second helps us recognize dead ends. The trouble is that the success of the first obstructs the operation of the second: a lifetime of getting our way creates the conviction that we can extricate ourselves from any situation. This is why we do battle to see if there is an escape. At a certain point, however, intelligent people stop the fight and acknowledge futility.

What, then, is it that the critics of pragmatism want it to do in "dealing" with death? I can see two possible and sensible demands. The first is to provide a way of integrating the fact of death into meaningful and satisfying lives. The second takes the form of making useful suggestions for how to live in the shadow of death, diminishing its power by delaying the inevitable. The first is a conceptual task; the second focuses on practical strategies. What I mean by "conceptual task" is the demand to develop forms of thinking to help us understand the complex relations between the process of living well and its termination. Valuable guidance in how to avoid dying is particularly important for pragmatism because of its interest in practical outcomes: concrete moral problems can serve only as illustrations in Kant's system of ethics, but their resolution functions as the ultimate test of the value of pragmatism.

There are ample conceptual resources in the history of philosophy to help pragmatists think about the end of life. The most useful idea may well be that of the life cycle, depicting birth and death as natural termini of individual existence. Birth as bursting on the scene and death as abrupt disappearance balance one another in the process of life. The balance is further supported by the symmetry of growth and decline every organism undergoes. Focus on this image enables us to view death as a natural and not extraordinary event, something that holds neither terror nor mystery.

The notion of the life cycle also reinforces our connection to nature. Our cats and dogs die, as do the squirrels in the yard. We may live longer and perhaps better than they, but we unite with them in our fate. The notion to combat is what Santayana characterized as the conviction that we are "too good for extinction," that what happens to "mere" animals cannot happen to us. A colossal sense of egotism hides behind such beliefs, reinforced by our refusal to be satisfied with however much life offers. Seventy or eighty years of existence should be enough to accomplish what we want, particularly since prior generations were lucky to have forty or fifty. Satisfactions are seasonal: A normal lifespan enables us to enjoy the exhilaration of childhood, the achievements of maturity, and the peace of old age. If we consider that the mayfly manages to do all of this in a day, the time available to us appears nearly endless.

The naturalness of death is further emphasized by the cycle of human vigor. As we age, the energy runs out and peace takes the place of striving. The very old witness a striking transformation: Having been an enemy, death comes to be a friend. People in the flower of life find it difficult to understand how anyone could welcome dying. But that is the energy speaking in them and the plans still hoping to be embodied. Only as one ages can one appreciate that there is something deeply appropriate in dying when our purposes are fulfilled, the work is done and there is no power left to start anew.

Knowledge of the social value of clearing the field for the next generation also enhances the private peace of dying at the right time. The gradual transfer of power and responsibility to the young is a fitting response to aging; at death, control of life and free decision making are completely ceded to those who come after us. Since others have stepped aside so we may have our day in the sun, this is as it should be. It serves as the foundation of intergenerational justice, securing the continuity and the integrity of communal life. On one reading, this transfer is the ultimate purpose of education, which is preparation for carrying forward the values and traditions of a society. As one nears death, there is something immensely satisfying in the thought that the affairs of the world are in good hands and that the young will carry on the projects we left behind.

Critics of pragmatism may well argue that this is too rosy a picture of life and death. Is the reality not far more bleak? Walt Whitman once confessed that he could not live another day if he believed that he is not immortal. He said:

> If all came but to ashes of dung,
> If maggots and rats ended us, then Alarum! for we are betray'd,
> Then indeed suspicion of death. Do you suspect death? if I were to suspect death I should die now,
> Do you think I could walk pleasantly and well-suited toward annihilation?

The dark underside of the desire never to die is a sense of the meaninglessness of striving in the face of extinction. The counterpart to Whitman's "To Think of Time" is Shelley's "Ozymandias," king of kings, whose greatest achievements get covered by the sands of time. Shelley's point is that in the end nothing remains: the generations that come after us forget our names, destroy our monuments, and lay waste to our plans. Strange and unintelligible customs take the place of our comfortable ways until, were we to return, we would no longer know our home. And then a catastrophe is likely to wipe out the human race, some event tragically self-wrought or else brought on by the dying of the sun. Imagine a world in which there is no one to appreciate the music of Mozart, the joy of laughter, the camaraderie of the corner pub. That is what we face. What is the point of doing anything if it is all undone and the death of everything precious leaves only a world of atoms moving in the dark?

This criticism represents a severe abuse of the power of foresight. Although the Rockies are ahead a thousand miles down the road, it is too soon to shift into low gear when driving through Missouri. We *know* that the Rockies are ahead with far greater assurance than anyone knows the death of our sun or of the universe. So what looks like foresight is really only forecast, and we are familiar with the fact that far more often than not, forecasts are erroneous. Even if we disregard this significant consideration, however, the possibility of distant disaster is an inadequate reason for ceasing our efforts and failing to enjoy the moment. Athletic teams work hard to win the championship, undaunted by the prospect that their achievement will not carry through to the next season. Couples beget children and lovingly raise them, undisturbed by the knowledge that eventually they will die. People sit in the sun and tan themselves, unmindful of the day when our middling star will no longer keep us warm.

It is sensible to concern ourselves with the near consequences of our acts, but not with what might flow from them in the unforeseeably distant future. Experience of what comes next teaches us what to do and what to abstain from, but only the power of language enables us to waste our energy wondering what might happen a million years from now. This is genuinely useless activity: it does not contribute to handling our problems now and its horror may immobilize us. It may sound harsh but is in fact the heart of sanity to say that what may happen in the hazy future has no relevance to our lives today. Moreover, the idea that events in the remote reaches of time can undo the value of what we love today amounts to the claim that nothing is intrinsically good, that everything is always at risk of having its value revoked. The kiss that leads to an unwanted child may be unfortunate in its consequences but nevertheless sweet at the time it is enjoyed. What is valuable in itself is insulated even from the immediate misfortunes of time; it is completely immune to what may come much later.

The optimistic pragmatist account of death is open also to another, much more serious, objection. We find young children dying of cancer, high school graduates killing themselves as they crash their cars, and individuals cut down by heart attacks and strokes in the prime of life. Their deaths are not good and valuable; they serve no purpose and cause mainly grief. Any glowing account of the appropriateness of death in its season must be balanced by a gloomy inventory of the sorts of death that occur out of season, at times and in ways that undercut human ambition and effort. In some circumstances, death *is* the enemy because it is poorly integrated into the stream of life.

The facts on which this objection is based are incontestable. Death sometimes comes at inappropriate times and takes cruel advantage of unsuspecting people. But pragmatists do not operate with the "feeble grasp of reality" of which William James accused Leibniz. They know that things do not always go well, that untoward circumstances or un-cooperative processes can disrupt even the best-directed existence. The expectation that nothing will trump our purposes is thoroughly unreasonable and the thought that we will always prevail is downright naïve. But lest we become too impressed with the frequency of untimely death, we need to distinguish the termination of life due to human desire or error from its end caused by uncontrolled natural events. A significant proportion of early deaths results from suicide, calculational mistake, carelessness, failing to act on what everybody knows, and luxuriant stupidity. Smokers, drunk drivers, drug addicts, daredevils, soldiers of fortune, and people who win Darwin Awards create their own ends. Absent their folly, many of them could reach a ripe old age and die in peace among their grandchildren.

The rest of early departures are caused by natural catastrophes, genetic construction errors, uncontrolled disease processes, and unpredictable accidents. People who dispose of themselves in slow or violent ways die because they have control over their fate; those who lose their lives in accidents or sickness leave us because they do not have adequate mastery of their lives. And that leads me to the practical advice pragmatists can give us concerning death. Their recommendation is that if life is satisfactory, we should avoid death for as long as we can. The reason why this sounds familiar—just as Aristotle's systematization of the valid forms of inference must have seemed familiar—is that all of us do it already nearly all the time. We do it when we eat, drink, drive carefully, get some sleep, visit the doctor, step out of the way of cars, refuse to take balloon rides with inexperienced pilots, try to learn more about our environment, and avoid midnight trips to inner-city parks.

The question of what pragmatists would have us do in relation to death has a simple answer: Fend it off one day at a time. For pragmatists, as in real life, there is no wholesale solution to anything, so we remain in a constant struggle to prevail. Every day we stay alive is a victory over death, to be celebrated as a grand achievement. Every meal strikes a blow on behalf of life; every time we wake up in the morning, we avoid permanent sleep. Each glorious breath keeps us from suffocating and every glass of clean water forestalls infection and possible death. Schopenhauer once said that walking is but a way of avoiding falling on our face, but it was clear that he would have been just as happy to see us in the mud. Similarly, all our labors in supporting life are ways of avoiding death, but pragmatists, and the rest of us, delight in its success.

In addition to private efforts to stay alive, the strategy also includes support for social measures to extend our days. The criminal code, police and courts, public sanitation, mass immunizations, pharmacological research, and institutions devoted to treating the ill are powerful instruments of extending life. They have been strikingly successful and as a result we live healthier, longer, happier, more pain-free, and more secure lives than any previous generation. That we die in the end is less significant than when the end comes: the ideal is to put off the moment until our ebbing energy gets us ready. At that point, we may experience the satisfaction of having lived well and the prospect of permanent peace.

# PART FIVE

# HUMAN ADVANCE AND
# FINITE OBLIGATION

# TWENTY-SEVEN

# THE RELEVANCE OF PHILOSOPHY TO LIFE

When the time came for our children to receive their oral polio vaccine, we took them to their pediatrician. Surprisingly, the first question the doctor asked was whether the parents themselves had had their medicine-soaked sugar cubes. Noting the puzzlement in our eyes, he explained that he viewed his job not as the narrow one of taking care of a few children, but as a broader mandate to promote public health. He was convinced, he said, that the well-being of young people is inseparable from the quality of their environment and that it is difficult, therefore, if not impossible, to safeguard their health without taking an interest in their families and in prevailing social conditions.

Not all physicians share this attitude. I cannot help thinking that those who do, though, take their responsibility more seriously than doctors satisfied to treat not the socially situated person but the disease. At any rate, I know that the more interested healer is the better one to have.

The contrast between a narrow and a broad conception of responsibility is not unique to medicine. In philosophy no less than in other professions, one may view oneself as a hired hand (or a hired mind?) paid to offer courses or to give lectures. But we may also think of our work as educating young people, as making available to them the skills necessary for a good life. The weight of tradition favors this latter view. The tenor of modern existence, on the other hand, encourages us to focus on professional standards and to be satisfied with a minimalist reading of our responsibilities.

In some fields, the distinction between these incompatible notions of the scope of responsibility is of little significance. Even if pharmacists, nurserymen, and typing instructors fail to go beyond the skimpiest demands of their standards of competence, they will not do much harm. To be sure, a broader sense of service could help them do more good; the pharmacist might find a generic substitute for the prescription and save people money. What is important in such fields is adequately captured by basic competence; beyond that, not a great deal is at stake. In medicine and philosophy, by contrast, the stakes are too high for the meeting of minimal standards to be enough. By not asking the additional question or not suggesting the innovative treatment, physicians can endanger their patients' lives. By failing to connect critical thought with the concerns of daily existence in the minds of their students, philosophers contribute to the impoverishment of personal life and the persistence of social irrationality.

Philosophy is an ancient instrument whose use is all but forgotten. It sits as mere decoration in the house of learning while the kitchen and the garage hum with activity. We need to learn to play the instrument again, to remind ourselves of the power of its music. We must go beyond scales and finger exercises until its melody becomes the soul of the house. Our music is the outcome and completion of the promising sounds of the kitchen, but also the tool that makes all that busy activity meaningful and joyous.

Because so much is at stake in philosophy, we cannot rest satisfied with a minimalist reading of our responsibilities. It is not enough to teach philosophy as a set of facts about what people once thought or as a set of verbal or conceptual skills. What Plato and Hegel believed has direct relevance to our lives today. And as even Groucho Marx knew, verbal skills can have important practical results. Our broader concerns must focus accordingly on the application of philosophical knowledge and skills to the pressing problems of personal and social life.

Philosophers today consider themselves academics who offer pure knowledge or, according to one view, none at all. The relevance or human significance or concrete result of their work appears distant from their minds. It is important, therefore, to inquire into the grounds of our broader obligations. Of these I see at least five, each powerful but none uncontroversial.

The purest source of obligation is fullness of soul. Such generosity used to be called divine; according to one account, God's creation of the world was itself the result of having wanted to share the goodness of existence with as many beings as possible. Stoics who felt no need of worldly goods explained their motivation for teaching their discipline as gratitude for what philosophy has done for them. And even today, those whose lives have acquired added meaning as a result of philosophical reflection share the enriching aspects of their field with authority, enthusiasm, and success rarely seen in the classroom.

The problem here is that in a world that views teaching philosophy as a job, few attain fulfillment through its study. For many today, even the ministry is a calling only in name; in reality, it is something one does for a living. Philosophy has become a profession in just this sense, enabling those who have never profited from its enriching wisdom to profit by telling others about it. The obligation to share the benefits one has received from philosophy cannot amount to much if they come to no more than the pleasure of an occasional argument, steady employment, and modest status in the academic world.

The second source of responsibility is more compelling. Society supports the university as the last and best hope of preparing its young people for life. The aim is emphatically not only, and not even primarily, to equip them with skills necessary for narrow social roles. They are to be acquainted, instead, with the best that human beings have thought and done, with a view to their repeating or improving upon these achievements. There is a tacit contract between the university and its social sponsors for it to be something different from a technical institute and something more than a haven of abstract research. Through its faculty, it must, of course, pursue the truth relentlessly and convey it to its students. But it is expected to do more: to establish the search for what is true and what is decent as permanent dispositions of young people. Our children are to emerge, accordingly, not only skilled and well informed, but also with secure habits and character traits and values. They are to be ready not merely to think straight but to act right, and specifically to act on the basis of what they think and to think about what they do.

No doubt this is what parents who pay for the college education of their children want and need. This is exactly what colleges and universities promise, if the mission statements in their catalogs are to be believed. What students actually get is another matter. When philosophers teach ideas without reference to their historical source, personal relevance, and social consequences, they renege on their responsibility to help students take charge of their lives. When they teach philosophy as a collection of puzzles and mistakes, or as a string of deft verbal moves, they abandon their obligation to make intelligence an effective force in life. Because parents, having been educated by the likes of us, do not know any better, we can get away with this. That is not something of which we should be proud.

The third source of our broader responsibilities is connected to this last. We are professors, teachers, educators. What we "profess" and teach is not neutral material. We devote our lives to reading, thinking, and writing about it; we convey it to our students without embarrassment, perhaps even with pride. Our posture toward our subject matter is one of interest and devotion; we act as if philosophy mattered and especially as if it mattered to us.

Can it matter if we fail to act on it? Demands for action are by no means unusual in the professions or in specialized fields of knowledge. The French chef who does not eat his own cooking but goes instead to Burger King for dinner is rightly an object of suspicion. The cancer researcher who smokes, the biologist who defends evolution in print but confesses commitment to creation on Sundays, the theorist of democracy who never votes are not cases of charming inconsistency: They constitute failures to live up to the commitments tacit in their professional activities. In just this way, philosophers who fail to embody the principles of their field in their personal lives are suspect: their words ring hollow so long as they remain words only. Devotion to reason in discourse combined with refusal to honor reason by bringing our actions in line with what we say reveals a basic incoherence, a break in the unity and integrity of the person.

Should our students attend to what we say or to what we do? It is reasonable for us to demand of ministers that they not preach what they are unwilling to practice. It is no less sensible for us to require of philosophers who, after all, claim to apply reason to every sphere, that they employ it fully in leading their own lives. The objection that a society ought not to demand that its ministers or its philosophers be better than other people makes a valid point. But it is one that belongs to the realm of excusing conditions or to the movement of forgiveness rather than to the discussion of proper expectations. For the requirement of the unity of theory and practice in our lives is not inflicted on philosophers from the outside. It is the natural result of our self-confessed commitment to the rule of reason.

The fourth fountainhead of our special responsibilities is the very nature of our subject matter. Mathematicians may have little obligation to do anything of a practical nature about their reasonings or results. But nearly everything in philosophy repudiates the idea that thinking is a terminal fact. The mathematical properties of infinity neither suggest nor demand physical application. By contrast, when we reflect on right action, criteria of justified belief, human rights, duties to our parents, standards of inference, and the good society, every result cries out for embodiment in our lives. Philosophical reasoning points beyond itself and can gain fulfillment only when it acquires influence over our actions. Those who wish to liberate philosophy from the demand for practical results must restrict its subject matter to the narrowest spheres of logic.

If it is wrong for professors not to act on what they teach, it is absurd for philosophers to disregard the demands their work articulates. Much of philosophy revolves around criteria, standards of what to think, what to believe, what to do. Such standards lay normative claims on our behavior. The claims are of two sorts. The first tell us how properly to do something, if we should care to undertake it—how to reason, for example, if we wish to think. The second decree what it is appropriate or fitting to do, quite apart from whether we want to do it or not. The commands that injustice be resisted, freedom preserved, and innocent lives saved fall in this category. Our lives abound in occasions when such claims make action mandatory. When they occur, what philosophers do must be exemplary. Those who know or set the standards must be the first to meet them. People who know the rules of implication must excel at inference; the moral philosopher must lead the moral life.

The fifth and final reason to think that we have special responsibilities derives from a widely accepted analysis of belief. According to this view, whose first great advocate was Plato and which is a hallmark of the American philosophical tradition, to believe something is, among other things, to have a tendency to act on it. Belief and action are, in this way, organically connected, demonstrating the unity of our cognitive and conative parts. If philosophers believe anything they teach, therefore, they must be prepared to act on it when the occasion arises. Conversely, if they fail to have their principles shape their behavior, we must conclude that they do not believe a word of what they teach. There is something contrived about doubt that does not penetrate to the level of action and something deceitful about beliefs concerning matters of substance that issue only in words. The only alternative to embodying our commitments in our lives is that of pursuing our profession without commitments and beliefs—a momentous fraud.

What are the broader responsibilities of philosophers? As with physicians, a list of specifics is neither possible nor appropriate. The first requirement is the realization that there are times when we must act. This engenders an alertness to opportunities for putting our principles into action. What we must do clearly depends on circumstances and on what each of us believes. There is, in this way, no ideological demand that philosophers be liberals or conservatives, that they support a free-market economy or welfare-state redistribution, that they love utilitarianism or deontology. Anything intellectually defensible is worthy to guide action, even if others believe differently and I might join them someday. The commitment of physicians to radical mastectomy may change as evidence accumulates and the effects of the procedure are better understood. But that is no reason for failing to implement it so long as it is defensible as the treatment of choice. Seeing what happens when we act on a belief, even a philosophical belief, is one of the tests of its validity; it is, therefore, a fundamental misunderstanding to withhold this trial because the conviction may turn out to be false.

We have two general areas of responsibility. The first is to bring our lives in line with our beliefs. Philosophers have, on the whole, not excelled at this. We tend to be no better, and in our feelings and actions we are no more rational, than ordinary people. One might even argue, I blush to admit, that in these respects we are below average. In looking over the long list of professional philosophers, we find distressingly many cases of mindless ambition, pettiness, arrogance, insensitivity, and a devastating lack of common sense and good judgment. The absence of even minimal decency lays waste to many colleagues and makes the lives of their mates and children unbearable. Not many chasms are greater than that between the professed high values and the despicable practice of some philosophers. There is work to be done here by all of us, and by some a staggering amount.

Our personal lives are framed in the context of a community. The second major field of our obligations is, accordingly, the social and political world that surrounds us. The injustice and irrationality of people cannot remain a matter of indifference to us. The inhumanity of large institutions demands a response. The callousness of some who are in power must be exposed. All of these, of course, are my value judgments, and I must be prepared to act them out. Your thoughts may be different from mine, but your responsibility to give them flesh in action is the same. The fact that the social world is so much larger and more powerful than you or I is no excuse for inaction. One's obligation is not to succeed, only to try and to do one's very best. In this way, even if we fail to change the world, at least we point our own souls in the right direction and convert a social defeat into personal victory.

My argument so far has been a plea for what is usually called the unity of theory and practice. What this notion of the integration of human effort actually means, however, is not altogether clear. At least three different ideas are referred to by the same phrase, and they have not been adequately distinguished. The first is what I shall call the unity of theory and practice in theorizing. Perhaps the staunchest proponent of this view, surprisingly, is George Santayana. Dismayed by the discrepancy between what philosophers believe when they act as ordinary human beings and what they find themselves affirming as a result of arcane reasonings, Santayana issued a call for honesty in our intellectual endeavors. Speaking of himself, as he thought the philosopher must, but suggesting universal applicability, he declared, "I should be ashamed to countenance opinions which, when not arguing, I did not believe."[1]

Such honesty yields radical results. Santayana's intention was not to tie philosophical thought to the tangled prejudices of humankind. He believed that philosophy needs instead to be the critical explication of what we unconsciously assume in our active moments. There are certain beliefs we enact when we operate in the world, such as that time and space are real and that we are surrounded by mind-independent things that our agency can affect. Our job as thinkers is to discover these tenets of "animal faith" or at least never to let our dialectic carry us to the point where we contradict them. In this way, our life activities determine or place limits on what we think, and as a result, our beliefs as active beings and our opinions as theorists always coincide.

This call for the unification of our theoretical and practical lives carries no prescription for broader action. It is explicitly restricted in application to how we ought to think. The second notion of the unity of theory and practice goes beyond it to disclose the full interconnectedness of action and thought. Many philosophers employ some such idea and give eloquent accounts of how our beliefs reflect what we do and our actions express, or ought to express, our thoughts. Sometimes the unity of the practical and the theoretical means simply the harmony of one's ethics and worldview. In other thinkers, it refers to the identity of two forms of consciousness or the equivalence of two different sorts of action. The breakdown of the unity is supposed to cause ruinous inversions or alienation; its recapture promises fulfillment, or the final perfection of the human frame.

All of this talk of unity, however, is talk only. This is what I call the unity of theory and practice *in theory*, for very few philosophers who embrace it go beyond writing books. Yet there is something devastatingly hollow about the demonstration that thought without action is hollow, when we find the philosopher only thinking it. We can say all the right things and we can add that saying them is not enough—but none of this helps us escape the world of words. And words can never encompass the broader forms of action nor serve as substitutes for them. There can therefore be no true unity of theory and practice in theory, in our ideas, in our books. It can exist only through the unified twofold agency of living persons.

I speak of the unity of theory and practice *in practice*, where real actions follow real thoughts. Philosophy at its best irresistibly breaks the bounds of thought, seeps out of books to love, embrace, and modify the world. Such unity cannot be found in the words of philosophers but only by comparing their books with what they do. Plato had it because he left for Syracuse, and Mill attained it by running for Parliament. Marx achieved it when he agitated for revolution and Spinoza reached it by quietly converting his passive emotions into active joy. We can all come near it by acting on what we believe, by making our books the authors of our deeds.

The very fact that we are philosophers burdens us with special obligations. This should present no surprise: a high calling exacts a high price. This means that if we are to be true to our profession, we must be ready for extensive and perhaps even painful action. We must not only lecture our students but also present ourselves as living examples of what we teach. Those who are after virtue in their philosophical theories should capture some of it in their personal lives.

# TWENTY-EIGHT

# BOTH BETTER OFF AND BETTER

*Moral Progress Amid Continuing Carnage*

To victims of twentieth-century atrocities, my argument may seem sinister and hollow. To intellectuals who equate sophistication with cynicism, it will appear naïve and perhaps shallow. To seekers after perfection who find each number wanting because it falls shy of the infinite, it will be a lesson in futility. But to the rest of us, what I have to say may serve as a useful reminder of how fortunate we are to live today and not even just a few hundred years ago. It may also evoke reasonable hopes for the future and establish a standard by which to measure the magnitude of the tasks on the road ahead.

I wish to show that in spite of the misery and wickedness that still remain in the world, the human race has enjoyed significant moral progress over the course of history. Only fools would deny that, on the whole, there has been striking material progress. But many believe, quite wrongly, that there is no connection between material and moral advancement or even that growth of comfort entails loss of character. At the very least, the ways in which being better off contributes to being better are poorly understood and inadequately appreciated. I hope to be able to clarify the connection.

The facts fall considerably short of proving John Stuart Mill's nineteenth-century hope that humankind is by nature a "progressive being."[1] There is no assurance that the positive changes achieved through centuries of effort will continue or that we have once and for all escaped the threats of nuclear annihilation, ideological repression, and murderous intolerance. I have, moreover, no desire to deny or explain away the evidence against moral improvement. Progress is not universal and unrelenting, and its presence is perfectly compatible with individual wickedness, with some continuing institutional discrimination and with pockets of unmitigated nastiness. Yet, one can deny its reality only by selective inattention, by the application of unreasonable standards or by astonishing ignorance of history.

Let me begin by acknowledging that the twentieth century is full of events ranging from the lamentable to the awful. Precise numbers are hard to come by, but it is clear that two world wars, the Holocaust, Stalinist purges, Japanese concentration camps, and the Chinese "Cultural Revolution" terminated the lives of more than 100 million individuals. Massacres in Cambodia, genocide in sundry African countries, ethnic cleansing in the Balkans, and other horrors added more than ten million dead in the last twenty years. Injustices against women and minorities continue everywhere. Religious intolerance, ethnic hatreds, and national rivalries contribute to the misery of hundreds of millions of people. Random violence erupts even in the most civilized countries, and fraud, lying, cheating, and coercion constitute ways of life all over the globe.

These facts cannot be denied. But they must be understood. The staggering number of those who died in wars in the last hundred years, for example, must be related to the vast increase in the human population since 1800. This does not explain or justify the killing, but it places it in historical context. There were not a hundred million people alive at the time of the Great Plague. That many killed in Descartes's day would have left few if anyone to reproduce the race. In the twentieth century, by contrast, the number constituted but a relatively small percentage of the global population. Moreover, a single evil intention without the aid of advanced technology can spell the doom only of a few victims; with access to weapons of mass destruction, it can destroy tens of thousands of people.

We must also consider that morality does not progress at the same rate everywhere. Offsetting massacres by Hutus and Tutsis cannot be blamed on civilized or morally advanced nations. Many of the horrors of Cambodia and Iraq must be laid at the door of dictators, who are among the morally least developed persons in the world. And participation in atrocities by many well-meaning people, though inexcusable, is at least in part testimony to the contagion of collective action and the relative powerlessness of individuals. Placing people in circumstances where decency demands heroic self-sacrifice is a telling but by no means complete measure of their moral quality.

Determining the moral level of a society is a complex affair, involving study of the practices and the sentiments of its people. As collections of living habits, practices are often at odds with one another, requiring examination of their relative strengths or of the frequency with which they are enacted. In looking for signs of the growth of decency, we must pay relatively little attention to rare heights of moral achievement and to exceptional degradation; as in assessing quality of life, what matter in the end are the repetitive patterns of everyday existence.

Even more revealing perhaps is what a given society accepts as commonplace and what, by contrast, is viewed as demanding excuse or explanation. In a disorderly, xenophobic world, for example, the occasional arrest, torture and murder of foreigners is a matter of course. When it happens, no special account of the event is needed; everyone knows and accepts that this may be the fate of intruders. In a law-abiding country that welcomes visitors, on the other hand, shooting at tourists from overpasses is considered an anomaly in need of explanation. Such accounts, moreover, are supposed to identify the causes of the event rather than serve as its justification. The point of understanding in a civilized world is the elimination of such incidents, not their exoneration.

In assessing the practices of various societies and historical epochs, we need to acknowledge an initial distinction between the material conditions of life and the moral qualities of individuals. Simple-minded utilitarians might suppose that only the level of happiness in a society matters much, and that is largely a function of the consequences of human actions rather than of the moral excellence of agents. But this distinction is, in the end, not very helpful. For happiness is by no means the only important value, and even if it were, it could not be detached from the internal disposition of people to favor creating it in themselves and in others. Mill himself acknowledges as much when he writes about the significance of choice in life and the intricate connections that obtain between character and well-being.[2]

So let me deal with these issues separately, and examine the ways in which prosperity enhances virtue only after I have considered each of them in detail. At first sight, the idea that we are better off than any previous generation may appear as what people nowadays call a "no-brainer." Consider an example. The philosopher Josiah Royce took a trip to Australia in 1888–89. He spent nearly three months at sea on the way there, out of touch with the rest of the world. He fretted ceaselessly at not being able to participate in the life of his family. His friends and his wife, in turn, were plagued by persistent worries about his health and well-being. An occasional telephone call would have allayed these concerns and made everyone involved feel happier or at least less uncertain, less angered, and less guilty.

Here is another example. The invention of the solenoid made it possible for cars to start at the turn of a key. Earlier versions of the automobile had to be hand-cranked at considerable effort at the front of the car below the radiator. From time to time, the crankbar would jerk, dislocating hand or arm. Less than a year before solenoids were first installed, when a young Detroiter cranked his car, the engine started and then backfired, transmitting violent motion to the crankbar, which hit him in the face, broke his jaw, and knocked out some of his teeth. The man developed general sepsis and died. He was the last fatality connected with the hand-cranked automobile engine.

There is no doubt that automobile drivers in the 1920s were better off than people who had had to ride in horsedrawn wagons a hundred years before, and that we live better than they did because we can get in our cars and start them without having to crank them in the weather. How could one deny this? Only by insisting that increase of comfort and decrease of suffering and risk constitute no improvements in life. This, in turn, can be justified only in one of two ways: we can assert that well-being carries no moral weight at all or that increments of it come at unacceptable cost. The first line of argument is absurd on the face of it. No sensible person can seriously entertain the notion that human suffering and delight should be thought insignificant. Even Kant, who came closest to this view, believing that happiness had no moral value, found an important role for it in satisfying our entire constitution.[3]

The second justification has at least some plausibility: We know that everything desirable comes at a price. But the claim that each technological advance, for example, leads to more misery than good is simply false. The use of penicillin, to take just one case, has admittedly caused a number of deaths and its availability may have contributed to less than optimal caution in sexual relations. But the millions of lives it saved is out of proportion to the relatively few whose loss or diminution may be attributed to it. On a simple cost-benefit basis, established and non-outmoded technologies are nearly always worth their price. Acknowledging this, opponents typically shift the ground from the discernible costs of progress to its more intangible effects in supposedly destroying human character. I will deal with this claim a little later.

Let me generalize the points my examples are designed to highlight. For most people in most of the industrially advanced countries, life today is strikingly easier, safer, richer in choices, more diversified, healthier, more just, longer, and more satisfying than ever before. We eat better, suffer less pain, are ravaged by fewer diseases, exercise greater control over our environment, face brighter prospects, have a better chance of enjoying worthwhile experiences, and live more peaceful lives than any previous generation.

To learn what life was like in prior centuries, we need to read about the travail of ordinary persons, not the exploits of the high and mighty. The little people who built the pyramids of Egypt and the cathedrals of medieval Europe were infested with parasites and found themselves at the mercy of tyrannical rulers and a poorly understood, terrorizing world. The peasants of the Black Forest Heidegger so admires[4] lived in cramped discomfort and suffered from painful degenerative ailments. People everywhere were decimated by war, malnutrition, persecution, tuberculosis, and venereal disease. The relatively few who survived past the age of twenty-five suffered from digestive malfunctions and rotting teeth.

Persons of the wrong religion were executed, people were deprived of property on the basis of accusations alone, and those in debt went to jail never to return.

A better understanding of the human body, the development of technology and the spread of democratic values made life better in large and small ways that are nearly impossible to detail. The best summary of these blessings is to note that they improve the human lot by increasing the range of our choices. We can now do things prior generations could hardly imagine the gods performing: sending messages to each other in the dark of night, making hot rooms cold by turning a knob, and growing food in desert sand. Such choices mean that we can determine our own good: we can still permit our teeth to rot or the heat to suffocate us, but we do not have to.

The oppressive force of necessity has been lifted from our shoulders and we can live as humans should, or at least as we desire. It is better if one out of four women don't die in childbirth and if lack of protein and calcium does not cripple one person out of every eight. It is better if people do not have to drink putrid water and eat rotting food, and if drunkenness is not the only relief from pain. It is better to live in a world in which hunger is a pleasant prelude to a meal instead of a gnawing menace that cannot be escaped. And it is better by far if families do not have to bury two children out of ten and see another three out of ten grow into physically or morally deformed adults.

A growing number of Americans believe that saying other ages and other cultures do not compare well with our own is unseemly or wrong. There is good reason for this: racist, nationalist, and ethnocentric affirmations of superiority constitute important elements of much recurrent human villainy. Furthermore, the idea of progress has on occasion been used as an instrument to justify such claims of comparative or transcendent excellence. We may rightly think, therefore, that it is best to avoid grand cross-cultural comparisons and to foster, instead, a generous appreciation of the virtues of other forms of life.

Such sentiments feel instinctively so right to us that it is tempting to adopt them. But their very popularity cuts against their truth. Prior ages were, and many cultures continue to be, not at all reluctant to declare their preeminence over all others. The fact that we relate to alien value systems with self-abnegating generosity is itself evidence of moral progress. But more: People in industrialized nations tend to be ahead of others when their practices are measured by generally, though perhaps not universally, accepted standards. They take better care of the sick and the disadvantaged, they have a keener and broader sense of justice, and they hold human life in higher regard than do individuals in less-developed countries. There is no better way to show that these are shared standards than by observing the choices of people all over the globe. Most of them do not think values are incommensurable; they have no trouble comparing their condition with ours, and when they do, they find theirs wanting. As a result, vast numbers of them prefer our opportunities and our caring—that is, our style of life—to their own. They vote with their feet in moving to industrialized countries or introduce modernizing reforms in their own.

As all good things, progress comes at a price. Heroic self-sacrifice may be more uncommon today, because it is less necessary. In many contexts, institutionalized care has replaced tender personal relations. We have lost the heartfelt closeness of fellow sufferers and the excitement of living in endangered communities. By no means the least, all or nearly all our hallowed values have been commercialized. But we are amply compensated for such losses. Individual generosity has placed 12 percent of our vast national wealth at the permanent service of education, the arts, and the helping professions. Government considers it a sacred obligation to take care of the sick and the elderly. And though it is lamentable that there remain causes whose support requires hunger strikes and nonviolent resistance, we must remember that such tactics work only in civilized countries where the perpetrators are not summarily murdered.

The growth of the middle class coincides with the development of better ways of taming the power of nature and of making it serve human purposes. The comfort and security we associate with middle class living is in no small measure the result of applying intelligence to the solution of the problems that face us. Even those who want to argue that humans lack good will or an ultimate vision of what would satisfy them cannot deny that ingenuity, inventiveness, and sustained labor have made human life immeasurably better.

Some high-minded critics of progress readily grant that, in material terms, life has undergone significant improvement in the past few hundred years. But they accord no moral significance to our growing comfort. A few go so far as to claim there is an inverse relation between well-being and virtue. They say that good living softens the will even as it hardens the heart. And, indeed, there is some evidence for this: in certain cases, the children of the well-to-do lose the work habits of their parents and some of those pampered with luxuries find little sympathy for people in need.

I have already indicated that in assessing what good there might be in the world, human welfare cannot be disregarded. Might it nevertheless be true that growing comfort entails moral loss? If only austerity can build character, our good fortune in living well and long must surely hurtle us into spiritual decline. Active virtues are likely to atrophy, the imagination may shrivel, and we will be tempted to turn inward to wallow in our happiness. We could end in the position of Nietzsche's last man, as small persons enjoying small pleasures in an abominably comfortable corner of the universe.[5]

Older people have from time immemorial charged the new generation with having lost the ancient virtues. In truth, announcing that the young lack character may be a way of saying that they have characters of which their elders do not approve. Every desire not immediately met and automatically sustained builds habits and drives; no generation lacks perseverance in the pursuit of its ends. But the ends change, and the young, growing up in the midst of plenty, may no longer hoard bottles and shopping bags—or money—in the way those who lived through the agony of the Great Depression could never overcome.

So austerity builds the sort of character needed to flourish under its strictures. Prosperity generates a different kind of person, one given to enjoying what life provides. This appears as profligate to children of the Depression as they seem irrationally pinch-fisted to those who never had to face their concerns. The question is not which group is right; they both are to the extent their attitudes are appropriate to their situations. Indefinitely delayed gratification is just what may get us over the hump in a time of shortage and uncertainty, but we would be fools not to fiddle and dance under the moon at the end of harvest.

People of plenty have as many virtues as the hardy indigent, even though what they do may look indulgent to those given to self-abnegation.

And their virtues are superior because of their superior means: when there is hardly enough for oneself, it is difficult to be generous. Flashes of heroic caring are always possible, and we heap special honor on those who take food out of their mouths to feed the hungry. But kindness is a more powerful disposition among people who do not suffer constant pain, and courage flourishes more easily when one's body is strong and one's feelings are educated. Magnanimity is not even possible for individuals without significant means and the sentiment of justice cannot readily take hold while people struggle to survive.

Contrary to the fears and warnings of luddites, the means our prosperous industrial world provides directly promote the growth of virtue. Consider the power of telecommunications. Medieval villages received virtually no news from the outside; their small worlds remained inescapably isolated from one another. By the time of the Vietnam War, the distant killing was replayed each night in our living rooms. Today, email, the telephone, CNN, and fax machines have forged indissoluble links between us and people around the globe. Once we know what happens to them, we cannot be indifferent to their fates: Sri Lankans and Kosovars evoke our sympathy as they solicit our aid. The resulting painful involvements—in Somalia and Bosnia and Kosovo—can be explained only by reference to caring. A primary motive for such costly interventions is the interest we take in human welfare everywhere.

Those who say that it is not in our national interest to dispatch troops to save innocent people or to stop humanitarian catastrophes far away take too narrow a view of what is a proper subject of concern for citizens and for human beings. The notion of the national interest must itself be put in the context of moral evolution. Hobbes's egoist, whose life was "solitary, poor, nasty, brutish, and short,"[6] may never have existed, but the human race did survive thousands of years of tribal warfare and clannish exclusiveness. The idea that our allegiance must extend beyond service to the local warlord and encompass others in a unified nation-state hundreds of miles away was a significant innovation in morality.

The notion of citizenship, pointing to democratic equality in mattering or, minimally, in not being overlooked, represents a momentous advance in the scope of caring. The idea of national interest extends protection and fellow feeling beyond the family, the tribe, the inhabitants of a region, and the subjects of a local authority. As such, the notion is a way station to universal human concern, which is now slowly beginning to take its place.

The same development in ideas occurred, much earlier, in religion with the emergence of universal faiths. Such religions as Christianity and Islam offer open enrollment to anyone prepared to confess certain beliefs. The proffered benefit of salvation is not restricted by birth or social status; it is available to human beings everywhere. This puts an end to aristocracy in religion and lowers, or raises, all persons to one level in the eyes of God.

Something similar happened also with the criminal code, which is the single most civilizing instrument ever devised. Those who think there has been no moral progress through the ages should recall that for thousands of years humans struggled without an impartially administered law protecting their lives and property. When laws proscribing and punishing criminal acts first emerged, as in the code of Hammurabi, they were a magnificent step in the direction of human security. Yet, they were supposed to govern the behavior of only those people whom local authorities had within their reach.

Even at the height of the Roman Empire, its criminal laws were thought to have bearing solely on its citizens and on the citizens of subjected nations. Until recently, laws of universal applicability were typically restricted to areas beyond national sovereignty, such as the sea. But from the middle of this century on, we have had a growing body of law that is supposed to set limits to the activity of humans everywhere and that takes preeminence over the legislative arrangements of nation-states.

The subject matter of these laws is as important as their scope: They are designed to protect human beings from inhumane treatment. The category of crimes against humanity includes many of the atrocities that tyrants and repressive regimes used to inflict routinely on suffering multitudes. Since the indictment of Milosevic, they can no longer do so believing that they will escape prosecution. The possibility that a sitting head of state would be indicted for war crimes committed against the citizens of his own nation would have been greeted with incredulous laughter even fifty years ago. Leaders of defeated powers had often lost their lives, but for an international court to hold a king or prime minister responsible while still in office was unprecedented in the history of the human race. To demand decency even, or especially, from the high and mighty is a stunning breakthrough in morality.

These remarkable developments came about as a result of growth of concern for human beings simply because they are human and not on account of their being of the same race or religion or nationality as we are. The increase of caring, in turn, had its source in large part in the material conditions that shape our lives. Rapid transportation, instant communication, and universal commerce make us participants in the lives of others. The leisure and wealth generated by highly efficient economies provide the wherewithal to aid our fellows. Without the infrastructure of the industrial world, large-scale concern for others would be impossible. One can readily suppose that there have been pockets of caring throughout human history, but nothing ever existed that comes even close to the magnitude, the reach and the institutional support of benevolence today.

At least two mechanisms support this growth of generosity; one is the way telecommunications have come to bolster the human imagination, the other the power and pervasiveness of commerce. The only sure source of decency is the imagination that enables us to place ourselves in the position of others. This splendid faculty makes it possible for us to do much more than empathize with those in pain; it propels us into the worlds of others to appreciate their self-justifications. But it is weak and quickly exhausts itself in the extraordinary efforts required to enter alien frames of mind. So while the imagination makes decency possible, it also imposes its own limits on the moral life.

Sensory contact with the distant functions as a mechanized imagination. Television brings us the distant scene and we are no longer required to construct for ourselves how others might live and what they believe. Crying children, a blood-splattered street, and people dazed from seeing the bomb go off present a reality hardly in need of interpretation; we respond to an immediacy more vivid, or at least more extensive, than what the mind creates. Sympathies expand as more of the world enters our consciousness until people we have never met, but whose images we see daily, become companions with a claim.

Even as early a writer as Benjamin Constant noted (1819) that "war and commerce are only two different means of achieving the same end, that of getting what one wants." Since commerce is "a milder and surer means of engaging the interest of others to agree to what suits [one's] own,"[7] little by little it takes the place of war. If we wage war to get people to surrender what we want, they are likely to resist; if we offer them something they want in return, they relinquish it freely. Moreover, trading keeps others productive so they may create more of the things we want, which means that we can trade again, whereas in war we may feel impelled to kill them.

Plutarch relates that Marcus Cato, in addressing the Roman senate, let a few fine figs drop out of his toga. When the senators indicated their admiration of the size and beauty of the figs, he remarked that "the place that bore them was but three days' sail from Rome."[8] If they wanted such figs, he said, they needed simply to kill the Carthaginians who grew them. The idea of setting up a trading post in Carthage seems not to have occurred to him.

Momentous changes take place in human relations when people realize that trade is a better way to relieve others of their goods than force. It is no overstatement that replacing war with commerce is a turning point in the moral evolution of humankind. Instead of wanting other people dead, we want them to live and prosper. Our relation to them becomes internal: in trade, their good is essentially linked to ours, so what harms them harms us, as well. A momentous expansion of the self follows inevitably. We begin to view our trading partners in the same favorable light in which we bathe ourselves. Their habits become interesting, their choices respectable, their fates important. We are ready to protect them, as we did in Kuwait, and admit them as valued persons into our community.

As all higher stages of development include a trace of what went before, trade retains a residue of playful or warlike competition. But this is a matter of clever gamesmanship rather than deadly combat. Its point is to gain an advantage over others, not to ruin them, for in killing them we would kill a part of ourselves. In this way, the growth of technology and the spread of commerce make powerful contributions to the moral betterment of the human race. They tie us to one another in fact and feeling, increasing both interdependence and caring. At a time when intellectuals were less cynical, we would have called them instruments of perfection. I am satisfied to call them tools of socializing humans or of unifying the human race.

Those who wish to argue that trade and wealth and communication change only our actions and not who we are, need to develop a better understanding of the intricate relations between "external" actions and the inner person. Everyone does things "out of character" from time to time, but normally the habits that constitute us are built out of repeated actions. What we do again and again penetrates the soul and shapes it in its image; it is impossible to act in a generous way over many years and yet remain a miser. Here and there, we can act as though we were brave or just or kind, but when we act consistently that way, no one can deny that we truly are. I conclude that, on the whole, humans today are not only better off but also better than previous generations. And by "better" I mean not only that we do good things more often, but also that we are, on the whole, morally more admirable people.

I remain unrepentant if this conclusion offends our sense of unworthiness. But my view will appear more convincing or at least less objectionable if I guard against two possible misunderstandings. I do not think that moral progress is destined to continue. Some unforeseen catastrophe or the wicked work of charismatic leaders may well reverse it. In any case, it is a slow process unlikely to move ahead without the committed work of many millions of people over long periods of time.

Further, I said that we are "on the whole" better than those who went before. Being on the whole better is consistent with there having been a few people in prior ages who were more virtuous than anyone living today, and it does not even suggest that we are in some absolute and final sense "good." All injustice has not been overcome, all pain has not been stilled, all needs have not been met. Probably they never will be. As we well know, indifference, deceit, ill will, even wickedness continue to flourish here as everywhere around the globe. We find throwbacks and face reversals again and again. The black holes of nastiness we continue to encounter set our tasks as educated human beings and especially as philosophers. But taking all of this into account, we still feel the tides of decency rising and see shafts of light to guide our actions and to feed our hope.

# TWENTY-NINE

# EDUCATION IN THE TWENTY-FIRST CENTURY

with Shirley M. Lachs

The fast pace of the modern world has at last defeated the risk-aversive conservatism of the human soul. We have come to accept, to expect, and even to welcome change. For a while, sound business practice was described as "management of change" and periodic alterations in product line, advertising, and the appearance of things have become standard, though by no means always effective, marketing techniques.

Surprisingly, the conversion of universities to primarily business institutions has not imbued them with this veneration of change. The marketing efforts of institutions of higher education have moved in line with the state of the art in the promotion of business, but the product line has remained largely unimproved. This may reflect the imperfect control administrations exert over slow-moving, recalcitrant faculties. The faculty's jealously guarded power over educational programs has made curricular innovation difficult to achieve, especially in traditional degree offerings. Administrations can start new programs here and there, but when it comes to the all-important bachelor's degree, for example, they are selling nineteenth-century lipstick to smear on twenty-first century lips.

The rapid development of the information industry may force major changes in the quiet hamlets of the academic world. At the very least, it is beginning to raise the question of what, if anything, the genteel and cumbersome residential university can offer beyond what is or will soon be available in information from the Internet. The question is likely to become more immediate with each annual increase of tuition. It will become pressingly urgent with the next major expansion of the Internet and once ordinary Americans begin to feel comfortable seeking information by electronic means.

At that point, the monopoly colleges and universities enjoy over credentialing young people may no longer be enough to justify and sustain their existence. They may face the fate of industries built on outmoded technologies. Just as email and the fax machine have displaced the telegraph, so learning at one's personal computer at home may squeeze out the lecture hall. Universities may go the way of Western Union.

Those who see college education with unclouded eyes readily admit that it is a tedious and inefficient process. Dull teachers, uninterested students, fragmented disciplines, and forced study unmotivated by real-life concerns make progress slow and the long-term retention of knowledge improbable. But what good would retention accomplish, in any case? The volume of information conveyed in the undergraduate classroom is a tribute to the cognitive achievements of the human race, but very little of it is of any direct value to young people trying to make their way in the world. Hoarding it is like stockpiling old bottles, shopping bags, and pieces of string with the justification that one never knows when they might come in handy.

Even the packaging of college level courses reveals the essential unconcern of faculty for the natural beat of intelligence. Curiosity is fed by problems we encounter and respects no disciplinary bounds. It takes us wherever we must go to get the answers we need. The results are memorable even without the attempt to memorize them. The typical college course, by contrast, covers a mound of loosely connected facts and theories in disciplinary isolation. The selection of topics rests in the hands of instructors who rarely bother offering a rationale for what they require or teach. The emphasis is on covering material, as if salvation or insight into the hidden recesses of reality depended on learning no less than the approved quantity of calculus or Chaucer.

Should it surprise us, then, that students show little interest in their work and that possibly as many as three in four cheat in writing papers and in taking exams? The fact that students admit to this level of dishonesty is a sign not of remorse but of open contempt of the system whose interest is in evaluating and not in educating them. If they must pass tests, they will pass them in whatever way is easiest or most effective; they see faculty talk of the dignity of learning and of the intrinsic value of knowledge as self-justification by funny little people who could never hold down regular jobs.

There is another side to faculty-student relations. Some young people come to admire some of their teachers and become their lifelong friends. A few find their lives changed or at least their purposes redefined as a result of meeting thoughtful adults who care. And more perhaps than we suspect carry away with them a small part of their teachers in happy memories, endearing habits, or a distant enthusiasm for the life of mind. But these are unplanned by-products of the system, not its primary goals.

Do such occasional fortuitous outcomes justify the expenditure of vast amounts of money and effort? The continued existence of colleges and universities is due as much to their power and position as to a vital need for their services. If the social inertia that allowed them to establish and maintain their power is swept aside by the electronic revolution, perhaps we should greet their decline as well deserved. No one grieves over the fate of the dinosaurs; why should we shed tears at the death of state universities?

Traditional defenses of liberal education are beside the point in the face of the electronic challenge. No one, after all, suggests that we abolish liberal arts colleges and send the next generation to engineering school. Reading good literature and having some idea of how the physical world operates may well be of great personal value to people, but they need not be connected with spending four years in a dorm. At question is not what good reflection and learning might do, but how best we can get people interested in and competent at pursuing them. Will schools of liberal education still provide something special when the sum of human knowledge is at the fingertips of anyone with modem and monitor?

The answer is clearly yes, and exploring it points us in the direction of what computers cannot give and what is, at least in one of its forms, the most neglected service of universities. Human immediacy in the form of new friends and the lasting companionship of peers constitutes one of the warmest and most worthwhile features of the residential experience.

Cynical outsiders among the students charge that many young people go to college to make contacts and to find mates, and they suppose that this is a devastating objection. But there is nothing wrong with making preparations for life at any time and in any context. In any case, the benefits of the campus are significantly broader: The mixing of students of differing values and lifestyles from varied family backgrounds, divergent social classes, and different parts of the world broadens their horizons and enriches their sympathies. They remember involvement in student organizations and adventures in the dorms with a fondness reserved for the best days of one's life.

Although such immediacy could be achieved by other means as well, the residential university is a convenient instrument for getting young people together under civilizing conditions. The educational value of this togetherness has never been fully utilized. Colleges and universities make occasional, halfhearted attempts to integrate what students do and learn in the residences with the intricacies of the curriculum, but faculty visits and dorm seminars fall far short of what could be done. Better coordination of practical life on campus with the abstract materials of the classroom offers a splendid opportunity for improving education and providing a more attractive alternative to the Internet.

Important as student camaraderie is, it does not constitute the most valuable contribution of the residential college to the growth of young people. Another sort of togetherness, inter-generational immediacy, defines the work of education. Surprisingly, this vital interaction between teachers and students is poorly understood and therefore inadequately supported by institutions of higher education.

Small colleges used to pride themselves on the close connection between professors and those enrolled in their classes. There were legendary figures in many schools whose devotion to young people structured or took over their lives: they were friends, advisers, savvy mentors, older brothers, loving uncles, and patient confidants to generations of students. They were available to listen and to help, to comfort, and to make small loans at any time of the day or year. Their students were their children or their grateful family, and the wells of their generosity seemed never to run dry.

This is an ideal that cannot be imposed on people. It was freely chosen by a few who viewed teaching as a calling and instinctively understood its profound, even sacred, significance. Though this may seem an absurdly romantic ideal to professional teacher-researchers today, there were and there continue to be some individuals who conduct their lives in its light. Nearly everything pulls against it: the busyness of the modern world, family obligations, the demands of the profession, even the physical distance at which faculty live from campus make it difficult to spend a great deal of time with students.

Colleges and universities, of course, acknowledge the significance of contact with students. They oblige faculty to hold office hours. They also operate advising systems and some of them organize hopelessly artificial "fireside chats" to encourage faculty to invite students into their homes. Such formal initiatives never amount to much. Many faculty members think of the mandated contact as a nuisance and an interruption; students quickly detect faculty displeasure or lack of interest and learn to stay away. The most effective student-faculty relationships may well occur in the labs when researchers take a promising student or two under their wings. But even there, the contact is limited and professional, and tends to lack depth of human encounter and of caring.

What makes extensive student-faculty immediacy so important? To understand this, we must get a clear grasp of what faculty, at their best, represent. In addition to being accomplished professionals, they are also expected to be mature human beings. The rigorous standards that govern hiring, retention, and promotion in a market where jobs are relatively scarce yield assurance of professional competence. Age, experience, and service in a humane and responsible institution make the expectation of maturity reasonable. The obvious fact that this demand frequently goes unmet is of no significance when we speak of what faculty do *at their best* or what they ought to be and do. That cars may not start and that mechanics may be unable to fix them present no threat to our knowledge of what they ought to or ought to be able to do.

In one respect, faculty are no different from other mature adults, contact with whom is of genuine value to young persons in the process of defining themselves. From another perspective, they are special, and especially useful for purposes of self-formation, because they have devoted their lives to intellectual pursuits that involve criticism and reflection. Persons of that sort will, of course, make their share of mistakes. But even their relations to their failures are likely to be, or at any rate ought to be, more intelligent than average. They tend to want to understand why they failed in order to prevent the same mistake from overtaking them again. Such reflection establishes habits that not only reduce costly errors in the conduct of life, but also provide a sweet sense of assurance that we can deal with problems.

Perhaps it is best to make the point we wish by calling attention to two different ways of storing knowledge. We safeguard the information we develop by writing it down, publishing it in books, or putting it on the Internet. We also stockpile knowledge in living human beings in the form of experience and the products of reflection. The information contained in books is inert; it does not reorganize itself as knowledge in persons does. It remains safe, unchanged, and accessible, always ready to be added to but never growing deeper or more complex than we made it.

What is stored in persons, by contrast, is living knowledge constantly in the process of transformation. Perhaps because much of it does not exist in the form of sentences, its depth is indeterminate; people questioned about what they know can surprise even themselves. This is because a single well-formed query can add to living knowledge by causing a reorganization of existing materials, the way a spark of electricity fuses hydrogen and oxygen to create water or in the fashion that tapping the side of a kaleidoscope rearranges colors into a new picture.

In more familiar language, asking people questions gives them an opportunity to think, draw on their experience and come up with something new. The demands of communication are such, moreover, that participants in the conversation may have to reformulate their questions and their answers in terms they have not used before and thereby contribute to the creation of novel ideas and insights.

Nothing like this is available in today's machines. We can learn new things by surfing the Net and those who are inventive about where to look can uncover a great deal. But often the information runs out before the questions do, and machines do not improvise. They are incapable, moreover, of particularizing their answers, that is, of adapting their information to the needs and situations of the people who want to know and presenting it in terms suited to their level of understanding and state of mind.

The simple way to say this is that we cannot have a conversation with Web sites. The more complete and more accurate way of putting it is that human beings are, among other things, vast collections of experience, organic systems of storing and using the living past. This is why talking with reflective older people can be so rewarding; their years of experience, crystallized into ideas, can give us stunningly rich perspectives on life. And this is also why it would be a great privilege to be able to question Plato or Napoleon one evening over a glass of wine. We have the words and know the exploits of the famous dead but, as a wonderful student used to say, we have a few more questions. No one can answer those questions but the people concerned and, alas, they took their share of knowledge with them to the grave.

What colleges and universities can offer that is unavailable from the PC is what they have always offered at their best: firsthand contact with remarkable people whose knowledge of their fields and whose experience of life have been integrated into the unity of a person. Such conversation is of benefit to both students and teachers. Students gain access to the accumulated wisdom of the human race through a dynamic medium that rewards searching and novel questions with thoughtful and often surprising answers. Teachers, in turn, find stimulation under the scrutiny of inquisitive young minds. Much human knowledge is unfocussed or tacit; the opportunities and irritations of dialogue force the articulation of thought and bring indistinct ideas to the clarity of explicit consciousness.

Sustained communication between mature scholars with a measure of life experience and young people in the early stages of charting their course meets the most exacting requirement of education: it results in the transmission of knowledge to a new generation. In assessing its value, we should not overlook the role it plays in creating new insights and in keeping established truths vibrant in the minds of those long familiar with them. Nor must we underrate the importance for the future of society of the intergenerational faith engendered by such nurturing contact.

Lectures on videotape, on audiotape and, if delivered from detailed, antique notes, even in the lecture hall come closer to the way knowledge is stored in books or on the Internet than to the manner in which it can be created and obtained through open questioning and collaboration. As a method of conveying information, lectures lack the speed and the free-ranging exploration typical of computer access to data. The information they present is rarely the reason for our interest in them; the source of their fascination is the eloquence and angle of vision of the lecturer. What makes such presentations worthwhile is the opportunity they afford of seeing and asking questions about how another human being perceives the world or some intriguing portion of it.

Laboratories have for centuries provided a setting for cooperative enterprises in which intellectual sparks can fly. But in scientific work, as in every activity in which persons meet, the central variable is the quality of the interaction. In spite of the claims of people who disguise nasty imperiousness as the defense of high standards, benevolent mentoring is not incompatible with the demand for top performance. To the contrary, high expectations in a friendly, supportive environment are more likely to bring results than the terror imposed by moody tyrants.

Hands-on education in scientific inquiry and laboratory investigation in which faculty adopt students as their junior partners are, therefore permanently valuable services electronic media cannot supplant. Their benefit derives from the same source as that of face-to-face work in the humanities and the social sciences. Searching, unimpeded intergenerational communication informs the young and stimulates their elders. The unpredictably rich results of questioning can make students the teachers of their teachers and their interchange a source of exhilaration and delight.

We are in greater need of what the residential college experience offers than perhaps any prior generation. Our world is disablingly busy. The demands of their jobs and of their complex lives make it difficult for parents to devote extensive attention to their children. Childcare workers and teachers, whose professional services are supposed to assure the moral growth and intellectual development of the young, are overwhelmed with people they must benefit. They cannot spend much time in direct personal contact with any of them. As a result, a significant number of individuals grow up without getting to know older, more experienced persons and without the benefit of feeling their sustained love.

This loss can be devastating. Inter-generational friendship is the sole method of handing down the habits of caring without which human life remains empty and often turns bitter. As any skill of the heart, this cannot be taught through words or through exercises devised by counselors. It is the grateful response of people to a happy childhood in a nurturing community, the desire to pay the next generation for what was received from the last.

Even at their best, residential institutions of higher education are poor substitutes for loving families. But they are among the few alternatives available today. College students are old enough to appreciate the deeper reaches of inter-generational friendship, yet not so jaded as to have ceased looking for warmth and guidance. Under the right circumstances, they can develop rich and caring relationships with their teachers. Though most of these remain temporary partnerships, some grow into lifelong commitments to intense mutual support.

The windstorm of the electronic revolution feels like a zephyr in the sheltered valleys of the academic world. Colleges and universities have not even started to assess the changes they will have to undergo to survive in the new world of the twenty-first century. They appear to trust in their credentialing power to stave off disaster. But before long, some reputable institutions are bound to recognize the windfall of offering legitimate degrees through electronic distance learning. This will set off a competitive stampede, resulting in a squeeze on prices. Will students short on money and time not prefer the cheaper and faster electronic degree to spending years at marginal institutions?

A painful consolidation of residential colleges and universities is as near a certainty as anything in the future can be. Rich schools are likely to survive, but even they will find their missions and their curricula transformed. To move in the direction of providing closer and more extensive contact with faculty, they will have to revamp their educational strategy.

The imaginative use of new technologies that alone makes this possible will, in the process, altogether transform the undergraduate program.

Full recognition that books and the classroom do not constitute effective ways of teaching facts is likely to revolutionize what teachers and students do. Electronic access to all the cut-and-dried material of education will liberate faculty from lengthy exposition and boring drill. Students will have all the facts they need at their fingertips, with easy machine checks that they got them right. Since they will uncover the facts as needed for the solution of problems, they will master them in their context and remember them better.

This should enable faculty members to attend to the tasks of education proper: to teaching skills of investigation, theory formation, and hypothesis testing, and to enhancing critical judgment and the scope and depth of appreciation. The resulting growth involves expansion of both the rigor of thought and the sweep of imagination, conferring on students some of the same pleasures critics, scientific investigators, and creative artists enjoy. We hardly dare say it: education might, in this way, become as joyous for students as it has always been for the best of their teachers.

We do not mean to suggest that Utopia is just around the corner. It never is. But the ingenuity of human beings has now put tools at our disposal that enable us to do what prior generations could not even dream. Transmission to the young of important portions of the accumulated knowledge of the human race need no longer exact the pain of dozens of years of rote memory. Much more material than any one person could ever remember is now available in response to simple commands typed into or spoken to machines.

Before long, we will find ourselves tied to our computers as we are tied to our cars; they will become integral elements of the self. The critical question is how we will learn to use this external memory for the purpose of improving human minds and, through them, human lives.

The effects of externalizing memory are likely to replicate the effects of finding a machine solution to providing the conditions of any important practice. The ease with which the activity can be performed makes for a vast increase in its frequency and a decline in the value we place on performing it the old way. So, for example, when writing was invented and accounts of past events could be stored in libraries or on walls, oral histories, passed from bard to bard, were nearly eliminated. And the advent of the typewriter brought with it a flood of writing, along with decreased appreciation of fine calligraphy.

Our veneration of the power of memory is also likely to evaporate as we learn to replace factual information stored in individual brains with communal data banks. Contests such as "The College Bowl" may come to look like freak shows without a point, much like the performances of people who try to play eight instruments at once to imitate an orchestra. Forcing students to remember large bodies of information and rewarding them for feats of recalling disconnected facts may appear sad or even bizarre to subsequent generations.

This is the context in which we must understand the impact computerized storage will likely exert on educational practices. Even a cursory assessment of how much time is spent on memory work suffices to indicate the extent of the changes we face. The optimistic interpretation of these impending events is that the development of technology is at last lifting from humans the burden of brute or unfitting activities. Dishwashers have liberated us from the daily imperatives of the sink and backhoes have taken over the hard work of digging. Why should the task of carrying with us the irrelevant details of the world not pass from us, as well? Thought and appreciation constitute more worthy uses of our time and capacity than storage of dead facts.

Such an optimistic account of developments is clearly better than the alternatives. But to make it acceptable, we must dispel a possible misunderstanding and call attention to a peril. When we speak of handing over the work of memory to machine substitutes of the human brain, we do not mean to imply that we will walk around with empty heads, unable to recall anything that happened to us. On the contrary, investigation and appreciation are themselves impossible without mastery, and that means storage and integration, of skills. Thought requires a subject matter held fast in memory and we cannot decide on the direction of inquiry without sustained knowledge of the shape of facts and of what about them needs to be explained.

Evidently, such contextualized ordinary memories are not what computers are in the process of replacing. Human minds, particularly the interested intellects of the young, are like flypaper: everything they come in contact with sticks to them. Such effortless remembering is a condition of operating in the world, and it enriches life in incalculable ways. Without it, we cannot know whether tires go on the car or as decorations around the neck. And we fail as friends if we are unable to distinguish strangers from those we love.

We have in mind, instead, the forced ingestion and periodic regurgitation in educational institutions of vast quantities of unrelated facts. At times when information is difficult to come by, such privately stored knowledge is invaluable, in just the way a flashlight comes in handy when the lights go out. But it is a mistake to organize education as if we perpetually faced the dark.

The danger confronting us is that our success has become our problem: the wonderful aids we have devised for mastering facts and understanding the world may diminish the felt seriousness of education. Traditionally, the discipline of compulsory memory work has carried the burden of conveying the momentousness of learning. The cry for a return to basics in education may, in fact, be simply the desire for effort and earnest respect to infuse the enterprise. Prosperity has supposedly made young people soft or unambitious. Since human nature, at least in its current incarnation, has no respect for the easy, eliminating the pressure of rote memory may make education painless or even fun, and thereby sap the energy with which we tackle it.

The long-term challenge facing educators at all levels is to find ways to sustain the motivation of students and to convey to them the life-creating power of appropriating the culture of the past. Fortunately, early indications point to success. Access to vast reaches of the Internet keeps young people riveted to their seats in front of monitors for hours. Such natural curiosity combined with desire for the companionship of caring adults should give teachers everything they need.

In any case, simple as access to information has become, there is nothing easy about interpreting and explaining the facts. Learning more about the world, therefore, will always be a challenge that the contagious excitement of good teachers can convert into the work of personal and intellectual growth.

# THIRTY

# LEARNING ABOUT POSSIBILITY

The physical world is a vastly complex place; human institutions, history, and traditional practices make it even more involuted. It takes the young many years to learn to operate in this environment. They get everything they know from others and from personal experience, but much more from the former because the latter is slow and limited in scope. Every human being we meet is in one way or another our teacher, conveying valuable information about the forces that surround us. But some humans educate us systematically or as a matter of their profession: their job is to teach us about how things stand in some area of life.

Such teaching can be part of an institution, though it need not be; marriage partners teach spontaneously and over many years what they will not accept from each other. The support educational institutions receive from their communities is due to the need to convey in a speedy and organized way the knowledge, values, and accepted practices of the culture. Professional teachers impart information and help their students develop useful skills for dealing with the complexities of the world. The emphasis is, understandably, on the actual; the function of education is to enable people to live longer and better lives.

In spite of the charge of irrelevance, undergraduate courses are devoted to the exploration of reality. Physics, chemistry, and biology deal with aspects or elements of the physical world; history lays bare what happened; sociology and economics uncover vast sets of interactions among human beings; even much of mathematics is focused on how it can help us understand the world. It may seem that fields of investigation specializing in the works of the imagination escape this tyranny of the actual, but students of literature are less interested in the luminous unreality depicted in stories than in how these symbols contribute to our ability to deal with the actual.

This interest in reality is natural and appropriate. "What else is there?" one could reasonably ask. Since human life is precarious and easily snuffed out, we have more than adequate motive for learning everything we can about how the world works and for trying to tilt it to our advantage. Those who know more are typically, though not always, better at bringing about desirable outcomes; the likelihood of their controlling their environment and obtaining what they want is higher than that of people operating without special skills and information. The philosophical tradition has always maintained that the object of knowledge is the real. The veneration of knowledge, to which Nietzsche so vehemently objected, is therefore at once the veneration of reality, a quiet surrender to what unquestionably *is*.

As Leibniz and others knew, however, the actual is but a tiny fragment of totality, surrounded on all sides by possibilities. Reality is embedded in an infinite field of what might, or might not ever, be. This is the world of the imagination, though among humans even the imagination is finite and can never do justice to the richness of the absurd, the baffling, the unforeseeable, the unintelligible, and the mind-numbingly large or complex. We cannot wrap our minds around the millionth prime number and cannot give content to how life might be different a hundred years from now.

The unfortunate oversight of possibility is supported by the general sense that the actual is natural—that there is something right about how things are and it would be inappropriate to try to change them. This feeling is ubiquitous, showing itself in how we relate to the house in which we grew up, the language we have been taught to speak, and even the table manners to which we have become accustomed. Alternatives to these and other habits tend not to occur to us: we simply do not see that anything we do is a selection from innumerable other things we could be doing and that even *how* we do things is optional and has only the weight of actuality to recommend it.

Educational systems are so busy teaching students about what is that they have no time and no taste for exploring alternatives. In any case, awareness of alternatives tends to make people think that everything is contingent, which might lead to questioning the status quo and thereby to destabilizing the entire system. Surely one of the reasons for discouraging speculation about how things could be different is that we might take matters in our own hands and change things to suit our desires. Even vision that differs from the conventional is considered illegitimate, as when her first grade teacher upbraided our daughter for having drawn a marvelously imaginative picture of the sun, in place of the conventional yellow orb with lines representing its rays. Hers was just an innocently different aesthetic vision; the presentation of alternative institutional arrangements, rules, and values is met with far more vigorous disapproval.

The guardians of the status quo do not welcome the consideration of possibilities because they make their living from existing arrangements. Institutions resist change even more mightily: they are conservative systems interested in safeguarding the actual, of which they are salient parts. Everything in the world seems to want to hold on to existence, which can be accomplished only by rejecting all other possibilities. Change is death to what exists now. Since it consists in the embodiment of some other possibility, the best way to stave it off is not even to acknowledge alternatives: The actual operates as if the myriad possibilities ready to replace it were not nipping at its heel.

Schools typically reinforce the tendency to suppress the possible. Social and political changes, for example, are presented as matters of the past whose sole legitimacy lies in having conducted us to our current, excellent system. Language is taught as it is supposed to be written, scientific theories are presented as facts, and even literary criticism restricts itself to a small number of canonical interpretations. Thomas Jefferson and his friends were inventive in how they spelled words; for us, any nonstandard spelling counts as error.

To be sure, some teachers announce proudly that they reject satisfaction with the actual and think of theirs as a subversive profession. They use ridicule or critical questioning to undermine the unthinking acquiescence of their students in whatever shape the world takes. They feel emboldened in their classrooms to say nearly anything they want and delight in creating the impression that in their opinion nothing is sacred. It seems invigorating to see them challenge every orthodoxy and question the legitimacy of all authority.

Young people speak and act as if they wanted to revolt against the authorities that surround them on every side, but they learn to treat power with respect early in life. Their talk of rebellion is no more than that: soon they make their peace with whatever institution accommodates them and however many mad rules it imposes on them. Rebellious undergraduate drugheads become lawyers in three-piece suits; anarchist artists who painted obscene frescoes on dorm walls learn to photograph cakes for magazine ads. Hardly any of them can imagine what will become of them precisely because no one taught them how to deal with possibilities and thereby fend off surrendering to what in their salad days they would have thought a nightmare.

Sadly, the bold talk of teachers has no more substance than the rebellious grumbling and foot-dragging of the young. Supreme courage in the classroom is little more than talk—in the hall and in the dean's or principal's office, teachers act as obedient officials of the institution. Principles seem to belong in the realm of discourse; reality demands compromise and adjustment. In this way, teachers learn to enact the living contradiction of mighty words and petty deeds, of never quite doing what they say one should. When students notice this, they lose all respect for their teachers. What good are words that never inspire acts?

All of this goes a long way toward explaining the tenuous life of possibilities in human society. They are difficult to envisage in detail and it is never enough to articulate them in words. The actual surrounds us on all sides; in stable societies, the weight of the status quo is such that we can hardly believe anything could be different from what it is. The possible can gain a foothold against the everlasting *is* only by being embodied in at least one life. It acquires credibility only by becoming actual or at least by having someone demonstrate the steps that will take us there.

The demonstration must be concrete and visible. Teachers who speak eloquently of social or institutional changes but never act on them fail to teach about possibility; outlining a future without embarking on bringing it about makes it look distant and unattainable. Literary critics who explain how novels should be written but never write one, social critics who stand on the sidelines observing the birth struggles of the new, and psychological counselors in the business of giving advice on which they tend not to act are enemies of the possible who masquerade as friends. They cheapen it by showing how little power it has to engage the soul and how easily those who profess allegiance to it can be discouraged from its pursuit.

Not surprisingly perhaps, those devoted to possibilities of harm appear more ready to take vigorous and steadfast action in pursuit of their vision. The literatures of heaven and hell are uneven in their specificity and quality: We can describe the tortures of the damned in exquisite detail but find ourselves oddly bereft of ideas when it comes to the rapture of the saved. Tamerlane, Hitler, and Saddam Hussein entertained clear notions of preferred futures for their victims, as do thieves, rapists, and masochist bureaucrats all over the globe. Such people have little trouble motivating themselves to act; their deeds and their imaginations appear to be welded together into a seamless nasty whole. People of good will, on the other hand, tend to be faint of heart when it comes to doing what they know they should. They suffer from self-doubt, hesitate, and talk themselves out of allegiance to a shining possibility by bringing to mind innumerable other alternatives. In the end, many of them find a proxy for action in an avalanche of words.

This discrepancy is particularly puzzling because in many instances benevolent people are protected from the consequences of their actions taken on behalf of ideals. College and university teachers, for example, enjoy the benefits of tenure, meaning that they can be fired only for crushing incompetence or gross moral turpitude. Such job security is the perfect cover for speaking one's mind and acting on one's convictions. Criticism of the institution and of the society beyond is protected speech, and so long as correlated actions do not violate the laws, they can be performed with impunity. Given the threat of bad publicity and expensive lawsuits, the likelihood of institutional retaliation is slim; its consequences are negligible.

For, after all, what could the administration of a university do to punish tenured in-house critics? They may be scheduled to teach at inconvenient times, forced to move their offices to the basement, and ordered to have their salaries frozen. In the grand scheme of things, however, *when* one teaches is of little significance. If one's office is a windowless cubicle, one can simply reduce the time spent there to the mandatory hour or two a week. Moreover, tenured professors earn a substantial salary, so making do without the annual two or three percent raise should not present a problem. At most, university administrators can make the life of critical faculty uncomfortable, which is a small price to pay for doing what a teacher should, namely explore possibilities so that a suitable ideal may be found and enacted.

Relative invulnerability does not embolden faculty to think and teach the possible. Tenure protects much more than classroom speech: Public criticism, peaceful protest, and investment of one's time and money are among activities one can support by evidence derived from one's field of specialization. Yet teachers show themselves to be a timid lot, always ready to sidestep commitment and find an excuse for not taking a stand. This lamentable lack of courage defines them as distant from the concerns of life and shining only so long as empty words suffice.

Timidity makes it impossible for teachers to fulfill their mission. Teaching the young involves activities that pull in different directions; the culture's practices and values must be handed on, but they must also be criticized and suitably revised. In doing the former, teachers act as servants of the past, giving a favorable account of the fruits of long experience. In doing the latter, they labor for the future, presenting ideas for how our practices can be improved. The first activity is centered on sketching the geography of what exists and explaining the rules governing it; the second is about the ways the possible can bring improvement to the actual. The first without the second yields stagnation, the second without the first creates chaos. When properly related, the two preserve what is of value from the past even as they encourage active dreaming about a better future.

Making established practices look attractive is a favored activity; this is what makes teachers beloved in the eyes of students who grow up to be pillars of society. Criticizing our comfortable values, on the other hand, makes instructors seem alien in their own world or troublemakers ungrateful for the good society lavishes on them. They need courage not so much to give voice to their own beliefs, which can range from the idiosyncratic to the absurd, but to express their dreams and point thereby to possibilities what may otherwise escape us. Without daring, teachers can only repeat the well-worn wisdom of the past, much of which is, in any case, available in books.

The critical stance toward current practices is as necessary in the sciences as it is in the humanities. Established methods and theories in physics, chemistry, and biology invite periodic challenge; at least some of them may have served us well in the past but now stand in need of imaginative revision or replacement. The social sciences are in a unique position to offer ideas concerning novel economic, social, and political arrangements, and the humanities have traditionally been a hotbed of new values and thoughts about better ways of treating our neighbors. At the very least, practitioners of all fields can have something useful to say about improvement of the institution in which they serve. Sharing those ideas is a minimal obligation and involves the development of possibilities considered, as it used to be said, under the form of the good.

Tenure in universities and colleges was instituted largely to protect faculty members in their vital activity of offering unpopular possibilities to their students, to administrators and to the public at large. Some may think that tenure confers a right to speak on faculty members and a collateral obligation on the institution not to fire them for the views they hold as professionals. This, however, is only part of the story. The right conferred carries with it a duty: faculty members are not only permitted to speak their minds without retaliation, they must do so. By extending tenure, an institution of higher education hires critics and pledges to pay them for the trouble they give. Those who do not present possibilities constituting at least tacit criticisms of the status quo fail to meet the conditions of their employment.

This failure is so widespread that at one point I suggested the possibility of requiring each tenured faculty member to advance at least two critical initiatives a year.[1] Not surprisingly, this idea captured the imagination of no one: administrators did not want to have to deal with in-house critics and teachers were concerned about their next raise. Artificial as the method may be, it addresses the real problem of faculties taking little interest in the governance of their institutions and timidly avoiding criticism of deans and presidents. Such behavior may make more time for advancing one's research agenda, but it does not improve the university one serves and whose care should be in all its employee's hands. A more natural way to enhance the role of possibilities in our lives is to make teachers fall in love with them. The changes must begin in kindergarten. Fortunately, in young children the imagination is as strong as the reality sense; all we have to do for them is not to crush the free play of their images and thoughts. Beyond puberty, when the actual lays siege to their minds, we must aid their resistance by showing that their teachers know how to think alternatives and rewarding them when they do likewise. The undergraduate curriculum needs to be changed to teach not only how things are, but also how they might have been, and may yet become, different. Even graduate and professional training have to be imbued with a sense of what is not, in order to take a full measure of the nature and limits of the real. The education of teachers in the love of possibilities must thus stretch from the time they first enter school as young students to the time they take retirement.

Embrace of possibilities may be confused with ready adjustment to inevitable change. But adjustment is serious work that belongs to the world of the actual. It lacks the free-ranging playfulness of considering alternatives and the excitement of the what-if. Moreover, there is a great deal of irrelevance in the range of possibilities: some have little or nothing to do with the world in which we live. We can imagine beings with eighty-two heads and kidneys, large as balloons, which encase them. We can think that clouds of methane gas sing the national anthem while small molecules scratch their tiny heads. Such fancies are certainly possibilities and they may have some use in the realm of humor. But they have little relation to the task of making life better and they make no contribution to recrafting reality. The possibilities we must always keep in mind are those relevant to the real but not now actualized, alternatives that help us understand the world in which we live or offer a blueprint for desirable change.

The most intriguing possibilities, which are at once the most difficult to bring into focus, cluster around our current fashion of conceiving the world. The way things appear to us has the authority of the objective and the natural. This takes attention away from the contingency of current arrangements and the contribution our thoughts make to how things seem to be. The French and the American revolutions opened our eyes to the possibility of new social and political orders; Darwin made it possible for us to view biology, and human beings, in a novel way. American pragmatism and postmodernist challenges are bringing home to us that how we think about the world is a vital element in its constitution and that such thoughts are within our power to change or to retain.

Inevitably, each new way of thinking freezes into place and, appearing natural and right, resists challenge. To counteract this tendency, we must keep reminding ourselves that modes of thought, no matter how entrenched, are optional. We can think of sex, for example, as duty within the context of holy matrimony or as casual recreation; of doctors as superior humans with unique access to the mysteries of the body or as useful health consultants; and of bureaucrats as powerful agents of obstruction or as servants of the public. Each mode of thought defines appropriate behavior and leads to consequences we may or may not desire. In the end, how we think should be determined by the consequences we want to achieve. This requires that we stand ready to exchange conceptual structures as if they were useful instruments. This is what the contemplation of possibilities is all about: in thinking of alternatives, we add tools to our tool chest. Nothing has a more profound effect on the world than a good idea.

# THIRTY-ONE

# MORAL HOLIDAYS

Let me begin with what may well be fighting words. Josiah Royce's intellect was doggedly one-directional; William James's mind, by contrast, showed signs of playful creativity. His relentless focus on evil places Royce among the most serious of philosophers; one can imagine him thinking with gritted teeth. James, on the other hand, displays moments of winking fun, such as when he invents the idea of moral holidays.

In his usual fashion, James does not spend much time explaining what moral holidays are. Aiming his comments at Royce, he assails the role of the Absolute in the moral life: if our obligations are infinite but God picks up the slack and completes what we leave undone, then we might as well break from our labors and let the Deity take over. The urgency of moral action abates the moment we feel assured that God presides over a universe in which the good inevitably prevails. In His infinity, God can do it all even if we "drop the worry of our . . . responsibility."[1] We can then take a moral holiday and "let the world wag in its own way, feeling that its issues are in better hands than ours."[2]

This leaves us with an intuitive but not very precise idea of what a moral holiday might be. A few moments of reflection reveals that there are at least four different notions of moral holiday and that James is not careful to draw distinctions between them. The first idea is the rejection of all moral rules and limits, the second the elimination of obligations, the third the disregard of what is supererogatory, and the fourth the lessening of effort usually associated with vacationing.

Only sociopaths of exceptional resolve and concentration can sidestep *all* moral constraints. Ordinary mortals find it nearly impossible to sustain immorality on a grand scale; even the cruelest and nastiest people tend to pay for their groceries and refrain much of the time, even if not always, from burning down their neighbors' houses. Suspending all moral rules is hard work and goes against the grain. Leading a thoroughly immoral life is as exhausting as being through-and-through moral: each of its constituent actions requires scrutiny, and we must make sure that the temptations of decency never prevail. This is hardly a holiday: It sounds more like the labored efforts of a conscientious person whose values became lamentably inverted.

The second notion of a moral holiday takes aim at obligations and announces that, for a while at least, they are suspended. Individual duties may be suspended for many reasons. Illness may make it impossible for us to do what we should, and greater obligations may overshadow some minor, ordinary duty. This concept of a moral holiday, however, goes far beyond lifting an obligation or two, sanctioning instead the wholesale temporary disregard of *all* obligations. So when I am on moral holiday in this sense, I can let my baby cry in the crib and the accident victim lie in a pool of blood—I am going to the beach and have, for the moment, no interest in doing what I should. Of course, not all of my actions are liberated from the rule of morality; I can still do good gratuitously, so long as it is not in response to a duty.

The third notion of a moral holiday is significantly narrower than the first two. It leaves us in the thrall of obligations but removes actions of supererogation. People on this sort of holiday remain, in a narrow sense of the phrase, moral agents, meeting their obligations and obeying obvious moral rules. They refuse, however, to go beyond the call of duty: they fill their roles adequately but are out of the office sharp at 5:00 o'clock.

Perhaps more than half the world is on such a holiday pretty much all the time, following rules but never going even a small part of the extra mile.

The last notion of a moral holiday is a little more difficult to articulate. Part of what a vacation means for many people is the opportunity to take a break from doing things for others. One might be inclined to help if help is desperately needed, and one would certainly not want to slough off important obligations. But life on vacation lacks the busy urgency of the everyday; the strenuous striving of the rest of the year is laid aside for the moment, and one can kick off one's shoes and head for the hammock. This is a time at which one does not look for things to do and considers it acceptable to be doing little or nothing. The fact that people on such holidays resist helping others does not mean that they go out of their way to serve themselves. Even activities of self-improvement are shelved, and what is perceived as a healing and wholesome laziness overtakes the soul. This is something like what James calls "the easy-going mood" that lets the world go its way without moving a finger to intervene.

I suspect that this fourth sense of the phrase comes closest to what James has in mind when he speaks of belief in the Absolute justifying moral holidays. His point is that if evil will inevitably suffer defeat and has already done so from the standpoint of eternity, then we may well declare a moratorium on effort; we *can* head for the hammock to contemplate the victory secured by God as we slip off to sleep. The name "moral holiday" may well be a misnomer for this attitude, for though it is a holiday, it is not an obviously or preeminently *moral* one. The people who enjoy such breaks from exertion do not dismiss the legitimacy of moral rules and obligations; they just do not feel called upon to follow them for a stretch of time.

If we take the matter further, Royce (as the friend of the Absolute whom James targets) is in even deeper trouble than it at first appears. Why should moral holidays be temporary events rather than permanent dispositions? Royce maintains that God makes up the difference between our noble aims and feeble efforts: He accomplishes what we set out to do but cannot achieve on our own. Royce inherited from Fichte the fateful idea that whatever demand can be satisfied does not constitute a proper duty, that Kant's idea of ought implying can must be set aside for the deeper and beautifully romantic notion that we are called upon to do what we can't. Anything finite might conceivably be attained, so the only way to assure that our obligations are worthy of us is to make them infinite. Royce declares that there is "no rest in Zion": our struggles never cease so long as we are mired in finitude, which means that they never cease.

But what motive do we have for engaging in the struggle with vigor? The distance between the finite good we can do and the infinite demanded of us is itself infinite, and that only an infinite being can traverse. This opens a marvelous opportunity for reducing our labors: If we do twice as much as we did last year, we are still infinitely removed from the goal, and if we reduce our effort to ten percent of that next year, we will be no further from meeting our obligations. Moreover, God must provide the same boost in both cases—he needs to close the gap between finite and infinite. Since only He can do that, why should we exert ourselves? If we do less, in one sense God does not have to do more than He would otherwise, and He will, in any case, do it all. The conclusion that we can do as little as we please and yet not imperil the perfection of the world seems inescapable. To load infinite obligations on finite beings is to let them escape with none.

James's attack has at least two prongs. Morally, it is repugnant to demand infinite achievements of the finite. Psychologically, if God supplements what we do and thereby raises it to a level adequate to meet our obligations, we have no incentive for doing much at all. Do these lines of reasoning raise fair objections to Royce? They would if he did not have a system of metaphysics and as a part of it a full account of human nature. But he clearly does, developed beautifully in *The World and the Individual*, and a central element of it consists of the claim that infinity is inscribed in our souls: the search for it is constitutive of what it means to be human.

"It is not satisfactory to be finite,"[3] Royce declares. All finite acts and facts are evil, and as such "leave us in disquietude, searching still for the Other, i.e., for true Being in its wholeness."[4] Having this drive or platonic *eros* for completion is precisely what it means to be a self, and the fact that the self's task in the finite world can never be fulfilled serves, astonishingly, as the premise that points to our immortality. In striving for union with God, we seek to be like Him, broadening our attention and expanding our loyalties. Royce can thus readily respond to James that there is nothing morally objectionable in letting human nature develop and express itself, and it does so in the search for the eternal. And as to motivation, we need no additional incentive if by nature our will is focused on the infinite.

I leave to one side the strikingly romantic nature of these ideas and offer only one comment. Remarkably for someone devoted to the expansion of attention, Royce pays little heed to what Hegel called mere "empirical details." Relentless and endless striving may well characterize commercial, industrial, and knowledge-based societies in the temperate zone, but it is not a feature of human beings everywhere. Ancient Athenians were satisfied with much less than infinity, significant numbers of Medieval Christians seeking union with God did not hope to find it through restless search for evils to defeat, and incessant yearning is alien to many cultures even today. The actual blinds us to distant variety and elevates the local into the universal.

One might suppose that James, respectful of human finitude and devoted to exploring the details of motivation, might be a friend of moral holidays. Even if our limits can expand, there is only so much good we can do; one person cannot stop the spread of AIDS or defeat starvation in Africa. Perhaps all of humanity acting in concert cannot either. Moreover, everyone needs some breathing room from obligations: we do better tomorrow if we spend an hour relaxing tonight. Moral holidays look, therefore, as useful and perhaps necessary breaks in the routine of life, enabling us to gather our forces and return stronger to the fray.[5]

This is the message James might have conveyed in his article entitled "The Gospel of Relaxation." And, indeed, in that essay he bemoans the breathlessness, anxiety, and convulsive "over-tension" he detects in the American character. He calls the intensity and agony of our approach to the world "bottled lightning"[6] and deplores the "absence of repose" in our lives. This is promising because it focuses on the hyperactivity that wants to correct everything in the world and leaves no time for quiet reflection and healing. He goes so far as to recommend to the students he addresses that they "fling away" their books the day before the exam and learn not to care about how well they do.[7] This sounds like an endorsement of moral holidays not only in the fourth sense of wholesome inactivity, but also in the second sense of failure to meet one's obligations.

By the end of the essay, however, it is clear that that is not what James has in mind at all. He does not want to reduce our labors or exempt us from what Royce would be happy to call "doing the Lord's work." He objects to our "absurd feelings of hurry" because they are inefficient. "If . . . living excitedly . . . would only enable us to *do* more . . . it would be different," he says.[8] As it is, the tension and anxiety that weigh on us because there is so much to accomplish, "are the surest drags upon steady progress and hindrances to our success."[9] Instead, James suggests, the better way to do everything we must is to clear our minds of worry about whether we are doing it or not. Then, we will be "calmly ready for any duty that the day may bring forth."[10] If we manage "genuinely" not to care about attaining what we should, we are more likely to succeed at our tasks than if we are dogged by perpetual concerns about our performance. What sounds like an invitation to take moral holidays quickly turns in this way into a recommendation of how to be maximally effective in the work that keeps us from going to the beach. James seems interested in improving our output rather than in limiting what we are supposed to do.

James thus appears imbued with something resembling the same moral fervor that animates Royce. In "The Moral Philosopher and the Moral Life," he makes his admiration of the strenuous mood clear. He argues that every desire is a demand for satisfaction and the essence of good is to satisfy these claims.[11] Demands are not directed at particular persons; anyone in a position to satisfy them is under obligation to do so. This throws the floodgates of generosity wide open, with each of us facing a universe that imposes indefinitely many duties on us. Such profusion of responsibilities leaves no room for moral holidays. Only the strenuous mood, teaching us to disregard stress and pain, makes it possible to meet our obligations. The endless labor of the Protestant ethic seems as central to James's moral metaphysics as it is to Royce's.

The similarity does not end there. The last few pages of "The Moral Philosopher and the Moral Life" suggest that God is no less significant for James than He is for Royce. James avers that finite demands are inadequate to evoke the deepest self-sacrificial commitments; it takes an "infinite demander"[12] to engage our sympathy and mobilize all our energies. He goes so far as to suggest that if God did not exist, we would be inclined to, and indeed ought to, "postulate" His existence. The Divine Being makes for a systematic moral universe in that His way of ordering the demands of living creatures is "the finally valid casuistic scale,"[13] and sincere belief in Him sets free the habits of endurance and courage necessary to do everything we must.

Yet these similarities, intriguing as they may be, do not go very deep. James is ready to wax poetic about the value of believing in God, but rarely does he give us more than a hint concerning what this Deity might be like. He is certainly not the Absolute of the idealists and, most important, He is not a being who compensates for our failures. For James, God does not play a consolatory function, assuring us that He will supplement our imperfect efforts. Contrary to Royce's view, we are left alone to do what needs to be done; all the action comes from human beings trying to make the world a little better. We postulate God for inspirational reasons: He is indispensable for letting "loose in us the strenuous mood."[14] So God's function in James is motivational, while in Royce it is metaphysical.

The contrast is even sharper in relation to our moral labors. The tasks that weigh on us, according to Royce, are infinite in number. We must defeat all evil and that, in the end, means that we must overcome finitude altogether. This remains forever impossible, and as a result we cannot escape frustration at our impotence. James, by contrast, burdens us only with indefinitely, but finitely, many obligations. Ideally, we are to satisfy every desire and meet every need. But James does not let philosophical enthusiasm obscure his marvelous reality-sense: he knows that gratifying some impulses is incompatible with satisfying others. Many parts of the ideal must, therefore, be "butchered," reducing the number of desires whose fulfillment falls to us. As a consequence, we can make genuine headway. Although hungers continue to arise, we can find technologically sophisticated ways in which many of them can be satisfied quickly: human intelligence is powerful enough to reorganize the world. If we want water, James reminds us, all we need to do is turn the faucet, and similar, equally forgotten but radical breakthroughs have occurred on many levels to make life immeasurably better. Even though he would not let us, in James's world we can afford to take a moral holiday.

The sorts of things we must rectify and what rectification consists in establish the final break between Royce and James. Royce sports a keener sense of evil than many of the medieval philosophers whose names begin with "Saint." He sees evil in the world and in the human soul; in the end, everything limited and partial falls under suspicion and requires to be corrected by integration into a larger whole. Royce's drive for overcoming evil, both moral and metaphysical, is so all-encompassing that it attempts to unite three elements that are difficult to reconcile. He welcomes concrete improvements in the human condition: the broadening of loyalties, the much-hoped-for elimination of aggressive wars and the possibility of a great community delight him. We might call this his American temper.

His soul, however, also harbors a romantic German metaphysician. To that Royce, all finite improvements count as nothing. Finitude itself is tainted and can be redeemed only by union with the infinite and the eternal. Halfway measures are of no value; empirical advances leave our condition morally—really, metaphysically—no better. In addition, there is the third Royce, whose plight is best understood in terms of Hegel's unhappy consciousness. When evil is thought to have penetrated the soul, we become our own enemies. The discord that comes of viewing oneself as both sinner and saint, of hating one's loves and loving one's hates as Royce puts it, rends the fabric of the self and makes satisfaction impossible to attain. As a result, nothing can be done with a good conscience and, though we are made in the image of God, nothing about us is holy. Under these circumstances, we cannot even *think* of taking a moral holiday; finitude and wickedness must be battled day and night. And yet the evil we fight cannot be overcome because the ones fighting it are evil.

James's thought, by comparison, is far simpler. He sees the concept of evil as derivative from the ideas of desire and satisfaction. If there is any room for the notion of evil in James's world, it is merely to mark that a need went unrequited or a want failed to be met. Evil is no more pervasive than the good; if anything, the opposite is true. Reasonable self-control in choosing, vigorous labor, social cooperation, and a bit of luck should enable us to satisfy many of our desires. Of course, we cannot satisfy them all: our wants notoriously conflict with one another, and when they do, some have to die shriveled on the vine. This, however, is just what comes of the innocent, natural profusion of life, and it is up to us to trim the luxuriant growths. The outcome may be tragic, and James boldly calls it that, but it is not nasty or disgusting or depraved.

James believes that each of our desires is justified from its own point of view. This contrasts nicely with Royce's idea that "an evil is, in general, a fact that sends us to some Other for its own justification."[15] The full force of this difference is best brought out by focusing on the sharply divergent reactions of the two thinkers to the defeat of evil. For Royce, this is cause for jubilation, for taking delight in crushing an enemy. Evil is a force without legitimacy and intrinsic value, a disobedient energy to be wiped out. In defeating it, we accomplish a divine mission and the heavens smile. If there is an equivalent in James to gaining victory over evil, it is the satisfaction of a desire too long denied. The proper response here is empirical enjoyment; what we had long wanted has at last come about. Royce glories in the elimination of an alien, negative reality, while James grieves the death of every impulse and being. In the end, it is not inappropriate to say that Royce believes in the fallenness of both humans and the world, while James, a child of the Enlightenment, affirms the fundamental goodness of everything that strives.

Several ideas offer themselves at this point as worthy reflections. The first concerns philosophers committed to radically different ideas living together in harmony. Despite superficial similarities of view, James and Royce are nearly as far from each other philosophically as two thinkers can be. Nevertheless, they managed to live for decades in the same department, respecting each other's talents and praising each other's achievements. Although James called Royce's *work* "a rotten tissue of reasoning,"[16] he also wrote: "How, then, O my dear Royce, can I forget you, or be contented out of your close neighborhood? Different as our minds are, yours has nourished mine, as no other social influence ever has, and in converse with you I have always felt that my life was being lived importantly."[17] Severe criticism of others' views is compatible with the most cordial of human relations and a hearty appreciation of their

444   HUMAN ADVANCE AND FINITE OBLIGATION

philosophical excellence in their chosen style and idiom. There is a lesson to be learned here.

A second reflection relates to the disturbing presence of the Absolute
in philosophical systems. Royce's work is replete with striking ideas, interesting arguments and illuminating analogies. Again and again, however, he is hampered in developing his insights by antecedent commitment
to an Absolute that is supposed to be both person and totality. His philosophy would have been more consistent had he allowed it to develop
from the vital finite realities that he, in his best moments, recognized
and embraced. It would have been also more sensible, had he not felt
himself carried to the obvious but unfortunate conclusion that everything finite is radically evil. James, burdened with his own inconsisten-
cies, saw clearly that the Absolute was philosophical dead weight, and he
wisely dispensed with it.

Third, preoccupation with evil and with the struggle to overcome it
distorts moral philosophy and stunts our generous impulses. Royce's
idea that an infinite process converts rottenness into perfection is satisfying to contemplate but suffers from three ruinous flaws. It postulates a
linear infinity, whose problems were thoroughly aired by Hegel and
whose motivational hold on finite beings is negligible. It makes us view
all things as broken and ourselves as never quite able to mend them. And
it burdens us with infinite obligations that we can never hope to meet.
Seeing anything as evil is one of the forms of blindness James was so
good at unmasking; it is the inability to see the world from the perspective of that being and to understand its self-justification. James was much
better at the imaginative extension of his sympathies than Royce.

That takes us back to moral holidays. To fight an infinite battle with
not a day out to let the smoke clear and to listen to the birds is nearly the
most terrible fate I can imagine. The fact that I might yell "Victory!"
makes little difference; Sisyphus also thinks he is winning before the rock
crushes his foot on the way back down the mountain. After a day of doing good, I want to listen to Mozart and drink a beer with unblemished
conscience and in the secure knowledge that this will make me a kinder
man in the morning. Royce does not allow me that, and James would
like to forbid it, too. For Royce, there is more evil to be vanquished in the
evening; for James, unmet desires continue to cry out for satisfaction.

Royce cannot accommodate my leisure; James could, but feels disinclined. I can appreciate the pressing urgency of need and want, but can one live a life of ceaseless service? What would life be without the song of birds, and what is the value of a philosophy that makes me feel guilty for listening to it?

What might a theory of moral holidays look like? It must start from the recognition that we have many obligations to others, but reject three views of these duties. Contrary to what some earnest moralists believe, our obligations are not infinite in number. The idea that our duties and our ability to meet them can never reach balance is devastating for the moral life. Moral psychology cannot be built on the perpetual frustration of our efforts; the thought that no matter how much we do, it is not enough extinguishes motivation and leaves us disillusioned with trying to make the world better. A limit to the demands on us, on the other hand, holds out hope of completion and sets clear and achievable objectives.

We must also repudiate the Fichtean view that even if our obligations are limited, they include tasks we cannot ever discharge. Our inability in this case is based not on the sheer volume of the demands on us, but on their nature. Fichte supposed that we have a duty to substitute laws of freedom for the mindless laws that govern the natural world.[18] This task is pompously momentous and logically impossible: our agency flows through the body, yet the body itself must be eliminated if freedom is to replace necessity. The duty some might suppose I have to change the foreign policy of my nation involves another sort of impossibility—"political impossibility," we might call it—but it frustrates sustained effort no less.

The third view of our duties a theory of moral holidays must repudiate is based on a curious inversion of the famous "ought implies can" proviso. Kant was right to insist that duties presuppose the ability to discharge them: we are not obliged to do what we cannot. With wildly generous spirit, however, some people insist that "can implies ought," meaning that it is mandatory for us to do all the good we can. This makes every valuable service we can perform for others a moral requirement and renders us slaves to our talents and possessions. So if I can use my lunch money for hunger relief in Darfur, I must do that; and the time I have after work ought to be spent caring for homeless people. Personal cost is irrelevant on this view; all that matters is that we employ our labor and inventiveness to the benefit of others.

Could one think of a demand more destructive of inner peace and joy in life than this? It reaches into the private recesses of our being and denies us the rest, the play and the freedom that make the grinding instrumentalities of life worth enduring. It tells us to sacrifice everything we like because others need it more than we do. It declares playtime with one's children unworthy by comparison with tutoring illiterate strangers. It denies us sleep and drives us mercilessly to emergency rooms, soup kitchens and orphanages to help the distressed and the diseased. Everyone's needs must be addressed under this regime but one's own; the relative privilege of those who have means and time must be paid for by self-sacrifice.

The idea that *can* implies *ought* travels in the company of a universalist ethics that refuses to distinguish obligations to those near and dear from duties to unknown multitudes around the globe. If I owe everything I can provide to everyone who can use it, I must not prefer meeting my children's needs to feeding the hungry in East Timor. Health care for my family cannot take precedence over curing the sick in India, and paying taxes to a nation-state is unjustified if the money could go to OX-FAM. There is no end to the mischief such views cause in the name of morality by imposing unreasonable demands on givers and creating outrageous expectations among recipients. These are the demands from which moral holidays are meant to shield us, and to do so while preserving our integrity if we choose to do less than everything we could.

A friend who works three jobs to support his family once told me, "It is so important to have a little time to do nothing." What he had in mind was a moral holiday in two senses of the phrase: a temporary turning away from moral demands and an inactivity that is morally justified. He saw the point of moral holidays, intuitively grasping that taking time out from moral concerns is, under certain circumstances, morally acceptable. Downtime is necessary in the way sleep is for animals, and it serves as eloquent affirmation of our finitude. We simply cannot do everything and cannot remain active without cease. The limits to our nature are neither evil nor something of which we can be proud; they are simply facts, like the rotation of nights and days, that we must learn to accept.

Under what conditions is time away from moral efforts justifiable? The easy answer is: Whenever a person needs it and circumstances permit. The need must be genuine and not contrived, occasional and not permanent. Extraordinary developments cancel moral holidays the way war terminates shore leave. But even an emergency of the magnitude of 9/11 is inadequate to command ceaseless service; the aid workers need time to eat and rest, or else soon they will join the victims. The difficult reality is, of course, that all these matters, as everything that relates to morality, require judgment. The need for respite must be assessed and measured against the need others have of help. From the standpoint of suffering people, everything looks like an emergency; yet, there is no algorithm to determine when all holidays must be put on hold.

The uncertainty that surrounds such judgments is no greater than we face in nearly every corner of life; at any rate, they are inadequate to bring the legitimacy of moral holidays into question. The case for them seems weaker, however, when clear duties are ignored to create private time. We do not think it alright to play the fiddle while one's neighbor's house goes up in flames, and there is something repulsive about overlooking massive suffering in the quest for spiritual peace. Yet, even in such circumstances, the case against moral holidays is by no means compelling. One might distance oneself from the fray because of inability to do much good; we may not have access to food to combat starvation or to water to quell the fire. Physical distance and cultural difference may also stand in the way of reaching out to those in need. Individual situations vary widely and there is no general principle on the basis of which those on holiday can be condemned.

The most objectionable cases of turning away from obligations may well be those in which people have the wherewithal to help others, yet choose to spend their substance in another way. Some years ago, a member of the Detroit Ford family hosted a wedding that cost over a million dollars. Newspapers wrote with outrage about what they saw as a gross display of selfishness. Editorial writers calculated how many people could have benefited if the money had been given to charity. Of course, no one noted that the money was *spent*, meaning that large numbers of people who provided useful services for the wedding were in fact benefited. But that consideration aside, were the parents justified in overlooking the urgent demands of the needy as they celebrated the beauty and good fortune of their child?

I find it hard to avoid the conclusion that they were. The money was, after all, theirs to use as they saw fit. There is nothing intrinsically immoral about large weddings; as over the top, they may offend our aesthetic sense, but constitute no moral violation. It may of course be true that the money could have been put to better use. That, however, is a matter of judgment, and such judgments leave room for discretion and personal taste. The most we can say about them is that they may fail to maximize the good even though, or perhaps precisely because, they permit significant freedom.

This casts a new and different light on moral holidays. They may be nothing more than temporary refusals to maximize value, that is, occasions on which we are satisfied with the good without seeking the best. Limits to our energy, time, attention, and readiness for self-sacrifice all point to a need for such events, and James at any rate should have seen this clearly. Royce probably saw it, but attributed it to the imperfection of our nature, which must be combated at all costs. For him, we are not allowed to take a moral holiday from suppressing our desires for moral holidays.

# THIRTY-TWO

# GOOD ENOUGH

No matter how well things go for us, we tend to dream of ways in which they could go better. Our love affair with the perfect may be an expression of Western restlessness or, more generally, the result of human desires in overdrive, but it unquestionably structures much of what we hope for and work to achieve. We want not only *more* of everything, but also *more perfect versions* of the goods we have and the experiences we enjoy. We seem to think that the world falls short of the ideal and that therefore everything needs to be improved.

This belief has become the grotesque mantra of the manufacturers of commercial goods, who advertise their products as "new and improved." But it is also embraced in cooking, where we seek surprising ways to enhance the taste of meals; in human relations, where we try to find the perfect friends; and in raising children, where they can never quite meet our expectations. It is not that we fail to know what is good; we just believe that nothing is good enough.

A particularly harmful version of the view that nothing is good enough hides in the claim that our duties are unending. Such diverse philosophers as Fichte, Royce, and Levinas maintain that no matter how much we do, we cannot fulfill our obligations; our efforts remain forever inadequate. The reason may be that what we are supposed to do is intrinsically impossible to achieve, that it exceeds our powers or that we have simply too many obligations; in any case, the best we can offer in moral exertion is not good enough. This reveals more clearly perhaps than anything else what is at stake. The demands on us are infinite even though our resources are clearly finite.

The perverse desire to heap infinite obligations on finite individuals guarantees moral failure. Similarly, demanding perfection of our experiences and relationships is a certain way of making life miserable. We do much better if we heed the counsels of finitude and refuse to seek what cannot be obtained. This involves both judgment and resolve: We must be able to decide what is good enough and willing to embrace it as sufficient for our purposes, that is, adequate to satisfy our desires. The romantic quest for the perfect destroys human relationships and converts what could be happy lives into the misery of endless seeking and striving.

The first task in exploring the geography of the good enough is to distinguish it from what merely will do. There is actually a double distinction here, encapsulated in the ideas of that which will do and that with which, in the absence of better instruments and experiences, we can make do. The latter clearly announces compromise: when we do not have what we need or want, we satisfy ourselves with something less that may serve as a substitute. As a child, my grandfather lacked Band-Aids and so had to put spider webs on cuts and bleeding bruises. Knives are plausible stand-ins for screwdrivers, and we settle for CDs when a live performance is unavailable. After a grand but failed love affair, people make do with whatever partner happens to be on hand, just as the threat of hunger inclines them to accept jobs for which they are overqualified.

To say that something will do, by contrast, is to endorse it as adequate. This judgment can express a broad range of attitudes from finding something barely satisfactory to thinking of it as fine. The variety is reflected in the many ways in which we say "This will do," sometimes conveying resignation, at others delighted surprise. The adequacy asserted means that some object or experience reaches at least a minimum level of acceptability, though in some cases it may be significantly better.

At the low end, for example, looking for cherry pie in the refrigerator but finding only a cookie, we might well decide that that will do; it may not be what we wanted, but it will still the desire for something sweet. At the other end, when searching the Internet gives us five million web pages on a subject, we may well decide after the first couple of dozen that that will be enough. The latter example makes it clear that the idea of something being adequate is not a judgment concerning a substitute; when tools or experiences are satisfactory, they are so on their own account. The way a lover kisses can be perfectly fine without the need for comparisons and without thinking that it is a replacement for someone else's style.

Considered as a continuum, the upper reaches of what will do adjoin the area of what is good enough. Things good enough are truly *good*, or colloquially speaking even *great*, in fact so good that they do not need to be better. This does not mean that they are perfect or that they could not perhaps be improved. But they are *good enough* for me or for us as finite, thoroughly limited beings operating under circumstances we may not be able to improve. It also does not mean that those satisfied by what is good enough settle for the dregs or live a compromise accepting shoddy goods. They enjoy what is fine and permit themselves to feel fulfilled, refusing to search for some elusive ideal.

Chess pie can be flawed in a variety of ways. The crust may be too soft, the taste not sweet enough, the consistency of the filling too loose. My wife and I were once given a pie that seemed to have none of these problems; it was sweet and soft and crunchy in all the right places. Conceivably, there can be better chess pies; a little extra lemon in the filling could tease the palate or a slightly crunchier crust could give more work for molars. But these were abstract and irrelevant considerations in eating the pie. It simply did not need to be better than it was; it was plenty good, and thus good enough. The same was true of a sunset I once saw on the shores of the Gulf of Mexico. The light danced on the waves, the huge orb was bathing in the water at the end of sight, the rest of the sky was white with terns and gulls. It is possible that the experience would have been better if the sun had set exactly where the water kissed the land or if the waves had been a little higher or the birds less numerous. But the moment had its integrity. The sight was magnificent and thus good enough. It did not need to be better.

The search for the perfect and the permanent seem to have an oddly close connection. In seeking the flawless, we seem to want something we will be able to remember forever. Perhaps we think of this permanence of memory as a warm home in the coldly changing world, something stable that will always welcome, accept and shield us. Having touched the perfect, even if only in one of its minor manifestations, gives the sense that our lives are justified, that something we have been or seen will always endure. This is one of the primary uses of the concept of God. The deity is supposed to hold all the achievements of the world in an eternal gaze, never permitting the perfect to sink under the waves of time. The flawless thus provides permanence or at least exemption from decay.

Whether true or not, this is a reassuring view, depicting the world as a cozy realm responsive to the good. The consolation is largely annulled, however, by the companion view, popular since Plato, that in ordinary life we can attain nothing perfect. To those committed to the search for some final good, this is a devastating prospect. Plato tried to counter its demoralizing effects by glorifying *eros*, the *drive* for perfection, even though it could deliver only meager results. Hegel understood the terrible contradiction between the dream of perfection and the fact of failure, of our being made in the image of God and yet succumbing to finitude and sin, and exposed it convincingly in the dialectical involutions of the Unhappy Consciousness.

What is there about perfection that exercises such a magical influence over the human mind? The traditional view has it that only in the infinitely perfect—that is, in God—can we find rest and satisfaction. But why should this be the case? Why should we not break off our search for the good when we find something good enough, without reference to whether it or something else could be better? Why is the good enough not good enough for us?

Some have thought that our very notion of the good is an idea of perfection, that we cannot know the value of anything without an absolute standard or exemplar. But where would we get such a standard? What we consider good is too closely tied to empirical desires to yield a notion that is pure or divine. Justice, power, mercy, and knowledge are matters of degree first; we have no idea of what a perfect version of any of these properties might be like. We can recite empty formulas, such as that omniscience is knowledge of all true propositions along with knowledge that each of an infinite number of false propositions is false. But this tells us nothing about lived omniscience—how it is, for example, for someone so well informed to be denied the delight of surprise.

In any case, we must first determine what it means to know anything at all before we can grasp the idea of knowing everything. This suggests that omniscience, and with it superlative levels of other desirable qualities, are abstract extrapolations of ordinary empirical achievements. We know that in this difficult world everything is tenuous and changing. The insecurity this begets drives us to imagine unfailing wisdom and goodness. Nothing shows better that perfection is a derivative ideal than the fact that we know so little of it; we have a precise idea of what it is to know that tomorrow is Sunday or that it is raining, but only the vaguest notion of an intuitive grasp of all reality.

The pursuit of perfection, therefore, is not the search for something definite and well known. The limits of human capacity and the vagueness of the ideal make attainment of perfection impossible, yet its lure ruins our satisfaction with what is clearly excellent and therefore good enough. Even if this is right, however, and I believe it is, one can sensibly ask for an account of the marks of the good enough. How can we know that an action, process, or experience does not need to be better? Are there generally recognizable signs that distinguish what is just good from what is so good that it is good enough in the sense of needing no improvement?

The wide compass of human natures, the differences among our likes, and the broad range of our experiences make the search for universal standards futile. A music lover may experience a performance of Schubert's *Trout* quintet as divine. Superior knowledge and acquaintance with other interpretations of the score may reveal to a music critic a host of problems in the same performance. To one, the evening may have been a luminous and exhilarating experience; the music was so good that it did not need to be any better. To the other, the tempo may have been too rapid or the pianist's playing mechanical. The same is true of virtually any experience: nothing is good enough in an absolute or nonrelational way. One has to be ready for the experience, possess an adequate background of appreciation, and believe that events of the sort are attractive. So to find something good enough is a spontaneous feeling evoked or judgment made on the basis of a relationship between events, persons, and their values.

Because determining that something is good enough involves a judgment, we may suppose that it is open to correction. And indeed it is, though only in the sense that what we find good enough at one time may not qualify as such later. This is the natural development of taste, as we become weary of repetition and may seek higher standards. There is, however, also an ineradicable feeling component in the experience of the good enough, and correcting that is impossible. We may never feel the same way about a similar experience, reserving enthusiasm only for what is rarified and finer, but that cannot annul the fact that at one point in our lives some process or event was thoroughly satisfying.

The spontaneity of our feelings distances the good enough from the highbrow by attaching, unpredictably, to commonplace sorts of objects and ordinary kinds of experiences. Nevertheless, we can be educated by being shown that what we thought good enough is easily outdone. A fine dish of home-cooked *coq au vin* can pale by comparison with what is available in good restaurants in France, and the next performance of Schubert's *Trout* may put to shame what we once thought divine. This does not eradicate the fact that what we now think weak was at an earlier time experienced as splendid. Although improvement of taste is in certain respects desirable, appreciation is a time-bound fact. Arguing that in light of some later judgment an earlier experience could not have been wonderful is futile, because what counts in the end is the direct enjoyment and not the then-unavailable knowledge.

Can we then be wrong when we say that some experience is good enough? Only in the limited sense of thinking that we would not have found it good enough had we had a richer trove of experiences or had we known more at the time. Since there are no objective standards in such matters, however, we cannot say that we *should* have held back our appreciation. Further, we cannot assert that it was a mistake to view the experience as good enough; we cannot even say that it would have been better had we not done so, because the experience of the good enough is valuable on any level of sophistication. We have no business grieving over the past; instead, we can cheer ourselves by thinking that we are getting less simple and more discerning.

Some may suppose that such a generally tolerant attitude is an invitation to settle for too little and thereby misses what is truly good enough. This objection originates in a stubborn misunderstanding of the notion of the good enough. Persons with the requisite faculty of appreciation and an appropriate set of values can experience events and objects of virtually any sort as good enough. This means neither lack of standards nor lack of judgment. Some people find thin beer and raw wine marvelous; others buy airbrush art for their homes. Although we may not agree with their choices, they are discriminating and selective, rejecting many objects as unsatisfactory. If experiences of their choice evoke in them the sense that drink and art need never be better, we can cheer them on in their enjoyment and leave the matter at that. Otherwise, we attempt to substitute our judgment for theirs by maintaining that what they think need not be better should be better, after all. The occurrence of experiences of the good enough deserves celebration independently of their content.

This, of course, does not hold for destructive processes. If some Serb commander announced that the ethnic cleansing his soldiers were conducting went so well that it needed no improvement, we would be rightly horrified. Our dismay, however, would not be directed at his experience of satisfaction, but at the awful source of it, and at that only because it involved murder, rape, and kidnapping. However electrifying they may seem to some, such activities must be proscribed. But to tell people that they should take satisfaction only in sophisticated activities and performances amounts to a reaffirmation of the hierarchy of values that has perfection at its apex.

How then should we think of the relation of the good enough to hierarchies of value? Are some experiences that are good enough of their kind better than good enough experiences of another kind? We have no reason to believe that that is so, at least from the standpoint of the feeling of satisfaction involved. It may nevertheless be true that some sources of satisfaction are deeper or richer or more variegated than others. Music lovers may experience no more than a general sense of delight at hearing

Schubert's *Trout*. Music critics, by contrast, can concentrate on the details and take pleasure in the flow of the melody, the interplay of the instruments, and the crystalline sound of the piano. Knowledge of relevant details enables critics to focus on more that they can find good enough—more that can satisfy—than ordinary people, and that makes their experience richer.

Yet, nothing is gained from excoriating music lovers for their shallow understanding of the performance. Those with greater knowledge may present them with the possibility of a more detailed grasp of what the music offers, and they may—if they wish—gain an education in auditory pleasure. People who know human nature, however, will do little more than nudge them in a direction; embarrassing them or lecturing them is of no avail. Too much knowledge of details and alternatives has its own problems: Critics find it more difficult to surrender to the experience and may know so much that they judge something good enough only on rare occasions. It may be best, therefore, to encourage enjoyment and create opportunities, but exert no pressure, for deepening its source.

Relatively little harm is likely to come from experiencing what to others may seem an inferior performance of music as good enough. But, moralists often urge, major disasters can result if we extend the idea of the good enough into morality. We may then experience middling efforts to make the world a better place or to respond to the needs of others as sufficient, and thereby perpetuate evil and injustice. Such halfhearted attempts at amelioration are, for them, never enough. Nothing short of a full-fledged war on poverty, ignorance, cruelty, discrimination and illness can be considered a good enough response to the evils that surround us. Anything less is neglect of our obligations to ourselves, to others or to God, an unconscionable preoccupation with our limits in the name of lessening our burdens.

I cannot think of myself as a moral monster, yet I am unable to detect any universal duties that tie me to humanity or the world. I have no problem identifying and acknowledging obligations to many people near and dear, and to animals whose care I have voluntarily assumed, but not to anyone and everyone, including individuals I have never met and those whom, for one reason or another, my agency is unable to reach. Such obligations, unlimited in scope, might be the ideological invention of persons devoted to keeping others miserable through failure or guilt-ridden for lack of trying.

Alternatively, the source of the idea of universal obligations may be a well-meaning and proper sense of horror at all the suffering in the world. The notion is supported, however, by a serious confusion. It would be better if there were no disease, poverty, and injustice, if people could live in peace with each other and if we did not have to eat living creatures to live. Still, the fact that the world could be better than it is does not imply that we are obliged to make it better. Even if it would be better if we tried to make things better, we cannot conclude that it is incumbent upon us to spend our lives in service to the good. The promise of improvement is inadequate to impose a moral obligation, which requires a closer or more stringent relationship between sufferer and agent, such as we have with family members and people we have promised to help. Being human or sentient or a fellow being in the world is close enough for concern and sympathy that may lead to action, but not for the demands of duty.

Up to a point, it is appropriate and good to encourage people to assume more obligations. It is important to keep in mind that when they embrace them, however, they do so voluntarily, and that there is a sharp limit to what they can do. Moreover, if world-improvement is what we have in mind, it is worth remembering that cleaning up one's little corner of it is a mighty start. Some can do much more, but no one can accomplish everything. So what counts as a good enough effort depends on the capacity of individuals and their circumstances. Bill Gates can offer heaps of money, the Mother Teresas of the world give much of their lives, but many others do all they can, and should, by raising a family and being kind to their neighbors.

Although occasions may arise in which we surprise even ourselves, most of us are neither saints nor heroes. Yet the world gets better if we do our share, if only we make an effort that is good enough. Feeling that we must fix everything is surely due to a perverted egoism propelled by the thought that nothing short of infinity is big enough for us. In reality, much less than infinity or perfection is good enough—must be good enough—because more we cannot reach. Of course, we can always take on one more task, support one more dependent and do one more good deed a day. The cat lady who has saved fifty-four cats may well find room for the fifty-fifth. Much as we can stretch, though, there is always a limit, and when we reach it, we should be able to look on what we have done and sincerely feel that it is good enough.

Here we see the advantage of the idea of the good enough. As affirmation of our finitude, it negates our Faustian tendency to want to have and do everything. It rejects the relevance of the ideal of perfection and strikes at the root of our compulsion to pursue unreachable ideals. It liberates us to the enjoyment of the possible without eliminating standards or moral effort. It enables us to still our will by achieving what we can and celebrating what we do. By no means least, it dissolves the eternal dissatisfaction that permeates Western industrial society, and it substitutes joy in the immediacies of life for all-encompassing guilt.

# EPILOGUE
## *Physician Assisted Suicide*

A persistent weakness of bioethics discussions is their abstraction. A nameless individual or someone designated by a capitalized letter, without personal background and value commitments, is supposed to have drifted into the emergency room and presents us with a thorny moral problem. The age and gender of the individual are indicated, and his/her condition is described in a neat paragraph. That is all we know of the "case," and that is supposed to be enough to come to a medically defensible and morally conscientious decision.

Physicians in emergency rooms may encounter such cases, but this way of presenting moral problems is ill adapted to getting sound answers. The current condition and future prospects of people cannot be detached from their histories. Treatment appropriate to them is not independent of their beliefs and values. Such abstract principles as "First, do no harm" and "Respect autonomy" lack meaning without an understanding of what, for the person involved, constitutes harm and counts as self-determination.

I will try to correct such vacuous abstractions by describing in considerable detail the ways and needs of a person seeking relief from existence. Her name was Magda, and she lived a long and rich life. She outlived a series of her physicians, all youngsters by comparison with her. She was massively healthy throughout life. Two broken hips in her nineties did not slow her down, and at 101 she cooked and needed no help to take care of herself.

Her husband died before she turned seventy. As she aged, her closest companions also went to the grave. Undaunted, she made new friends and reached out to people she had known as a child. Over decades, she saw these buried as well. Eventually, only two or three friends remained, and they lived so far away that she could keep only in telephone contact with them.

Although Magda had no life-threatening illness, her organs began to fail. Macular degeneration robbed her of her sight, and she lost much of her hearing. She learned to walk with a cane, then with a walker, and finally gave up walking altogether, except for a step or two when someone would lift, steady, and support her. Her mind remained clear, which made things more difficult because she saw and understood how her life was closing down.

A vibrant woman who loved life and enjoyed its activities, Magda resisted the closing hour. She employed every mechanical aid available to support her organs. She had always been fiercely independent and did not find it easy to have to rely on others for help with a growing number of activities. Her tendency was to offer help rather than to seek it, and her inabilities took a heavy toll on her self-image. She said that she was angry because she could no longer even attempt what she used to do without effort.

Magda understood how, as we age, the horizon narrows and the activities of life become impossible to sustain. Still, she thought it was an indignity that she could not take care of her own private functions and could communicate with others only with great difficulty. At 103, she suffered compression fractures and found that moving caused excruciating pain. Going to bed became torturous, so she learned to live and sleep in a recliner. She had to wear diapers and rely on her son to clean her.

A mild case of pulmonary hypertension did not hold hope of terminating her life quickly. Living longer seemed to her utterly pointless: the pain, the indignity, and the growing communicative isolation overshadowed her native optimism and the joy she had always taken in being alive. She decided that she had had enough and was ready to die. She had foreseen this possibility in her younger years and stockpiled sleeping pills so that when the time came she could commit suicide. But the pills disappeared in the chaos of her apartment, and she was, in any case, unable to leave her chair to get them. She decided not to eat or drink, but there was enough love of life left in her to make this a regimen she could not sustain.

This leads us to the moral problem. Is it acceptable to provide her with aid in dying? Here is a more pointed way of putting it: Is it not outrageously wrong to let her shriek in pain and live disgusted with her condition for months and possibly years?

It may be worth mentioning that this was the story of my mother.

In the name of what value past, present or future could one deny Magda help with finishing her life? Clearly, no past value is at stake: her days of delight and generosity were over and would never return. The past has an integrity all its own, opening itself to grateful memory without ever changing. There is reason to be thankful for lives of kindness and sharing, but what was achieved in the past neither calls for nor justifies maintaining an existence after it turns barren.

Magda's life near its end has no present value. If we added up the positive aspects of her pained existence in the recliner and deducted her anguish, embarrassment, sorrow, and frustration, the sum would come in as a high negative number. Further deducting her sense that she is a burden on everyone and that her will is violated if she cannot die, we get an overwhelming indication that nothing in her present justifies continued life.

There are occasions when the hope of future good makes it appropriate to grit our teeth and fight through painful times. Cancer patients have reason to subject themselves to surgery, radiation, and chemotherapy. Husbands and wives divorcing suffer through dark days in anticipation of a better life. Soldiers endure the pains of basic training and young doctors the sleepless exhaustion of internship, expecting something better at the end of torture. Nothing like this relates even vaguely to Magda. She had no future; all she could anticipate was release whenever it would come "naturally," that is, without the help of any human being.

She made it clear to me and to others that receiving no help in dying amounted, in her view, to abandonment. "Don't let me live like this," she pleaded, "No human being should be made to endure such a fate." I cannot think that in this assessment she was wrong. With pity in our hearts, we do not permit our animal companions to suffer: we ease them out of life with sorrow, painlessly. By contrast, we seem to take no pity on human beings, forcing them to live to the end, no matter how miserable they are. Visitors from another planet would find this a baffling and indefensible cruelty.

Animal life is cheap but human life is sacred, some might be tempted to say. Just exactly what is it that makes for this difference? The usual answer is that animals are valuable only as instruments, adding to our comfort and enjoyment, but humans represent an intrinsic and perhaps infinite value. As ends in themselves, possibly the only ones this side of God and the angels, humans deserve respect: We are not to shorten their lives or interfere with their fortunes. This is a hugely improbable position, a theory we may embrace in words but never honor in practice.

If we are to do nothing to extend human life, we have no business going to the doctor, taking medicines, driving cautiously and even eating. And if we must not shorten our existence, hundreds of activities, including smoking, eating beef, overwork, and worry, become morally unacceptable. The human race has pronounced judgment on this theory long ago by happily taking control of human life, extending and shortening it according to what seems sensible and good at any given time. If slow and long-term self-destruction escapes moral censure, the immediate termination of life in suicide cannot be morally condemned.

This argument aside, however, we can ask what confers intrinsic value on human life. The idea that humans claim extraordinary status for humanity is immediately suspect. Does it not sound like special pleading or species-ist foolishness? Cats maintain that humans are there to serve them and lions affirm their superiority by killing and eating everything in sight. If we could converse with chimpanzees and porpoises, would they not instruct us to view our existence as of no special concern because we are merely instrumental to their good? Those who do not spend time observing animals make the mistake of thinking that they lack value systems and intelligence.

The supposed intrinsic value of humans must be due either to some relationship or to a special feature of their lives. The prime candidate for the relation is the Deity who is supposed to have created us and placed us in a privileged position above the beasts. Without reference to something identifiably special in our experience, this relationship remains a theological supposition in need of evidence. That leaves the claim that there is something unique in human experience, something whose extinction would represent a momentous loss. The uniqueness of any feature of human experience is questionable, but let us make the best case for the view and say that the characteristic we are looking for is the conscious and intelligent enjoyment of life.

One can readily see that such enjoyment is of great value. In fact, it may be the only genuine good in the world. But if this is what constitutes the intrinsic value of human beings, what becomes of that value when conscious and intelligent enjoyment is no longer possible? This was Magda's problem: Her days of delight were over, and she could no longer perform the activities that make life worthwhile. She faced only suffering, and if the source of the intrinsic value of human existence consists of intelligent joy, then toward the end her life was without value.

Opponents of suicide may here respond that intrinsic value can never be lost. That which is valuable in and of itself relies on nothing beyond itself for its value. For this reason, it is immune to changes in its surroundings: since nothing external gave it value, nothing external can take it away.

Unfortunately, this argument is flawed. It confuses essence with existence, the characteristic of an object or experience with its presence. Certain experiences are valuable in and of themselves and it may well be impossible to separate them from their value. But that does not mean that such events must happen or always do. Being special on account of a unique brand of intelligent enjoyment does not guarantee that that enjoyment will always be available to humans. So long as it is at hand, it may well be wrong to hasten death. But in Magda's case and in many others, the enjoyment is unavailable, eliminating the special status of humans and the obligations that go with it.

Opponents of suicide can attempt to reformulate their view by insisting that what makes humans special, and imposes restrictions on hastening their death, is not a set of events or experiences but the very constitution of human nature. Followers of Kant maintain that our uniqueness is due to our rationality or to the spontaneity of the human mind. It is notoriously difficult to give a precise account of what it means to possess reason, especially if this single factor is to be responsible for separating humans from all other animals.

The fact is that many species of animals show themselves capable of reasoning. Their behavior reveals that they understand what counts as evidence and can move unhesitatingly from premises to conclusions. In the sphere of morality, Kant believes that reason enables us to decide on our actions totally independently of desires and external pressure. But if such performances serve as conditions of being human, the large majority of our fellows belong to a different species. We cannot be sure that anyone in the human race has ever reached a level of purity of intention to satisfy Kant. Moreover, how can we maintain that reason is the hallmark of the human in the teeth of all the irrationality that surrounds us? Thinking of reason as a faculty present in all of us, if only potentially, amounts to embracing an unwarranted opinion.

Obviously, arguments on the basis of the quality of life and the constitution of human nature do not prevail against suicide. Yet, many people who object to the practice do so for social or political reasons. On the social side, they think that permitting it sets a dangerous example; they fear mass suicides and the possibility that, not understanding what they do, children will join adults in terminating their lives. Politically, they maintain that the state has a legitimate interest in the protection of human life. They imagine that without legislation banning the practice, older people, the sick, the disabled, and the poor will likely be forced to end their days.

The fear of mass suicides is altogether groundless. We do not have to outlaw starvation to get people to eat; living is sufficiently joyous and the alternative sufficiently frightening to motivate people to hang on with all their might. The way to reduce child suicides is by parental love and car-

ing and not by laws of whose existence the young are in any case unaware. Unavoidably, some young, jilted romantics will kill themselves
under any regime, but here, too, the best hope of reducing their number
is social vigilance and the investment of time to help them over their
despair, rather than legislation and threats of punishment.

From the standpoint of justice and the protection of human life, there
is nothing to fear from morally accepting and legally permitting suicide.
The Oregon experience of legalization yielded significantly fewer suicides than had been anticipated. It is possible, of course, that heartless
people will exert pressure on the old, the sick and the less fortunate to
remove themselves before their time, but this can occur whether suicide
is legal or not. If there is evidence of it, laws can be introduced to control
the unfeeling and, in any case, adequate safeguards can be developed
against abuse when suicide is aided by physicians.

The state's interest in protecting life raises a troubling issue concerning the range of its power. Sometimes, this is expressed by the question
of who owns our persons or our lives. The metaphor of ownership can be
misleading, but it is useful because it points to social arrangements of
which slavery was an integral part. The great historical development of
banning slavery established the untouchable independence of human
individuals. If no other person can own us, no group of people—such as
the state—can either.

That God, having created us, has lost or ceded ownership control was
clear as early as the Garden of Eden. He can order us about, but whether
we obey him is a question for us to decide. The idea that we are somehow
God's "children" and therefore lack the right to make decisions about
our lives confers no credit on religion. One would want to make the commitment to a faith and its God as a responsible adult, with an understanding of the prospects and the costs. Acting like a child in such
matters of the gravest import does not give moral credit to individuals
and can hardly be acceptable to God.

The myth of a social contract carries a vital message concerning the
relationship of citizens to their states. It reminds us that nations are derivative organizations built on the consent and cooperation of individual
human beings. The state can impose a variety of demands and limitations on its citizens, though only ones that promote the common good.

For example, a system of taxation, setting limits to one's control of one's earnings, is justified so long as the money extracted is used for projects that cannot be undertaken by individuals and that benefit everyone.

The state can and should protect individuals from others who may want to harm them. It exceeds its legitimate power, however, if it sets out to protect sensible people from themselves, interfering in the way they choose to run or end their lives. Specifically, keeping a person such as Magda going beyond the time she reasonably decides to be done with life is an abomination; there is no value in the name of which government officials can insist that she continue to suffer. The existence of people in excruciating pain, hardly capable of moving and without the prospect of improvement, contributes nothing to the common good. Striving to make suicide unavailable to them reminds one of hell where devils torture sinners instead of letting them expire in peace.

Since neither God nor the state owns us, we must learn to be our own masters. This is appropriate in many of the activities that make life interesting and precious, but especially when it comes to decisions concerning the quality and quantity of existence. People who choose to live as drunkards or as deans must be allowed to make their own decisions and bear the consequences. It is especially important for end of life choices to be left in the hands of directly affected individuals. Telling others what they should do is for the most part wrong, but making others carry on the burden of a horrible life when they want to be set free is nothing short of wanton cruelty.

The followers of Kant and Mill appear to agree in describing freedom as self-determination. The agreement, however, is only verbal because the selves they have in mind differ sharply. For Kant, the self that is to determine itself is what we might call the "higher" or rational element in us. This means that free actions are supposed to be devised solely by reference to duty or other stern moral values, without taking into account the influence of others or what we may desire. A free action is, in this way, inevitably also a moral action, and an immoral act is at once unfree.

Mill, by contrast, views freedom as the ability to do what we desire. The self that determines our actions is the everyday agent we know, motivated by needs and wants and seeking its happiness in a changeable, treacherous world. Here freedom means the absence of external constraint, that is, the ability of people to frame purposes and to carry them out. Free or autonomous actions are therefore not necessarily moral; as Adam and Eve in the Garden of Eden, we can succumb to temptation and choose the wrong alternative.

The point of the contrast is not that Kant recommends the righteous path and Mill is satisfied with the willful search for happiness. Both of them embrace moral standards, but Kant thinks happiness has nothing to do with them. He finds it difficult to identify with the everyday ambitions of ordinary people, restricting morality to the realm of austere duty. Mill, on the other hand, understands the yearning for untrammeled movement that frames the moral life; he attaches high value to being able to do what we want. Morality, for him, is constituted by desires freely formed and actions freely performed or restrained, enabling us to grow into responsible adults.

Kant and Mill represent the two great strands of accounting for moral action. Deontology, growing out of Kant, measures moral performance by its adherence to duty; teleology, perfected by Mill, insists on assessing the consequences of what we do. Oddly, Kant and Mill agree that suicide is impermissible, but neither has an argument that adequately supports that conclusion. Kant thinks that suicide constitutes disrespect for human life: when we commit it, we use ourselves as a means to relieving us of some undesirable condition. Mill believes that suicide and selling oneself into slavery do not fall within the range of our freedom because they are irreversible: Choosing to destroy oneself is to put a permanent end to one's freedom to choose.

Kant's argument is unconvincing because we use ourselves (and others), unobjectionably, as means in the course of ordinary life. I use myself to acquire the skill of playing the piano when I make myself practice, and I use the pilot to get me to my destination when I take a trip on an airplane. What makes such actions morally acceptable is that when I undertake them, I do not use humans as means *only*, but respect their freedom by asking for their consent. That is precisely what happens in suicide. Designed to relieve a horrible situation, it does so with the sufferer's consent. Further, we can reasonably ask if it does not show greater respect for human life to terminate suffering rather than to let someone like Magda struggle for months with despondency and pain.

Mill's argument against suicide is equally weak. The irreversibility of the choice of self-destruction is shared by every decision. When I marry, I change my life permanently; choices that were once open disappear. In deciding to settle in one part of the country, I surrender a host of possibilities, and in choosing a profession I disable myself to practice many others. Admittedly, these choices close off many activities but not all, whereas killing oneself is, presumably, an end to everything. This distinction is irrelevant in Magda's case. She was able to do very little and nothing that satisfied, so the loss of all is a net gain because it ends the suffering.

Another way to look at this is to examine duties and consequences more systematically. In taking my life, do I violate a duty? The language of obligation is not well adapted to capture the relation of individuals to themselves. We commit ourselves to values, formulate plans, undertake projects, and engage in activities as a result of what we want and what we think is good. We do not believe that we owe it to ourselves to do these things or that we are duty bound to perform them. We do have obligations to others: parents, for example, have a duty to stay alive so they may take care of their underage children. But no such obligation existed in Magda's case. Her husband and her close friends had died long ago, her son had grown old, and her grandchildren were busy with their lives. No duty held her attached to existence.

Utilitarian or teleological calculation of the consequences of Magda's committing suicide yields a similar result. She had little on the positive side of the ledger. A few distant friends had the pleasure of occasional conversations with her, and her son and daughter-in-law took delight in bringing her food she particularly liked. For the most part, she ate only a few morsels. Her days were indistinguishable from her nights; her pain medication left her without knowledge of who or where she was, and when she awoke to a moment of lucidity, all she could call for was an end to it. Sadly, much as she would be missed, her suicide would have reduced the misery and thereby added to the net sum of good in the world.

The first stage in arguing that physician assisted suicide is morally permissible consists in showing that committing suicide is not always wrong. If we can find even one case in which the intentional termination of life by a human being is clearly justified, the abstract claim that it is always wrong is roundly defeated. The logic of the argument is that a single counterexample destroys a general theory. Magda's case is just such an example: no good could emerge from forcing her to continue to suffer. This establishes the legitimacy of suicide at least in some cases. The next task is to show that it is morally acceptable for doctors to aid people when they wish legitimately to terminate their existence.

The modern world values life and makes it difficult for people to end it. People who want to kill themselves by jumping from high places find it difficult to identify a suitable venue. The windows of skyscrapers do not open and high fences protect the walkways on bridges. Slitting one's arteries is a bloody and distasteful affair. Most people do not have guns or are untutored in their use. In any case, one might miss, as did the German generals when they tried to commit suicide after their unsuccessful attempt on Hitler's life. That leaves pills, with which everyone today is thoroughly familiar. They hold the hope of a smooth and rapid transfer, the painless end to pain and misery.

Unfortunately, however, people do not know the power of pills: they tend to be ignorant of which ones end life and which put them in the hospital. In any case, ordinary people have no access to powerful drugs without the intervention of doctors, and physicians are notoriously reluctant to make drugs suitable for suicide available to their patients. The question of why doctors should assist in suicides is easy to answer: the medical profession has monopoly power over drugs. Since society conferred this vast and lucrative power on physicians, they are under an obligation to help individuals who have a legitimate reason to hasten their death.

The standard objection to this consists of reminding us that doctors are supposed to return us to health rather than aid our demise. But what if health is never to be restored? There was simply no hope of improvement in Magda's situation; at her age, any intervention was like trying to stop the tides. Would it not be appropriate for her physician to offer help when she cried out to die? This question opens a distinction between two conceptions of the proper function of physicians, one narrow and one much broader.

The restricted notion is characterized by the claim that physicians should treat diseases so that their patients may recover. This tends to be the view of medical specialists, who arrive on the scene to practice their marvelous art and depart as soon as the problem gets resolved. One might think of them as hired guns employed by the sheriff to help restore order in town. They have little interest in their patients as people, asking little about the values and personal history of the individuals they treat. Such information is not necessary for the cure and may in fact interfere with it; doctors are supposed to solve problems by means of pills or surgery and, when all goes well, return patients to their normal lives.

The broader conception of the task of medicine was in complete possession of the field a hundred and fifty years ago when many physicians lived in small communities and cared for their patients from birth to death. Doctors in those days took an interest not only in the physical status but also in the psychological condition and social relationships of their patients. In the belief that personal health is inseparable from the flourishing of society, some went so far as to demonstrate vital concern for the well-being of the families and communities of their patients. Family practice physicians come closest to this conception today, though financial pressures make it difficult even for them to spend much time with their patients.

Not surprisingly, doctors who subscribe to the dominant narrow conception of their duties have difficulty understanding how they could be called on to aid a patient's suicide. Their role is to treat the disease and, when there is nothing further they can do, to declare the case one of medical futility, making room for hospice care and palliative measures. The idea that patients have life histories, purposes, desires, values, and fervently held beliefs appears irrelevant; the possibility that they might not want to waste away waiting for death is given no consideration. The result is that just when we need good doctors the most, they become unavailable.

Even if the broad conception of physician duties is no longer viable, we must insist that doctors help us through every stage of life. They need to provide empathy no less than specialist knowledge and learn to view their contributions to our lives as informed suggestions and kindly advice. Most important, they must be there for their patients at the great crises of life, helping in the difficult task of making decisions concerning the dark days. This does not mean that they have to stand ready with pill or syringe to honor every wish of the depressed. Unless they have personal or religious objections to suicide, however, they must be on hand to provide, when appropriate, the means to a peaceful and dignified departure.

The original version of the Hippocratic Oath forbids physicians to make deadly drugs available to their patients. It is essential, however, to remember that in the days of Hippocrates people did not live very long. Many died in the prime of life and virtually no one reached old age in a debilitated condition. Magda would have expired long before she reached her hundred and third birthday and hence would not have needed physician help to terminate her life. Enlisting doctors in the quest for a peaceful and dignified death is a need and an activity unique to the contemporary world. It grew out of the success of medicine in keeping people alive and the political decision to control drugs and vest their distribution in the medical profession. The vast and continuing increase in the number of the very old will likely intensify the pressure on physicians until our laws come to reflect the moral acceptability of terminating life.

Does this mean that suicide is morally permissible at any age and under all conditions? Not at all. Here it may be useful to distinguish between what we are free to do and what is good to undertake. A generous reading of human freedom leaves it open for adults to finish the book of life at any time they desire. If they are young and healthy, their doing so is a lamentable error. But they are at liberty to do what is sad and wrong, as Adam and Eve were when they disobeyed God's command. The source of the liberty is the fact that no one has a right to force life on people when they want to die.

Friends and neighbors incur responsibilities when people they know decide to exit life. They must speak with them, stressing the beauty and goodness of life, along with the irreversibility of death. They have to ask them to reconsider or at least to wait until they see more clearly. If they can truthfully say it, they might even indicate how much they mean to their friends and how intensely they will be missed. Just as God did not use His power to stop Adam and Eve, the freedom of individuals blocks us from employing force to prevent their suicide. We cannot be expected to stand idly by while people kill themselves, yet morally we can stop them only by persuasion.

This means that exercising freedom is by no means the same as following moral rules. The freedom to commit suicide gives us more operational leeway than moral principles allow: We have the right to terminate our lives even if it is wrong to do so. But healthy young adults who propose to kill themselves cannot demand aid from others. Helping someone commit an immoral act is itself immoral, so there can be no obligation to provide gun or pills. The situation is altogether different with suicide that is justifiable. As in trying to do what is right or at least permissible, so here also, one can legitimately enlist the aid of friends and physicians. Such a right to ask, if exercised, imposes an obligation on those in a position to help.

Naturally, the duty is dissolved if the request violates the physician's moral commitments. It is binding if aid is just bothersome or inconvenient. The demand is valid even if meeting it is dangerous or may lead to severe repercussions. This is why Dr. Kevorkian must be seen as a pioneer who was willing to risk criminal censure to affirm in his actions the responsibility of the medical profession for help with suicide. Many found his manner of providing deadly drugs to terminal patients disquieting or even grisly, but he used a parked van only because honest ways of committing suicide are banned in hospitals. The objection to his efforts that the people he aided in dying were not his patients is fatuous; he stepped in only because the attending physicians did not shoulder their responsibility.

How can we tell whether a proposed suicide that requires physician assistance is morally acceptable? There are no easy answers to such questions. In the moral life, everything is a matter of judgment, with no recipe for making them. A careful examination of the facts, conscientious reflection on the values involved and a savvy understanding of needs and alternatives will still not guarantee the correct result. It may be helpful to remember Magda's case and use it as a measure by which other problem situations may be evaluated. Her predicament establishes a standard that other potential cases of physician-assisted suicide must approximate.

First, there must be adequate reasons for terminating life, and they have to be both objective and subjective in nature. On the subjective side, nihilistic mood and temporary despondency do not amount to a justification. We have to begin with objective facts: The patient must be near the end of life and in significant pain or discomfort. The phrase "near the end of life" is vague and requires case-by-case interpretation. No one knew how close Magda was to the end of her life, but it was clear that past her hundred and third year, with pulmonary hypertension, she could not live very long. A precise number of days or weeks that would govern universally is impossible to postulate, but we know that, in most cases, a life expectancy of a year or more would be too long.

As important as the amount of time left is the quality of it. People who are likely to be able to operate to the end and then slip away peacefully are not candidates for physician assistance in killing themselves. Sick persons who are not in excruciating pain but experience their debility as a crushing burden, on the other hand, may well be justified in seeking help to get permanent relief. In any case, if people have significant obligations they can discharge only by living on, they forfeit the right to look for help with dying. How significant these duties need to be is another question to which there is no general answer. Having promised someone to go to lunch next month is obviously not weighty enough; earning money to feed one's children who would otherwise go hungry clearly is.

A few common sense provisos need to be added at this point. Even if it is morally acceptable for people to seek expert help in hastening death and for doctors to provide it, patients do not have the right to approach *any* physician with their request. There must be an established doctor-patient relationship between the parties that makes the call for help legitimate. Furthermore, it is wise for society to establish a variety of safeguards to make abuse of the practice of physician-assisted suicide difficult and improbable. The state may require application to a board, examination of the patient by at least one physician uninvolved in the case and a waiting period. Regular reassessment of the practice may suggest additional safeguards and procedures.

It took multiple calls to Magda's physician to get him to order hospice on the scene. When representatives of this worthy organization arrived, they brought a powerful morphine solution. They assured her caregivers that any dosage necessary to still her pain and any frequency of applying the drug was acceptable. This was an invitation to suicide, assisted in this case not by a physician but by benevolent hospice nurses. Hiding behind the double-effect of morphine, they offered pain relief at the price of depressed lung function and accelerated death. Our current laws make it impossible to help needy people die peacefully without this subterfuge.

# Notes

### INTRODUCTION BY PATRICK SHADE

1. Lachs is also one of the founding members of its key organization, the Society for the Advancement of American Philosophy.

2. The exception to this organizational principle occurs in Part IV, since it makes most sense to couple "Aristotle and Dewey on the Rat Race" and "Improving Life," even though *In Love with Life* was written in the interim.

3. This second article is significant not only in extending the original argument, but also in relating the thought of personalist Borden Parker Bowne to Lachs's own emendations to pragmatism. Lachs thus helps link pragmatist ideas to philosophers other than the traditional figures of Peirce, James, and Dewey.

4. The triad of desire-act-satisfaction is a permutation of the unity of "intent-act-consequence" Lachs discussed in his theory of mediation. The value of each triad is that it articulates a phenomenon that has not only a clearly recognizable unity but also distinct parts.

5. "To Have and to Be" is Lachs's first article focused on meaningful living, and it proved to be a very important one. It has enjoyed multiple publications and was revised to constitute Chapter 3 of *Intermediate Man*.

### 1. THE IMPOTENT MIND

1. A. C. Ewing, *The Fundamental Questions of Philosophy* (New York: Macmillan, 1951), 127.

2. See my "Epiphenomenalism and the Notion of Cause," *Journal of Philosophy* 60 (1963): 141–46.

3. A. E. Taylor, *Plato: The Man and His Work* (New York: Meridian Books, 1956), 198.

4. Ibid.

5. William James, *The Principles of Psychology*, ed. Frederick H. Burkhardt, Fredson Bowers, and Ignas K. Skrupskelis (Cambridge, MA: Harvard University Press, 1981), 1:145.

6. John Stuart Mill, *A System of Logic* (London: Longmans, 1959), 263.

7. J. B. Pratt, *Matter and Spirit* (New York: Macmillan, 1922), 20.

## 2. SANTAYANA'S PHILOSOPHY OF MIND

1. George Santayana, *The Realm of Spirit* (New York: Charles Scribner's Sons, 1940), 18. Hereafter referred to as *RS*.

2. George Santayana, *Scepticism and Animal Faith* (New York: Charles Scribner's Sons, 1923, reprinted 1955), 274. Hereafter referred to as *SAF*.

3. *SAF*, 130.

4. George Santayana, *The Realm of Matter* (New York: Charles Scribner's Sons, 1930), 140. Hereafter referred to as *RM*.

5. *RM*, 139.

6. *SAF*, 273.

7. Ibid., 274.

8. George Santayana, *The Realm of Essence* (New York: Charles Scribner's Sons, 1927), 128.

9. *RS*, 46.

10. *RM*, 111.

11. On this issue see my "Epiphenomenalism and the Notion of Cause," *Journal of Philosophy* 60 (1963): 141–146.

12. George Santayana, "A General Confession," in *The Philosophy of George Santayana* (La Salle, Ill.: Open Court, 1940), 17.

13. *SAF*, 217.

14. *RS*, 94.

15. *RM*, 93.

16. *SAF*, 208.

17. *RM*, 90.

## 3. FICHTE'S IDEALISM

1. Johann G. Fichte, *The Science of Knowledge*, ed. and tr. Peter Heath and John Lachs (New York: Appleton-Century-Crofts, 1970; reissued by Cambridge University Press, 1982).

2. Ibid., 98.

3. I acknowledge my indebtedness for this interpretation of Spinoza to H. F. Hallett's excellent *Benedict de Spinoza* (London: Athlone Press, University of London, 1957).

4. Fichte, *Science of Knowledge*, 9ff.

5. Fichte devotes considerable effort and ingenuity to the attempt to show that Kant held no such view.

6. Fichte, *First Introduction* to the *Wissenschaftslehre,* in *Science of Knowledge,* 12–16.

### 4. PEIRCE, SANTAYANA, AND THE LARGE FACTS

1. Presidential Address, delivered to the Society for the Advancement of American Philosophy, Cleveland, Ohio, March 2, 1979.

2. George Santayana, *Scepticism and Animal Faith* (New York: Dover, 1955), viii. *SAF* hereafter.

3. Charles S. Peirce, *Collected Papers,* 8 vols. (Cambridge, MA: Harvard University Press, 1931–58), 6:33.

4. Ibid., 1:42.

5. Ibid., 5:314.

6. Ibid., 5:267.

7. Ibid., 6:270.

8. Ibid., 1:673.

9. Ibid.

10. Ibid., 6:264.

11. Ibid., 6:429.

12. Ibid., 5:311.

13. Ibid., 1:673.

14. *SAF,* x.

### 5. THE TRANSCENDENCE OF MATERIALISM AND IDEALISM IN AMERICAN THOUGHT

1. *The Science of Knowledge,* ed. and trans. P. Heath and J. Lachs (Cambridge: Cambridge University Press, 1982), 9ff.

2. *Ludwig Feuerbach and the Outcome of Classical German Philosophy* (New York: International Publishers, 1941), 21.

3. George Santayana, *The Realm of Spirit* (New York: Charles Scribner's Sons, 1940), 293.

4. George Santayana, *The Realm of Matter* (New York: Charles Scribner's Sons, 1930), 10.

### 7. TWO VIEWS OF HAPPINESS IN MILL

1. *Utilitarianism* in *Collected Works of John Stuart Mill, vol. X: Essays on Ethics, Religion, and Society,* ed. J. M. Robson (Toronto: University of Toronto Press, 1969), 210.

2. Ibid., 236.

3. See also Mill's comments on happiness as a by-product of the ordered or meaningful life apropos of his appreciation of Carlyle's anti-self-consciousness

theory: *Autobiography*, ed. J. Stillinger (Boston: Houghton Mifflin, 1969), 85–86.

4. Mill, *Collected Works*, X:236.

## 12. PUBLIC BENEFIT, PRIVATE COST

1. I wish to express my thanks to Professors John Howie and Henny Wenkart for helpful suggestions in formulating these ideas.

## 13. LEAVING OTHERS ALONE

1. Josiah Royce, *The World and the Individual*, Second Series (New York: Macmillan, 1923), Lecture VIII.

2. William James, "The Moral Philosopher and the Moral Life," in *The Will to Believe and Other Essays in Popular Philosophy*, ed. Frederick H. Burkhardt, Fredson Bowers, and Ignas K. Skrupskelis (Cambridge, MA: Harvard University Press, 1979), 145ff.

3. James Rachels, "Killing and Starving to Death," *Philosophy* 54 (1979): 159–72.

## 15. THE ELEMENT OF CHOICE IN CRITERIA OF DEATH

1. President's Commission for the Study of Ethical Problems in Medicine and Biomedical and Behavioral Research, *Defining Death* (Washington, DC: Government Printing Office, 1981), 77.

2. Ibid., 28.

## 16. HUMAN NATURES

1. Concerning the decisions involved in the definition of death, see my "The Element of Choice in Criteria of Death," in *Death: Beyond Whole-Brain Criteria*, ed. Richard M. Zane (Dordrecht: Kluwer Academic, 1988), 233–51.

## 17. PERSONS AND DIFFERENT KINDS OF PERSONS

1. Borden Parker Bowne, *Personalism* (Boston: Houghton Mifflin, 1908), 266.

2. Ibid., 263.

3. Ibid., 266.

4. Ibid., 80.

5. Ibid., 74.

6. Ibid., 76.

7. See the preceding essay in this volume.

8. Bowne, *Personalism*, 274.

### 18. GRAND DREAMS OF PERFECT PEOPLE

1. Norman Daniels, "Normal Functioning and the Treatment-Enhancement Distinction," *Cambridge Quarterly of Bioethics* 3 (2000): 309–22.

### 20. TO HAVE AND TO BE

1. Thomas Hobbes, *Leviathan* (London, 1943), 30.

2. Aristotle, *Nicomachean Ethics,* 1094a 3–5.

### 23. ARISTOTLE AND DEWEY ON THE RAT RACE

1. George Santayana, *Scepticism and Animal Faith* (New York: Dover, 1955), 217.

2. John Dewey, *Experience and Nature,* in *The Later Works, 1925–1953,* ed. Jo Ann Boydston (Carbondale: Southern Illinois University Press, 1988), 1:271.

3. Ibid.

4. Ibid., 272.

5. Ibid., 271.

6. Ibid., 275.

7. Ibid.

8. Ibid., 277.

9. G. E. Moore, *Principia Ethica* (Cambridge: Cambridge University Press, 1951), chap. 3.

10. Dewey, *Experience,* 275–76.

11. Ibid., 271.

12. Ibid.

13. William James, *Pragmatism* (Cambridge, MA: Harvard University Press, 1975), 139.

14. Dewey, *Experience,* 271, 276.

### 24. IMPROVING LIFE

1. Harry Frankfurt, "On the Usefulness of Final Ends," *Iyyun* 41 (January 1992): 4.

2. Ibid., 15.

3. John Lachs, "Aristotle and Dewey on the Rat Race," in *Philosophy and the Reconstruction of Culture: Pragmatic Essays After Dewey,* ed. John J. Stuhr (Albany: SUNY Press, 1993), 97–109. "Rat Race" hereafter.

4. John Dewey, *Art as Experience,* in *The Later Works, 1925–1953,* ed. Jo Ann Boydston (Carbondale: Southern Illinois University Press, 1987), 10:202.

5. Ibid., 201.

6. See "Rat Race."

7. G. W. F. Hegel, *Phenomenology of Spirit*, trans. A. V. Miller (Oxford: Oxford University Press, 1977), 111–19.

8. Ibid., 116.

9. Epictetus, *The Handbook* (Indianapolis: Hackett, 1983), 13.

10. Aristotle, *Nicomachean Ethics*, trans. Terence Irwin (Indianapolis: Hackett, 1985), 273–75.

11. Immanuel Kant, *Foundations of the Metaphysics of Morals*, in *Critique of Practical Reason and Other Writings in Moral Philosophy*, trans. Lewis White Beck (Chicago: University of Chicago Press, 1949), 82.

12. Ibid., 225–34.

13. A good example of Dewey's critique of modern institutional life may be found in John Dewey, *Experience and Nature*, in *The Later Works*, 1:271–77.

14. Ibid., 66.

15. Dewey presents a good discussion of his idea of natural histories in *Experience and Nature*, 69–99.

16. Ibid., 275–76.

17. Dewey, *Art as Experience*, 201.

18. Dewey, *Experience and Nature*, 275.

19. Dewey, *Art as Experience*, 201.

20. Dewey, *Experience and Nature*, 277.

21. Ibid., 272.

22. Aristotle, *Nicomachean Ethics*, 275.

23. I discuss chains of mediation and the resultant alienation in *Intermediate Man* (Indianapolis: Hackett, 1981).

24. *Experience and Nature*, 275–76.

### 25. STOIC PRAGMATISM

1. John Dewey, *Democracy and Education, The Middle Works, 1899–1924*, ed. Jo Ann Boydston (Carbondale: Southern Illinois University Press, 1985), 9:52.

2. William James, "The Moral Philosopher and the Moral Life," in *The Will to Believe and Other Essays in Popular Philosophy*, ed. Frederick H. Burkhardt, Fredson Bowers, and Ignas K. Skrupskelis (Cambridge, MA: Harvard University Press, 1979), 154.

3. Ibid., 153.

4. Larry Hickman reminds me that in *A Common Faith* Dewey shows awareness of the need for acceptance. Just as in some places (see below) Seneca comes near to being a pragmatist, so here, Dewey embraces an important element of stoicism. At these times, they approximate being stoic pragmatists.

5. Epictetus, *The Handbook*, trans. Nicholas White (Indianapolis: Hackett, 1983), 13.

6. Ibid., 20.

7. Ibid.

8. Immanuel Kant, *Critique of Pure Practical Reason*, trans. Lewis White Beck (Chicago: University of Chicago Press, 1950), 221.

9. *The Stoic Philosophy of Seneca*, ed. and trans. Moses Hadas (Garden City, N.Y.: Doubleday, 1958), 222-23.

10. Ibid., 93-94.

11. Ibid., 102.

12. Epictetus, *The Handbook*, 11.

13. Vincent Colapietro remarks that, according to pragmatism, tools are transformed in the act of using them. This may well be true in exceptional cases, such as when I use a knife to turn screws, but it is clearly not the norm. No such transformation occurs when I board my scheduled flight or don a hat.

14. Jose Medina rightly argues that both the pragmatist and the stoic are stringent critics of values and practices. In stoic pragmatism, each adds an important critical principle to the work of the other: the former insists on gauging the efficacy of actions, the latter on assessing their futility.

15. Richard Shusterman reminds me that sometimes only acceptance can improve one's situation, viz., that in some cases only by being a stoic can one achieve pragmatic amelioration. The widespread phenomenon of aging people throwing themselves into youthful activities and failing at them comes immediately to mind.

### 27. THE RELEVANCE OF PHILOSOPHY TO LIFE

1. George Santayana, *Scepticism and Animal Faith* (New York: Dover, 1955), 305.

### 28. BOTH BETTER OFF AND BETTER: MORAL PROGRESS AMID CONTINUING CARNAGE

1. John Stuart Mill, *On Liberty*, in *Essential Works of John Stuart Mill*, ed. Max Lerner (New York: Bantam, 1961), 264.

2. See Section III of *On Liberty*.

3. Immanuel Kant, *Critique of Practical Reason*, ed. and trans. Lewis White Beck (Chicago: University of Chicago Press, 1949), 227ff.

4. Martin Heidegger, "Being, Dwelling, Thinking," in *Poetry, Language, Thought*, trans. Albert Hofstader (New York: Harper and Row, 1971), 160ff.

5. Friedrich Nietzsche, *Thus Spoke Zarathustra*, in *The Portable Nietzsche*, trans. Walter Kaufman (New York: Viking, 1954), 130.

6. Thomas Hobbes, *Leviathan*, in *Hobbes Selections*, ed. F. J. E. Woodbridge (New York: Scribner's, 1930), chapter 13.

7. Benjamin Constant, "The Liberty of the Ancients Compared with That of the Moderns," in *Political Writings*, trans. and ed. Biancamaria Fontana (Cambridge: Cambridge University Press, 1988), 313.

8. Plutarch, *The Lives of the Noble Grecians and Romans*, trans. John Dryden (New York: Random House, 1932), 431.

### 30. LEARNING ABOUT POSSIBILITY

1. John Lachs, *A Community of Individuals* (New York: Routledge, 2003), 9.

### 31. MORAL HOLIDAYS

1. William James, *Pragmatism*, ed. Frederick H. Burkhardt (Cambridge, MA: Harvard University Press, 1975), 41.

2. Ibid.

3. Josiah Royce, *The World and the Individual*, Second Series (New York: Macmillan, 1923), 363.

4. Ibid.

5. James flirts with the idea that moral holidays are wholesome and valuable. In "On a Certain Blindness in Human Beings," for example, he exalts the mysteries of "sensorial life" and asserts that "the holidays of life are its most vitally significant portions, because they are, or at least should be, covered with just this kind of magically irresponsible spell" (*Talks to Teachers on Psychology and to Students on Some of Life's Ideals*, ed. Frederick H. Burkhardt, Fredson Bowers, and Ignas K. Skrupskelis [Cambridge, MA: Harvard University Press, 1983], 149. But he does not say that the holidays of which he speaks are *moral* holidays, and he generally shies away from endorsing breaks in our earnest efforts to improve the world.

6. William James, "The Gospel of Relaxation," in ibid., 122.

7. Ibid., 128.

8. Ibid., 125.

9. Ibid.

10. Ibid., 129.

11. *The Will to Believe and Other Essays in Popular Philosophy*, ed. Frederick H. Burkhardt, Fredson Bowers, and Ignas K. Skrupskelis (Cambridge, MA: Harvard University Press, 1979), 153.

12. Ibid., 161.

13. Ibid.

14. Ibid.

15. *The World and the Individual*, Second Series, 380.

16. *The Correspondence of William James*, vol. 9, ed. Ignas K. Skrupskelis and Elizabeth M. Berkeley (Charlottesville: University of Virginia Press, 2001), 120–21.

17. Ibid., 320–21.

18. J. G. Fichte, "Second Introduction to the Science of Knowledge," in *The Science of Knowledge*, trans. P. Heath and J. Lachs (Cambridge: Cambridge University Press, 1982), 83.

# Further Reading

PROLOGUE

For related overviews of Lachs's work, see my entry "John Lachs" in the *Dictionary of American Philosophers*, ed. J. Shook (Bristol, UK: Thoemmes Continuum, 2005), 1390–1393. An interview, addressing important questions raised by a graduate student interlocutor, is Matthew Flamm's "Cheering on Life: A Conversation with John Lachs," *Kinesis: Graduate Journal in Philosophy* 27 (2000): 4–24.

PART I

"Epiphenomenalism and the Notion of Cause" (*MP* 29–34) offers an analysis pertinent to both "The Impotent Mind" and "Santayana's Philosophy of Mind." Its chief argument is that the epiphenomalist cannot subscribe to any of three views of causation (the activity view, the entailment view, or the regularity view). To save epiphenomenalism, though, Lachs takes his cue from Aristotle's distinction between activity (*energeia*) and process (*kinesis*), interpreting mind as the form or activity of the body so that "the relation of physiological process to mental act is that of the potential to the actual or that of the first entelechy to the second" (*MP* 34). This interpretation has the merit of rendering mind both effectless and fully actual, thereby taking the sting out of the adjective "impotent." Importantly, Lachs continues to invoke the activity/process distinction throughout his career. Its first appearance is in "Epiphenomenalism and the Notion of Cause," though "Santayana's Philosophy of Mind" offers a fuller exposition.

Related works in the philosophy of mind concerning epiphenomenalism include "Angel, Animal, Machine: Models for Man" (*MP* 5–15). Lachs here identifies three advantages epiphenomenalism enjoys over materialism: its simplicity and higher initial probability, its ability to explain intentionality, and its capacity to accommodate the experiential insights of dualism—including moral lessons—without rejecting or unnecessarily limiting science. "The Proofs of Realism" (*MP* 89–119) offers a detailed analysis of Santayana's critical realism. Lachs concludes that Santayana is right in his general account of realism, showing realism to be a tenet of animal faith, but encounters difficulties in the details (especially those concerning symbolism involved in perception). Written with colleague Michael Hodges, "Meaning and the Impotence Hypothesis" (*MP* 35–52) defends epiphenomenalism against charges raised by proponents (including Wilfrid Sellars) of "the semantic tie principle." More recently, Lachs argues in "Peirce and Santayana on Purposes" (*CI* 187–191) that these two philosophers' different views of purposiveness can be traced to their disagreements about the efficacy of mind.

For readers interested in Lachs's fuller consideration of Santayana's philosophy, should consult his two books, *George Santayana* (Boston: Twayne, 1988) and *On Santayana* (Belmont, CA: Wadsworth, 2006). (Sadly, the manuscript of Lachs's first monograph on Santayana's philosophy was lost when the briefcase containing it was stolen.) Lachs has representative works on Santayana from each decade of his career. In the early "Matter and Substance in the Philosophy of Santayana" (*The Modern Schoolman* 44 [1966]: 1–12), he unearths the various senses Santayana gives to substance, matter, and existence and offers a reinterpretation of Santayana's claim to be a materialist. This article is important to Lachs's later critiques of Santayana's ontology, for example, those presented in "The Transcendence of Materialism and Idealism in American Thought" and "Primitive Naturalism." Lachs clarifies Santayana's treatment of animal faith and stresses the importance of action in "Belief, Confidence and Faith" (*MP* 141–156). As the title suggests, "The Enduring Value of Santayana's Philosophy" (*Overheard in Seville* [1988]: 1–13) assesses dominant positions in Santayana. Lachs embraces Santayana's naturalistic relativism, while he is critical of his treatment of matter and of his embrace of epiphenomenalism. He argues that if we begin with Cartesian assumptions, epiphenomenalism offers the reasonable position, but he hints that those assumptions may be flawed. A more recent article, "Animal Faith and Ontology" (*SP* 174–181), argues that Santayana has two dominant tendencies: to develop both a system of animal faith and a complete ontology. Lachs, as we have seen in "Primitive Naturalism," favors the former.

Lachs productively contrasts Santayana with philosophers other than Peirce in a number of articles. In "Thinking in the Ruins: Two Overlooked Responses to Contingency" (*Overheard in Seville* 13 [1995]: 1–8; later developed in the monograph, *Thinking in the Ruins: Wittgenstein and Santayana* [Nashville: Vanderbilt University Press, 2000]), he again teams up with colleague Michael Hodges to give attention to the neglected views and resources Santayana and Wittgenstein offer us with respect to responding to contingency. Both share a suspicion of the quest for certainty and an embrace ordinary practices. In "The Difference God Makes" (*SP* 144–158), Lachs examines how belief in God accounts for divergent views of eternity held by Santayana and Royce.

Readers interested in Lachs's treatment of Fichte should consult the Introduction to his translation (with Peter Heath) of *The Science of Knowledge* (New York: Appleton-Century-Crofts, 1970; reissued by Cambridge University Press, 1982). J. Douglas Rabb offers a critique of Lachs's view in "Lachs on Fichte," *Dialogue: Canadian Philosophical Review* 12 (1973): 480–485. In "Pre-Socratic Categories in Fichte" (*MP* 203–212), Lachs examines the role of the ideas of activity and passivity in the pre-Socratics, Plato, Descartes, Berkeley, Spinoza, Kant and Fichte. Lachs contends that Fichte's attempt to understand how the active posits the passive generates a system that emphasizes the practical. In "Is There an Absolute Self?" (*The Philosophical Forum* 19 [1988]: 169–181), Lachs argues, contra Mandt, that Fichte shows both parts of a whole whose ground is the absolute self. This article shows that Lachs's work on Fichte likely influenced his interpretation of selves as mediated (see Part II for more on mediation). In "The Insignificance of Individuals" (*CI* 141–154), Lachs investigates the different value given to the individual by German thinkers (including Fichte) and American pragmatists (including Santayana).

Finally, Lachs's discussion of other metaphysical issues can be found in articles on God and critiques of colleagues. The former includes "Omniscience" (*Dialogue* 1 [1963]: 400–402) and "Two Concepts of God" (*MP* 53–66), in which Lachs argues that omniscience because, by its nature, it precludes the possibility of knowing what a surprise is. He also contends, in keeping with his epiphenomenalism, that divine knowledge and power are inconsistent, since knowledge occurs outside of time and is inefficacious. Lachs critiques the relevant positions of other philosophers in "Consciousness and Weiss' Mind" (*The Review of Metaphysics* 13 [1959]: 259–270), "Self-Identity without a Self" (*MP* 227–244), and "The Social Construction of Human Nature" (*The Philosophy of Paul Weiss*, ed. Lewis E. Hahn, The Library of Living Philosophers, vol. 23 [Carbondale: Southern Illinois University Press, 1995], 73–83)—three articles in which his teacher, Paul Weiss, comes under fire—as well as "Artless Metaphysical Belief" (*Pacific Philosophy Forum* 6 [1967]: 50–68), which critiques Arthur W. Munk's refutation of naturalism. "God's Action & Nature's Way" (*Idealistic Studies* 12 [1973]: 223–228) offers three challenges to John Cobb's view of God, with special consideration given to the theme of causation.

## PART II

Lachs's first publication on moral philosophy, "Santayana's Moral Philosophy" (*MP* 120–140), provides a clear exposition of many of Santayana's themes that recur in later articles, most notably those that form the basis of his commitment to pluralism and tolerance. Since Santayana did not develop a systematic ethic, Lachs here aims to "develop and enlarge upon the ethical position that is the natural complement of his ontology" (122). He agrees with Santayana that the good is relative to one's nature and that, while there is enough in common between different human natures to form societies and make possible a workable morality, natures differ enough that there is no universal human nature. Goods are absolute insofar as our natures are not matters of opinion, and the challenge for each individual is to know herself so that she understands the conditions of her goods and also has available the larger perspective that makes the harmonization of competing goods possible. Lachs and Santayana recommend tolerance of others' goods, both when they do not conflict with my own and when we are able to cultivate spirit's unique perspective on our lives. These themes will recur in later articles, most notably Lachs's own arguments for pluralism in "Human Natures" (see Part III).

Lachs's engagement with J. S. Mill begins in the first article of this section, and two later articles show him a sympathetic interpreter. The first is his entry on Mill in *Ethics in the History of Western Philosophy*, ed. Robert J. Cavalier, James Gouinlock and James P. Sterba (New York: St. Martin's Press, 1989), 244–270. As can be expected, the article canvasses Mill's life and ideas, paying special attention to his utilitarianism and view of liberty. The second article, "Mill and Constant: A Neglected Connection in the History of the Idea of Liberty" (*History of Philosophy Quarterly* 9 [1992]: 87–96), explores twelve "clusters of belief" that link Mill and Benjamin Constant's view of liberty. Included among these are the belief that individuals' rights are grounded in human nature, that self-regarding actions must be free from government control, and that individual self-development goes hand in hand with progress of the human race.

The attention to individual agency found in "A Community of Psyches" is complemented by the discussion in "The Insignificance of Individuals" (*CI* 141–154). Also relevant is "Operational Independence" (*SP* 127–139), in which Lachs argues that "[e]very denial of individual agency or operational independence is its affirmation: the action might serve some imagined social good, but it is executed by an individual person" (134).

Lachs's theory of mediation develops in a series of articles in the late 1970s, including "Mediation and Psychic Distance" (with Michael Hodges in *Theories of Alienation*, ed. R. F. Geyer and D. Schweitzer [Leiden: Nijhoff, 1976], 151–167) and "I Only Work Here: Mediation and Irresponsibility" (*Ethics, Free Enterprise, and Public Policy*, ed. Richard T. DeGeorge and Joseph A. Pichler [New York: Oxford University Press, 1978], 201–213), but finds its fullest statement in *Intermediate Man* (Indianapolis: Hackett, 1981), a unique and original work that is both sophisticated and accessible to a nonacademic audience. The book enjoyed two printings as well as a British publication as *Modern Man and Responsibility* (London: Harvester). Chapters address mediation in interpersonal and institutional contexts. Lachs ends the book with a more optimistic appraisal of education's role in reimmediation than we find in "Public Benefit, Private Cost." Two later works, "Persons and Technology" (*RPL* 113–125) and "Immediacy and De-Alienation" (*Alienation, Community, and Work*, ed. Andrew Oldenquist and Menace Rosier [New York: Greenwood Press, 1991], 119–130) further develop the theory. The former anticipates themes in "Public Benefit," but the latter, offers new suggestions concerning the role sympathy and informed imagination can play in reimmediation. Importantly, Lachs also has the manuscript of a sequel, *The Cost of Comfort*, which he has been reluctant to let go. I hope that it will make its way to a publisher in the near future.

Lachs was an early writer on issues in medical ethics and his reflections on the trying matters with which this developing technology confronts us continue to the present. (See, for instance, the epilogue in this volume.) His first publication in this area, "Humane Treatment and the Treatment of Humans" (*RPL* 170–175), addresses euthanasia. Lachs argues that the only humane treatment of "humans" in an ongoing vegetative state is to refuse to treat them as humans. He supports a comparable conclusion in "Resuscitation," (*RPL* 176–180), and "Active Euthanasia" (*RPL* 181–187). He disputes Daniel Callahan's objections to euthanasia and assisted suicide in "When Abstract Moralizing Runs Amok" (*RPL* 188–194), arguing that "in the end, our lives belong to no one but ourselves. The limits to such self-determination are set by the demands of social life" (194), These include considerations such as whether persons soliciting help in dying can demonstrate that they are of sound mind, that their desire is enduring, and that both their subjective and objective conditions make their wish sensible. Two later articles on aging and death are "Dying Old as a Social Problem" (CI 129–138) and "Is Aging a Disease?" (*HEC Forum* 16 [2004]: 173–181). Finally, Lachs considers the dynamics that affect the patient-physician relation in "Personal Relations Between Physicians and Patients" (*RPL* 199–205).

The themes of "Leaving Others Alone" are further developed in a forthcoming book of the same name.

Central to the development of his view of choice-inclusive facts is Lachs's reflections on the pluralism and relativism. These are presented briefly in "Santayana's Moral Philosophy" (*MP* 120–140). An early critique of Joseph Fletcher's Christian relativism, "Dogmatist in Disguise" (*RPL* 62–69), develops key moves Lachs will employ when attacking dogmatism in "Relativism and Its Benefits." After "Relativism," Lachs adopts the terminology of "relationalism" to distinguish his position from the more common and vicious versions of relativism that suggest that values are arbitrary. Lachs addresses these concerns in "How Relative Are Values? or Must a Nazi Be Irrational and Why the Answer Matters" (*RPL* 40–49) and "Values and Relations" (*RPL* 29–39). The latter article extends Lachs's argument by tackling the objection that relationalism appears to leave us incapable of explaining moral error and improvement. In response, Lachs contends that the distinction between long-term and short-term satisfaction, which relationalism embraces, enables us to account for both error and improvement. The article is also significant in that it was published with Erazim Kohák's response ("Why Is There Something Good, Not Simply Something? Reflections on the Ontological Status of Value," same volume, 10–20), as well as Lachs's own further reply ("Is Everything Intrinsically Good," 20–24). Kohák's concern is that relationalism leaves us with the vexing question, "how can a relation between two intrinsically worth-less entities give rise to value?" (11) Lachs's reply is that relations beget new properties, as when we combine letters to create words, new units with additional meaning.

The theme of tolerance central to these papers is also addressed in "Grand History and Ordinary Life" (*RPL* 70–78). It can also be found in Lachs's more recent reflections on William James's discussion of human blindness ("Human Blindness," *SP* 88–95).

A significant early article in which Lachs considers the moral implications of the designation "human" appear in his first article on medical ethics, "Humane Treatment and the Treatment of Humans" (*RPL* 170–175). Most articles, however, defending and applying his view of human natures issue from the same period as "Human Natures." "The Philosophical Significance of Psychological Differences Among Humans" (*RPL* 243–253) critiques essentialist approaches and emphasizes the moral status of the designation "human." In "What Humans Did Not Make" (*CI* 37–46), an article critical of constructivists, Lachs attends to the varied contributions humans make to reality, offering examples that result from our acts, our choices, our thoughts, and our feelings. Arguing that "our values constitute the ratio cognoscenti of our natures" (307), Lachs proposes that we consider ourselves to be a "valuational species" ("Valuational Species," *CI* 47–58). Human natures are thus to be distinguished (and related) by the valuational affinities of individuals.

Lachs has had a longstanding interest in the welfare of philosophy and the role of the philosopher in society. Early articles concerning philosophy's status can be found in "Graduate Programs in the Undergraduate College" (*The Journal of Higher Education* 36 [1965]: 121–130). "From College to University" (*Liberal Education* 52 [1966]: 277–280), and "Philosophy and American Studies" (in *Challenges in American Culture*, ed. Ray B. Brown [Bowling Green: Bowling Green University Popular Press, 1970], 47–54). In "Reflections on Current French Philosophy" (*Journal of Speculative Philosophy* 10 [1996]: 19–23; *RPL* 11–16), Lachs expresses concerns that philosophers continue to pursue lines of thought that lead to isolation and irrelevance. (A critical response is provided by Lachs's Vanderbilt colleague Charles Scott in the same volume.) Lachs's call for philosophers to aid in the public discourse about timely issues (including those concerning bioethics) can be found in Part IV of *The Relevance of Philosophy to Life* and Part III of *A Community of Individuals*. Most recently, his critique of the discipline can be found in the articles that constitute Chapter 1 of *Stoic Pragmatism* (3–27). He there sounds the same theme, calling on philosophers to resume the "traditional tasks of providing moral guidance to individuals and assuming a critical stance toward questionable social practices" (13).

## PART IV

Both of the first two essays here, "To Have and to Be" and "Drugs," were later revised to become chapters 3 and 8, respectively, of *Intermediate Man*. The context of mediation dominates in the revisions, but the overall treatment of the meaning of having and of drug experimentation remain the same.

The other chapters of *In Love with Life* are all suitable complements to "Loving Life," especially since the book was conceived as a whole. Here I will note three chapters of special interest. In chapter 2, Lachs turns to the challenge posed by those who profess to hate life. He argues that hatred of some things is based on love of others and so does not amount to unconditional hate. Moreover, he contends that seeking to expand the scope of the self by identifying with others and their joys provides an important antidote to such hatred, for then there is less to hate and more to love. Chapter 4 examines the conditions that affect our choice of activities; these include our abilities, opportunities, previous satisfactions, social standards, and the value of variety. Chapters 6 and 7 address being tired with life and facing death. With respect to the latter, Lachs couples recognition of our own insignificance with an embrace of the satisfactions possible for each of life's stages.

The notion of activity—in distinction from the concept of process—that forms the heart of the duo "Aristotle and Dewey on the Rat Race" and "Improving Life" is a topic Lachs addressed throughout his career. Early treatments can be found in nearly all of Lachs's discussions of epiphenomenalism, Santayana's philosophy, and mediation.

Stoic pragmatism is the focus of a recent monograph of the same name (Bloomington: Indiana University Press, 2012). Of particular importance is the chapter "The Past, The Future, and The Immediate" (*SP* 28–40), which traces the history of pragmatism and notes its preoccupation with the future—a natural consequence, Lachs notes, of its stress on action. Critical of this emphasis, Lachs argues that we should not overlook the significance of the present, for "people who suffer from painful terminal diseases have little hope of amelioration or even Deweyan growth. For them, embrace of a happy moment is all the 'quality' life can offer. Abstracted from regrets for the past and worry about the bleakness of the future, their present can shine with the joy of fading light" (38). A similar emphasis on the present can be found in earlier discussions of Santayana's philosophy as well as in "Transcendence in Philosophy and in Everyday Life" (*CI* 73–81). Contending that "transcendence today is the search not for a reality beyond the everyday but for a value of unquestioned finality in daily life" (75), Lachs charts the development of the transcendent through Kant, Schopenhauer, and Santayana. Santayana democratizes Schopenhauer's insight that absorption in beauty offers us the only viable route to transcendence when he "opens the possibility of joyous absorption in the present and in anything present to consciousness" (78). As such, we are able to immerse ourselves in the immediate, an act which provides a liberating counterweight to guilt about the past and anxiety concerning the future.

Lachs's reflections on death, stemming back to the 1970s articles on bioethics, emphasize the significance of life's different seasons. Additional discussions of death not already noted in the readings for previous sections, include Lachs's treatment of the desire for immorality in "The Vague Hope of Immortality" (*CI* 83–94). Lachs examines different phenomena that might fuel such a desire—e.g., the natural expansion of the self to include others, our love of life, and the desire for unmitigated satisfaction—but concludes that we have no viable idea of an afterlife. His view of the self as an active and energetic but finite being underlies the discussion, and forms the basis of the antiperfectionism that constitutes the core topic of part of Part V.

PART V

"The Relevance of Philosophy to Life" is a title that at once indicates one of
Lachs's fundamental commitments as well as the title of both an article and
a book (Nashville: Vanderbilt University Press, 1995). Readers who find the
article short on concrete examples need only turn to the book, for each chapter is designed to expound on this commitment. Also relevant is the 1996
article, "Intellectuals and Courage" (reprinted *CI* 5–10). Here Lachs explores
reasons intellectuals hesitate to criticize institutions; he nevertheless argues
that they have an obligation to contribute to public dialogue.

Lachs's appraisal of our material and moral improvement in "Both Better and
Better Off" was the focus of an edition of *The Journal of Speculative Philosophy* 15, no. 3 (2001) (reprinted *CI* 97–108). Four commentators—Cynthia
Willet, Dennis Schmidt, Andrew Light, and Nikita Pokrovsky—offered critical responses.

Lachs has written on educational matters throughout his career. In the first
such article, "Graduate Programs in the Undergraduate College" (*The Journal of Higher Education* 36 [1965]: 121–130), he urges that we identify the goal
of liberal arts with development of *personality*, not development of the professional. A comparable message is defended in the later "Teaching as a Calling" (*CI* 15–21). Lachs's view of mediation also influenced his guarded hopes
for education. The last chapter of *Intermediate Man* recognizes education as
a source of reimmediation, though only if we revise many of our practices.
Lachs teams up with his wife, a former teacher, to provide a fuller discussion
of the needed revisions in "Education and the Power of the State: Reconceiv-
ing Some Problems and Their Solutions" (*RPL* 133–151). The Lachses call for
immediacy at all levels; administrators, teachers, parents, and students must
all participate. For instance, school leaders should seek ways to ensure education is a perennial part of the public's agenda and that teachers pursue
their craft as a calling that requires caring interactions as readily as a passion for the subject matter on which they focus. Written in the hopes that
students will continue to exercise their powers of reflection in the world beyond academia, "Courage and Critique" is a recent commencement speech
(slightly altered and published as "A Reflection on Courage" in *SP* 139–142)
in which Lachs highlights the forces that make challenging the status quo
difficult. He nevertheless encourages his audience to resist the temptation to
agree with the crowd and to choose safety above all else. Lachs thus extends
his call for integrating thought and deed, theory and practice, to students as
well as teachers.

Two related articles examine the educative value of social life more broadly. In
"Professional Advertising in an Ignorant World" (*RPL* 126–32), Lachs contends

that to counteract the ignorance that mediation breeds, professionals have an obligation to advertise in manner that educates the public of the services they have to perform. Lawyers receive special attention in "Law and the Importance of Feelings" (*RPL* 152–159). Characterizing these professionals as thirds in the service of thirds (laws), Lachs argues that the cooling distance lawyers represent in the legal process can be damaging, especially if the loss of direct contact means that parties fail to feel they have been included and so do not accept the rulings handed down to them.

The theme of antiperfection is an outgrowth of Lachs's consistent attention to human finitude, with respect to both abilities and duties. It is thus linked to his writings on leaving others alone (see Part II). "Human Blindness" (*SP* 88–95) offers an analysis of ten forms of blindness that lie at the heart of our finite existence. While he considers the advantages to ameliorating these, Lachs argues against attempts to eliminate blindness altogether. He concludes the essay by urging that "we must not forget our finitude and we must try to remember that much as blindness is, in the abstract, a lamentable condition, in concrete life it protects us from being overwhelmed by reality."

# Index

**AMERICAN PHILOSOPHY**

*Douglas R. Anderson and Jude Jones, series editors*

Kenneth Laine Ketner, ed., *Peirce and Contemporary Thought: Philosophical Inquiries.*

Max H. Fisch, ed., *Classic American Philosophers: Peirce, James, Royce, Santayana, Dewey, Whitehead, second edition.* Introduction by Nathan Houser.

John E. Smith, *Experience and God, second edition.*

Vincent G. Potter, *Peirce's Philosophical Perspectives.* Edited by Vincent Colapietro.

Richard E. Hart and Douglas R. Anderson, eds., *Philosophy in Experience: American Philosophy in Transition.*

Vincent G. Potter, *Charles S. Peirce: On Norms and Ideals, second edition.* Introduction by Stanley M. Harrison.

Vincent M. Colapietro, ed., *Reason, Experience, and God: John E. Smith in Dialogue.* Introduction by Merold Westphal.

Robert J. O'Connell, S.J., *William James on the Courage to Believe, second edition.*

Elizabeth M. Kraus, *The Metaphysics of Experience: A Companion to Whitehead's "Process and Reality," second edition.* Introduction by Robert C. Neville.

Kenneth Westphal, ed., *Pragmatism, Reason, and Norms: A Realistic Assessment—Essays in Critical Appreciation of Frederick L. Will.*

Beth J. Singer, *Pragmatism, Rights, and Democracy.*

Eugene Fontinell, *Self, God, and Immorality: A Jamesian Investigation.*

Roger Ward, *Conversion in American Philosophy: Exploring the Practice of Transformation.*

Michael Epperson, *Quantum Mechanics and the Philosophy of Alfred North Whitehead.*

Kory Sorrell, *Representative Practices: Peirce, Pragmatism, and Feminist Epistemology.*

Naoko Saito, *The Gleam of Light: Moral Perfectionism and Education in Dewey and Emerson.*

Josiah Royce, *The Basic Writings of Josiah Royce.*

Douglas R. Anderson, *Philosophy Americana: Making Philosophy at Home in American Culture.*

James Campbell and Richard E. Hart, eds., *Experience as Philosophy: On the World of John J. McDermott.*

John J. McDermott, *The Drama of Possibility: Experience as Philosophy of Culture.* Edited by Douglas R. Anderson.

Larry A. Hickman, *Pragmatism as Post-Postmodernism: Lessons from John Dewey.*

Larry A. Hickman, Stefan Neubert, and Kersten Reich, eds., *John Dewey Between Pragmatism and Constructivism.*

Dwayne A. Tunstall, *Yes, But Not Quite: Encountering Josiah Royce's Ethico-Religious Insight.*

Josiah Royce, *Race Questions, Provincialism, and Other American Problems, expanded edition.* Edited by Scott L. Pratt and Shannon Sullivan.

Lara Trout, *The Politics of Survival: Peirce, Affectivity, and Social Criticism.*

John R. Shook and James A. Good, *John Dewey's Philosophy of Spirit, with the 1897 Lecture on Hegel.*

Josiah Warren, *The Practical Anarchist: Writings of Josiah Warren.* Edited and with an Introduction by Crispin Sartwell.

Naoko Saito and Paul Standish, eds., *Stanley Cavell and the Education of Grownups.*

Douglas R. Anderson and Carl R. Hausman, *Conversations on Peirce: Reals and Ideals.*

Rick Anthony Furtak, Jonathan Ellsworth, and James D. Reid, eds., *Thoreau's Importance for Philosophy.*

James M. Albrecht, *Reconstructing Individualism: A Pragmatic Tradition from Emerson to Ellison.*

Mathew A. Foust, *Loyalty to Loyalty: Josiah Royce and the Genuine Moral Life.*

Cornelis de Waal and Krysztof Piotr Skowroński (eds.), *The Normative Thought of Charles S. Peirce.*

Dwayne A. Tunstall, *Doing Philosophy Personally: Thinking about Metaphysics, Theism, and Antiblack Racism.*

Erin McKenna, *Pets, People, and Pragmatism.*

Sami Pihlström, *Pragmatic Pluralism and the Problem of God.*

Thomas M. Alexander, *The Human Eros: Eco-ontology and the Aesthetics of Existence.*

John Kaag, *Thinking Through the Imagination: Aesthetics in Human Cognition.*

Kelly A. Parker and Jason Bell (eds.), *The Relevance of Royce.*

W. E. B. Du Bois, *The Problem of the Color Line at the Turn of the Twentieth Century: The Essential Early Essays.* Edited by Nahum Dimitri Chandler.

Nahum Dimitri Chandler, *X—The Problem of the Negro as a Problem for Thought.*

John Lachs, *Freedom and Limits.* Edited by Patrick Shade.

Morris Grossman, *Art and Morality: Essays in the Spirit of George Santayana.* Edited by Martin A. Coleman.